WAR,
POLITICS,
and
DIPLOMACY

WAR,

POLITICS,

and

DIPLOMACY

Selected Essays

By GORDON A. CRAIG

WEIDENFELD AND NICOLSON
5 Winsley Street, Oxford Circus, London W.1

First published in Great Britain in 1966

Printed in the United States of America

To

Charles Grant Craig

Foreword

THIS COLLECTION OF ESSAYS is the result of more than twenty years' preoccupation with problems of war and diplomacy. My interest in military affairs was awakened by Hans Delbrück's monumental *History of the Art of War,* which first made me aware of the intimate relationship that exists between a society's military institutions and its political and social organization and of the reciprocal and varied influences they exert upon each other. All of the themes touched on in the first two sections of this book grew, one way or another, out of Delbrück, although my treatment of them has profited from the early influence of Edward Mead Earle, a pioneer in American military studies, with whom I had the good fortune to work while I was reading *The Art of War* for the first time.

The essays on diplomatic history also show the mark of illustrious models, particularly that of my teachers at Princeton and Oxford, Raymond James Sontag, B. H. Sumner, and Sir Llewellyn Woodward. More recently, a happy collaboration with Hajo Holborn and Felix Gilbert introduced me to the technical aspects of diplomacy and, especially, to the problems of negotiation in a time in which war and revolution have destroyed the old homogeneity of the international community. These interests are reflected in the third section of this volume.

The chapter on the diplomacy of new nations was given as part of the Haynes Foundation Lectures in 1961 and was intended as a highly tentative appraisal of one aspect of the diplomatic revolution of our times. In the five years that have passed since its publication, circumstances have changed in some of the states mentioned, and the whole piece has a hortatory ring that may seem inappropriate for a historian.

Even so, aside from minor changes of wording and the addition of a few notes, I have not sought to revise it or bring it up to date. The problem posed, and our attitude toward it, are much the same as they were five years ago.

I am grateful to various publishers for permission to reprint articles that originally appeared elsewhere and have acknowledged this at the foot of the first page of the chapters in question.

G. A. C.

Stanford, California
March, 1966

Contents

Part Three. DIPLOMACY

PART ONE

THE ART OF WAR

1. Command and Staff Problems in the Austrian Army, 1740-1866

On 18 June 1857 the Austrian army celebrated the hundredth anniversary of the founding of the Order of Maria Theresa, that association of officers who had been awarded the right of membership for actions of personal initiative which had contributed significantly to victories for Austrian arms. The Chancellor of the Order was old Prince Metternich, and he lavished upon the arrangements the same care that he had given to the organization of the Congress of Vienna in 1814. At the commemorative banquet at Schönbrunn, which was attended by representatives of all the regiments of the army, Emperor Francis Joseph was presented with a bullet from the field of Kolin, set in gold and accompanied by a plaque which was engraved with the names of Field Marshal Daun and all the other soldiers who had won the first Maria Theresa Crosses on the day of that victory over Frederick of Prussia. Later, against the background of the Gloriette, there were *tableaux* depicting scenes from the history of the army since Maria Theresa's day, speeches by court actors in honor of those who had given their lives for the Habsburg cause, and a dramatic portrayal of an episode from the battle of Aspern. The day's festivities ended with a performance of Schiller's play *Wallenstein's Camp*.[1]

It is melancholy to reflect upon how quickly this proud tribute to Austria's military greatness was followed by the humiliating defeats that robbed the Habsburg monarchy of its influence and possessions in Italy

"Command and Staff Problems in the Austrian Army" was first published in Michael Howard, ed., *The Theory and Practice of War* (London: Cassell and Co., Ltd., 1965; New York: Frederick A. Praeger, 1966). Reprinted with permission of the publishers.

[1] Egon Conte Corti, *Mensch und Herrscher: Wege und Schicksale Kaiser Franz Josephs I* (Graz, Vienna, 1952), pp. 190–91.

and Germany and handed it over to an uncertain future. For this precipitate fall from glory, which stunned contemporary Europe,[2] various reasons have been given—notably, the Empire's lack of national unity and the unreliability of some of its subject nationalities, its grave weaknesses in financial resources and administration, and the deficiencies in weaponry that resulted from inadequate military expenditure.[3] These factors were undeniably important. It is the contention of this paper, however, that the defeats of 1859 and 1866 were equally influenced by serious problems of civil-military relations and unresolved differences of attitude with respect to the art of war which were rooted in the very past celebrated by Metternich's theatrical set-piece in 1857.

I

It was entirely appropriate that the celebration should have included a play about Wallenstein, for although that enigmatic figure had met his death at Eger more than a century before Maria Theresa came to the throne, his influence lived on in her army and that of her successors. It was, indeed, from the remnants of the mercenary force raised and trained by Wallenstein that Austria's first standing army was created, when Emperor Ferdinand III commissioned nine foot regiments and ten regiments of horse at the close of the religious wars.[4] In the eighteenth century some of those same regiments fought against Frederick on Bohemian battlefields where Wallenstein's army had maneuvered; and a century later the Hessen Cuirassiers who distinguished themselves at Skalitz and Langenhof could claim legitimate descent from the Pappenheimers mentioned in Schiller's play, and at least three other regiments had a similar ancestry.[5] In Wallenstein's castle at Gitschin, the capital of that Duchy of Friedland which Ferdinand II created for his Captain General after the Battle of the White Mountain, Emperor

[2] For examples of newspaper opinion after the defeat of 3 July 1866, see Gordon A. Craig, *The Battle of Königgrätz: Prussia's Victory over Austria, 1866* (Philadelphia, Pa., 1964), pp. ix, x.

[3] For emphasis on the financial question and the inadequacy of military spending, see Oskar Regele, *Feldzeugmeister Benedek: Der Weg nach Königgrätz* (Vienna, 1960), especially pp. 108 ff., 290–384.

[4] Edmund Glaise von Horstenau, "Oesterreichs Wehrmacht im deutschen Schicksal," in Josef Nadler and H. Ritter von Srbik, ed., *Oesterreich: Erbe und Sendung im deutschen Raum* (Salzburg and Leipzig, 1937), p. 207.

[5] Alfons Freiherr von Wrede, *Geschichte des K. u. K. Mährischen Dragonerregiments Fr. Franz IV Groszherzog vom Mecklenburg Schwerin No. 6* (Brünn, n.d.), pp. 5, 560 ff.

Francis I spent five weeks in 1813; and it was there that Metternich, Nesselrode, and Wilhelm von Humboldt held some of the negotiations that preceded Austria's adhesion to the Grand Alliance against Napoleon.[6] Thus, Wallenstein had at least a tenuous connection with the subsequent victories of the armies led by Schwarzenberg and Radetzky. Gitschin was also the scene of a day-long fight between an Austro-Saxon force and the Prussian First Army in June 1866, a battle which might have been won if it had not been for failures of communications with the Supreme Command in the rear.[7]

But Wallenstein's influence upon the Austrian army assumed other forms than these, and more unfortunate ones. After all, the most memorable thing about the *Friedländer* was that he had been an ambitious man and possibly a treasonable one; and the obscurity of his motives had led the same Emperor who had rewarded him with a duchy for his victories to divest him of power and, possibly, to encourage his assassination. Performances of Schiller were not needed to keep this memory alive. It is not too much to say that there was always a kind of Wallenstein complex in Vienna, which created grave civil-military problems and troubled command relationships in the army throughout the modern period.

It is striking that there was hardly a ruler or chief minister after Maria Theresa's time who was not in some measure suspicious of outstanding field commanders. The great Empress was perhaps exceptional in this respect because, unlike most of her successors, she was capable of gratitude. She never forgot that Daun's victory at Kolin had marked a major turning-point in Austria's fortunes, and she remained loyal to the Field Marshal long after her ministers and allies had begun to clamor for his recall on the grounds that his excessive circumspection stood in the way of complete victory over Frederick. Daun repaid his Empress's support by working indefatigably to modernize and make an efficient fighting force out of an army that had in 1740 been a disorganized welter of units without leadership, armament, or training; and he left to his successor Lacy a basically sound organization and a fighting force that was generally considered to be as good as Prussia's.[8]

[6] Anna von Sydow, ed., *Wilhelm und Caroline von Humboldt in ihren Briefen* (Berlin, 1910), IV, 40; Theodor Fontane, *Der deutsche Krieg von 1866* (2 vols.; Berlin, 1871–72), I, 205–6.

[7] Craig, *op. cit.*, pp. 74–78.

[8] Friedrich Walter, "Feldmarschall Leopold Joseph Graf Daun und Feldmarshall Gideon Ernst Freiherr von Laudon," in Hugo Hantsch, ed., *Gestalter der Geschichke Oesterreichs* (Innsbruck, Vienna, 1962), pp. 263, 274.

The two most gifted field commanders in the period that stretched between the Seven Years' War and the creation of the alliance of 1813 had less happy relations with their sovereigns. Laudon, the victor at Olmütz and Kunersdorf and Glatz, was a better strategist than Daun and was infinitely more offensive-minded. He also, however, enjoyed a popularity greater than any Austrian commander since Eugene of Savoy. This hardly ingratiated him with Joseph II, who found no employment for the Field Marshal's talents. Laudon was relegated to a retirement that lasted almost a quarter of a century, until in 1789, a year before he died, he was hurriedly summoned to extricate the Emperor from the complications of a badly planned war against the Turks and displayed his old mastery, for the last time, by capturing the stronghold of Belgrade.[9]

Worse was the treatment meted out to the man who is sometimes called Austria's greatest *Feldherr* after the time of Eugene. In all of his campaigns, Archduke Charles had to contend with the suspicion of his brother, Francis I, and the open hostility of the Emperor's ministers, who did not hesitate to question his strategy or even his direction of operations. In 1793, for instance, when the young Archduke, in what was virtually his baptism of fire, drove the French revolutionary army of Dumouriez out of the Austrian province of Belgium, these initial victories were vitiated by the persistent refusal of the Emperor, acting on the advice of his minister Thugut, either to strengthen the Austrian forces in the west or to use diplomatic means to secure a more effective alliance with Prussia. When French pressure was renewed at the beginning of 1794, Charles was denied the over-all command that his previous victories justified; and the Austrian army of the west, badly led, was smashed by Jourdan at Fleurus.[10] Two years later, when the critical situation on the Rhine made it impossible to deny Charles supreme command, Thugut arranged to have a tool of his own, Lieutenant Field Marshal Count Bellegarde, appointed as his deputy and, through him, interfered with the operations against the enemy. Despite the resultant annoyance and confusion, Charles fought a masterful double campaign against Jourdan and Moreau, defeating them separately and forcing their armies back across the Rhine.[11] But even this did not stop ministerial incursions into the operational field or reduce the suspicions with which Charles was regarded in Vienna.

[9] *Ibid.*, p. 274.

[10] H. Rössler, *Oesterreichs Kampf um Deutschlands Befreiung* (Hamburg, 1940), I, 102–4.

[11] *Ibid.*, pp. 109–11.

The Archduke made enemies in the capital partly because he did not restrict his activities to the military sphere. With great conviction, he held that a nation's foreign policy must be determined on the basis of a proper assessment of its resources, and particularly of its military strength and potential. In the Austrian case, this precept was often flouted. Increasingly in 1796 and 1797 Charles felt that the government was seeking to achieve objectives that were beyond the reach of an army whose vigor and spirit had been worn down by incessant campaigning; and he did not hesitate to travel to Vienna to press his case. These occasional forays were resented and feared by ministers who, for their part, never had any compunction about meddling in Charles' own sphere of competence, and they also aroused the indignation of his brother. In 1797, when the Archduke came to the capital in his capacity as commander on the Italian front, and warned that peace should be sought because troop morale was at the breaking point, he was, as he said ruefully, simply "hunted out of Vienna."[12] The young Bonaparte subsequently proved that all of Charles' fears were justified, but this won him no credit. After the government had been forced to submit to the peace of Leoben, Charles was relieved of his post in Italy and sent to Mannheim in disgrace, to take up command of the Rhine Army once more but with strict orders to remain at his new headquarters unless given specific authorization to leave it.[13]

Charles' position did not improve with the passage of time. During the War of the Second Coalition, incessant ministerial interference brought him to the point of resignation, a step which he reconsidered only after the Emperor accused him of insubordination. Once more he won smashing victories in the field, this time over Masséna in Switzerland, but once more they were thrown away by politically inspired changes in the allied command structure, which allowed the French to recover.

The complete lack of coordination between political and military strategy that resulted from all this brought Austria to the nadir of its fortunes at Marengo in 1800. At long last, Thugut was forced from office, and there was a popular demand for a grant of greater authority to the one Austrian soldier who seemed to be capable of beating the French in the open field. To this feeling the Emperor yielded: Charles was appointed President of the Supreme War Council in January 1801 and six months later was made War and Naval Minister as well. With the whole military establishment unified in his person, he was now

12 *Ibid.*, p. 112.
13 *Ibid.*, pp. 112–13.

in the position to carry through reforms he had long believed essential. But this opportunity was of limited duration. For a brief period Charles was permitted to effect changes in disciplinary codes and training, in recruitment and staff work; but in 1805 the Emperor undid the very basis of these reforms by destroying the newly created unity of the military system, re-establishing the *Hofkriegsrat* as a separate body, and depriving Charles of any influence over it. He even undermined the Archduke's authority in the army command by dismissing his chief aides and saddling him with a quartermaster whose views were diametrically opposed to his own—a General Mack, who Francis believed had military gifts as great as his brother's. These demoralizing changes coincided with the outbreak of the war of 1805, during which Charles was sent to the Italian front, too far away to prevent Mack's crushing defeat at Austerlitz, which destroyed everything that had been accomplished since the beginning of the century.

After 1805 Charles took up the task of reform once more,[14] successfully enough to prepare the army for the great effort of 1809 and for the first clear defeat of Napoleon in battle, the Austrian victory at Aspern. But if Aspern was the height of Charles' career, it was also its end, not merely because it was followed by Wagram, but because he was from now on to be excluded from posts suited to his talents. Despite his great services to the state, there was no disposition to appoint him to supreme command again. When the great hour of liberation struck in 1813, neither the Emperor nor his chief minister Metternich wanted him, and the latter said, "We need a commander who makes war, not one who is a politician. The Archduke wants to be Minister of Foreign Affairs as well, and that is not compatible with the functions of a commander."[15]

The operational direction of the campaign that led to Leipzig and eventually to Napoleon's abdication fell, therefore, not to Charles but to Field Marshal Karl Philip Prince Schwarzenberg, a competent but not inspiring *Feldherr*, whose system of command Clausewitz (perhaps a biased observer) described as "hesitant and lacking determination."[16] Schwarzenberg was too circumspect to dabble in politics and too dull

[14] For details, see Ludwig Jedlicka, "Erzherzog Karl, der Sieger von Aspern," in Hantsch, *op. cit.*, p. 319; R. Lorenz, "Erzherzog Karl als Denker," in August Faust, ed., *Das Bild des Krieges im deutschen Denken* (Stuttgart and Berlin, 1941), I, 258–59.

[15] Oskar Regele, *Feldmarschall Radetzky: Leben, Leistung, Erbe* (Vienna, 1957), p. 118.

[16] Karl von Clausewitz, *Vom Kriege* (ed., Werner Hahlweg) (16th ed.; Bonn, 1952), p. 222.

to acquire a popular following large enough to worry the politicians in Vienna. Even so, he was not entirely spared the kind of interference that had plagued his predecessor. In September 1813 his Chief of Staff, Radetzky, urged him to impress upon the Emperor the necessity, not only of increased material support, but also of less court interference in the sphere of strategical planning. "Every operational plan which we have so far proposed," he wrote, "has been greeted with opposition as soon as we spoke of putting it into effect. Everybody has something to say in the way of criticism, but no one ever tries to put forward a better proposal."[17] In December 1813 the momentum of the Austrian drive toward France slowed when the Emperor and his aides objected to the army's crossing the Rhine. When Radetzky pressed for a continuation of the offensive, Francis said jokingly that it looked as if he would have in the end either to imprison or to behead him because of his operational ideas, and one of the Emperor's councilors asked spitefully, "Are you trying to be smarter than Prince Eugene?"[18]

Differences between generals and politicians are not uncommon in wartime, and it would be difficult to find a nation whose history was entirely free of civil-military conflict. The striking feature of the Austrian case, however, is the fact that such conflict was so continuous that it became a kind of law of Austrian politics. Even in the great crisis of 1848–49, when the fate of the dynasty depended on the vigor and skill of its soldiers, the court and the politicians found time to indulge their now traditional suspicion of outstanding military talent; and the new Emperor Francis Joseph joined them in this exercise. On 13 February 1849, during the Hungarian campaign of Field Marshal Windischgrätz, the *Wiener Zeitung* reported a rumor that the Emperor intended to honor the commander by making him Duke of Friedland. This evocation of Wallenstein's name, with what seemed to the Emperor to be an implication that he would himself become a mere tool in the arms of the military, annoyed Francis Joseph and made him responsive to those politicians and soldiers who wanted to pull Windischgrätz down for reasons of their own. In April 1849, the Field Marshal was recalled from Hungary, on the grounds that his campaign against the rebels had bogged down and that he had nothing further to offer but the unpleasant prospect of Russian intervention to save the Austrian cause. He was replaced by *Feldzeugmeister* Ludwig Freiherr von Welden, who had played an active part in the conspiracy against him and who had

[17] Regele, *Radetzky*, p. 137.
[18] *Ibid.*, p. 162.

boasted of the ease with which he would dispose of the Hungarian troubles. As in the case of other such changes of command in Austrian history, the results were not happy. Welden's confidence evaporated within a month of his appointment, and he began to clamor, in almost panic-stricken tones, for the very course he had earlier described as unnecessary. In May Russian aid was solicited after all, and intervention followed.[19]

It has to be admitted that the soldiers often invited suspicion. Archduke Charles had had independent views about foreign policy which suggested to some an unwillingness to stay within his proper sphere. Windischgrätz, on the eve of his Hungarian campaign, had written a letter to the Emperor asking that no ministerial decisions on major issues be made without prior consultation with him, a request which Francis Joseph must surely have remembered when the Wallenstein article appeared in the *Wiener Zeitung*. Haynau, the Austrian commander in the mopping-up phase of the Hungarian revolution, was so arrogant in his exchanges with Vienna and so adamantly opposed to any form of ministerial control or even advice that he had to be recalled.[20]

There were enough incidents of this kind in the years of revolution to make the Emperor thoroughly distrustful of the commanding generals of his army, including the now revered Radetzky, whose headquarters—"*cette boutique de Vérone,*" as Metternich called it—he came to regard as a center of potential subversion.[21] This feeling persuaded him to go beyond the tactics of control used by his predecessors—ministerial interference with command matters, the practice of burdening commanders with deputies and aides whose views were incompatible with their own, and the like—and to concentrate all important matters of command, troop dispositions and movements, and personnel in his own hands. Since it was impractical to suppose that he could deal with all these matters personally, he established a Central Military Chancery to handle them and placed at its head his Adjutant General, Karl Ludwig Count Grünne von Pinchard. The son of one of Archduke Charles' aides, Grünne was a man of natural wit, great energy, and limitless vanity. His practical knowledge of the military art, however, was as exiguous as his confidence in his military judgment was great, and he almost automatically opposed those who knew more about soldiering than he did himself. Thus, he played a leading role in turning the

19 Corti, *op. cit.*, pp. 16–25.
20 *Ibid.*, pp. 4 f., 57–58, 60.
21 *Ibid.*, p. 172.

Emperor against Windischgrätz, and he was always critical of the savior of Austria's Italian provinces, whom he once described as "that old ass Radetzky." To place command matters completely in the hands of this political general—for that was the practical result of the Emperor's decision, and it remained so for the next ten years—could only be productive of trouble if another great crisis should arise. And Austria's history was never free of crisis for very long.[22]

II

The confusion and inefficiency that were caused in command relationships by what has here been called the Wallenstein complex were made worse as a result of attitudes and habits of mind within the officer corps itself, which originated at least as far back as the Battle of Kolin. That battles are often won by personal initiative is true, and that willingness to assume responsibility should be inculcated in any army's officer corps is equally so; but the efficiency of a military machine depends nevertheless upon the maintenance of a delicate balance between freedom and subordination. There was no Austrian Kleist to dramatize the importance of the latter quality, and it was not among the values most highly honored by the Order of Maria Theresa. At the risk of exaggeration, indeed, it may be suggested that the mystique of that order was largely responsible for the frequent instances of departure from and disobedience to orders by regimental, brigade, and even corps commanders in Austrian campaigns. To win the Cross of Maria Theresa was the ambition of every officer, and, since it could be won only by an act of individual bravery, a nice observance of orders often seemed inexpedient.

Imperceptibly this led the average Austrian officer to place a higher valuation upon individualism than upon system and—by extension—upon qualities of the spirit than upon those of the mind. In the Prussian army of the Old Dessauer's time and even later there had been a lot of expressed scorn for "ink-splashers" and "pedants,"[23] but this was much diminished after the reforms of the Napoleonic period. In Austria, it continued at least as late as the disaster of 1866. Resistance to any

[22] On Grünne, see, *inter alia,* Joseph Redlich, *Emperor Francis Joseph of Austria: A Biography* (New York, 1929), pp. 43 ff., 91–92; Edmund Glaise von Horstenau, *Franz Josephs Weggefährte* (Zurich, Vienna, 1930), pp. 37 ff.; Corti, *op. cit.,* pp. 6–7, 27.

[23] See Gordon A. Craig, *The Politics of the Prussian Army 1640–1945* (new ed.; Oxford, 1964), p. 25.

systematic study of the business of war was fairly general outside of the technical branches of the service; and, with the higher charges of the army in the hands of great nobles who regarded war as a kind of blood sport, there was little pressure upon junior officers to change their attitude. When the future Field Marshal Mollinary started his career as a cadet in the Sixteenth Infantry Regiment in Treviso in 1837, he served under a colonel who left all matters of education and training in the hands of an adjutant who was incompetent to deal with them. In consequence, "nothing was done for the theoretical education or improvement of the officers and cadets. Nobody even bothered to see that the not inconsiderable number of them who had not mastered the verbal usages peculiar to the regiment were kept working at them."[24] Conditions like these were, unfortunately, not confined to Treviso.

After 1848 there was a tendency in high places not merely to disregard learning but to distrust it. This at least was the Emperor's reaction to the defection of many of the Italian and Hungarian officers during the year of revolution. Francis Joseph was soon declaring, in a marginal note on a reform proposal submitted to him, that the "strength of the army lies not so much in educated officers as in loyal and gallant ones," adding that this should be borne in mind when command positions were filled in the future.[25] In practice, this attitude could only lead to discrimination against officers who were too conspicuously "learned," and this was indeed the case during the years of Grünne's influence.

It is clear that the evolution in Austria of anything corresponding to a modern general staff system would be strongly influenced by these attitudes, for the general staff is supposed to be the seat of intelligence, the brain of the army. In the broadest sense, a general staff has two functions:

> first, the systematic and extensive collection in time of peace of specific information which may be important to the future conduct of operations or to proper preparation for future operations; and, second, intellectual preparation for the future conduct of operations either through systematic development of skill for the handling of contingently anticipated situations or through the elaboration of specific plans for war, or both.[26]

The second function generally includes the training of a corps of specifically designated staff officers who can serve at army, corps, brigade,

[24] Anton Freiherr von Mollinary, *Sechsundvierzigjahre im oesterreich-ungarischen Heere, 1833–1879* (Zurich, 1905), I, 39.

[25] Corti, *op. cit.*, p. 27.

[26] Dallas D. Irvine, "The Origin of Capital Staffs," *Journal of Modern History*, X (1938), 165.

and division headquarters and give appropriate information and advice to commanding officers. In Austria, the machinery for the accomplishment of these tasks was developed, but the results were nonetheless hardly impressive.

As in other countries, the Austrian general staff system had its origins in the eighteenth-century quartermaster general's staff, an organization charged with the totality of arrangements necessary for the quartering of troops in the field. In Maria Theresa's time, a start was made toward widening the functions of this staff (which originally resembled an engineering corps) and adjusting them to the changing nature of war. Field Marshal Daun was a man who regarded war as a "comprehensive science" which had to be learned. In his view, a true commander had to have knowledge of tactics and weapons and maps, of the resources of his own and other countries, and of the technical problems of command, and he must, in addition, have some sense of strategical theory. "Intelligence and strength are the only decisive things in warfare," he told his royal mistress. "Intelligence is the most important quality for officers, just as good morale is for the common soldier." Believing this, Daun encouraged the Empress in her support of her new military schools at Wiener-Neustadt and bent his own energies toward such tasks as the improvement of cartographic work, the beginning of serious operational studies, and the introduction of yearly maneuvers for the army.[27]

The momentum which Daun gave to the development of a staff system was not maintained in the years that followed, although Joseph II showed some fleeting interest in the subject.[28] It was not until the Archduke Charles' reforms in the years 1800–1809 that new progress was made. Like Daun, Charles was insistent that good commanders were not born but made, and that the future of the Austrian state would depend to a significant degree upon the quality of its military education. Charles sought to systematize officer training so that it would be continuous from the level of subaltern all the way up to the rank of general. At the same time, he set about reorganizing the quartermaster general's staff by removing from it all officers who had been serving as adjutants or administrators and converting it into a body exclusively devoted to strategical and operational duties, the preparation of technical and cartographic studies, the accumulation of intelligence about foreign armies, and other modern staff functions. This systematization was carried further after 1809, when Radetzky was chief of the quartermaster general's

27 Walter, *op. cit.*, pp. 263–65.

28 Ernst Benedikt, *Kaiser Joseph II, 1741–1790* (2d ed.; Vienna, 1947), p. 180.

staff. In 1810 this body was reorganized to provide separate sections for cartography, intelligence and communications, war archives, general staff corps (service with army and divisional commands), and service with legations and embassies abroad (the beginning of a system of military attachés).[29]

All this represented progress, although no more than was being made by other states in this period. In the years after 1815, unfortunately, while other countries (especially Prussia) continued to develop the efficiency and authority of their general staffs, the reverse was true in Austria.

One reason for this was that the chief of the quartermaster general's staff occupied a relatively modest position in the military hierarchy. Archduke Charles had hoped to make the holder of this position the Supreme War Council's chief adviser for all operational and strategical matters, and an imperial decree of 1809 had actually defined the chief's position in those terms. But he was never given enough rank to hold his own with the department chiefs (*Hofkriegsräte*) in the Supreme War Council, and his influence was always checked by military bureaucrats who, Radetzky once said, knew about as much "of the army, its spirit and its needs as they do about the Sultan's Divan."[30] Another reason was financial. As early as 1820, the Emperor felt it necessary to order that in the autumn maneuvers of that year no costly experiments (the throwing of bridges across the Danube and the like) be attempted and that observers pay their own expenses. Similar curtailments were made all through the period before 1848, and other economies hampered the development of staff training. Financial stringency also played a part in the failure to expand the general staff corps, with the result that, when the revolution burst upon the empire, there were only eleven trained general staff officers available for service with the army in Italy, which at that time comprised some 70,000 men.[31]

But more important than these things was the widespread disregard of the importance of learning as a military virtue, which diminished the prestige of staff work even in the eyes of some of those who became staff officers. In 1811 Radetzky had said (with perhaps a premonition of what was to happen) that vigilance would have to be exercised lest general staff work become "a fertile ground for lucky mushrooms" (*Glückspilze,* careerists) and lest "a glib tongue, a good seat on a horse,

[29] On all this, see Jedlicka, *op. cit.,* p. 319; Lorenz, *op. cit.,* pp. 258 ff.; Regele, *Radetzky,* pp. 88, 398–401.

[30] Mollinary, *op. cit.,* I, 62–63; Regele, *Radetzky,* pp. 397–98.

[31] Regele, *Radetzky,* p. 226; Mollinary, *op. cit.,* I, 118.

and a good supply of technical terms be considered sufficient to qualify a man for staff service."[32] When the later Chief of the General Staff Beck was assigned as a lieutenant to the Operations Bureau of the *chef* of the Vienna army command in 1851, he found conditions that justified Radetzky's fears. With a few exceptions, all of the officers on the staff were "happy idlers, who either had names that showed they belonged to the high nobility or possessed powerful protectors." Among them was the son of the horse-dealer who took care of the commanding general's stable. A year later, when Beck qualified for admission to the War College, he discovered that that organization, in the very first year of its existence, was adapting itself to prevailing values. The emphasis was on rote learning, and horsemanship played an excessive role in the curriculum.[33]

After Emperor Francis Joseph had established his Military Chancery in 1849 and given his full confidence to Count Grünne, the reduction of the influence of the General Staff and of staff officers in general became a matter of formal policy. Grünne made the newly established adjutants corps the executive agency for his directives, and, on army and divisional staffs, adjutants who reported directly to him usurped functions that had once been performed by members of the general staff corps. Mollinary, who watched this system operating in Italy in 1849 and saw the Emperor's Adjutant General Schönhals do everything in his power to disrupt the work and countermand the directives of Radetzky's brilliant *chef*, Heinrich Freiherr von Hess, admitted that the adjutants were generally talented, energetic and patriotic men, but added that they were unschooled in the art of war and, perhaps for that very reason, resented the staff officers, who were.[34] After the suppression of the revolutionary disorders, Grünne saw to it that Hess, who had been made chief of the quartermaster general's staff, was not only bypassed, even in strategical matters, but publicly humiliated as well; and, since Hess was not the kind of man who fought back, the influence of his staff reached bottom in the 1850's.[35] Deprived of authority, money, and prestige, there was little it could do to keep alive the important truth that war is a complicated business which can be mastered only by intelligence and application.

The effects of this were noticed by at least one sapient foreign observer. In 1854, the Prussian military attaché, Prince Kraft zu Hohen-

[32] Regele, *Radetzky*, pp. 399–400.
[33] Glaise von Horstenau, *Franz Josephs Weggefährte*, pp. 31 ff.
[34] Mollinary, *op. cit.*, I, 118–19.
[35] *Ibid.*, I, 250; Glaise von Horstenau, *Franz Josephs Weggefährte*, pp. 37–38.

lohe-Ingelfingen, an artillery officer whose batteries were to help blast Austrian troops off the height of Chlum on 3 July 1866, observed the annual maneuvers of the Austrian army. All branches of the service, he noted, were suffering from grave deficiencies of training and equipment, and "the exercises of combined arms demonstrated that the unit leadership, as well as the over-all command, was in a childish condition, which surprised me."[36] The following year saw no improvement. The maneuvers were badly planned and executed and, since there were no critiques, seemed rather pointless. After one day's exercises, Hohenlohe met the Austrian artillery general, Bauer von Bauernfeld, riding slowly back to quarters and asked him why he seemed so glum. Bauer answered, "*G'lernt hob i nix!*" ("I haven't learned anything!")[37]

Unfortunately for Austria, it was not in maneuvers alone that the results of this deliberate flight from intelligence were perceptible.

III

On the eve of the Italian war of 1859, there was a flare-up of that civil-military incompatibility which had prevented proper coordination between force and diplomacy in the days of the Archduke Charles. Relations between the military chiefs and the ministry of Count Buol-Schauenstein had deteriorated rapidly during the Crimean War, for in that conflict Buol had worked energetically for intervention on the side of the western powers, while the soldiers (including Grünne, who for once found himself on the side of Windischgrätz and Hess) stood either for neutrality or for loyalty to the old Russian alliance. In an audience with the Emperor after the Paris Conference of 1856, the Austrian ambassador to Paris, Count Hübner, accused the soldiers of being directly responsible for Austria's present isolation. They had made intimations of assistance to Russia which the government had never intended, and by doing so they had increased Russia's resentment, while discrediting the government in the eyes of the English and the French. Dabbling in politics, said Hübner violently, had become a military disease, and he went on to cite examples from the year 1849. The Emperor, on the whole, seemed to agree with him.[38]

The diplomats got their own back in 1859 by disregarding military considerations entirely in the planning of national policy. In his dealings

[36] Prinz Kraft zu Hohenlohe-Ingelfingen, *Aus meinem Leben, 1848–1871* (4 vols.; Berlin, 1897–1907), I, 280 ff.

[37] *Ibid.*, I, 337.

[38] Corti, *op. cit.*, p. 172.

with the Italian and French governments, Buol used tactics that were calculated to make war inevitable, while at the same time he refused to admit to his colleagues that the situation was serious enough to justify the soldiers' demands for an urgent and comprehensive armaments program. In meetings of the Emperor's advisers, he persistently denied that France was serious about supporting the Piedmontese government in any hostilities that might ensue; and he dropped broad hints about prospective Austrian alliances with Prussia, the German states, and even Great Britain. He agreed that the Archduke Albert, the son of Archduke Charles and a distinguished soldier in his own right, should go to Berlin and try to win a Prussian promise of aid in the event of French intervention, but then undercut this mission by despatching an ultimatum to Piedmont without informing Albert that he intended to do so. Finally, having created a situation in which war in the most unfavorable conditions was inevitable—Hess had persistently warned that an ultimatum would invite disaster, and he was right—Buol washed his hands of the whole business. At a meeting of the ministers on 27 April 1859, Grünne pointed out that the soldiers had a right to know who exactly were their enemies, what precisely were their objectives, and who specifically might come to their assistance, and he asked fretfully what had become of all of Buol's fine promises. The minister answered blandly that negotiations were continuing but that he regarded the situation as similar to that which had obtained when Maria Theresa came to the throne. In any case, he added, "the answers to the questions posed by His Majesty's Adjutant General no longer lie in the diplomatic sphere; full responsibility for giving the decisive answers lies now with the military."[39]

The damage done by this classic case of faulty civil-military coordination was now compounded by military maladroitness arising from the intellectual slackness of the last half century. This is not the place for a detailed account of the Italian campaign of 1859;[40] but a few items from the sorry record are worth noting. The Austrian army marched into Italy without an adequate supply system, or accurate intelligence of enemy strength and capabilities, or even reliable maps to guide its movements. Thanks to Grünne, it was led not by Hess, who knew Italy, where he

[39] For Buol's policy, see *ibid.*, pp. 212 ff., 220–21; H. Ritter von Srbik, *Deutsche Einheit* (Munich, 1935 et seq.), II, 340 ff., 353.

[40] See, *inter alia*, the accounts in W. von Willisen, *Die Feldzüge der Jahre 1859 und 1866* (Leipzig, 1868); Heinrich Friedjung, ed., *Benedeks nachgelassene Papiere* (Leipzig, 1901); and H. von Moltke, *Militärische Werke*, III (Berlin, 1904). An interesting recent sketch is Anton Freiherr von Bechtolsheim, "Vor 100 Jahren: Magenta," in *Wehrwissenschaftliche Rundschau*, IX (1959), 427–54.

had served as Radetzky's *chef* in 1849, but by Franz Count Gyulai, a court favorite who had so little confidence in his own abilities that his cautious fumbling ruined troop morale before he had made real contact with the enemy. At the same time, he was deaf to the advice of others and was soon on such bad terms with his chief of staff, Kuhn, that they corresponded only in writing. Conditions at Gyulai's headquarters were so confused that one commander said that the spectacle turned his stomach. There was no clear chain of command, and unit commanders were constantly receiving contradictory orders from two or more higher officers and continually having to recall their troops from one pointless mission in order to despatch them on another equally so. Because of this sort of thing, what slim chance there had been of defeating the Italians separately before the French came up in strength was lost, and by the beginning of June Gyulai's forces were in full retreat across the Ticino. Magenta was fought on 4 June 1859 and led to new withdrawals so precipitate that headquarters lost all control over the subordinate commands.[41]

Gyulai was relieved of his post on 18 June, and the Emperor assumed personal command of the army, with Hess at his side—but with Grünne there too, and all of Grünne's staff. This changeover did not improve the situation, since it soon transpired that all orders issued by Hess had to be verified by Grünne's Chancery before being forwarded. Mollinary, who visited headquarters at this time, records a scene that sums up everything that was wrong with the direction of the war. When the army high command departed from Villafranca, it did so in a long row of handsome carriages, the Emperor and an aide leading the procession, followed by the archdukes, then the Adjutant General, then the other generals assigned to the Military Chancery, and then the swarm of wing adjutants. At the very end of the line came an ordinary *Postkalesche* drawn by two unprepossessing horses: transportation for the chief of the quartermaster general's staff! Hess climbed in wearily and after a few moments said to Mollinary, "You can have no conception of *how* I suffer!"[42]

IV

On 24 June, Solferino completed the discomfiture of the Austrian army and the discrediting of those who had brought it to this sorry pass. Buol had already been dismissed; Hess, worn out by age and disappoint-

[41] Glaise von Horstenau, *Franz Josephs Weggefährte,* pp. 50–65; Corti, *op. cit.,* pp. 221–33.

[42] Mollinary, *op. cit.,* II, 44.

ment, submitted his resignation; Grünne tried to shore up his position but came under such sharp attack from people like Hübner that the Emperor was forced to let him go. The Hofburg was suddenly filled with new faces. Rechberg, a careful diplomat of the Metternich school, took over Buol's functions. Lieutenant Field Marshal Franz Folliot de Crenneville, a soldier who knew infinitely more about war than Grünne had known, and who was a good, if occasionally overcritical, judge of men, assumed the post of First Adjutant General. The whole military establishment was reorganized, what had been the Supreme War Council being transformed into a Ministry of War and placed under the leadership of August Count Degenfeld-Schonburg, an energetic man who was determined to correct the weaknesses revealed in Italy. Finally, the most popular soldier since Radetzky and the hero of Solferino, Feldzeugmeister Ludwig August von Benedek, was made chief of the quartermaster general's staff.[43]

This change of order had the effect of reducing the civilian-military differences that had been productive of so much harm in the years from 1854 to 1859, for Rechberg got along rather well with the soldiers. Its effects upon the efficiency of the army were also marked, but mixed. There can be little doubt that the excellent performance of the Austrian artillery and cavalry in the war against Prussia, and particularly in the battle of Königgrätz, owed much to the vigor with which Degenfeld tackled problems of weaponry, supply, and training in those arms. On the other hand, the War Minister was also at least partly responsible for drawing false conclusions from his observation of French tactics in 1859 and, as a result, for placing excessive emphasis upon shock tactics in Austrian training in an age in which battles were to be decided by firepower. This prejudice in favor of the bayonet, which was shared by the Emperor himself, was strengthened by the successes won by Austrian troops in Denmark in 1864, although these victories were gained, as shrewd Prussian observers noted, at excessive cost in lives.[44]

Leaving this aside, it is notable that in one vital area no improvement was made: namely, in the general staff system. No change could really be expected here unless someone with authority encouraged a general change of attitude toward the role of intelligence in war. Benedek, who

[43] On Crenneville and Degenfeld, see H. Ritter von Srbik, *Aus Oesterreichs Vergangenheit* (Salzburg, 1949), pp. 116–18. On Benedek, see Friedjung, *op. cit.*, pp. 1–250 *passim,* and especially 63, 134, 175, 183, 265; and Regele, *Benedek,* pp. 261–89.

[44] On this subject, see Craig, *Königgrätz,* pp. 8–10; Hohenlohe-Ingelfingen, *op. cit.*, III, 105–6; Srbik, *Aus Oesterreichs Vergangenheit,* p. 118.

perhaps possessed the necessary personal weight to accomplish this, was not sufficiently interested to try. For one thing, he did not have the time to do so: in addition to being chief of the quartermaster general's staff and head of the general staff corps, he held the post of Governor of Hungary until October 1860 and was then appointed commander of the Second Army in Italy. This meant that most of his staff work had to be carried on by deputies, first by General von Ramming and later, from 1861 to 1864, by Lieutenant Field Marshal Nagy. This was hardly an arrangement designed to enhance the authority or prestige of the general staff.

But more important was the fact that Benedek—and this was true also of Archduke Albert, whose influence in the army, if not on the public, was as great as Benedek's[45]—was more interested in preserving what was often called "the old army spirit" than he was in advancing the uses of intelligence and the skills associated with staff work. A member of the Order of Maria Theresa himself—he had won his cross at Curtatone in May 1848[46]—Benedek believed that wars were won by courage, discipline, and *élan,* and these were the qualities he sought to encourage in his peacetime commands. On the other hand, officers who sought to win his approbation by arranging operational exercises or writing tactical studies received no encouragement.[47] These things bored him. He was, as Chief of Staff Beck's biographer has written, "an opponent of any kind of scholarly activity by soldiers."[48]

Not even Benedek's most recent biographer has been able to point to much in the way of achievement during his term as chief of the quartermaster general's staff.[49] Some changes of procedure were introduced into the cartographic, historical, and archival sections; the role of the staff in the program of the *Kriegsschule* was broadened; and a railway section was established. To avoid the kind of friction that had existed at army and corps headquarters in 1859, the influence of the adjutants corps was reduced, although it is worth noting that Benedek opposed this reform and that it was not complete. On the other hand, much was not done: the position of the quartermaster general's staff remained ambiguous, as Benedek's successor pointed out in a memorandum in 1865; the relationship between its chief and the head of the Operations Section in

45 Srbik, *Aus Oesterreichs Vergangenheit,* pp. 109 ff.
46 Friedjung, *op. cit.,* pp. 74–75.
47 Mollinary, *op. cit.,* II, 108.
48 Glaise von Horstenau, *Franz Josephs Weggefährte,* p. 71.
49 See Regele, *Benedek,* pp. 171 ff.

the Ministry of War was never made clear; and he had no effective control over the selection of *chefs* for the different army corps.[50]

Most critical was the failure to impress the officer corps in general with a sense of the vital importance of a good staff system. None of the glamor that had been associated with the Prussian staff system since Scharnhorst's time attached itself to the Austrian quartermaster general's staff. It had, indeed, to a distressing degree, remained "a fertile ground for *Glückspilze,*" and this was widely known. When Beck was working in the cartographic section in these years, he was charged with the task of making a military geographical survey of central Germany, based on reports that were to be sent home by another staff officer working in Germany. This second officer, however, disappeared into the casinos of Bad Ems and, when Beck pleaded for material, told him to dig it out of Baedeker.[51] Nor was this sort of dry rot confined to the junior ranks. Henikstein was able to write in 1865, "I ask myself whether it is not shameful that we have four *chefs* on army staffs at the present time who are completely incompetent."[52]

When Henikstein became vocal about these deficiencies, the man who was to lead the Northern Army against Prussia in 1866 refused to take his friend's complaints seriously. Benedek had already advised his successor, when Henikstein insisted that he did not have the necessary talent to be chief of staff, that he worried too much. Let him take the job for a while. After all, if something important like a war should come along, he could always give it up and take command of a corps![53] This advice, which neatly expressed Benedek's unflattering opinion of the role of intelligence in war, explains why the Austrian staff system was almost as confused and ineffective in 1866 as it had been in 1859.

There is reason to believe that, after his fall from grace, Benedek began belatedly to doubt the validity of the philosophy of war which he had shared with the great majority of the officer corps of the Austrian army. "How could we prevail against the Prussians?" he said sadly to a visitor. "We have learned so little, and they are such a studious people."[54]

[50] Eugen Frauenholz, "Feldmarschalleutnant Alfred Freiherr von Henikstein im Jahre 1866," *Münchener Historische Abhandlungen,* Series 2, III, 34 ff.

[51] Glaise von Horstenau, *Franz Josephs Weggefährte,* p. 71.

[52] Frauenholz, *loc. cit.*

[53] *Ibid.*

[54] Friedjung, *op. cit.,* p. 406.

2. Problems of Coalition Warfare: The Military Alliance Against Napoleon, 1813-14

For some six generations now, the campaigns of 1813 and 1814 in Germany and France have exercised a powerful fascination over the minds of historians, and it is understandable that this should be so. It would be difficult to find another time in the modern age as full of dramatic crises as the autumn that saw Napoleon's strength and reputation broken at Leipzig and the spring that witnessed his brilliant but unavailing attempts to break out of the ring of steel that forced him toward surrender. To members of an older generation, the spectacle of this greatest of Great Captains fighting tenaciously but with shrinking resources to save the New Order he had created possessed all the qualities of classical tragedy, and they studied the details of his last campaigns with admiration for the flashes of inspiration that lightened the gathering pall of defeat and with sympathy for the desperate twistings and turnings that preceded the end. "The campaign of 1814," wrote a British historian in a book that appeared a century after the events it described, "is certainly a wonderful example of what Napoleon's genius could do in circumstances which . . . had become so desperate that no other general of the time would have attempted to make head against them."[1]

Napoleon doubtless has as many admirers today as when that judgment was written fifty years ago. But circumstances alter cases and even have the power to change the prescription of the glasses through

"Problems of Coalition Warfare" was originally presented at the United States Air Force Academy, Colorado, in March 1965 as the seventh annual Harmon Memorial Lecture in Military History, and was later privately printed by the Academy. It is reprinted with the Academy's permission.

[1] F. Loraine Petre, *Napoleon at Bay, 1814* (London, 1914), p. 203.

which the historian peers back at the past. What we see in history and the things in it that stir our active interest are largely determined by our own experience and by the perplexities of our own time; that is why, living as we do in a country which, in the last quarter of a century, has fought two wars in alliance with other powers and is presently a member of the greatest peacetime alliance in history (although admittedly one that is very difficult to hold together), we are apt to be less interested in the purely military features of the last struggle against Napoleon than in those things that mirror our current and recent concerns. The tactical virtuosity of Napoleon will make a weaker claim upon the attention of our historians than do the problems of the coalition that opposed him—particularly such things as the difficulties its members experienced in establishing an effective command structure, their incomplete success in reaching agreement on war aims and the repercussions this had on their operational efficiency, and the problems caused within their alliance by imperfect governmental control over commanders in the field, which threatened to expand the war against Napoleon to a new and frightening dimension. All of the thorny problems with which western statesmen have wrestled during the Second World War, the Korean conflict, and the troubled history of NATO can be found, in hardly altered form, within the anti-Napoleonic coalition, a fact that suggests that certain problems are endemic to military alliances, which may or may not be comforting.

I

At the outset of the autumn campaign of 1813, Napoleon had at his disposal about 442,000 combat troops, of whom 40,000 were cavalry, supported by 1,284 guns. The bulk of this army, about 314,000 men, was concentrated north of the Bohemian mountains in an arc extending from Dresden to Liegnitz in Silesia; a force of 70,000 under Oudinot was poised on the southern border of Mark Brandenburg, within striking distance of Berlin; an observation corps under Margeron was bivouacked at Leipzig; and Davout commanded a mixed force of Frenchmen and Danes at Hamburg. Another 80,000 men were in garrison in the Elbe fortresses and those of Prussia and Poland, and an additional 43,000 stood in reserve.[2] The Emperor had largely repaired the losses that had forced him to accept an armistice after his successes over the

[2] Freiherr von Freytag-Loringhoven, *Kriegslehren nach Clausewitz aus den Feldzügen 1813 und 1814* (Berlin, 1908), p. 11.

Russians and the Prussians at Lützen and Bautzen in May.[3] He was still short of supplies and deficient in certain arms, but his new troop levies, while raw, were commanded by battle-tried veterans; their spirit was good; they could shoot; and French tactics—the advance in column—required no special skill in execution. In addition, the army had the great advantage of fighting on interior lines under the sole direction of a man of energy and purpose. (See Map I.)

Napoleon's opponents were superior to him in every category but the last. The original Russo-Prussian alliance had now been strengthened by the adhesion of Sweden, whose Crown Prince, the former French Marshal Bernadotte, had brought a force of 35,000 troops to Pomerania in May,[4] and—a more important addition—by that of Austria, whose forces swelled the allied total to some 570,000 effectives, plus reserves and fortress troops. This force was, however, split into three widely separated groups: a mixed Prussian-Russian-Swedish force under Bernadotte based on Berlin (the so-called Northern Army); the Silesian Army (Prussians and Russians commanded by Field Marshal Blücher) at Breslau; and the larger Bohemian Army (Austrians, plus Russian and Prussian contingents) stationed south of the Erzgebirge under the command of Field Marshal Prince Schwarzenberg. For successful employment against a determined and centrally positioned opponent, this federated force needed an effective command structure and a strategical plan that was accepted by all its members.

With respect to the first of these, it became clear, once Austria had joined the alliance, that supreme command would have to be vested in an Austrian general. The Russians and the Prussians had shown no particular talent for strategical direction during the spring campaign, and the defeats suffered at Lützen and Bautzen had been due on the one hand to Prussian impetuosity and inattention to detail and on the other to Emperor Alexander's penchant for superseding his commander-in-chief at crucial moments in battle and then becoming discouraged and relinquishing command when things went wrong.[5] Bernadotte, who was

[3] On the reasons for his seeking an armistice, see Colonel F. N. Maude, *The Leipzig Campaign 1813* (London, 1908), pp. 142–43; and J. F. C. Fuller, *A Military History of the Western World* (New York, 1955), II, 464–65.

[4] On Bernadotte's role in the subsequent campaign, see Franklin D. Scott, *Bernadotte and the Fall of Napoleon* (Cambridge, Mass., 1935).

[5] See Friedrich Carl Ferdinand Freiherr von Müffling, *Aus meinem Leben* (Berlin, 1815), pp. 36 ff.; *Die Befreiungskriege,* herausgegeben von der Deutschen Gesellschaft für Wehrpolitik und Wehrwissenschaften (Berlin, 1938), p. 25; E. F. Henderson, *Blücher and the Uprising of Prussia against Napoleon, 1806–1815* (London, 1911), pp. 105, 108; Andrei A. Lobanov-Rostovsky, *Russia and Europe, 1789–1825* (Durham, N. C., 1947), pp. 249–50.

Mecklenburg
Strelitz
Stettin
POMERANIA
Wittenberge
KINGDOM OF WESTPHALIA
Brandenburg
Berlin
Northern Army
Havel
Oder
Küstrin
Warthe
Netze
GRAND DUCHY OF WARSAW
Posen
Magdeburg
Spree
Frankfurt
Elbe
Wittenberg
3.K.K.
XII.
VII.
IV.
Oudinot
Mulde
Torgau
Freistadt
Lissa
2.K.K.
Bober
Glogau
Margaron
Leipzig
Gr. Görschen
Saale
Elster
Neiße
SAXONY
Lausitz
Meißen
Napoleon
G.
Bautzen
II
Görlitz
Bunzlau
VI.
Ney
V.
III.
Trachenberg
Silesian Army
Sacken
Katzbach
Liegnitz
Jauer
Hundsfeld
Dresden
Stolpen
Pirna
I.K.K.
Rumburg
Sonnenstein
Lilienstein
Königstein
VIII.
Zittau
XI.
Neukirch
Kähn
Striegau
Kanth
Breslau
5.K.K.
Peterswalde
4.K.K.
Schreiberhau
Langeron
Balkenhain
York
Landeshut
Pahlen
Schweidnitz
Reichenbach
SILESIA
Div. Bubna
Erz Geb.
Eger
Bohemian Army
Gitschin
Direction of approach of Barclay's Unit of the Silesian Army
BOHEMIA
Prag
Moldau
Königgrätz
0 10 20 30 40 50 60 70 80 90 100 km.
1:1750000.
Allied forces
French forces
Position in August, 1813, at the recommencement of hostilities

Map I

accorded a degree of respect that he did not subsequently justify by his actions in the campaign—(it was mistakenly believed by Emperor Francis of Austria, among others, that the Swedish Crown Prince knew the most intimate secrets of Napoleon's art of war and would turn them against its author[6])—had not supplied enough troops to the alliance to qualify for the post. No one was clearer about this than the Austrian Chancellor Metternich, whose devious diplomatic campaign during the spring and summer of 1813 had been accompanied by an armament effort of great energy, which had brought Austrian troop strength, by August, to 479,000 officers and men, including 298,000 combat troops.[7] Metternich was determined that this contribution should receive the recognition it deserved and that he should be entitled to name the supreme commander. "The important thing," he wrote to one of his associates on 13 August, "is to have the decisive voice in the determination of the military dispositions, and to maintain against everyone—as I have been emphasizing to the Emperor Alexander—the principle that the power that puts 300,000 men into the field is the first power and all the others only auxiliaries."[8]

The Tsar ceded this point, but not without an attempt to influence the selection of the supreme commander. The logical choice, he suggested, would be the first man who had ever defeated Napoleon in the open field, Archduke Charles of Austria, the victor at Aspern in 1809, and the best possible chief for his general staff would be the Swiss Antoine Henri Jomini, formerly *général de brigade* in the French Army and *chef* to Marshal Ney. Alexander's proposal is still intriguing to the historian who likes to speculate about might-have-beens. Next to Clausewitz, Jomini was the best known military theorist of the first half of the nineteenth century and the most incisive analyst of Napoleon's methods of war; a partnership between him and the Archduke Charles, who, more than any other soldier of his day, enjoyed the love and admiration of Austrian troops, might have been a happy and fruitful combination.[9]

[6] Helmuth Rössler, *Oesterreichs Kampf um Deutschlands Befreiung* (2 vols.; Hamburg, 1940), II, 148.

[7] On the financial and other obstacles that had to be overcome before this was possible, see *ibid.*, pp. 132–33, 221.

[8] Oskar Regele, *Feldmarschall Radetsky: Leben, Leistung, Erbe* (Vienna, 1957), p. 118. On Metternich's sense of military affairs and the coordination between his military policy and his diplomacy, see *ibid.*, p. 108.

[9] On Jomini, see the essay by Crane Brinton in Edward Mead Earle, ed., *Makers of Modern Strategy: Military Thought from Machiavelli to Hitler* (Princeton, N.J., 1943), pp. 77–92. On Archduke Charles, see Rössler, *op. cit.*, I, pp. 109–50; Ludwig Jedlicka, "Erzherzog Karl, der Sieger von Aspern," in Hugo

Or again, it might not: their common prejudice in favor of the methodical position warfare characteristic of the eighteenth century would not have commended them to the commanders of the Silesian Army, who were, in any case, scornful of French renegades like Bernadotte, Moreau, and Jomini. Moreover, it is possible that Jomini shone to best advantage in the study rather than in the field; the Silesian Army's quartermaster general wrote later that Jomini's advice to the Tsar during the fighting around Dresden in August 1813 was so impractical that no one ever took him seriously again.[10]

The partnership between the Tsar's candidates never had an opportunity to prove itself, because Metternich never considered it seriously. He was aware not only that Jomini was a member of Alexander's military suite, but that Archduke Charles was in love with Alexander's sister Caroline and hoped to secure the Tsar's permission to marry her.[11] In these circumstances, the two nominations promised to give the Russians a preponderance of influence at Supreme Headquarters. Even if that had not been true, the relationship between Charles and his brother, the Emperor Francis, had never been an easy one, and Charles had a record of conflict with civilian authorities that dated back to the 1790's and was regarded (not wholly justly) as a commander who was not amenable to governmental control.[12] Metternich expected to have enough troubles with his allies without compounding them with differences within the Austrian camp. He said at this time: "We need a commander who makes war, not one who is a politician."[13]

With all this in mind, therefore, the chancellor decided not to take Alexander's advice. With his sovereign's approval, he selected a man of Charles' age but of different temperament, the forty-two-year-old Karl Philip Prince Schwarzenberg. A soldier without personal ambition, who admired Metternich and enjoyed his confidence, Schwarzenberg deserves a better reputation than that given him by historians, who have perhaps been unduly influenced by Clausewitz's biased and second-hand criticism of his generalship.[14] The new supreme commander's talents

---

Hantsch, ed., *Gestalter der Geschicke Oesterreichs* (Innsbruck, Vienna, 1962); R. Lorenz, "Erzherzog Karl als Denker," in August Faust, ed., *Das Bild des Krieges im deutschen Denken,* I (Stuttgart and Berlin, 1941); and Hans Delbrück, *Geschichte der Kriegskunst* (new ed.; Berlin, 1962), IV, 503.

10 Müffling, *Aus meinem Leben,* p. 82.

11 Rössler, *op. cit.,* II, 149–50, 234–35.

12 See above Chapter 1, pp. 7 ff.

13 Regele, *op. cit.,* p. 118.

14 See, *inter alia,* Karl von Clausewitz, *Vom Kriege* (ed. Werner Hallweg) (16th ed.; Bonn, 1952), pp. 16, 222.

were, to be sure, more diplomatic than strictly military, and it was probably a good thing that this was so. Like Dwight D. Eisenhower in another great coalition 130 years later, his great gift was his ability, by patience and the arts of ingratiation, to hold together a military alliance which, before Napoleon was finally defeated, comprised fourteen members, and to persuade the quarreling monarchs and their field commanders to give more than lip service to the alliance's strategical plan. This was not, as we shall see, an easy task, or one that could be performed with perfect or continuous success.

In the strategical direction of the war, Schwarzenberg's chief assistants were Lieutenant Field Marshal Count Radetzky von Radetz, the Chief of his General Staff, and Lieutenant Field Marshal Freiherr von Langenau, a Saxon officer who defected to the allies in the summer of 1813 and who served as head of the operations section.[15] Radetzky, the future hero of the Italian campaign of 1848–49, was the author of the strategical plan that guided the movements of the three armies during the autumn campaign of 1813, although his claim to this distinction has been contested by the Russians and the Swedes. As early as May 1813, foreseeing Austrian intervention in the war, he had laid an operational plan before his chief; in June, when he met the Tsar's Quartermaster General Toll at Gitschin, he had found that officer in complete agreement with his views; and in July, when the allies gathered (without Austrian participation) at Trachenberg, they accepted an operational plan sponsored by Bernadotte and Toll which was very similar to Radetzky's original plan and which was later amended to make it correspond even more closely to his concept.[16]

Based upon the strategy of attrition—and hence depreciated by all Prussian-German military publicists until the time of Hans Delbrück on the mistaken assumption that *Ermattungsstrategie* was an inferior form of war[17]—Radetzky's plan was intended to make Napoleon split his forces, to wear himself out in constant movement, and, in the end, having lost the advantage of interior lines because of the constriction of territory he controlled, to fight against armies advancing simultaneously

[15] On Langenau, an able but vain and ambitious soldier, see Regele, *op. cit.*, p. 178.

[16] On the Trachenberg talks, see *ibid.*, pp. 124 ff.; Scott, *op. cit.*, pp. 84 ff.; Generalleutnant von Caemmerer, *Die Befreiungskriege 1813–1815: ein strategischer Überblick* (Berlin, 1907), pp. 41 ff.; Rudolf Friederich, *Die Befreiungskriege 1813–1815* (Berlin, 1912), II, 34–41; and, for some biting comments, Müffling, *Aus meinem Leben*, pp. 56–57.

[17] For a discussion of this view, which was based essentially on a misreading of Clausewitz, see below, chapter 4, pp. 73–77.

against his center, flanks, and communications. The method of achieving this he described as a coordinated advance by the three allied armies in such a manner that each of them would act offensively against detached French units but would withdraw if Napoleon sought to concentrate his forces against it, always refraining carefully from becoming involved in a major fight with a superior force, "lest the principal objective of the joint operation be lost," namely, "to strike the final blow with assurance."[18] In general, as he wrote years later, the plan called for "the Austrian army to be the pivot, while the allies would form the swinging wings."[19]

Although this plan won general acceptance, difficulties arose as soon as it was put into effect, partly because of the gap that always exists between paper plans and actual operations, but also because of limitations upon the authority of the supreme commander which manifested themselves as soon as fighting began on 17 August. During the whole of the autumn campaign of 1813, life was enormously complicated for Schwarzenberg and Radetzky by the presence of three of the allied sovereigns at, or uncomfortably close to, general headquarters. These rulers had to be briefed on all specific operational plans and, when they were consulted, often gave less weight to the advice of the supreme commander than they did to their private military advisers. Of the latter there were many. Emperor Francis placed great confidence in General Duka, a courtly desk general with whom Radetzky did not always see eye to eye. King Frederick William III of Prussia relied upon the judgment of his adjutant general Karl Friedrich Freiherr von dem Knesebeck, a man who had played an important role in the reform of the Prussian army but who, as an adviser on operations, was timorous and vacillating, excessively respectful of Napoleon's capacities, and inclined to believe that a strictly defensive posture was the best way of dealing with him.[20] As for the Russian Emperor, he was surrounded by clouds of professional soldiers from all the countries on the map, chief among whom were his own countrymen Wolkonsky, Arakcheiev, and Diebitsch and the Frenchmen Jomini and (until he was killed at Dresden) Moreau. Life at general headquarters was one continual war council, in which all of these royal advisers subjected operational plans to niggling criticism or proposed substitutes of their own. Before the campaign was

[18] Regele, *op. cit.*, pp. 121 ff.

[19] *Ibid.*, p. 126.

[20] On Knesebeck's reforming activities, see W. O. Shanahan, *Prussian Military Reforms, 1786–1813* (New York, 1945), pp. 75 ff., 226. On his presence at Supreme Headquarters, see Rössler, *Oesterreichs Kampf*, II, 152.

far advanced, the usually mild-mannered Schwarzenberg was writing, "It is really inhuman what I must tolerate and bear, surrounded as I am by feeble-minded people, fools of every description, eccentric project-makers, intriguers, asses, babblers, criticasters; I often think I'm going to collapse under their weight."[21]

Fully as irritating as this constant criticism was the tendency of the monarchs—like a group of early Charles de Gaulles—to withdraw troops from the joint command for their own purposes, or to threaten to do so out of personal pique. From the very beginning of the campaign, Emperor Alexander reserved exclusive command over Russian contingents in the Bohemian Army, as well as over the sizable Russian reserve, and Schwarzenberg could not always count on their presence in the line of battle when they were needed. As early as September 1813, the commander-in-chief was complaining to his sovereign that this uncertainty subjected him to pressures and tempted him to make concessions that might be dangerous to the state interest and the common cause; it was essential, he argued, that Russian troops be placed under the effective control of the supreme command.[22] Emperor Francis, unfortunately, had no power to satisfy this demand, and Schwarzenberg was forced to go on worrying about the Russians until Napoleon was overthrown. Nor was he concerned about them alone. There were moments during the autumn campaign, and particularly during the spring campaign in France, when the King of Prussia intimated to the Silesian Army command that he thought it advisable to avoid committing Prussian troops to battle, since further losses might weaken Prussia's voice when the peace talks began.[23] As for the Crown Prince of Sweden, he not only tried to keep his own forces intact but made incessant demands for the assignment of additional Russian and Prussian corps to his command—in order to gratify his self-esteem, one must suppose, since he was very chary of using what was granted him.

Orders from the supreme command were transmitted to the Northern and Silesian armies by the monarchs themselves or by their military plenipotentiaries on Schwarzenberg's staff, the Russian General Toll and the Prussian General von Hake. But instructions were not always carried out in the manner intended, for conditions at the army level were not dissimilar to those that prevailed at the supreme command. In

[21] Regele, *op. cit.*, p. 136.

[22] Hugo Kerchnawe and A. Veltze, *Karl Fürst zu Schwarzenberg* (Vienna, 1913), pp. 166–67.

[23] Müffling, *Aus meinem Leben*, pp. 149 ff.; Generalleutnant von Janson, *Geschichte des Feldzuges 1814 in Frankreich* (Berlin, 1903–1905), II, 98.

the Silesian Army, there were differences between Blücher and his *chef* Gneisenau, on the one hand, and Müffling, the Quartermaster General, and some of the corps commanders on the other. York and Langeron, in particular, were worried by Blücher's lack of caution and sought, by means that sometimes verged on insubordination, to restrain it; and instructions from Schwarzenberg sometimes got lost in the clash of personalities. In the Northern Army there were similar difficulties. Bernadotte was suspicious of all orders emanating from the supreme command lest they overtax his resources and make it impossible for him to attain his real objective in the war, which was the acquisition of Norway for Sweden. The Prussian and Russian corps commanders, Generals von Bülow and Winzingerode, suspected him of sacrificing their troops for his private interest, while saving his own, and, before the campaign in Germany was over, they were accusing him of carrying on secret negotiations with the French. The Crown Prince, on his side, complained continually that he could not count on his generals obeying him.[24]

In the face of these disruptive factors on every level of the command structure, it is remarkable that the strategical task confronting the allies was carried out at all, let alone within a bare three months. To direct a widely separated group of armies toward a common goal and a decisive battle in an age in which there were no railways and few good roads, and no telephone or telegraph, was a formidable enough undertaking even without the trouble caused by administrative duplication, international professional jealousies, and personal feuding within the separate commands. That it was accomplished was doubtless a tribute to the patience and forbearance of Schwarzenberg, but it was certainly due more to the general fear of Napoleon and the common awareness that he was still far from being beaten. The divisive factors were always held in restraint by the common danger, and the allied war plan was enabled to achieve its objective.

Thus it was that, despite the brilliance of Napoleon's employment of his depleted forces and despite some discreditable episodes on the allied side—York's disinclination to accept direction from army headquarters during the fight on the Katzbach[25] and the panic that inspired the monarchs and their staffs when Napoleon appeared like an apparition before Dresden[26]—the first four weeks of the autumn campaign were, on balance, gloomy ones for the French Emperor. Oudinot was beaten

[24] *Ibid.*, pp. 80–81; Scott, *op. cit.*, pp. 99 ff.
[25] Müffling, *Aus meinem Leben,* pp. 61 ff.
[26] Henderson, *op. cit.*, pp. 134–35.

at Grossbeeren by Bernadotte, MacDonald on the Katzbach by Blücher, Vandamme at Kulm by a mixed force working for once with superb coordination,[27] Ney at Dennewitz by Bülow. Prevented by Radetzky's strategy from concentrating against a single enemy, worn out by constant movement, Napoleon slowly fell back upon Leipzig, where he found himself threatened by the three converging allied armies and elected to risk battle against them. The resultant Battle of the Peoples, which extended over three days of hard fighting, was marred by faults of tactical coordination and breakdowns of command efficiency on the part of the allies and by a stubborn refusal on the part of the Swedish Crown Prince to commit anything but his artillery to the common effort—he is reported to have said, "Provided the French are beaten, it is indifferent to me whether I or my army take a part, and of the two, I had much rather we did not"[28]—but, when it was over, Napoleon's armies were broken and caught up in a retreat that was not to stop short of the Rhine. Despite their failure to devise a perfectly functioning command system, the allies had succeeded in liberating all of Germany.

II

Henry A. Kissinger has written recently:

> As long as the enemy is more powerful than any single member of the coalition, the need for unity outweighs all considerations of individual gain. Then the powers of repose can insist on the definition of war aims which, as all conditions, represent limitations. But when the enemy has been so weakened that each ally has the power to achieve its ends alone, a coalition is at the mercy of its most determined member. Confronted with the complete collapse of one of the elements of the equilibrium, all other powers will tend to raise their claims in order to keep pace.[29]

This describes very well what happened to the allied coalition after the battle of Leipzig. The military-technical questions that had troubled the allies in the past continued to be a source of irritation, but they became far less important than the political divisions which now threatened to destroy the alliance utterly.

It was not, of course, immediately clear that "the enemy [had] been

[27] Rudolf Friederich, *Geschichte des Herbstfeldzuges 1813* (Berlin, 1904), II, pp. 41 ff.

[28] Scott, *op. cit.*, p. 114.

[29] Henry A. Kissinger, *A World Restored* (new ed.; New York, 1964), p. 109.

so weakened that each ally [had] the power to achieve its ends alone." When the allied sovereigns and their military advisers gathered in Frankfurt-am-Main in November in order to discuss the future course of the war, there was no agreement as to Napoleon's strength and capabilities. Blücher, scornful of what he called "the swarm of monarchs and princes . . . that spoils everything" might feel that "it is perfectly certain that, had we all, without delay, crossed the Rhine, Napoleon would by this time be suing for peace,"[30] but York was of a different opinion, pointing out that his corps had already lost two-thirds of its effectives, and York's views, laid before the King by Knesebeck, impressed that ruler.[31] Bernadotte, who had by now diverted his attention to a campaign in Denmark for the possession of Norway, took the view (perhaps natural, given his interests) that a campaign in France might jeopardize everything that had been won so far, a position shared by the Austrian General Count Bubna, who had the ear of Emperor Francis and who believed that an advance into France would provoke a national rising beyond the power of the allies to control. "We must," he said, "carefully avoid driving a people to desperate resolves by insults to its honor."[32] Among the allied sovereigns only Alexander was anxious for an immediate advance into France, and even his optimism was momentarily dampened by the doubts of his generals and the signs of war weariness among his troops.

The Tsar's periods of self-restraint were never, however, of long duration, and Napoleon's failure to make use of the opportunity given him by the pause at Frankfurt in order to secure a peace settlement on the basis of the Rhine frontier led the Russian ruler to renew his pleas for a reopening of hostilities. And from the moment when the Rhine was crossed in late December, Alexander's self-confidence and his ambition grew until they assumed grandiose proportions. As Sorel has written, he began to fancy himself as "the Agamemnon of the new Iliad." He began to revert to dreams of his youth, in which he had determined one day "to reconstitute Europe and assume the place usurped by Napoleon in the domination of the continent." He wanted now to take vengeance

> for the insults he had suffered . . . to persecute the war relentlessly, to show no moderation to the perfidious enemy, but to destroy his army and overthrow his power. . . . He would dominate France, a Latin Poland,

[30] Henderson, *op. cit.*, p. 197.

[31] F. von Cochenhausen, "Vor 125 Jahren: Politische und militärische Führung im Feldzug 1814," in *Wissen und Wehr*, XX (1939), 81–82.

[32] Müffling, *Aus meinem Leben*, p. 90.

give new institutions to the land of Montesquieu, give a king to the Revolution. The destiny yearned for since Tilsit was now being fulfilled; the hour had struck for the revelation of his genius.[33]

None of this was lost on Metternich, who realized that Alexander's fantasies, if unchecked, could lead to a costly prolongation of the war, ending, not in a restoration of European order, but in a complete subversion of it, in the Russian interest. Years later, the elder Moltke was to say that the trouble with the Russians as allies was that they always came too late, and then were too strong. Metternich must have felt something of this. The Russian forces were fresher than those of their allies and their reserves were larger; their losses at Leipzig, in comparison with Austria's and Prussia's, had been very low; if the Tsar decided that they were strong enough to secure his objectives in defiance of his allies, then the consequences might be very grave indeed. A peace settlement must therefore be arranged with Napoleon before France had become so weakened that Alexander would conclude that he could go it alone; and whatever military operations were authorized must support this political strategy.

To persuade Napoleon to conclude peace and to restrain Alexander were, therefore, the two poles of Metternich's policy from the winter of 1813 onward. He had hoped to end the war in December on terms that would leave France the boundaries of the Rhine and the Alps. When Napoleon refused to treat on that basis, the Austrian chancellor reluctantly agreed to a renewal of hostilities. But he and Schwarzenberg refused to consider the kind of headlong offensive against the Rhine fortresses that was advocated by Alexander and the chiefs of the Silesian Army. Instead, they proposed and, after much haggling, persuaded their allies to accept a plan which called for an advance of the Bohemian Army in a great looping movement through northern Switzerland into the Franche-Comté and thence to the plain of Langres, where it would threaten Napoleon's communications. Meanwhile, the Silesian Army would cross the Rhine and advance through the Palatinate to Metz and eventually to the Marne, where it would fall in on the right wing of the Bohemian Army.[34] It was a strategy designed to avoid bloody encounters, while exerting the kind of pressure on Napoleon that would induce him to negotiate seriously. Metternich was quite explicit on this

[33] A. Sorel, *L'Europe et la Révolution française* (Paris, 1904), VIII, 185–86.

[34] See Cochenhausen, *op. cit.*, pp. 82 ff. for Gneisenau's objections to this plan and the amendments which freed the Silesian Army from the original restrictions placed on it.

point, instructing Schwarzenberg in January 1814 to advance "cautiously" and "to utilize the desire of the common man in France for peace by avoiding warlike acts."[35] (See Map II.)

The lengthy debate over this plan had exacerbated relations between Metternich and Emperor Alexander,[36] and they did not improve in the weeks that followed, as the sovereigns moved toward France in the wake of the soldiers. Exasperated by the long delays, the Tsar was soon openly accusing Schwarzenberg of sabotaging a genuine war effort, and his references to Metternich were hardly more flattering. By the time the monarchs had reached Basel in mid-January, Alexander was so exercised that he announced that he was opposed to any further negotiations with Napoleon—indeed, that he intended to demand the Corsican's abdication; he let it be known, in addition, that he considered the Crown Prince of Sweden, Bernadotte, as a logical successor to the throne.

To this body blow Metternich replied in kind. On 16 January he instructed Schwarzenberg, whose troops were now at Langres, to avoid any further forward action until the political situation had been clarified; simultaneously he urged the King of Prussia to order Blücher to stand at Metz. The time had come, the Austrian statesman saw, for a showdown and a redefinition of purpose. "All our engagements are fulfilled," he wrote to one of his ministers:

> All former goals of the coalition have been not only achieved but exceeded. Now we must get clear once more about our purpose, for it is with alliances as with all fraternizations: if they do not have a strictly determinate aim, they disintegrate.[37]

Metternich found an ally in the British Foreign Secretary, Lord Castlereagh, who arrived at Basel on 18 January. The Englishman was appalled when he learned of Alexander's plans for the future government of France, and was also disturbed by the violence of tone employed by Alexander's supporters in the Silesian Army, from which an intemperate memorandum from Gneisenau's pen had just arrived, demanding an immediate advance on Paris. After a long and exasperating interview with the Tsar, who was in one of his most exalted moods,

[35] Kissinger, *op. cit.*, p. 112.

[36] This was partly caused by the Swiss issue, for Alexander did not want to violate the neutrality of the country of his old tutor La Harpe. On this and other aspects of the dispute, see Gustav Roloff, *Politik und Kriegführung während des Krieges von 1814* (Berlin, 1891), p. 28.

[37] *Ibid.*, pp. 35–36; Kissinger, *op. cit.*, p. 113.

Map of the 1814 Campaign in France

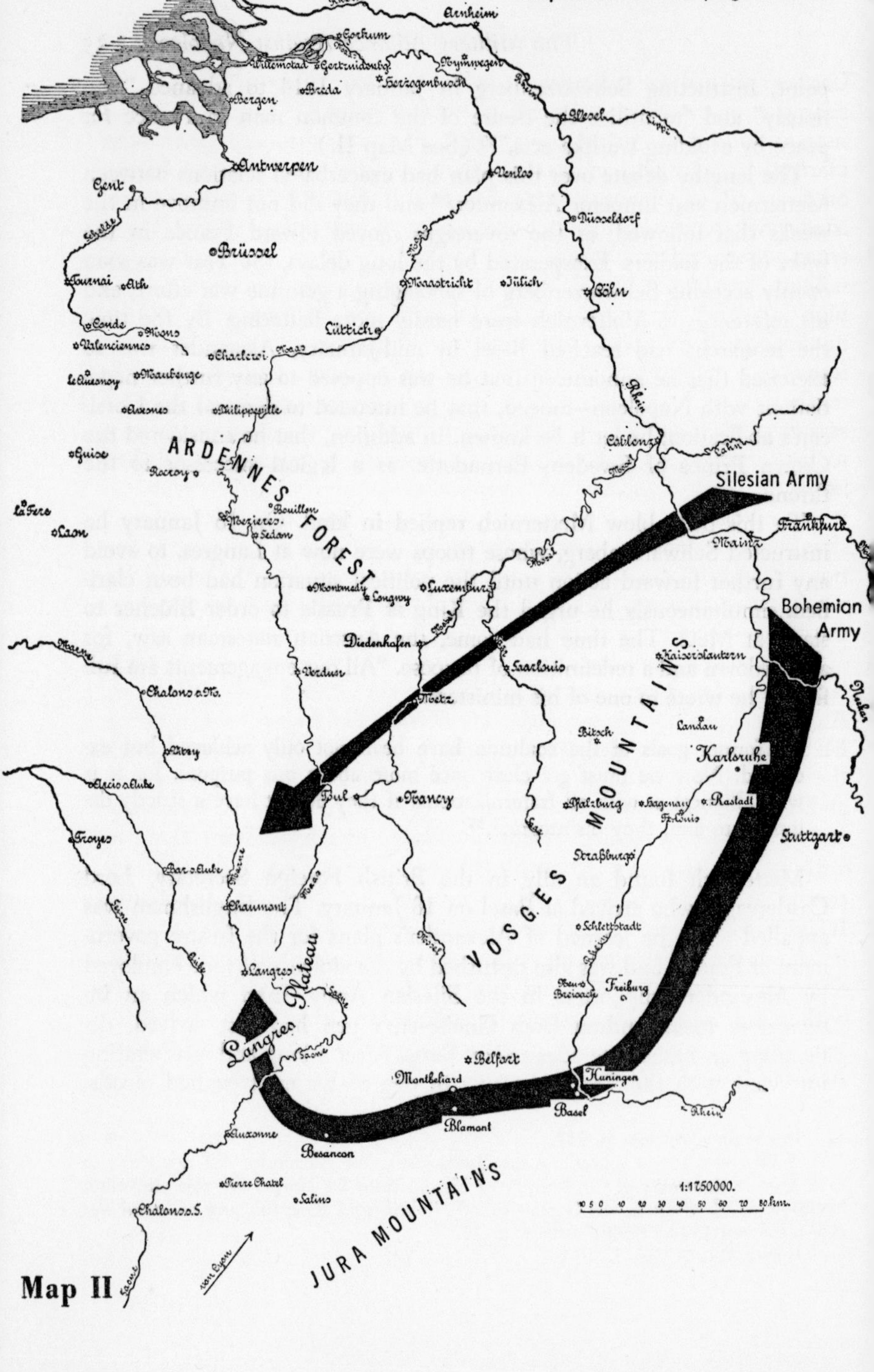

Map II

Castlereagh had no difficulty in agreeing with Metternich that a redefinition of the aims of the alliance was necessary.[38] Armed with this support, and the private knowledge that the Prussian Chancellor Hardenberg felt the same way and that even the Tsar's closest advisers, Stein and Pozzo di Borgo, were dismayed by his plans for Bernadotte, Metternich went on the offensive against both Alexander and Gneisenau. From Schwarzenberg he extracted a report that painted the military situation in hardly encouraging hues, since it underlined the high incidence of illness and desertion in the Bohemian Army, the disaffection of the local population, the difficulties of supply, the still formidable resources of Napoleon, and other factors that threw doubt on the feasibility of an easy advance on the French capital.[39] Using this as a basis for argument, he wrote an alarmed memorandum of his own to Emperor Francis, pointing out that success in the war so far had been the result of a carefully coordinated politico-military strategy in which operations and negotiations went hand in hand. This strategy should not be abandoned lightly, although that seemed to be the intention of Alexander and Gneisenau. Before steps were taken which—in view of the facts stated by Schwarzenberg—might well be disastrous, the four powers must consult on fundamental questions.[40]

The Austrian Emperor agreed with this view entirely, as did Hardenberg and the Tsar's own foreign minister, Nesselrode. Even so, Alexander did not immediately give way. The showdown between Metternich and his imperial antagonist came on 26–27 January, when the chancellor warned that, if Russia intended to force Napoleon's abdication, Austrian troops could no longer participate in the campaign, and Alexander responded by threatening to march on Paris alone or with his Prussian ally. These threats were less serious than they appeared, however; or at least, once made, they induced second thoughts. It did not take much counting on his fingers to convince the Tsar that it would not be easy to defeat Napoleon without Austrian assistance, or much ratiocination to remind Metternich that he could not safely withdraw from the war, since a Russo-Prussian defeat or a Russo-Prussian victory in a campaign in France would be equally dangerous to Austrian interests. A private conversation between chancellor and Tsar

[38] See C. K. Webster, *The Foreign Policy of Castlereagh, 1812–1815* (London, 1931), pp. 200–203.

[39] That Schwarzenberg's picture was not an exaggerated one, as most Prussian historians have been inclined to argue, is shown by a report of Sir Charles Stewart of 28 February 1814, cited in *ibid.*, p. 219 n.

[40] Roloff, *op. cit.*, pp. 45–46.

on 28 January somewhat relieved the acerbity of their relations and paved the way for more general talks; and on 29–30 January, at Langres, the allies agreed that military operations should be resumed under the direction of Schwarzenberg, who would pay "appropriate attention to military expediency" (a graceful way of saying that he would proceed in accordance with his own methodical plan rather than in the manner desired by Gneisenau). At the same time, negotiations would be opened at Chatillon with Napoleon's representative Caulaincourt to explore the possibility of a peace settlement on the basis of the frontiers of 1792, with Napoleon, presumably, remaining on the throne, since the Tsar had privately promised to refrain from interfering further in dynastic matters.[41]

It is indicative of the constant but sometimes curious interrelationship of politics and war that this undoubted political victory for Metternich should now have been upset by an unforeseen military success. On 29 January, Blücher's army, advancing on Brienne, became unexpectedly involved in heavy fighting with Napoleon's main force, and, although it was rolled back to Trannes, received strong reinforcements from Schwarzenberg and renewed the fight at La Rothière on 1 February. By eight o'clock in the evening, the French line had been broken and Napoleon's grenadiers were retreating in disorder toward Brienne, leaving 3,600 dead, 2,400 prisoners, and 73 guns on the field. Allied casualties were almost as high, but Schwarzenberg and Blücher had won a clear moral victory, defeating Bonaparte decisively for the first time on his own soil.[42]

This splendid success had the unfortunate effect of reviving all of the Tsar's ambitions, and he had no compunction about violating the agreement just made at Langres. He instructed Razumowsky, his representative at Chatillon, to do everything in his power to delay a successful issue of the talks there; he refused to consider a French request for an armistice; and he began to talk once more of marching on Paris, dethroning Napoleon, and giving the French people a king of his own choosing. The kind of threat that had restrained him at Langres now seemed to have lost its effect. The Tsar had used his strong personal influence over the wavering Frederick William III to win a promise from that sovereign that he would stand by him through thick and thin.

41 *Ibid.*, pp. 49 ff.

42 For descriptions of the battle, see Janson, *op. cit.*, I, 169–214, and Friederich, *op. cit.*, III, 99 ff. Müffling, *Aus meinem Leben*, pp. 137 ff., defends Schwarzenberg's conduct of the battle against the charges made in Clausewitz, *Der Feldzug von 1814* (Berlin, 1835).

Now, thanks to the blow suffered by Napoleon at La Rothière, Alexander could—as an American historian has written recently—

> seriously contemplate withdrawing the 61,000 Russian troops from Schwarzenberg's Bohemian Army, joining them to Blücher's Silesian Army, two-thirds of which were Russian anyway, and leaving the Austrians to their own devices. Were Alexander to try it and were he to succeed, his hegemony on the continent would be an accomplished fact.[43]

For Metternich this was a grim prospect. But he was rescued by Napoleon—or perhaps, more accurately, by his antagonists within the allied camp, Blücher and Gneisenau. The impetuosity that had become the hallmark of the Silesian Army had long worried some of their professional colleagues. General Müffling, who in later life was to become a distinguished and influential Chief of the Prussian General Staff, had noted during the spring campaign that his chiefs spent more time making inspirational speeches to their troops than in providing for their security, and that Gneisenau's conspicuous weakness was his failure to plan carefully, his excessive emphasis upon bravery as the determinant of victory, and his confidence in his own ability to inspire it whenever it was needed.[44] In the days before La Rothière, Schwarzenberg had remarked on the same dangerous tendencies and had written:

> Blücher, and still more Gneisenau—for the old fellow has to lend his name—are urging the march on Paris with such perfectly childish rage that they trample under foot every single rule of warfare. Without placing any considerable force to guard the road from Chalons to Nancy, they rush like mad to Brienne. Regardless of their rear and of their flanks, they do nothing but plan *parties fines* at the Palais Royal. This is indeed frivolous at such an important moment.[45]

It was probably inevitable that this disregard of the fundamental rules of war would catch up with Blücher and Gneisenau sooner or later; and it did so in the second week of February when, in the neighborhood of Bautemps-Etoges, Napoleon fell like a thunderbolt upon their over-extended and hopelessly disarticulated forces and proceeded to defeat them corps by corps, inflicting more than 15,000 casualties in five days

[43] Enno E. Kraehe, *Metternich's German Policy:* I. *The Contest with Napoleon, 1799–1814* (Princeton, N.J., 1963), p. 296.
[44] Müffling, *Aus meinem Leben,* pp. 33–34, 36 ff.
[45] Henderson, *Blücher,* pp. 206–7.

of fighting and almost bagging Blücher himself in an ambush at Montmirail.[46]

The news of this shattering reverse caused a near panic at supreme headquarters, and the phlegmatic Castlereagh noted with disgust that this affected not only the princes of the lesser German states but the Tsar as well. Only a few days ago, Alexander had been talking of marching on Paris alone; now he was clamoring for an armistice.[47] But this sudden imperial collapse did have the happy effect in the end of reducing the tensions within the alliance and preparing the way for ultimate victory. It enabled Metternich to isolate the Tsar diplomatically when he was most conscious of the slump of his military fortunes, and by threatening a separate peace on the part of Austria and the lesser German states, to force him, on 15 February, to adhere to a formal interallied agreement, stipulating that military operations and diplomatic negotiations should continue side by side but that, regardless of the fate of either, France's borders should in the end remain those of 1792, that, if Napoleon accepted these, he would remain on the throne but that, if he were deposed, the allies would regard the Bourbon pretender Louis XVIII as his successor, and that, if Paris were occupied by the allies, they would administer it in common.[48]

These terms assured France of an honorable place in the postwar balance of power under a ruler with a claim to legitimacy. They relieved Metternich of his fears that the country might be depressed into the position of a Russian satellite and, because they did so, permitted him to view the reopening of military operations in a more relaxed mood, even to the extent of agreeing that the Silesian Army should be authorized to start once more for Paris (although only after it had been reinforced by Russian and Prussian units detached from Bernadotte's inactive Northern Army, since—as Castlereagh said—Blücher was clearly "too daring to be trusted with a small force").[49] At long last, the first days of March saw the beginning of the resolution of the political differences that had weighed so heavily upon the alliance and slowed down operations on so many occasions; and, after the treaty of Chau-

[46] Accounts of the battle are to be found in Janson, *op. cit.*, I, 237 ff.; Friederich, *Befreiungskriege,* III, 116 ff.; Henderson, *op. cit.*, pp. 217 ff.; Petre, *op. cit.*, pp. 55 ff.; Cochenhausen, *op. cit.*, pp. 88–89.

[47] Webster, *op. cit.*, p. 218.

[48] Kraehe, *op. cit.*, I, 297 ff.

[49] Webster, *op. cit.*, p. 220. See Hans Delbrück and G. Pertz, *Das Leben des Feldmarschalls Grafen Neidhardt von Gneisenau* (Berlin, 1880), IV, 82 ff.; and E. von Conrady, *Leben und Wirken des Generals Carl von Grolman* (Berlin, 1894–96), II, 193–94.

mont of 4 March had confirmed and elaborated the agreement of 15 February and had converted the coalition into a permanent alliance, the total military resources of the partners could be turned, without let or hindrance, against Napoleon. There followed in quick succession the battles of Craonne, Laon, and Arcis sur Aube, and, on 31 March, the allies entered Paris.

III

From what has been said above, it will have become clear that it was not only imperfect command relationships and differences on war aims that caused internal strains within the anti-Napoleonic coalition, but that the problem of civil-military relations also played an important role. Even before Austria had joined the alliance, Metternich was expressing doubts whether the Prussian army was an entirely reliable instrument of its government, and during the campaigns of 1814 and 1815 British statesmen also came to regard the behavior of Prussian soldiers with misgivings.

Although most nineteenth-century German historians sought to deny it, the war of liberation against Napoleon began with an act of insubordination by the Prussian military against its royal commander. Tension between King Frederick William III and his soldiers had existed since 1809, when the King had refused to join Austria in the campaign that ended at Wagram. Frederick William was a melancholy and pessimistic man who had more faith in the genius of Napoleon than in the ability of his people or his army to oppose him effectively,[50] and he turned a deaf ear to the counsel of soldiers like Gneisenau who urged him to resort to the *levée en masse* in order to free his country. His attitude embittered the patriotic party, and, when the King capitulated to Napoleon's pressure in 1812 and placed Prussian troops at his disposal, this feeling turned to a suppressed fury. "We shall receive the fate we deserve," Gneisenau wrote of the King's action. "We shall go down in shame, for we dare not conceal from ourselves the truth that a nation is as bad as its government." And again, with something bordering on contempt: "The King stands ever by the throne on which he has never sat."[51]

When Napoleon's fortunes changed in Russia and the long retreat from Moscow began, Blücher, Gneisenau, Grolman, Clausewitz, and

[50] See Max Lehmann, *Scharnhorst* (Leipzig, 1886–87), II, 295.
[51] Gerhard Ritter, *Staatskunst und Kriegshandwerk,* I (Munich, 1954), 104.

others once more raised the cry of war and, when the King did not respond, became increasingly critical of him and his chosen ministers—notably Hardenberg—and increasingly inclined to a rebellious forcing play which would bring Prussia into the war on Russia's side. The capitulation of Napoleon's Prussian auxiliary corps, led by General York, to the Russians at Tauroggen in December 1812 was such an action, and it was bitterly resented by the King, even after he had yielded to the popular enthusiasm aroused by it and had summoned his people to arms.[52] The way in which Prussian intervention had been effected was not lost on foreign observers. The Austrian minister in Breslau wrote home in February 1813: "Under the guise of patriotism, the military and the leaders of the sects have seized complete control of the reins of government, and the chancellor [Hardenberg] is swept along by the stream."[53]

Few things have so disturbing an effect upon statesmen engaged in a common war effort as the thought that the soldiers might begin to take important decisions into their own hands. The nervousness shown by our own allies during the Korean War as they observed the behavior and read the press releases of General Douglas MacArthur is a case in point. And it was parallelled throughout the campaigns of 1813 and 1814 by the apprehension of Prussia's allies as they listened to the complaints and objections and demands of the Silesian Army commanders, their constantly reiterated opposition to any form of restraint, their violent criticism of the strategy of the supreme command, and their ill-disguised contempt for "the diplomats," whom Blücher once called "*Schuften* who deserve the gallows."[54]

Disturbing enough during the months leading up to Napoleon's fall, the soldiers' impatience with governmental control reached new heights after Napoleon's return from Elba and his second defeat. Blücher's headquarters in Paris in 1815 was a center of disaffection in which insubordination was the order of the day. Only the intervention of the British prevented Blücher from levying a contribution of 100 million francs on the people of Paris and from taking other measures for which he had neither royal nor allied authorization. Colonel Hardinge, the British liaison officer at his headquarters, reported that the King of Prussia was experiencing the gravest of difficulty in checking "the very unusual

[52] On the debate among historians on the question of whether Tauroggen was an act of insubordination, see Gordon A. Craig, *The Politics of the Prussian Army, 1640–1945* (new ed.; Oxford, 1964), p. 59 n.

[53] Lehmann, *op. cit.,* II, 514.

[54] Ritter, *op. cit.,* I, 106 ff.

spirit of political interference existing in this army and its reported intimate connection with popular feeling in Prussia."[55] The autumn of 1815 was marked by a lengthy dispute between Hardenberg and Blücher's headquarters over occupation policy, and the Field Marshal's open disobedience of instructions forced the King to intervene in October with an order explicitly stating that the chancellor was to be regarded as the final authority in political matters. Blücher and his most radical adviser Grolman were clearly trying to do what Moltke was to attempt in 1870 and Ludendorff was to succeed in doing in 1916—namely, to supersede the civilian authorities in a vital area of war policy.[56] The spectacle of their doing so alarmed Castlereagh, who admitted that he looked "with considerable anxiety at the tendency of [Prussian] politics" and noted that "the army is by no means subordinate to the civil authorities,"[57] and it led Emperor Alexander to say to a group of his generals: "It is possible that some time we shall have to come to the aid of the King of Prussia against his army."[58]

Metternich was less concerned over the effects of the behavior of Blücher and his colleagues upon the authority of the Prussian crown than he was over the threat it represented to the common interests of the alliance. He sensed what it is easier for us, with twentieth-century experience, to recognize: namely, that the Silesian Army commanders were fighting, or wanted to fight, a different kind of war than the allied sovereigns and ministers. The latter—and this was true even of Emperor Alexander, whose enthusiasms were always restrained before they went too far by a cool appreciation of state interest—were fighting for political objectives; the Prussian soldiers were fighting for ideological ones. In Blücher's headquarters, Gneisenau, Grolman, and the others rubbed shoulders with fantasts and demagogues like Arndt, Görres, and Jahn and partook of that mystical nationalism which turned the war against Napoleon into a fight against evil, a struggle against the anti-Christ and his minions. Gneisenau's quarrels with Schwarzenberg were not really about strategy; they were, at least to Gneisenau, about something much more fundamental, about faith, about religion. When he pressed for a headlong drive toward Paris, he talked of it as a crusade. "Destiny brought us here," he wrote to Stein in January 1814.

55 Webster, *op. cit.*, p. 463.

56 Ritter, *op. cit.*, I, 115–16.

57 H. G. Schenk, *The Aftermath of the Napoleonic Wars* (New York, 1947), pp. 116–17.

58 Friedrich Meinecke, *Das Leben des Generalfeldmarschalls Hermann von Boyen* (Stuttgart, 1895–99), II, 73.

> We must take revenge for the so many sorrows inflicted on the nations, for so much arrogance, so that the principle *discite justitiam moniti non temnere divos* may be observed. If we do not do that, then we are miserable wretches, who deserve to be shocked out of our lazy peace every two years and to be threatened with the scourge of slavery.

And again:

> We must answer the visits of the French to our cities by visiting them in theirs. So long as that does not happen, our revenge and triumph will be incomplete. If the Silesian Army gets to Paris first, I shall at once have the bridges of Austerlitz and Jena blown up, as well as the Arc de Triomphe.[59]

In these words, and in the behavior of Blücher in Paris in 1815, we sense a spirit which, if uncontrolled, could only expand the war to new dimensions of bitterness and devastation and make a viable peace settlement impossible. In them we find already an intimation of the ideological passions which were, in the twentieth century, to make it so difficult to keep war within the limitations that statecraft requires. Metternich and Castlereagh had every reason to be alarmed.

IV

When one reviews the history of the Grand Alliance of 1813–15 and contemplates the serious deficiencies of the command relationships, the fundamental differences in political ambition and objective between the partners, and the dangers posed by the insubordination and ideological incompatibility of the Prussian soldiers, it is not immediately easy to understand how the coalition managed to survive even the first winter of the war. It did so, of course, because of the existence of that almost elemental force mentioned only occasionally in these pages—Napoleon Bonaparte himself, formidable even on a stricken field, endlessly resilient and resourceful, always ready to strike hammer blows against the weak points in the coalition arrayed against him. The pressure exerted by the mere knowledge that Bonaparte was still at large, reinforced as it was by his sudden and dreadful appearances, was enough to hold the alliance together in moments of crisis and eventually to persuade it to consolidate its resources in such a way that victory became possible.

59 Ritter, *op. cit.*, I, 110–11.

It is always dangerous to attempt to draw lessons from history, and there are, in any event, profound differences between the Grand Alliance discussed here and the great peacetime alliance of which we are a part today. Even so, at a time when we hear so much about the crisis of NATO and when so much is written about the difficulties of reforming its command structure or resolving the strategical and political differences of its members, it may be useful to reflect that others have found it possible to live with administrative deficiencies and conflicts of interest and yet to be effective partners, and that we may do so too, provided we remember why our alliance was established in the first place and provided we do not lose sight of the fact that our Bonapartes too are always in the near distance and that their menace is undiminished. The Grand Alliance of 1813–15 is interesting because it is a kind of prototype of all alliances, with all the troubles to which they are heir. Its history may be a source of encouragement to us if we note that its internal divisions were deeper and more fundamental than those which affect the Atlantic Alliance today, but that it survived and was victorious.

3. The Military Cohesion of the Austro-German Alliance, 1914-18

SOMEWHERE IN THE LABYRINTHINE WAYS of Karl Kraus' interminable moon drama *Die letzten Tage der Menschheit,* a character called the Grumbler comments on the military alliance of the Central Powers and says that it reminds him of a partnership between Eskimos and natives of the Congo. How, he asks, could one expect military success from an association between a people that had made lack of system a way of life and another that seemed to deify order and live for it alone?[1]

That there was a certain temperamental incompatibility between the Germans and their Austro-Hungarian allies is doubtless true. Long before 1914, the well-trained, scientifically minded Prussian staff officers who had any contact with Austrians in similar positions were puzzled or shocked by the levity with which their southern colleagues went about the business of soldiering. In 1854, Prussia's first military attaché to Vienna, Prince Kraft zu Hohenlohe-Ingelfingen, tried to explain to his Austrian colleagues how one used the *Kriegsspiel,* that time-tested method of training staff officers, and was asked by one of his auditors how you won money at it;[2] and there must have been many other instances of this sort of thing. During the First World War, German officers were inclined to react more violently than Prince Hohenlohe had to this unintellectual approach to the art of war and to what they considered to be congenital Austrian inefficiency and muddle; and they

"The Military Cohesion of the Austro-German Alliance" is reprinted from *The Journal of Modern History,* XXXVII, No. 3 (September, 1965), with the permission of The University of Chicago Press.

[1] Karl Kraus, *Die letzten Tage der Menschheit* (Zurich, 1945), p. 225, Act II, scene 2.

[2] Prince Kraft zu Hohenlohe-Ingelfingen, *Aus meinem Leben, 1848–1871* (4 vols.; Berlin, 1897–1907), I, 296.

were often driven to extremes of fury by another characteristic of their allies—a tendency to accept and even to take a certain melancholy pride in their own fecklessness. The Austrian ability to regard some incredible foul-up with a mixture of resignation and aesthetic enjoyment and with the comment *"Da is halt nix zu machen"* or *"Das is halt unsere Schlamperei"* must have brought many a narrow-gutted northerner close to apoplexy.

This difference in temperament and its varied manifestations had the effect, at different times and in different sectors of the battle front, of complicating relations between the allies and diminishing the effectiveness of their joint effort. Even so, it is hardly adequate to account for the faults of strategical coordination, the failures of communication, and the general incoherence of the alliance that will be treated here. These things had their roots rather in the failure of the allies, in the years before the outbreak of the war, to formulate a joint war plan that would have had a reasonable chance of success—a failure, incidentally, for which the Germans bear as much responsibility as do the Austrians. If one must speak of *Schlamperei,* it should at least be noted that it occurred on both sides of the alliance.

I

When the great crisis of 1914 arose, it was, or should have been, clear to the general staffs of Germany and Austria-Hungary that if they permitted matters to come to open hostilities they would find themselves confronted with a coalition of at least three powers (France, Russia, and Serbia) which would possess a military superiority of about 1.5 million fighting men (5 million to 3.5 million). If either the principles of classical strategy or the simple rules of common sense had been observed, this situation should have required from them a truly joint effort, an effective exploitation of interior lines, an offensive concentration against one major antagonist coupled with an essentially defensive posture on other fronts, and careful attention during this offensive lest the theater of war be compressed so as to threaten the vital interests of either ally. In an essay written in 1941, the former German Chief of General Staff Ludwig Beck wrote: "The numerical superiority of the enemy in 1914 required that the German and Austro-Hungarian forces exploit the interior lines in accordance with a coordinated (*einheitlichen*) plan and that the latter forces be protected against exposure to an isolated defeat by superior Russian forces."[3] In actuality, however, the Central Powers paid no attention to these precepts. Instead, they launched offensives not on one front but on three—the Germans striking through Belgium into France, and the Austrians attacking simultaneously on the Galician and the Drina-Save fronts.

If one seeks an explanation for this operational disarticulation, which, as we shall see, had very grave results, one will find it, first of all, in lack of communication between the two armies and their staffs in the prewar period. Ludendorff once wrote that, in contrast to the alliance of the western powers, the Austro-German combination was a political but not a military association;[4] and there is a good deal of truth in this. Certainly there was, from the time of the elder Moltke onward, a minimum of anything that could be called joint planning. During his term as Chief of Staff, Count Schlieffen, according to the testimony of one of his most brilliant juniors, did not trust the ability of the Austrians to keep secrets and was, consequently, disinclined to make them privy to his plans.[5] He communicated with them as infrequently as possible and, when he made proposals, did so with scant courtesy or consideration for Austrian views. His decision to shift the focus of German action in case of war from the eastern to the western front—which could not but have a serious effect on Austrian war dispositions—was made independently and passed on to Vienna belatedly; and in the subsequent period the German Chief of Staff showed no desire to advise his allies concerning the necessary adjustments in their own line of battle.[6]

Schlieffen's taciturnity offended Austrian susceptibilities so seriously in the end that his successor felt called upon to do something to allay resentment in Vienna. It cannot be said, however, that he improved communications between the two armies in any fundamental way. Essentially, Moltke the younger was no more favorably inclined to a true measure of joint planning than Schlieffen himself had been. Freytag-Loringhoven and others among his aides have testified that he always had a plausible excuse for not increasing contacts or establishing working relationships between the German and Austro-Hungarian staffs;[7] and, in fact, communication and consultation between the two

[3] "West- oder Ost-Offensive 1914?" in Ludwig Beck, *Studien* (ed. Hans Speidel) (Stuttgart, 1955), p. 158.

[4] Erich Ludendorff, *Kriegführung und Politik* (3d ed.; Berlin, 1923), p. 63.

[5] Erich Ludendorff, *Meine Kriegserinnerungen* (Berlin, 1920), p. 46.

[6] Edmond Glaise von Horstenau, *Franz Josephs Weggefährte* (Zurich, Leipzig, Vienna, 1930), pp. 346–53, 377–78.

[7] Freiherr von Freytag-Loringhoven, *Menschen und Dinge wie ich sie in meinem Leben sah* (Berlin, 1923), p. 199.

rmies was virtually confined to that exchange of personal letters between Moltke and his opposite number, Conrad von Hötzendorf, about which so much has been written. The striking feature of this intermittent correspondence, which extended from 1908 to 1914, was that t at no time touched upon the subject of coordinated direction of operaions in a future war (a subject which was absent also from Moltke's nly lengthy commentary on the two-front war, his memorandum of 913) and that in all matters affecting the military cohesion of the allince it was singularly imprecise. The exchanges did make it clear that, vhen war came, Germany would attack on the western front with the ulk of its forces and that, until a decision had been reached there, the urden and the direction of the war on the eastern front would be in Austrian hands. But no war aim or objective was specified in the east, no strategy prescribed, no concrete measures provided for; even Moltke's romise of an active offensive across the Narew in the event of Austrian ffensive action in Galicia was more a moral pledge than a concrete lan of action and was, in any case, progressively drained of meaning y the changes that took place in the relations of the Great Powers between 1909, when it was made, and 1914.[8] How little the two allies vere prepared for an effective and united war effort in 1914 is shown y the plea of the German military attaché in Vienna to Moltke's *Oberquartiermeister* on 1 August 1914:

> It is high time that the two general staffs consult now with absolute frankness with respect to mobilization, jump-off time, areas of assembly, and precise troop strength. . . . I take the liberty of begging Your Excellency once again to persuade His Excellency the Chief that the measures necessary to provide for cooperation and coherence in the operations against Russia must be taken with the greatest possible speed. Everyone has been relying upon the belief that the two chiefs of staff had worked out these most intimate agreements between themselves.[9]

[8] On this correspondence and the so-called pledge of 1909, see, *inter alia,* Feldmarschall Conrad, *Aus meiner Dienstzeit* (5 vols.; Vienna, Berlin, 1921), I, 380–84, 631–33, II, 85, 144; Oesterreichischen Bundesministerium für Heereswesen and Kriegsarchiv, ed., *Oesterreich-Ungarns letzter Krieg, 1914–1918* (Vienna, 1931 *et. seq.*), I, 332–35; August von Cramon, *Deutschlands Schicksalsbund mit Oesterreich-Ungarn: von Conrad von Hötzendorf zu Kaiser Karl* (Berlin, 1932), chap. 1; Gerhard Ritter, *Staatskunst und Kriegshandwerk,* II (Munich, 1960), 299–307; Oskar Regele, *Feldmarschall Conrad: Auftrag und Erfüllung, 1906–1918* (Vienna, 1955), pp. 264–69.

[9] "Besass Deutschland 1914 einen Kriegsplan?" in Beck, *op. cit.*, p. 102. See also August Urbanski von Ostrymiecz, *Conrad von Hötzendorf, Soldat und Mensch* (Graz, 1938), p. 247.

Last-minute entreaties of this nature had no effect upon the two chiefs of staff. Moltke and Conrad may have been subject to occasional twinges of doubt, but these were never as strong as their faith in the strength of their own forces and their confidence in the military effectiveness of their ally. A long line of distinguished military critics, including Hans Delbrück, Georg Wetzell, and Gerhard Ritter, have pointed out that the Schlieffen Plan, in either its original or its modified form was a gamble with relatively slight chance of success;[10] but Moltke continued to believe that the German Army could finish the war in the west in forty days, and he seems never to have asked himself what would happen if it did not. The most competent postwar commentators on Austrian operations—a group that includes Winston Churchill and the Austrian strategist Alfred Krauss—have questioned the realism of Conrad's decision to go on the offensive against the Russians in Galicia after his northern army had been weakened by the shipment of eighty battalions to the Serbian front and after his right flank had been endangered by Rumania's decision to remain neutral;[11] but the Austrian Chief of Staff was convinced that his army had a greater chance of success if it took the offensive than if it stood on the Carpathian line and awaited the Russian attack.

Nor did the Germans seek to dissuade Conrad from what General Krauss later called his "attack into the blue."[12] On the contrary, with full knowledge of Austria's difficulties in Serbia, they actually requested the Austrian offensive in Galicia in the hope that it would take pressure off their own forces in East Prussia, and they showed considerable anxiety when it was delayed until 22 August.[13] This German request showed a faith in the capability of the Austrian Army that was as unwise as Conrad's confidence that the German Army could not only achieve its western objectives on schedule but also make an offensive

[10] Georg Wetzell, *Der Bündniskrieg* (Berlin, 1937); Gerhard Ritter, "Das Verhältnis von Politik und Kriegführung im Bismarckischen Reich," in *Deutschland und Europa: Festgabe für Hans Rothfels* (Munich, 1951), pp. 92–94, and *Staatskunst und Kriegshandwerk,* II, especially 245–66; and, on Delbrück's criticisms, Ernst Kabisch, *Streitfragen des Weltkrieges, 1914–1918* (Stuttgart, 1924), pp. 29–31.

[11] Winston S. Churchill, *The Unknown War: The Eastern Front* (New York, 1931), pp. 120–22; Alfred Krauss, *Die Ursachen unserer Niederlage* (2d ed.; Munich, 1921), pp. 113–15 and especially 130–34; Hermann von Kuhl, *Der Weltkrieg, 1914–1918* (2 vols.; Berlin, 1929), I, 24.

[12] Krauss, *op. cit.,* p. 134.

[13] Freytag-Loringhoven, *op. cit.,* p. 221; Josef Graf Stürgkh, *Im deutschen Grossen Hauptquartier* (Leipzig, 1921), p. 30.

thrust across the Narew toward Siedlice (behind Warsaw) at the very moment when its East Prussian forces had been defeated at Gumbinnen and were contemplating a retreat behind the Vistula.

It is difficult to study the campaigns of 1914 without being impressed by the incompleteness of Austro-German planning for their joint military venture and the dearth of their knowledge about each other, and without being convinced that the major share of the responsibility for this must be assigned to the stronger of the allies. In the military literature of the west, and particularly in the United States, the German General Staff has been accorded a high degree of veneration. It is time that it was pointed out that it went to meet its greatest test with only the most rudimentary knowledge of the strength, organization, command structure, national composition, and tactical forms of the Austro-Hungarian Army, to say nothing of the state of that army's morale, the cumbersomeness and inefficiency of its reserve system, and such potentially important technical questions as the unsatisfactory state of its munitions reserves and the deterioration of its strategical rail net in comparison with Russia's during Conrad's term as Chief of Staff. Even a man like Ludendorff, who had served before 1914 in the mobilization section of the German General Staff, was forced to admit: "I learned about conditions in Austria-Hungary only during the war. Before then I had no opportunity."[14] Germany's military plenipotentiary at Conrad's headquarters wrote: "There were very few people in Germany who had any degree of knowledge about our ally and its army. Hence the surprise over the fact that there were Austrians who did not understand German!"[15] Moltke's remark to the Austrian liaison officer Stürgkh in August 1914—"You have a good army. You'll beat the Russians"[16]—was typical of the prevailing ignorance which permitted the Germans to entertain the same kind of unreasonable expectations with respect to their ally's front as they did in the western theater of war. When the German Quartermaster General von Stein wrote Freytag-Loringhoven a few weeks later that the striking force of the Austro-Hungarian Army was not very impressive, Freytag answered: "It was our job in the general staff to get an accurate picture of the capabilities of the Austro-Hungarian army *before* the war began."[17] Unfortunately for both allies, that job had not been done.

[14] *Meine Kriegserinnerungen*, p. 91.

[15] August von Cramon, *Unser Oesterreich-Ungarischer Bundesgenosse im Weltkriege* (Berlin, 1920), p. 43; Regele, *op. cit.*, p. 291.

[16] Stürgkh, *op. cit.*, p. 30.

[17] Freytag-Loringhoven, *op. cit.*, p. 232.

II

The first result of all this was the wholly uncoordinated offensive on three fronts with which the Central Powers began the war and which eventuated in serious setbacks on all three, as well as in the virtual destruction during the battles around Lemberg of the flower of Austria's junior officer and noncommissioned officer corps, a blow from which the Imperial and Royal Army never recovered.[18] The second result was the mutual disenchantment that troubled relations between the allies for the rest of the war and made any true measure of military cohesion impossible. The failure of their western offensive and their subsequent inability to support operations on the eastern front to the extent originally envisaged made the Germans sensitive to Austrian reproaches about lateness and inadequacy of assistance and sometimes led them to counter with accusations of inefficiency and lack of steadfastness on the Austrian side. As early as September 1914 Emperor William II was pointing out with some asperity to the Austrian General Stürgkh that the German Eighth Army in East Prussia had repelled, and in part destroyed, a greatly superior Russian force of twelve army corps, while the Austrians in Galicia, roughly equal in strength to the Russians opposing them, were clamoring for German support.[19] This was an argument that was, incidentally, to be repeated *ad nauseam* by postwar German military publicists; during the war, this kind of invidious comparison became increasingly frequent as the Austrian need of assistance grew; so too did the German tendency to claim credit for all successes won by mixed units and to blame all setbacks on the *"schlappen Oesterreicher."*[20]

On the Austrian side the disillusionment was equally profound. Conrad, who called the German defeat on the Marne a "declaration of insolvency" on the part of the Germans, said later that the greatest mistake he had made during the war was placing unlimited confidence in the German high command.[21] After the autumn campaigns of 1914 he never recovered his trust in its competence or, for that matter, in its good faith. Refusing to admit that the circumstances of August 1914

[18] *Oesterreich-Ungarns letzter Krieg,* I, 319–21, 335–38; General Max Hoffmann, *Der Krieg der versäumten Gelegenheiten* (Munich, 1923), p. 53; Churchill, *op. cit.,* pp. 228–29.

[19] Stürgkh, *op. cit.,* p. 40.

[20] Regele, *op. cit.,* pp. 299–300, 482–87; Urbanski, *op. cit.,* p. 237.

[21] Regele, *op. cit.,* p. 266.

made impossible the execution of the German supporting thrust against Warsaw promised in 1909, he chose to blame the failure of his Galician offensive, as he once said to Josef Redlich, upon German refusal to honor a solemn promise.[22] In January 1915 Conrad shocked General Stürgkh, fresh from German headquarters, with the question: "Well, what are our secret enemies the Germans up to, and what is that comedian the German Emperor doing?"[23] This lingering resentment and Conrad's fixed idea that the German officers assigned to his and other Austrian headquarters were either spies or control officers seeking to deprive him of independence did not create an atmosphere that was conducive to harmonious working relationships. During the Vistula operations of the last months of 1914, the instances of friction between the allies were numerous and unedifying, on the operational as well as the staff level.[24]

This unhappy state of affairs was reflected in the subsequent period in the allies' failure to make any progress toward improving joint-command relationships, as well as in an increasing degree of strategical incoherence that was to reach its height in June and July 1916. With respect to the command question, the ideal arrangement would have been some kind of united supreme command with authority over all fronts. There is no evidence that this was discussed, let alone settled, before 1914, although the reasons for this failure to achieve a joint command, as Falkenhayn says in the introduction to his memoirs, are obscure.[25] From his correspondence with Moltke, and particularly from the imprecise arrangement of 1909, Conrad appears to have concluded that there would be a division of command, with the Austrian *Armee Oberkommando* (AOK) supreme on the eastern front. Even when the weakness of German troop strength in the east invested this conception with a certain amount of logic, the Germans resisted it. When joint operations began on the Silesian front in September 1914, the German *Oberste Heeresleitung* (OHL) wired to General von Hindenburg: "The independence of the army will be maintained even in conditions

[22] *Schicksalsjahre Oesterreichs 1908–1919: Das politische Tagebuch Josef Redlichs* (2 vols.; Vienna, 1953–54), I, 270. See also Conrad's letter of August 28, 1914, to Count Bolfras in Conrad, *op. cit.*, IV, 563–64.

[23] Stürgkh, *op. cit.*, p. 116.

[24] C. R. M. F. Cruttwell, *A History of the Great War, 1914–1918* (Oxford, 1934), pp. 79–90; Hoffmann, *op. cit.*, pp. 61–62; Freytag-Loringhoven, *op. cit.*, p. 246. On Conrad's attitude toward the liaison officers, see Stürgkh, *ibid.*, p. 133.

[25] Erich von Falkenhayn, *Die Oberste Heeresleitung, 1914–1916* (Berlin, 1920), p. 5. See also Conrad, *op. cit.*, IV, 259.

of common operations with the Austrians." A month later, when Conrad suggested that the nine German divisions fighting side by side with thirty-eight Austro-Hungarian divisions in the campaign in southern Poland be subordinated to command by the AOK, his suggestion was opposed by the German Emperor.[26] The fact that the German Ninth Army was responsible not to the AOK but to the German headquarters at Mézières was a complicating factor during the whole campaign.[27]

As German troop strength increased all along the eastern front, it was the Germans who began to propose plans of joint command and the Austrians who resisted. Conrad's arguments against any degree of subordination to German authority were always cogent and often plausible, and he made great play with the point that the Germans simply did not understand the peculiarities of the Austro-Hungarian military system and would be incapable of directing the operations of Slavic troops with intelligence and sympathy. There can be no doubt, however, that his personal embitterment had made him incapable of any detached judgment of the question of command; by 1916 he had persuaded himself that the Germans were bent upon reducing his country to the status of a satellite. "The Germans are cold, compromising calculators," he wrote to the Emperor's adjutant general. "It is part of their method to portray us as weaklings and inferiors and to belittle our accomplishments so as to be able to step forward arrogantly and deprive us of all rights."[28]

The allies managed to achieve a measure of effective cooperation during the Gorlice-Tarnow campaign of 1915. But the system of command employed there was complicated (the German general, Mackensen, was in effective command of all German and Austrian troops in the sphere of attack but received his instructions from the Austrian AOK, which in turn agreed to communicate with the German Chief of Staff Falkenhayn before important decisions[29]), and it was not employed in later operations. Even during the Gorlice drive there were instances of disagreement and signs of bad blood between the allies, and these increased in number during the Serbian and Montenegrin operations later in the year. Even so, these operations were models of

[26] Paul von Hindenburg, *Aus meinem Leben* (Leipzig, 1920), p. 101.
[27] Conrad, *op. cit.,* V, 178.
[28] Regele, *op. cit.,* p. 285.
[29] Cruttwell, p. 174; Cramon, *Bundesgenosse,* p. 14. On Austro-German cooperation in planning the Gorlice battle, see *Oesterreich-Ungarns letzter Krieg,* II, 297–309; Hoffmann, *op. cit.,* p. 105; Cramon, *Deutschlands Schicksalsbund,* p. 101.

strategical harmony compared with what happened in 1916, when the absence of a supreme directorate for the war effort led to another example of the kind of incoherence that had been so damaging in 1914.

We need not become involved here in the much controverted question whether Conrad could have knocked Italy out of the war in the spring of 1916 if Falkenhayn had given him the nine divisions he requested (although it should perhaps be noted that the Austrian writer who has come down most heavily on Conrad's side in this matter has rested his case on the hardly disinterested testimony of David Lloyd George[30]). It is surely necessary in a discussion of the military cohesion of the Austro-Hungarian alliance only to point to what happened: namely, that when his request for the German divisions was declined, with reasons given, Conrad implemented his Italian plan on his own, without the necessary reserves to continue pushing it until the Italians collapsed; that he mounted his offensive after withdrawing some strength from the Russian front (how much is a matter of dispute); and that he did so after the German commitment at Verdun had become so heavy that Falkenhayn's ability to react to new pressure on any front had been seriously reduced. As is well known, new pressures came, in June 1916, when General Brusilov broke the Austrian front at Lutzk, took an entire army of 250,000 prisoners with all its guns, and advanced thirty-seven miles.[31]

This Austrian collapse made it impossible for Conrad to block an increase of German authority over the eastern front. After a stop-gap solution that made Hindenburg commander on the whole northeastern sector and assigned a German chief of staff to the Austrian commander in the southeast, the command question was regulated in September 1916 when Hindenburg and Ludendorff replaced Falkenhayn in the German OHL. The German Emperor now became supreme commander of the allied forces on all fronts, with Hindenburg acting in his name. If the Austrian AOK did not like his decisions it could protest, and the question could then be subject to decision by the two sovereigns.[32]

[30] Urbanski, *op. cit.*, p. 341. See David Lloyd George, *War Memoirs* (London, 1933–36), III, 1454–58.

[31] On the background of this defeat see, *inter alia, Oesterreich-Ungarns letzter Krieg*, IV, 359–74; Cramon, *Bundesgenosse*, pp. 57–64; Kabisch, *op. cit.*, pp. 217–19; Falkenhayn, *op. cit.*, p. 205. See Ritter, *Staatskunst und Kriegshandwerk*, III, 224–25.

[32] Generaloberst Arz, *Zur Geschichte des grossen Krieges 1914–1918* (Vienna, 1924), pp. 126–27; Cramon, *Bundesgenosse*, pp. 66–73; Edmond Glaise von Horstenau, *Die Katastrophe* (Vienna, 1929), pp. 57–58.

This arrangement soon proved to be of limited usefulness. As Ludendorff wrote later: "We had no clear conception of the internal condition of our ally's armies and could not therefore decree that, for example, only so and so many divisions should remain on Austria's Italian frontier. In practice, reciprocal agreements were necessary."[33] Moreover, it was not always possible to reach such agreements, for in November 1916 Emperor Francis Joseph died, and his successor Charles proved to be as resistant to German direction as Conrad always was. The fact that the new sovereign assumed personal control over his armies in itself disturbed the new command arrangement and forced adjustments in it. In addition, the Emperor's sensitivity in matters of form led him to fancy slights where none was intended, and his earnest desire for peace at home and abroad obtruded itself upon the conduct of military operations in ways that offended and alarmed his ally. For a time, Charles convinced himself that he might promote the cause of peace by forbidding his troops to resort to offensive aerial bombardment or to the use of gas and certain other weapons, a policy that merely surrendered advantage to the enemy, who was not bound by similar gestures of self-denial. More serious in German eyes was Charles' amnesty decree of the spring of 1917 which freed the leaders of the Czech subversive movement. The Germans believed that this helped destroy what was left of the morale of the loyal components of the Austro-Hungarian army, while encouraging the defection of the disloyal, and they attributed the betrayal of Carzano to the Italians and the treason of the 19th Division on the eastern front in July 1917 directly to Charles' amnesty decree.[34]

By this time the military effectiveness of the Austro-German alliance was beyond salvation, or even improvement, by adjustments in command relationships or better communications or more frequent planning sessions. After its heavy losses during the so-called Kerenski offensive of July 1917 and its last victory at Caporetto (the pleasure of which was diminished by the fact that the breakthrough had been spearheaded by seven German divisions commanded by General von Below), the Austro-Hungarian Army was worn out. Not even the withdrawal of the Russians from the war checked its progressive disintegration, and there was no hope that it could make any significant contribution to Ludendorff's spring offensive of 1918, although the fate of both empires was riding on that desperate throw. It is significant, however, that the last example of long-distance cooperation between Austrian and German

[33] Ludendorff, *Kriegserinnerungen*, pp. 202–3.

[34] See, for instance, Arz, *op. cit.*, pp. 132–37; and Cramon, *Bundesgenosse*, pp. 92 and especially 112–13.

forces suffered from the same lack of coherence as the earlier ones. When the German OHL accepted an Austrian plan for an offensive between the Brenta and the Piave in June 1918, in the hope that it might bring some relief to the western front, the Austrian AOK proceeded, without consulting its ally, to change that approved plan to one involving a series of uncoordinated actions along the whole front between the Pasubio and the Adriatic. In the judgment of the British historian C. R. M. F. Cruttwell, "No attack in the war was so uselessly fritted away and dispersed over so wide a front."[35] One hundred and fifty thousand men were lost, and the Austro-Hungarian Army was permanently paralyzed, without any perceptible effect on the front in France.

In their critiques of the German war plan of 1914, General Ludwig Beck and Professor Gerhard Ritter have agreed that a return to the conception of the elder Moltke would have offered greater chances of military success, at least at the outset of the war, than the application of the Schlieffen Plan. Whether this is true and, if true, whether this would have made for a greater degree of military cohesion in the alliance of the Central Powers are questions that cannot be answered with any degree of assurance fifty years after the fact. It may be suggested, however, that a war effort begun with a joint success on a common front would have avoided some of the prejudices and resentments that plagued the alliance from 1914 onward and might have made it easier for the allies to solve technical problems that hampered the efficiency of their operations throughout the war.

[35] Cruttwell, *op. cit.*, p. 599.

4. Hans Delbrück: The Military Historian

HANS DELBRÜCK, whose active life coincided almost exactly with that of the second German Empire, was at once military historian, interpreter of military affairs to the German people, and civilian critic of the General Staff. In each of these roles his contribution to modern military thought was noteworthy. His *History of the Art of War* was not only a monument to German scholarship but also a mine of valuable information for the military theorists of his day. His commentaries on military affairs, written in the pages of the *Preussische Jahrbücher,* contributed to the military education of the German public and, during the First World War especially, helped them comprehend the underlying strategic problems which confronted the General Staff. His criticisms of the high command, written during the war and in the period following it, did much to stimulate a reappraisal of the type of strategical thinking that had ruled the German army since the days of Moltke.

The military leaders of Germany have always placed great emphasis on the lessons that can be drawn from military history. This was especially true in the nineteenth century. It had been Clausewitz' ideal to teach war from purely historical examples; both Moltke and Schlieffen had made the study of military history one of the responsibilities of the General Staff.[1] But if history was to serve the soldier, it was necessary that the military record be an accurate one and that past military events be divested of the misconceptions and myths which had grown up around them. Throughout the nineteenth century, thanks to the

"Hans Delbrück: The Military Historian" is reprinted with the permission of the Princeton University Press from Edward Mead Earle, ed., *Makers of Modern Strategy: Military Thought from Machiavelli to Hitler* (Princeton, 1943).

[1] See Hajo Holborn, "Moltke and Schlieffen: The Prussian-German School," in Earle, *op. cit.,* pp. 179, 190.

influence of Leopold von Ranke, German scholars were engaged in the task of clearing away the underbrush of legend which obscured historical truth. But it was not until Delbrück had written his *History of the Art of War* that the new scientific method was applied to the military records of the past, and it is this that constitutes Delbrück's major contribution to military thought.

It was not, however, his sole contribution. In the course of the nineteenth century the basis of government was broadened and in the western world generally the voice of the people was felt increasingly in every branch of governmental administration. The control of military affairs could no longer remain the prerogative of a small ruling class. In Prussia, the embittered struggle over the military budget in 1862 was an indication that the wishes of the people and their representatives with regard to matters of military administration would at least have to be given serious consideration in the future. It seemed important therefore for the safety of the state and the maintenance of its military institutions that the general public should be educated to a proper appreciation of military problems. The military publications of the General Staff were designed not only for use in the army but also for more general consumption. But the writings of professional soldiers, devoted as they were to accounts of single wars and campaigns, were in general too technical in style and content to fulfill the latter function. There was a genuine need for instruction in elements of military affairs on a popular level.[2] Delbrück felt this need and tried to supply it. In all of his writings he considered himself as interpreter of military affairs to the German people. This phase of his work was most marked during the First World War, when, in the pages of the *Preussische Jahrbücher*, he wrote monthly commentaries on the course of the conflict, explaining on the basis of available materials the strategy of the high command and of Germany's opponents.

Finally, especially in his later years, Delbrück became a valuable critic of the military institutions and the strategical thinking of his time. His study of the military institutions of the past had shown him, in every age, the intimate relationship of war and politics, and had taught him that military and political strategy must go hand in hand. Clausewitz had already asserted that truth in his statement that "war admittedly has its own grammar, but not its own logic" and in his insistence that war is "the continuation of state policy by other means." But the Clausewitz

[2] See Delbrück, "Etwas Kriegsgeschichtliches," *Preussische Jahrbücher*, LX (1887), 607.

dictum was too often forgotten by men who remembered that Clausewitz had also argued for the freedom of military leadership from political restrictions.[3] Delbrück returned to the Clausewitz doctrine and argued that the conduct of war and the planning of strategy must be conditioned by the aims of state policy and that once strategical thinking becomes inflexible and self-sufficient even the most brilliant tactical successes may lead to political disaster. In Delbrück's writings in the war years, the critic outgrew the historian. When he became convinced that the strategical thinking of the high command had become antithetical to the political needs of the state, he became one of the foremost advocates of a negotiated peace. After the war, when the Reichstag undertook to investigate the causes of the German collapse in 1918, Delbrück was the most cogent critic of Ludendorff's strategy, and his criticism grew naturally from the precepts he had drawn from history.

I

The details of Delbrück's life may be passed over quickly.[4] He himself summed them up tersely in 1920 with the words: "I derived from official and scholarly circles, on my mother's side from a Berlin family; I had war service and was a reserve officer; for five years I lived at the court of Emperor Frederick, when he was Crown Prince. I was a parliamentarian; as editor of the *Preussische Jahrbücher,* I belonged to the press; I became an academic teacher."

Delbrück was born in November 1848 in Bergen. His father was a district judge; his mother, the daughter of a professor of philosophy at the University of Berlin. Among his ancestors were theologians, jurists, and academicians. He received his education at a preparatory school in Greifswald and later at the universities of Heidelberg, Greifswald, and Bonn. He showed an early interest in history and attended the lectures of Noorden, Schäfer, and Sybel, all men deeply inspired by the new scientific tendency that was Ranke's contribution to scholarship. The influence of Ranke was clearly evident in Delbrück's doctoral disserta-

[3] H. Rothfels, "Clausewitz," in Earle, *op. cit.,* p. 105.

[4] Delbrück himself has written brief autobiographical sketches in *Über die Glaubwürdigkeit Lamberts von Hersfeld* (Bonn, 1873), 78; *Die Geschichte der Kriegskunst im Rahmen der politischen Geschichte* (4 vols.; Berlin, 1900–1920), I, vii–viii; and *Krieg und Politik* (Berlin, 1918–1920), III, 225 ff. See also J. Ziekursch in *Deutsches biographisches Jahrbuch* (1929). An excellent account of Delbrück's life is given in Richard H. Bauer's article in Bernadotte Schmitt, ed., *Some Historians of Modern Europe* (Chicago, 1942), 100–127.

tion, which was a critical and highly devastating appraisal of the writings of a German chronicler of the eleventh century.[5] Delbrück showed that these writings, long accepted as genuine by historians, were in large part unreliable and, in doing so, revealed for the first time the critical acumen which was to distinguish his later work.

As a student, Delbrück was keenly interested in political problems and was a staunch advocate of German unity. It was not until after 1870, however, that he was convinced that Bismarck's policy would attain that unity.[6] Nevertheless, feeling that war with France was inevitable, he enlisted in the army in 1867, saw active duty in the war of 1870, and remained a reserve officer until 1885.

From 1874 to 1879, Delbrück was tutor of Prince Waldemar, the son of the crown prince. His position not only placed him on terms of intimacy with the members of Frederick's court but gave him an excellent insight into the political problems of his time. Meanwhile, he had remained true to his early determination to become a historian and in 1881 was successful in obtaining a post at the University of Berlin, beginning a distinguished academic career which was to last until 1920. Although his research and his lectures occupied most of his time, Delbrück found an opportunity to take an active part in politics as well. From 1882 to 1885 he was a member of the Prussian Landtag and from 1884 to 1890 of the German Reichstag. As a parliamentarian, he was always, however, more of an observer than an active participant, and he regarded himself as "the scholar in politics."[7]

In addition to these activities, he was a publicist of weight and reputation. He served as editor of the *Staatsarchiv,* an annual collection of official and diplomatic documents, and of Schulthess' *Europäischer Geschichtskalender,* a publication that annually reviewed the events of the preceding year. In 1883 he was appointed to the editorial board of the *Preussische Jahrbücher,* and, after 1890, he became the sole editor of that vigorous publication. It was in the pages of this journal that Delbrück wrote his military commentaries during the war and, in the post-war years, his bitter attacks on the war-guilt clause of the Treaty of Versailles.

Even before he had begun his career at the University of Berlin, Delbrück had turned his attention to the study of military history. As a soldier, during spring maneuvers at Wittenberg in 1874, he had read

[5] *Über die Glaubwürdigkeit Lamberts von Hersfeld.* See Bauer, *op. cit.,* 101–2.
[6] *Krieg und Politik,* III, 226.
[7] *Ibid.*

Rüstow's *History of Infantry,* and he later spoke of that event as having determined his choice of career. It was not, however, until 1877 that he turned seriously to the study of warfare. In that year he was given the opportunity of completing the editing of the memoirs and papers of Gneisenau which had been begun by Georg Heinrich Pertz. As he immersed himself in the history of the War of Liberation, he was struck by what seemed to be a fundamental difference in the strategical thinking of Napoleon and Gneisenau on the one hand and Archduke Charles, Wellington, and Schwarzenberg on the other. As he carried his investigations further in the biography of Gneisenau with which he followed his editorial task,[8] the difference seemed more marked, and he sensed that nineteenth-century strategy in general was strikingly different from that of the previous century. He read Clausewitz for the first time and held long conversations with the officers attached to Frederick's court. While he did so, his interest was heightened, and he determined to seek the basic and determining elements of strategy and of military operations.

His first lectures at the University of Berlin were on the campaign of 1866. But thereafter, he turned his mind to the past, lecturing first on the history of the art of war from the beginning of the feudal system, and then pushing his researches even further back into the period between the Persian Wars and the decline of Rome. He began a systematic study of the sources in the ancient and medieval periods and published short studies of the Persian Wars, the strategy of Pericles and Cleon, the tactics of the Roman maniple, the military institutions of the early Germans, the wars between the Swiss and the Burgundians, and the strategies of Frederick the Great and Napoleon. Meanwhile, he encouraged his students to make equally detailed studies of special periods. Out of these lectures and monographs grew Delbrück's *History of the Art of War in the Framework of Political History,* the first volume of which appeared in 1900.[9]

[8] Delbrück, *Das Leben des Feldmarschalls Grafen Neidhardt von Gneisenau* (Berlin, 1882).

[9] *Geschichte der Kriegskunst im Rahmen der politischen Geschichte.* The work is in seven volumes, but only the first four can be considered Delbrück's own. The fifth volume (1928) and the sixth (1932) were written by Emil Daniels; a seventh volume (1936) was written by Daniels and Otto Haintz. The first four volumes will be treated here. All citations will be made from the first edition. A second edition of the first two volumes appeared in 1908 and a third edition of the first volume in 1920. None of the corrections or additions in these later editions made essential differences in the original work.

II

From the date of the publication of the first volume, the *History of the Art of War* was the butt of angry critics. Classical scholars resented the way in which Delbrück manhandled Herodotus; medievalists attacked Delbrück's section on the origin of the feudal system; patriotic English scholars were furious at his slighting of the Wars of the Roses. Many of the resultant controversies have been written into the footnotes of the later editions of the work, where the fires of academic wrath still smolder. But in its main outlines the book stands unaffected by the attacks of the specialists and it has received its meed of praise from such widely separated readers as General Groener, Defense Minister under the Weimar Republic, and Franz Mehring, the great socialist publicist. The former referred to it as "simply unique";[10] the latter as "the most significant work produced by the historical writing of bourgeois Germany in the new century."[11]

Of the four volumes written by Delbrück, the first discusses the art of war from the period of the Persian Wars to the high point of Roman warfare under Julius Caesar. The second volume, which is largely concerned with the early Germans, treats also the decline of Roman military institutions, the military organization of the Byzantine Empire, and the origins of the feudal system. The third volume is devoted to the decline and near disappearance of tactics and strategy in the Middle Ages and concludes with an account of the revival of tactical bodies in the Swiss-Burgundian Wars. The fourth volume carries the story of the development of tactical methods and strategical thinking to the age of Napoleon.

In Proust's novel *The Guermantes Way*, a young officer remarks that "in the narrative of a military historian, the smallest facts, the most trivial happenings, are only the outward signs of an idea which has to be analyzed and which often brings to light other ideas, like a palimpsest." These words are a reasonably accurate description of Delbrück's conception of military history. He was interested in general ideas and tendencies rather than in the minutiae that had crowded the pages of earlier military histories. In his introduction to the first volume of his

[10] Wilhelm Groener, "Delbrück und die Kriegswissenschaften" in Emil Daniels and Paul Rühlmann, eds., *Am Webstuhl der Zeit, eine Erinnerungsgabe Hans Delbrück dem Achtzigjährigen . . . dargebracht* (Berlin, 1928), p. 35.

[11] Franz Mehring, "Eine Geschichte der Kriegskunst," *Die Neue Zeit* (Erganzungsheft, No. 4, 16 October 1908), p. 2.

work, he specifically disclaimed any intention of writing a completely comprehensive history of the art of war. Such a work, he pointed out, would necessarily include such things as "details of drill with its commands, the technique of weapons and of the care of horses, and finally the whole subject of naval affairs—matters on which I have either nothing new to say or which I don't for a moment comprehend." The purpose of the history was stated in its title: it was to be a history of the art of war in the framework of political history.[12]

In the introduction to his fourth volume, Delbrück explained this in greater detail. The basic purpose of the work was to establish the connection between the constitution of the state and tactics and strategy. "The recognition of the interrelationship between tactics, strategy, the constitution of the state, and policy reflects upon the relationship [between military history and] world history and has brought to light much that until now has been hidden in darkness or left without recognition. This work has been written not for the sake of the art of war, but for the sake of world history. If military men read it and are stimulated by it, I am pleased and regard that as an honor; but it was written for friends of history by a historian."[13]

At the same time, however, Delbrück realized that, before any general conclusions could be drawn from the wars of the past, the historian must determine as accurately as possible how those wars had been fought. It was precisely because he was intent on finding general ideas which would be of interest to other historians that Delbrück was forced to grapple with the "trivial happenings," "the smallest facts" of past campaigns; and, despite his own disclaimer, his reappraisal of those facts was of great value not to historians alone but to soldiers as well.

The "facts" were to be found in the great volume of source material which had been inherited from the past. But many of the sources of military history were obviously unreliable and were no better than "wash-room prattle and adjutants' gossip."[14] How was the modern historian to check these ancient records?

Delbrück believed that this could be done in several ways. Provided the historian knew the terrain in which past battles were fought, he could use all the resources of modern geographical science to check the reports which were handed down. Provided he knew the type of weapons and equipment used, he could reconstruct the tactics of the battle in a logical manner, since the laws of tactics for every kind of

[12] *Geschichte der Kriegskunst,* I, xi.
[13] *Ibid.,* IV, Preface.
[14] *Ibid.,* I, 377.

weapon could be ascertained. A study of modern warfare would supply the historian with further tools, for in modern campaigns he could judge the marching powers of the average soldier, the weight-carrying capacity of the average horse, the maneuverability of large masses of men. Finally, it was often possible to discover campaigns or battles, for which reliable reports existed, in which the conditions of earlier battles were reproduced almost exactly. Both the battles of the Swiss-Burgundian Wars, for which accurate records exist, and the Battle of Marathon, for which Herodotus was the only source, were fought between mounted knights and bowmen on the one side and foot soldiers armed with weapons for hand-to-hand fighting on the other; in both cases, the foot soldiers were victorious. It should be possible, therefore, to draw conclusions from the battles of Granson, Murten, and Nancy that could be applied to the Battle of Marathon.[15] The combination of all of these methods Delbrück called *Sachkritik.*[16]

Only a few applications of the *Sachkritik* need be mentioned. Delbrück's most startling results were attained by his investigations of the numbers of troops employed in the great wars of the past. According to Herodotus, for instance, the Persian army that fought against Athens in the fifth century B.C. numbered over 4 million men. Delbrück pointed out that this figure could not be considered reliable: "According to the German order of march, an army corps, that is 30,000 men, occupies about three miles, without the baggage trains. The marching column of the Persians would therefore have been 420 miles long, and, as the first troops were arriving before Thermopylae, the last would have just marched out of Susa on the other side of the Tigris."[17]

Even if this awkward fact could be explained away, none of the fields on which battles were fought were big enough to hold armies as large as those in Herodotus' accounts. The plain of Marathon, for instance, "is so small that some fifty years ago a Prussian staff officer who visited it wrote with some astonishment that a Prussian brigade would scarcely have room enough there for its exercises."[18]

On the basis of modern studies of the population of ancient Greece, Delbrück estimated the size of the Greek army which faced Xerxes at

[15] Delbrück used this last method in his first account of the Persian Wars, *Die Perserkriege und die Burgunderkriege: zwei combinierte kriegsgeschichtliche Studien* (Berlin, 1887).

[16] *Geschichte der Kriegskunst,* I, Introduction.

[17] *Ibid.,* I, 10.

[18] Delbrück, *Numbers in History: Two Lectures Delivered before the University of London* (London, 1913), p. 24.

about 12,000 men. It was a citizen army trained to fight in a rude phalanx but incapable of tactical maneuvering. The Persian army was a professional army, and the bravery of its soldiers was admitted even in the Greek account. "If both things were true, the size [of the Persian army] as well as its military bravery, then the ever-repeated victory of the Greeks would remain inexplicable. Only one of the two things can be true; hence, it is clear that the advantage of the Persians is to be sought not in numbers but in quality."[19] Delbrück concludes that, far from having the mass army described by Herodotus, the Persians were actually inferior in numbers to the Greeks throughout the Persian Wars.

The account of Herodotus had long been suspect, and Delbrück's criticism was by no means wholly original. But his real contribution lay in the fact that he applied the same systematic methods to the numerical records of every war from the Persian Wars to those of Napoleon. Thus, in his discussion of Caesar's campaigns in Gaul, he clearly demonstrated that Caesar's estimates of the forces pitted against him were, for political reasons, grossly exaggerated. According to Caesar, the Helvetians, in their great trek, numbered 368,000 persons and carried three months' provisions with them. To Delbrück the numerical estimate smacked of the fabulous; but it was Caesar's remarks on the Helvetian food supply that enabled him to prove it so. He pointed out that some 8,500 wagons would be required to carry such provisions and, in the condition of roads in Caesar's time, it would be quite impossible for such a column to move.[20] Again, in his discussion of the invasion of Europe by the Huns, Delbrück effectively disposed of the belief that Attila had an army of 700,000 men by describing the difficulties which Moltke experienced in maneuvering an army of 500,000 men in the campaign of 1870. "To direct such a mass unitedly is, even with railroads, roads, telegraphs, and a general staff an exceedingly difficult task. . . . How could Attila have led 700,000 men from Germany over the Rhine into France to the Plain of Chalons, if Moltke moved 500,000 with such difficulty over the same road? The one number acts as a check on the other."[21]

Delbrück's investigations of numbers have more than a mere antiquarian interest. At a time when the German army was being taught to seek lessons in history, the destroyer of myths helped it avoid the drawing of false conclusions. In war and the study of war, numbers

[19] *Geschichte der Kriegskunst,* I, 39.
[20] *Ibid.,* I, 427.
[21] *Numbers in History,* p. 18.

were of the highest importance.[22] Delbrück himself pointed out that "a movement which a troop of 1,000 men executes without difficulty is a hard task for 10,000 men, a work of art for 50,000, an impossibility for 100,000."[23] No lessons can be drawn from past campaigns unless an accurate statement of the numbers involved is available.

Sachkritik had other uses. By means of it, Delbrück was able to reconstruct the details of single battles in a logical manner, and his success in doing so made a profound impression upon the historical section of the German general staff. General Groener has attested to the value of Delbrück's investigation of the origins of that oblique battle order which made flanking possible;[24] while it is well known that his scientific description of the encircling movement at Cannae strongly influenced the theories of Count Schlieffen.[25] But it is his account of the Battle of Marathon which is perhaps the best example of the skill with which Delbrück reconstructed the details of past battles, the more so because it most clearly illustrates his belief that "if one knows the armament and the manner of fighting of the contending armies, then the terrain is such an important and eloquent authority for the character of a battle, that one may dare, provided there is no doubt as to the outcome, to reconstruct its course in general outline."[26]

The Greek army at Marathon was composed of heavily armed foot soldiers, formed in the primitive phalanx, the maneuverability of which was restricted to slow forward movement. It was opposed by an army inferior in numbers but made up of highly trained bowmen and cavalry. Herodotus had written that the Greeks had won the battle by charging across the plain of Marathon some 4,800 feet and crushing the center of the Persian line. Delbrück pointed out that this was a physical impossibility. According to the modern German drill book, soldiers with full pack could be expected to run for only two minutes some 1,080 to 1,150 feet. The Athenians were no more lightly armed than the modern German soldier, and they suffered from two additional disadvantages.

22 General Groener made explicit acknowledgment of Delbrück's contribution. See Groener, *op. cit.*, p. 38.

23 *Geschichte der Kriegskunst*, I, 7.

24 Groener, *loc. cit.* The oblique battle order, first used by the Theban Epaminondas, bears a striking resemblance to that used by Frederick the Great at Leuthen in 1757. On Epaminondas, see *Geschichte der Kriegskunst*, I, 130–35.

25 *Geschichte der Kriegskunst*, I, 281–302. Graf Schlieffen, *Cannae* (Berlin, 1925), p. 3.

26 *Geschichte der Kriegskunst*, II, 80. Delbrück used the method not only for the Battle of Marathon but also in his reconstruction of the Battle of the Teutoburger Wald.

They were not professional soldiers but civilians, and many of them exceeded the age limit required in modern armies. Moreover, the phalanx was a closely massed body of men which made quick movement of any kind impossible. An attempted charge over such a distance would have reduced it to a disorganized mob which would have been cut down by the Persian professionals without difficulty.[27]

The tactics described by Herodotus were obviously impossible, the more so because the Greek phalanx was weak on the flanks and, in any encounter on an open field, could have been surrounded by Persian cavalry. It seemed obvious to Delbrück that the battle was not fought on the plain of Marathon proper but in a small valley to the southeast where the Greeks were protected by mountains and forest from any flanking movement. The fact that Herodotus speaks of the opposing armies delaying the engagement for days shows that Miltiades, the Athenian commander, had chosen a strong position, and, given the tactical form of the Greek army, the position in the Brana Valley was the only one possible. Moreover, that position dominated the only road to Athens. To reach the city, the Persians were forced to dispose of Miltiades' army or give up the whole campaign, and they chose the former alternative. The only logical explanation of the battle, then, is that the Persians, despite their numerical inferiority and inability to use flanking tactics, made the initial attack, and Miltiades, shifting at the crucial moment from the defensive to the offensive, crushed the Persian center and swept the field.[28]

To the casual reader, the *History of the Art of War,* like many a work before it, is a mere collection of such battle pieces. But the care with which Delbrück reconstructed battles was necessary to his main purpose. He felt that by the study of key battles the student could acquire a picture of the tactics of an age and from that he could proceed to the investigation of broader problems.[29] For the key battles are important not only as typical manifestations of their age but as mileposts in the progressive development of military science. In a sense, Delbrück, like

27 Ulrich von Wilamowitz upheld the Herodotus story by arguing that the goddess Artemis had given the Greeks sufficient strength to make the charge, and he issued a stern reproof to scholars who minimized the military contributions of the deities. Delbrück's refusal to accept this explanation led to a controversy with J. Kromayer, who came to Wilamowitz' aid. The battle was fought out in the pages of the *Historische Zeitschrift* (XCV, 1 ff., 514–15) and the *Preussische Jahrbücher* (CXXI, 158–59) and, like most of Delbrück's controversies, left the parties involved unreconciled.

28 *Geschichte der Kriegskunst,* I, 41–59.

29 *Ibid.,* I, 417.

Proust's young officer, believed that past battles were "the literature, the learning, the etymology, the aristocracy of the battles of today." By reconstructing single battles he sought continuity in military history, and thus his *Sachkritik* enabled him to develop the three major themes that give his work a meaning and a unity found in no previous book on the subject: namely, the evolution of tactical forms from the Persians to Napoleon, the interrelationship of war and politics throughout history, and the division of all strategy into two basic forms.

Delbrück's description of the evolution of tactical bodies has been called one of his most significant contributions to military thought.[30] He was interested in discovering the reasons for the military supremacy of the Romans in the ancient world. Searching for a key to this problem, he came to the conclusion that their success rested on the excellence of their tactical forms. It was the gradual evolution of the primitive Greek phalanx to the highly coordinated tactical body used by the Romans which comprised "the essential meaning of the ancient art of war."[31] Turning then to the modern period, Delbrück argued that it was the revival of tactical bodies, not unlike the Roman, in the Swiss-Burgundian Wars and their improvement and perfection to the age of Napoleon which gave unity to modern military history.

The turning point in the history of ancient warfare was the Battle of Cannae,[32] where the Carthaginians under Hannibal overwhelmed the Romans in the most perfect tactical battle ever fought. How were the Romans able to recover from that disaster, to defeat the Carthaginians, and eventually to exercise military supremacy over the whole of the ancient world? The answer is to be found in the evolution of the phalanx. At Cannae, the Roman infantry was formed in a body essentially the same as that which had won the Battle of Marathon. The basic weaknesses of the phalanx had delivered the Roman army into Hannibal's arms. The exposed flanks and the inability of the Roman rear to maneuver independently of the mass of the army made it impossible for the Romans to prevent the encircling tactics employed by the Carthaginian cavalry. But in the years following Cannae, striking changes were introduced into the Roman battle form. "The Romans first articulated the phalanx, then divided it into columns (*Treffen*), and finally split it up into a great number of small tactical bodies which were

30 F. J. Schmidt, Konrad Molinski, and Siegfried Mette, *Hans Delbrueck: der Historiker und Politiker* (Berlin, 1928), p. 96. Eugen von Frauenholz, *Entwicklungsgeschichte des deutschen Heerwesens,* II, vii.

31 *Geschichte der Kriegskunst,* II, 43.

32 *Ibid.,* I, 330 ff.

capable, now of closing together in a compact impenetrable union, now of changing the pattern with consummate flexibility, of separating one from the other and of turning in this or that direction."[33] To modern students of warfare this development seems so natural as to be hardly worthy of notice. To accomplish it, however, was extremely difficult, and only the Romans, of all the ancient peoples, succeeded. In their case it was made possible only by a hundred years of experimentation —in the course of which the army changed from a civilian to a professional army—and by the emphasis upon military discipline which characterized the Roman system.[34]

The Romans conquered the world, then, not because their troops "were braver than all their opponents, but because, thanks to their discipline, they had stronger tactical bodies."[35] The only people who successfully avoided conquest by the Romans were the Germans, and their resistance was made possible by a natural discipline inherent in their political institutions and by the fact that the German fighting column, the *Gevierthaufe,* was a tactical group of great effectiveness.[36] Indeed, in the course of their wars with the Romans, the Germans learned to imitate the articulation of the Roman legion, maneuvering their *Gevierthaufe* independently or in union as the occasion required.[37]

With the decline of the Roman state and the barbarization of the empire, the tactical progress that had been made since the days of Miltiades came to an end. The political disorders of the age following the reign of the Severi weakened the discipline of the Roman army and gradually undermined the excellence of its tactical forms.[38] At the same time, as large numbers of barbarians were admitted into the ranks, it was impossible to cling to the highly integrated battle order that had been devised over the course of centuries. History had shown that infantry was superior to cavalry only if the foot soldiers were organized in strong tactical bodies. Now, with the decline of the state and the consequent degeneration of tactics, there was a growing tendency, in the new barbarian empires of the west and in Justinian's army as well, to replace infantry with heavily armed mounted soldiers.[39] As that tend-

[33] *Ibid.,* I, 380.

[34] *Ibid.,* I, 381; see also I, 253: "The meaning and power of discipline was first fully recognized and realized by the Romans."

[35] *Ibid.,* II, 43.

[36] *Ibid.,* II, 45 ff.

[37] *Ibid.,* II, 52–53.

[38] *Ibid.,* II, 205 ff. This chapter, entitled "Niedergang und Auflösung des römischen Kriegswesens," is the key chapter of the second volume.

[39] *Ibid.,* II, 424 ff.

ency gained the upper hand, the days when battles were decided by infantry tactics died away, and Europe entered a long period in which military history was dominated by the figure of the armed knight.[40]

Delbrück has been accused of maintaining that the development of military science stops with the decline of Rome and starts again with the Renaissance,[41] and the accusation is justified. The essential element in all warfare from the days of Charlemagne to the emergence of the Swiss infantry in the Burgundian Wars was the feudal army. This, in Delbrück's opinion, was no tactical body. It depended upon the fighting quality of the single warrior; there was no discipline, no unity of command, no effective differentiation of arms. In this whole period, no tactical progress was made, and Delbrück seems inclined to agree with Mark Twain's Connecticut Yankee, that "when you come to figure up results, you can't tell one fight from another, nor who whipped." It is true that at Crécy, the English knights dismounted and fought a defensive battle on foot and that, at Agincourt, dismounted knights actually took the offensive; but these were mere episodes and cannot be considered as forecasts of the development of modern infantry.[42]

It was among the Swiss in the fifteenth century that the independent infantry was reborn. "With the battles of Laupen and Sempach, Granson, Murten, and Nancy we have again a foot soldiery comparable to the phalanx and the legions."[43] The Swiss pikemen formed themselves in bodies similar to the German *Gevierthaufe;*[44] and, in the course of their wars against the Burgundians, they perfected the articulated tactics used by the Roman legions. At Sempach, for instance, the Swiss infantry was divided into two bodies, one holding a defensive position against the mounted enemy, the other delivering a decisive blow on the enemy's flank.[45]

The revival of tactical bodies was a military revolution comparable to that which followed Cannae. It was this revival, rather than the introduction of firearms, which brought feudal warfare to an end. At Murten, Granson, and Nancy the new weapons were employed by the knights but had no effect upon the outcome of the battle.[46] With the restoration of the tactical body of infantry as the decisive one in warfare, the

40 *Ibid.*, II, 433.

41 T. F. Tout, in *English Historical Review,* XXII (1907), 344–48.

42 *Geschichte der Kriegskunst,* III, 483. For a penetrating criticism of Delbrück's discussion of medieval warfare, see Tout, *loc. cit.*

43 *Geschichte der Kriegskunst,* III, 661.

44 *Ibid.*, III, 609 ff.

45 *Ibid.*, III, 594.

46 *Ibid.*, IV, 55.

mounted soldiers became a mere cavalry, a highly useful but supplementary part of the army. In his fourth volume, Delbrück discussed this development and the evolution of the modern infantry to the age of the standing army and concluded with an account of the revolution in tactics made possible by the French Revolution.

The attention that Delbrück pays to the emergence of tactical bodies serves not only to give a sense of continuity to his military history but also to illustrate the theme which he considered basic to his book, namely, the interrelationship of politics and war. In every period of history, he pointed out, the development of politics and the evolution of tactics were closely related. "The Hopliten-Phalanx developed in quite a different manner under the Macedonian Kings than it did in the aristocratic Roman *Beamten-Republik*, and the tactics of the cohort were developed only in relationship with constitutional change. Again, according to their nature, the German *hundreds* fought quite differently from the Roman cohorts."[47]

The Roman army at Cannae, for example, was defeated because of the weakness of its tactics. But contributory to that weakness was the fact that the army was composed of untrained civilians rather than professional soldiers and the additional fact that the constitution of the state required that the high command alternate between the two consuls.[48] In the years following Cannae, the necessity of a unified command was generally recognized. After various political experiments were tried, P. C. Scipio was in the year 211 B.C. made general in chief of the Roman armies in Africa and assured of continued tenure for the duration of the war. The appointment was in direct violation of the state constitution, and it marked the beginning of the decline of republican institutions. The interrelationship of politics and warfare is in this case apparent. "The importance of the Second Punic War in world history," Delbrück writes, "is that Rome effected an internal transformation that increased her military potentiality enormously"[49] but that at the same time changed the whole character of the state.

Just as the political element was predominant in the perfection of Roman tactics, so also the breakdown of tactical forms can be explained only by a careful study of the political institutions of the later empire. The political and economic disorders of the third century had a direct effect on Roman military institutions. "Permanent civil war destroyed the cement which till now had held the strong walls of the Roman army

[47] *Ibid.*, II, 424.
[48] *Ibid.*, I, 305.
[49] *Ibid.*, I, 333.

together, the discipline which constituted the military worth of the legions."[50]

In no part of the *History of the Art of War* does Delbrück include a general discussion of the relationship of politics and war. But, as he moves from one historical epoch to another, he fits the purely military into its general background, illustrating the close connection of political and military institutions and showing how changes in one sphere led of necessity to corresponding reactions in the other. He shows that the German *Gevierthaufe* was the military expression of the village organization of the German tribes and demonstrates how the dissolution of German communal life led to the disappearance of the *Gevierthaufe* as a tactical body.[51] He shows how the victories of the Swiss in the fifteenth century were made possible by the fusion of the democratic and aristocratic elements in the various cantons, and the union of the urban nobility with the peasant masses.[52] And, for the period of the French Revolution, he shows how the political factor, in this case "the new idea of defending the fatherland, inspired the mass [of the soldiers] with such an improved will that new tactics could be developed."[53]

That politics and war were closely related had been accepted as a truism even before Delbrück's time. But it was a truism which had to be studied from every angle and illustrated by actual events. Delbrück's service to military theorists lay in the systematic manner in which he illustrated the interplay of political and military factors in every age.

The most striking of all of Delbrück's military theories was that which held that all military strategy can be divided into two basic forms. This theory, formulated long before the publication of the *History of the Art of War*, is conveniently summarized in the first and fourth volumes of that work.[54]

Under the influence of Clausewitz' book *On War*, the great majority of military thinkers in Delbrück's day believed that the aim of war is the complete destruction of the enemy's forces and that, consequently, the battle which accomplishes this is the end of all strategy. Delbrück's first researches in military history convinced him that this type of strategical thinking had not always been generally accepted and that there were long periods in history in which a completely different

[50] *Ibid.*, II, 209.
[51] *Ibid.*, II, 25–38, 424 ff.
[52] *Ibid.*, III, 614–15.
[53] *Ibid.*, IV, 474.
[54] *Ibid.*, I, 100 ff.; IV, 333–63, 426–44.

strategy ruled the field. He discovered, moreover, that Clausewitz himself had admitted the possibility of the existence of more than one strategical system. In a note written in 1827, Clausewitz had suggested that there were two sharply distinct methods of conducting war: one which was bent solely on the annihilation of the enemy; the other, a limited warfare, in which such annihilation was impossible either because the political aims or political tensions involved in the war were small or because the military means were inadequate to accomplish annihilation.

Clausewitz did not live long enough to do more than suggest the existence of the two forms; Delbrück determined to accept the distinction and expound the principles inherent in each. The first form of warfare, to which Clausewitz had devoted the book *On War,* he named *Niederwerfungsstrategie* (the strategy of annihilation). Its sole aim was the decisive battle, and the commanding general was called upon only to estimate the possibility of fighting such a battle in a given situation.

The second type of strategy Delbrück called variously *Ermattungsstrategie* (the strategy of exhaustion) and two-pole strategy. It was distinguished from the strategy of annihilation by the fact "that the *Niederwerfungsstrategie* has only one pole, the battle, whereas the *Ermattungsstrategie* has two poles, battle and maneuver, between which the decisions of the general move." In *Ermattungsstrategie,* the battle is no longer the sole aim of strategy; it is merely one of several equally effective means of attaining the political ends of the war and is essentially no more important than the occupation of territory, the destruction of crops or commerce, and the blockade. This second form of strategy is neither a mere variation of the first nor an inferior form. In certain periods of history, because of political factors or the smallness of armies, it has been the only form of strategy that could be employed. The task it imposes on the commander is quite as difficult as that required of the exponent of the strategy of annihilation. With limited resources at his disposal, the *Ermattungsstrategie* must decide which of several means of conducting war will best suit his purpose, when to fight and when to maneuver, when to obey the law of "daring" and when to obey that of "economy of forces."

> The decision is therefore a subjective one, the more so because at no time are all circumstances and conditions, especially what is going on in the enemy camp, known completely and authoritatively. After a careful consideration of all circumstances—the aim of the war, the combat forces, the political repercussions, the individuality of the enemy commander, and of the government and people of the enemy, as well as his own—the

general must decide whether a battle is advisable or not. He can reach the conclusion that any greater actions must be avoided at all cost; he can also determine to seek [battle] on every occasion so that there is no essential difference between his conduct and that of one-pole strategy.[55]

Among the great commanders of the past who had been strategists of annihilation were Alexander, Caesar, and Napoleon. But equally great generals had been exponents of *Ermattungsstrategie*. Among them, Delbrück listed Pericles, Belisarius, Wallenstein, Gustavus Adolphus, and Frederick the Great. The inclusion of the last name brought down upon the historian a flood of angry criticism. The most vocal of his critics were the historians of the General Staff who, convinced that the strategy of annihilation was the only correct strategy, insisted that Frederick was a precursor of Napoleon. Delbrück answered that to hold this view was to do Frederick a grave disservice. If Frederick was a strategist of annihilation, how was one to explain away the fact that in 1741, with 60,000 men under his command, he refused to attack an already beaten army of only 25,000, or that, in 1745, after his great victory at Hohenfriedberg, he preferred to resort again to a war of maneuver?[56] If the principles of *Niederwerfungsstrategie* were to be considered the sole criteria in judging the qualities of a general, Frederick would cut a very poor figure.[57] Yet Frederick's greatness lay in the fact that although he realized that his resources were not great enough to enable him to seek battle on every occasion, he was nevertheless able to make effective use of other strategical principles in order to win his wars.

Delbrück's arguments did not convince his critics. Both Colmar von der Goltz and Friedrich von Bernhardi entered the lists against him, and a paper warfare ensued that lasted for over twenty years.[58] Delbrück,

[55] Delbrück, *Die Strategie des Perikles erlaütert durch die Strategie Friedrichs des Grossen* (Berlin, 1890), pp. 27–28. This work is Delbrück's most systematic exposition of the two forms of strategy.

[56] *Preussische Jahrbücher,* CXV (1904), 348–49.

[57] In the *Strategie des Perikles,* Delbrück wrote a parody that showed that the application of such criteria to Frederick's campaigns would prove him a third-rate general. For this he was accused in the Prussian Landtag of maligning a national hero.

[58] A full account of the controversy, with bibliography, appears in *Geschichte der Kriegskunst,* IV, 439–44. See also Friedrich von Bernhardi, *Denkwürdigkeiten aus meinem Leben* (Berlin, 1927), pp. 126, 133, 143.

The most thorough and judicious criticism of Delbrück's strategical theory is that of Otto Hintze, "Delbrück, Clausewitz und die Strategie Friedrichs des Grossen," *Forschungen zur Brandenburgischen und Preussischen Geschichte,* XXXIII (1920), 131–77. Hintze objects to the sharp distinction which Delbrück draws between the strategy of Frederick's age and that of Napoleon and insists that

who loved controversy, was indefatigable in answering refutations of his theory. But his concept of *Ermattungsstrategie* was rejected by an officer corps trained in the tradition of Napoleon and Moltke and convinced of the feasibility of the short, decisive war.

The military critics completely missed the deeper significance of Delbrück's strategical theory. History showed that there could be no single theory of strategy, correct for every age. Like all phases of warfare, strategy was intimately connected with politics, with the life and the strength of the state. In the Peloponnesian War, the political weakness of Athens in comparison with that of the League that faced it determined the kind of strategy Pericles followed. Had he attempted to follow the principles of *Niederwerfungsstrategie,* as Cleon did later, disaster would have followed automatically.[59] The strategy of Belisarius' wars in Italy was determined by the uneasy political relations between the Byzantine Empire and the Persians. "Here as always it was politics which determined the administration of the war and which prescribed to strategy its course."[60] Again, "the strategy of the Thirty Years War was determined by extremely complicated, repeatedly changing political relationships," and generals like Gustavus Adolphus, whose personal bravery and inclination toward battle were unquestioned, were nevertheless compelled to make limited war.[61] It was not the battles won by Frederick the Great which made him a great general, but rather his political acumen and the conformity of his strategy with political reality. No strategical system can become self-sufficient; once an attempt is made to make it so, to divorce it from its political context, the strategist becomes a menace to the state.

The transition from dynastic to national war, the victories of 1864, 1866, and 1870, the immense increase in the war potential of the nation seemed to prove that *Niederwerfungsstrategie* was the natural form of war for the modern age. As late as 1890, Delbrück himself, despite his insistence on the relativity of strategy, seems to have believed that this was true.[62] Yet in the last years of the nineteenth century, the mass army of the 1860's was being transformed to the *Millionenheer* which

---

Frederick was at once a *Niederwerfung*- and an *Ermattung*-strategist. He also questions Delbrück's interpretation of Clausewitz' intentions, as does Herbert Rosinski in *Historische Zeitschrift,* CLI (1935). See Delbrück's answer to Hintze, *Forschungen zur Brandenburgischen und Preussischen Geschichte,* XXXIII (1920), 412–17.

[59] *Geschichte der Kriegskunst,* I, 101 f.

[60] *Ibid.,* II, 394.

[61] *Ibid.,* IV, 341.

[62] *Strategie des Perikles,* chapter 1.

fought in the First World War. Might not that transformation make impossible the application of the strategy of annihilation and herald a return to the principles of Pericles and Frederick? Was not the state in grave danger as long as the general staff refused to admit the existence of alternate systems of strategy? These questions, implicit in all of Delbrück's military writings, were constantly on his lips as Germany entered the war.

III

Since Delbrück was Germany's leading civilian expert on military affairs, his writings in the war years 1914–18 are of considerable interest. As a military commentator, his sources of information were in no way superior to those of other members of the newspaper and periodical press. Like them, he was forced to rely on communiqués issued by the general staff, stories that appeared in the daily press, and reports from neutral countries. If his accounts of the war were distinguished by a breadth of vision and understanding not usually found in the lucubrations of civilian commentators, it was due to his technical knowledge of modern war and the sense of perspective he had gained from his study of history. In his monthly commentaries in the *Preussische Jahrbücher,* one can find a further exposition of the principles delineated in his historical works and especially of his theory of strategy and his emphasis upon the interrelationship of war and politics.[63]

In accordance with the Schlieffen strategy, the German army swept into Belgium in 1914 with the purpose of crushing French resistance in short order and then bringing the full weight of its power against Russia. This was *Niederwerfungsstrategie* in its ultimate form, and Delbrück himself, in the first month of the war, felt that it was justified. Like most of his fellows, he had little fear of effective French opposition. The instability of French politics could not but have a deleterious effect upon France's military institutions. "It is impossible that an army which has had forty-two war ministers in forty-three years will be ca-

[63] The articles that Delbrück wrote in the *Preussische Jahrbücher* are collected in the three-volume work called *Krieg und Politik* (Berlin, 1918–19). To the articles as they originally appeared Delbrück added occasional explanatory notes and a highly interesting summary statement. The best article on Delbrück's war writings is by General Ernst Buchfinck, "Delbrücks Lehre, das Heer und der Weltkrieg," in *Am Webstuhl der Zeit,* pp. 41–49. See also M. von Hobohm, "Delbrück, Clausewitz und die Kritik des Weltkrieges," *Preussische Jahrbücher,* CLXXXI (1920), 203–32.

pable of an effectively functioning organization."[64] Nor did he feel that England was capable of continued resistance. Her past political development, he believed, would make it impossible for her to raise more than a token force. England had always relied on small professional armies; the institution of universal conscription would be psychologically and politically impossible. "Every people is the child of its history, its past, and can no more break away from it than a man can separate himself from his youth."[65]

When the first great German drive fell short of its goal, however, and the long period of trench warfare set in, Delbrück sensed a strategical revolution of the first importance. As the stalemate in the west continued, and especially after the failure of the Verdun offensive, he became increasingly convinced that the strategical thinking of the high command would have to be modified. In the west at least, defensive warfare was the order of the day, a fact "the more significant since, before the war, the pre-eminence of the offensive was always proclaimed and expounded with quite exceptional partiality in the theory of strategy fostered in Germany."[66] Now, it was apparent that conditions on the western front approximated those of the age of *Ermattungsstrategie*. "Although this war has already brought us much that is new, nevertheless it is possible to find in it certain historical analogies: for example, the Frederician strategy with its impregnable positions, its increasingly strengthened artillery, its field fortifications, its infrequent tactical decisions and its consequent long withdrawals presents unmistakable similarities with today's war of position and exhaustion [*Stellungs- und Ermattungskrieg*]."[67] In the west, reliance upon the decisive battle was no longer possible. Germany would have to find other means of imposing her will upon the enemy.

By December 1916 Delbrück was pointing out that "however favorable our military position is, the continuation of the war will scarcely bring us so far that we can simply dictate the peace."[68] A complete and crushing victory of German arms was unlikely, if not impossible. That did not mean, however, that Germany could not "win the war." Her inner position not only separated her opponents but enabled her to retain the initiative. Her strength was so formidable that it should not

[64] *Krieg und Politik,* I, 35.

[65] Delbrück's views on England's weakness as a military power were most clearly developed in an article of April 1916. See *Krieg und Politik,* I, 243 ff.

[66] *Ibid.,* II, 242.

[67] *Ibid.,* II, 164; see also I, 17.

[68] *Ibid.,* II, 97.

be difficult to convince her opponents that Germany could not be defeated. While a firm defensive in the west was sapping the will of Allied troops, the high command would be well advised to throw its strongest forces again the weakest links in the Allied coalition—against Russia and Italy. A concentrated offensive against Russia would complete the demoralization of the armies of the Tsar and might very well precipitate a revolution in St. Petersburg. A successful Austro-German offensive against Italy would not only have a tremendous moral effect in England and France but would threaten France's communications with North Africa.[69]

In Delbrück's opinion, then, Germany's strategy must be directed toward the destruction of the enemy coalition and the consequent isolation of England and France. In this connection, it was equally important that no measures be adopted which might bring new allies to the western powers. Delbrück was always firmly opposed to the submarine campaign, which he rightly feared would bring the United States into the war.[70]

But in the last analysis, if the war was to be won by Germany, the government would have to show a clear comprehension of the political realities implicit in the conflict. Since the war in the west had become an *Ermattungskrieg,* the political aspect of the conflict had increased in importance. "Politics is the ruling and limiting factor; military operations are only one of its means."[71] A political strategy must be devised to weaken the will of the people of France and England.

In the political field, Delbrück had felt from the beginning of the war that Germany suffered from a very real strategical weakness. "Because of our narrow policy of Germanization in the Polish and Danish districts of Prussia, we have given ourselves the reputation in the world of being not the protectors but the oppressors of small nationalities."[72] If this reputation were confirmed in the course of the war, it would give moral encouragement to Germany's enemies and would jeopardize the hope of ultimate victory. Turning to history, Delbrück argued that the example of Napoleon should serve as a warning to Germany's political leaders. The emperor's most overwhelming victories had served only to strengthen the will of his opponents and to pave the way for his ultimate defeat. "May God forbid that Germany enter upon the path of

69 Buchfinck, *op. cit.,* p. 48.
70 *Krieg und Politik,* I, 90, 227 ff., 261.
71 *Ibid.,* II, 95.
72 *Ibid.,* I, 3–4.

Napoleonic policy. . . . Europe stands united in this one conviction: it will never submit to a hegemony enforced upon it by a single state."[73]

Delbrück believed that the invasion of Belgium had been a strategical necessity;[74] but it was nonetheless an unfortunate move, for it seemed to confirm the suspicion that Germany was bent upon the subjugation and annexation of small states. From September 1914 until the end of the war, Delbrück continued to insist that the German government must issue a categorical disclaimer of any intention of annexing Belgium at the conclusion of hostilities. England, he argued, would never make peace as long as there was danger of German retention of the Flanders coast. The first step in weakening the resistance of western powers was to state clearly that Germany had no territorial desires in the west and that her war aims would "prejudice in no way the freedom and honor of other peoples."[75]

Perhaps the best way to convince the western powers that Germany was not seeking world domination was to make it apparent that Germany had no objection to a negotiated peace. Delbrück had favored such a peace ever since the successful Allied counteroffensive on the Marne in September 1914. He firmly believed that the war had been caused by Russian aggression and saw no reason why England and France should continue to fight the one power that was "guarding Europe and Asia from the domination of *Moskowitertum.*"[76] As the war was prolonged, he was strengthened in his conviction that a sincere willingness to negotiate would win for Germany a victory that arms alone would be powerless to effect; after the entrance of the United States into the war, he openly predicted defeat unless Germany's leaders used that weapon. He was, therefore, enthusiastic about the passage by the Reichstag of the Peace Resolution of July 1917,[77] for he felt that it

[73] See *ibid.,* I, 59, and the article entitled "Das Beispiel Napoleons," *ibid.,* II, 122 ff.

[74] *Ibid.,* I, 33.

[75] *Ibid.,* II, 97.

[76] *Ibid,* I, 18.

[77] The Peace Resolution, passed by the Reichstag by 212 votes to 126, stated in part: "The Reichstag strives for a peace of understanding and a lasting reconciliation among peoples. Violations of territory and political, economic, and financial persecutions are incompatible with such a peace. The Reichstag rejects every scheme which has for its purpose the imposition of economic barriers or the perpetuation of national hatreds after the war. The freedom of the seas must be secured. Economic peace alone will prepare the ground for the friendly association of the peoples. The Reichstag will actively promote the creation of international organizations of justice. But so long as the enemy governments dissociate themselves from such a peace, so long as they threaten Germany and her allies with

would do more to weaken the resistance of the western powers than any possible new offensive upon the western front.

Delbrück never for a moment wavered in his belief that the German army was the best in the world, but he saw that that best was not good enough. Throughout 1917 he hammered away at one constant theme: "We must look the facts in the face—that we have in a sense the whole world leagued against us—and we must not conceal from ourselves the fact that, if we try to penetrate to the basic reasons for this world coalition, we shall ever and again stumble over the motive of fear of German world hegemony. . . . Fear of German despotism is one of the weightiest facts with which we have to reckon, one of the strongest factors in the enemy's power."[78] Until that fear was overcome, the war would continue. It could be overcome only by a political strategy based on a disclaimer of territorial ambitions in the west and a willingness to negotiate.

Just as the conditions of the present war were, to Delbrück, comparable in some ways to those of the eighteenth century, so was this heightened emphasis upon the political aspects of the war in full accordance with the principles of *Ermattungsstrategie* as practiced by Frederick the Great. When the German army had taken the field in 1914, it had staked all on the decisive battle and had failed. Delbrück would now relegate military operations to a subordinate position. The battle was no longer an end in itself but a means. If Germany's political professions failed at first to convince the western powers that peace was desirable, a new military offensive could be undertaken and would serve to break down that hesitation. But only such a coordination of the military effort with the political program would bring the war to a successful issue.

In his desire for a political strategy that would be effective in weakening the resistance of the enemy, Delbrück was bitterly disappointed. It became apparent as early as 1915 that strong sections of German public opinion regarded the war as a means of acquiring new territory not only in the east but in the west of Europe. When Delbrück called for a declaration of willingness to evacuate Belgium, he was greeted by a howl of abuse and was accused by the *Deutsche Tageszeitung* of being "subservient to our enemies in foreign countries."[79] The changing fortunes of war did not diminish the desire for booty, and the powerful

conquest and domination, then so long will the German people stand united and unshaken, and fight till their right and the right of their allies to live and grow is made secure. United thus, the German people is unconquerable."

[78] *Krieg und Politik,* II, 187.

[79] See R. H. Lutz, ed., *Fall of the German Empire* (Hoover War Library Publications, No. 1), p. 307.

Vaterlandspartei, the most important of the annexationist groups, exercised a strong influence on the governments that ruled Germany. Not only did the German government not make any declaration concerning Belgium, but it never made its position clear on the question of a negotiated peace. When the Peace Resolution was being debated in 1917, Hindenburg and Ludendorff threatened to resign if the Reichstag adopted the measure. After the passage of the resolution, the influence of the high command was exerted so effectively that the government did not dare to make the resolution the keystone of its policy. As a result of the so-called crisis of July 1917, the western powers were encouraged to believe that the Reichstag's professions were insincere and that Germany's leaders were still bent on world domination.

To Delbrück the crisis of July had a deeper significance. It showed within the government a dearth of political leadership and a growing tendency on the part of the military to dominate the formulation of policy. Germany's military leaders had never been known for their political acumen, but in the past they had generally followed the advice of the political head of the state. Although at times reluctantly, Gneisenau had subordinated his views to those of Hardenberg, and Moltke had bowed to Bismarck's political judgment. Now, in the time of Germany's greatest crisis, the military were taking over completely and there was among them no man with a proper appreciation of the political necessities of the day. For all their military gifts, Hindenburg and Ludendorff still thought solely in terms of a decisive military victory over the western powers, a *Niederwerfung* that would deliver western Europe into their hands. It was with a growing sense of despair that Delbrück wrote: "Athens went to her doom in the Peloponnesian War because Pericles had no successor. We have fiery Cleons enough in Germany. Whoever believes in the German people will be confident that it has not only great strategists among its sons but also that gifted statesman in whose hands the necessity of the time will place the reins for the direction of foreign policy."[80] But that gifted statesman never appeared; and the fiery Cleons prevailed.

It was, consequently, with little confidence that Delbrück watched the opening of the German offensive of 1918. "It is obvious," he wrote, "that no change can be made in the principles I have expounded here since the beginning of the war, and the dissension with regard to our western war aims remains."[81] Strategy, he insisted, is not something in the abstract; it cannot be divorced from political considerations. "The

[80] *Krieg und Politik,* III, 123.
[81] *Ibid.,* III, 63.

great strategical offensive should have been accompanied and reinforced by a similar political offensive, which would have worked upon the home front of our enemies in the same way as Hindenburg and the men in field gray worked upon the front lines." If only the German government had announced, fourteen days before the opening of the offensive, that they firmly desired a negotiated peace and that, after such peace, Belgium would be evacuated, what would the result have been? Lloyd George and Clemenceau might have regarded these claims as signs of German weakness. But now, as the offensive rolled forward, "would Lloyd George and Clemenceau still be at the helm? I doubt it very much. We might even now be sitting at the conference table."[82]

Because of the failure to coordinate the military and political aspects of the war, Delbrück felt that the offensive, at most, would lead to mere tactical successes and would have no great strategical importance. But even he did not suspect that this was the last gamble of the strategists of annihilation, and the suddenness and completeness of the German collapse surprised him completely. In the November 1918 issue of the *Preussische Jahrbücher,* he made a curious and revealing apology to his readers. "How greatly I have erred," he wrote. "However bad things looked four weeks ago, I still would not give up the hope that the front, however wavering, would hold and would force the enemy to an armistice that would protect our boundaries." In a sentence which illustrates the responsibility he felt as a military commentator to the German people, he added, "I admit that I often expressed myself more confidently than I felt at heart. On more than one occasion, I allowed myself to be deceived by the confident tone of the announcements and reports of the army and the navy." But despite these mistakes in judgment, he could, he said, be proud of the fact that he had always insisted that the German people had a right to hear the truth even when it was bad, and, in his constant preaching of political moderation, he had tried to show them the road to victory.[83]

It was in this spirit also that Delbrück made his most complete review and most searching criticism of the military operations of the last phase of the war. This was in two reports he made in 1922 before the Fourth Subcommittee of the commission set up by the Reichstag after the war to investigate the causes of the German collapse in 1918. In his testimony before the subcommittee, Delbrück repeated the arguments he had made in the pages of the *Preussische Jahrbücher,* but the removal of censorship restrictions enabled him to give a much more detailed

[82] *Ibid.,* III, 73.
[83] *Ibid.,* III, 203–6.

criticism of the military aspect of the 1918 offensive than had been possible during the war.[84]

The main weight of Delbrück's criticism was directed against Ludendorff, who conceived and directed the 1918 offensive. In only one respect, he felt, had Ludendorff shown even military proficiency. He had "prepared the attack, as regards both the previous training of the troops and the moment for taking the enemy by surprise, in a masterly manner, with the greatest energy and circumspection."[85] But the advantages of this preliminary preparation were outweighed by several fundamental weaknesses and by gross mistakes in strategical thinking. In the first place, the German army on the eve of the offensive was in no position to strike a knockout blow against the enemy. Its numerical superiority was slight, and, in reserves, it was vastly inferior to the enemy. Its equipment was in many respects equally inferior, and it was greatly handicapped by a faulty supply system and by insufficient stocks of fuel for its motorized units. These disadvantages were apparent before the opening of the offensive but were disregarded by the high command.[86]

Ludendorff was sufficiently aware of these weaknesses, however, to admit the impossibility of striking the enemy at that point where the greatest strategical success could have been won. In his own words, "tactics were to be valued more than pure strategy." That meant, in effect, that he attacked at those points where it was easiest to break through and not at those points where the announced aim of the offensive could best be served. The strategical goal of the campaign was the annihilation of the enemy. "In order to attain the strategical goal—the separation of the English army from the French and the consequent rolling-up of the former—the attack would have best been arranged so that it followed the course of the Somme. Ludendorff, however, had stretched the offensive front some four miles farther south because the enemy seemed especially weak there."[87] The defensive wing of the army

[84] The Delbrück testimony is reproduced in full in *Das Werk des Untersuchungsausschusses der Deutschen Verfassunggebenden Nationalversammlung und des Deutschen Reichstages 1919–1926. Die Ursachen des Deutschen Zusammenbruchs im Jahre 1918,* Series Four, III, 239–73. Selections from the Commission's report, but only a very small portion of the Delbrück testimony, is found in R. H. Lutz, ed., *The Causes of the German Collapse in 1918* (Hoover War Library Publications, No. 4).

[85] *Die Ursachen des Deutschen Zusammenbruches,* III, 345; Lutz, *The Causes of the German Collapse,* p. 90.

[86] *Die Ursachen des Deutschen Zusammenbruches,* III, 246.

[87] *Ibid.,* III, 247.

under Hutier broke through at this point, but its very success handicapped the development of the offensive, for its advance outpaced the real offensive wing under Below which was operating against Arras. When Below's forces were checked, "we were forced with a certain amount of compulsion to follow the line of [Hutier's] success. . . . Thereby the idea of the offensive was altered and the danger of dispersing our forces evoked."[88]

In short, by following the tactical line of least resistance Ludendorff began a disastrous policy of improvisation, violating the first principle of that *Niederwerfungsstrategie* he professed to be following: "A strategy that is not predicated upon an absolute decision, upon the annihilation of the enemy, but is satisfied with single blows, may execute these now in this place, now in that. But a strategy which intends to force the decision, must do it where the first successful blow was struck." Far from obeying this precept, Ludendorff and Hindenburg operated on the principle that, when difficulties developed in one sector, new blows could be struck in another.[89] As a result, the grand offensive degenerated into a series of separate thrusts, uncoordinated and unproductive.

The cardinal fault of the offensive was the failure of the high command to see clearly what could be accomplished by the German army in 1918 and the failure to adapt its strategy to its potentialities. Here Delbrück returned to the major theme of all his work as historian and publicist. The relative strength of the opposing forces was such that the high command should have realized that the annihilation of the enemy was no longer possible. The aim of the 1918 offensive, therefore, should have been to make the enemy so tired that he would be willing to negotiate a peace. This in itself would have been possible only if the German government had expressed its own willingness to make such a peace. But once this declaration had been clearly made, the German army in opening its offensive would have won a great strategical advantage. Its offensive could now be geared to the strength at its disposal. It could safely attack at the points of tactical advantage—that is, where success was easiest—since even minor victories would now have a redoubled moral effect in enemy capitals.[90] The high command had failed in 1918 and had lost the war because it had disregarded the most important lesson of history, the interrelationship of politics and war. "To come back once more to that fundamental sentence of Clausewitz, no

[88] *Ibid.*, III, 346.
[89] *Ibid.*, III, 250–51.
[90] *Ibid.*, III, 253–54.

strategical idea can be considered completely without considering the political goal."[91]

IV

The military historian has generally been a kind of misfit, regarded with suspicion both by his professional colleagues and by the military men whose activities he seeks to portray. The suspicion of the military is not difficult to explain. It springs in large part from the natural scorn of the professional for the amateur. But the distrust with which academicians have looked on the military historians in their midst has deeper roots. In democratic countries especially, it arises from the belief that war is an aberration in the historical process and that, consequently, the study of war is neither fruitful nor seemly. It is significant that in his general work *On the Writing of History,* the dean of military historians, Sir Charles Oman, should entitle the chapter that deals with his own field "A Plea for Military History." Sir Charles remarks that the civilian historian dabbling in military affairs has been an exceptional phenomenon, and he explains this by writing: "Both the medieval monastic chroniclers and the modern liberal historiographers had often no closer notion of the meaning of war than that it involves various horrors and is attended by a lamentable loss of life. Both classes strove to disguise their personal ignorance or dislike of military matters by depreciating their importance and significance in history."[92]

The prejudice that Oman resented was felt equally keenly, throughout his life, by Hans Delbrück. When, as a relatively young man, he turned his talents to the study of military history, he found that the members of his craft too often regarded his specialty as one not worthy of the energy he expended upon it. While the Prussian academicians were not so ready as the English liberal historians to regard war as an unnatural occurrence, they were not convinced that excessive absorption in the study of military affairs entitled a man to academic recognition and the promotions and emoluments that went with it. Delbrück's advancement to a full professorship was certainly delayed by his insistence that the history of war was quite as important as the deciphering of Roman inscriptions,[93] and, throughout his life, he was constantly

[91] *Ibid.,* III, 253.

[92] Sir Charles Oman, *On the Writing of History* (New York, n.d.), pp. 159–60.

[93] J. Ziekursch, "Delbrück," *Deutsches Biographisches Jahrbuch* (1929).

arguing the legitimacy of his historical field. At the beginning of his career, he pleaded that there was a crying need for historians "to turn not only an incidental but a professional interest to the history of war."[94] In his last years, long after he had won a secure position in academic circles, he lashed out once again in the pages of his *World History* at those who persisted in believing "that battles and wars can be regarded as unimportant by-products of world history."[95]

Delbrück's importance in the history of military thought has been contested almost as bitterly as were his academic privileges. Many of the discoveries of his *Sachkritik* have been questioned or dismissed as unoriginal, while his theory of strategy has never been generally accepted either by historians or by military men. But there is no doubt that the *History of the Art of War* will remain one of the finest examples of the application of modern science to the heritage of the past and, however modified in detail, the bulk of the work stands unchallenged. Moreover, in an age in which war has become the concern of every man, the major theme of Delbrück's work as historian and publicist is at once a reminder and a warning. The coordination of politics and war is as important today as it was in the age of Pericles, and strategical thinking that becomes self-sufficient or that neglects the political aspect of war can lead only to disaster.

[94] Delbrück, "Etwas Kriegsgeschichtliches," *Preussische Jahrbücher,* LX (1887), 610.

[95] Delbrück, *Weltgeschichte* (Berlin, 1924–28), I, 321.

PART TWO

CIVIL-MILITARY RELATIONS

5. Portrait of a Political General: Edwin von Manteuffel and the Constitutional Conflict in Prussia

THE HISTORY OF GERMAN LIBERALISM in the nineteenth century is a sad story of repeated but vain attempts to restrict the prerogatives of the crown and to limit its absolute control over the armed forces of the state. Perhaps the most dramatic of these attempts occurred in the 1860's when the lower house of the Prussian parliament sought, by exercising its budgetary rights, to strengthen its influence in military questions. This constitutional struggle marked Bismarck's debut as a statesman, and the successful defense of the royal power of command is usually associated with his name. But, while Bismarck deserves the credit for having fashioned the strategy which produced the liberal defeat, there were others whose efforts in the royal cause were almost equally important. One of these was the Chief of the Military Cabinet, Edwin von Manteuffel, a man whose policies were decisive in preserving for the army the dangerous freedom from parliamentary control which it enjoyed until 1918.

I

The career of Edwin von Manteuffel has attracted the attention of few historians outside of his own country.[1] The fascination that Bis-

"Portrait of a Political General" is reprinted from *Political Science Quarterly*, LXVI, No. 1 (March, 1951), with the permission of the publishers, The Academy of Political Science, Columbia University.

[1] Standard histories rarely mention him, and even special studies in English have done him scant justice. An exception is Chester W. Clark's *Franz Joseph and Bismarck: The Diplomacy of Austria before the War of 1866* (Cambridge, Mass., 1934), which includes a careful treatment of Manteuffel's policy as Governor of Schleswig.

marck's personality has exercised upon the minds of foreign students is perhaps chiefly responsible for this but can scarcely justify it, for Manteuffel is easily the most important of the "political generals" who crowded the German stage in the nineteenth century. For forty years he served the Prussian state in a variety of capacities. He was active in the backstage politics of the revolutionary year 1848 and had considerable influence in the drafting and revision of the Prussian constitution. In the 1850's he was despatched on frequent diplomatic missions, especially during the Crimean War, and demonstrated a high degree of talent as a negotiator.[2] From 1857 to 1865 he was Chief of the Military Cabinet, the King's private military bureau, and of the Division for Personal Affairs in the War Ministry, the office that governed officer selection. In the wars of 1866 and 1870, he was conspicuously successful as a field commander and, in recognition of this, was appointed commander of the troops that occupied France until 1873. Finally, after a retirement of six years, broken frequently by diplomatic missions, he ended his career as *Statthalter* in Alsace-Lorraine from 1879 until his death in 1885.[3]

The career thus hastily sketched was active and honorable, but it fell far short of Manteuffel's own hopes. An avid reader of history and a life-long friend of Ranke,[4] he was also an incurable romantic. Thus, in his study of the past, his imagination was captured by figures like Epaminondas and Hannibal and Wallenstein, men who had combined in their persons both military and political genius. It is not difficult to infer, from his own correspondence, that he sought to model his career after these giants of the past and to become the greatest soldier and the greatest statesman of his own age.[5] This dream was never fulfilled;

[2] See Kurt Borries, *Preussen im Krimkrieg* (Stuttgart, 1930), pp. 168 ff., 260 ff.

[3] A good brief account of Manteuffel's career will be found in Kurt von Priesdorff, *Soldatisches Führertum* (Hamburg, 1936), VII, 150–67. See also article by B. von Poten in *Allgemeine deutsche Biographie* (Leipzig, 1906), LII, 176–86.

[4] After Manteuffel's death, Ranke wrote: "He had more understanding of my writings and a greater spiritual sympathy than was granted me elsewhere in the world." Leopold von Ranke, *Sämmtliche Werke* (Dritte Gesamtausgabe, Leipzig, 1890), LIII-LIV, 653. See also Elisabeth Schmitz, *Edwin von Manteuffel als Quelle zur Geschichte Friedrich Wilhelms IV* (Berlin, 1921), pp. 76–77; Ludwig Dehio, "Manteuffels politische Ideen," *Historische Zeitschrift*, CXXXI (1925), 45–46; Wilhelm Gradmann, *Die politischen Ideen Edwin von Manteuffels und ihre Auswirkungen in seiner Laufbahn* (Düsseldorf, 1932), especially pp. 24 ff.; and the many letters from Ranke to Manteuffel in Ranke, *Neue Briefe* (Bernard Hoeft and Hans Herzfeld, eds.) (Hamburg, 1949).

[5] Dehio, *op. cit.*, pp. 63–64. "I thought earlier," Manteuffel wrote to Münster in St. Petersburg, "of naming my first born sons Leuctra and Mantinea."

despite the honors that crowded his last years, Manteuffel must have died with a sense of failure. Certainly his later career was embittered by his knowledge that his military triumphs had gone without popular recognition and that his accession to political eminence was made impossible by the tremendous prestige of Bismarck. The honors of his position as a *Statthalter* were overshadowed by the realization that, in the eyes of most future historians, he would be not another Epaminondas but a figure of the second grade.

In his own day, Manteuffel's burning ambition caused him to be feared by the liberal opposition, to whom he was "an unwholesome man in an unwholesome place,"[6] and to be regarded with tolerant amusement or resigned irritation by his colleagues, to whom he seemed "a fantastic corporal"[7] or a "Bayard with a faint touch of Don Quixote."[8] Yet there was, in his ambition, nothing ignoble. Even Bismarck, who thought him a dangerous rival, admitted that "Manteuffel is of noble metal. For him reason of state far transcends personal interest."[9] Schweinitz, the long-term ambassador in St. Petersburg and one who was certainly not uncritical of Manteuffel, also minimized the element of personal ambition in his character. "A burning love for his country," he wrote, "true piety, enthusiasm for the noble and the sublime filled this true Prussian heart; Christian humility and classical greatness of soul united in this man and made him, to whom nature had given the bent to fanaticism, a model of those virtues upon which Prussia's greatness is founded."[10]

These judgments are more just than those of observers who were alienated by Manteuffel's vanity or who saw in him only the self-seeker. If Manteuffel yearned for greatness he did so only that his greatness might give him an opportunity to serve his country. Unlike the star-struck Wallenstein of Schiller's drama—the complete text of which he was reputed to have memorized—the fantasy in his own temperament

[6] This was Carl Twesten's phrase, in his pamphlet *Was uns noch retten kann* (1861).

[7] So Bismarck in 1857. Erich Eyck, *Bismarck: Leben und Werk* (Zurich, 1943–44), I, 281–82.

[8] Alfred Dove, quoted in Dehio, *op. cit.*, p. 42. For Ranke's judgment of Manteuffel's critics see *Neue Briefe*, p. 559.

[9] H. Goldschmidt, "Mitarbeiter Bismarcks im aussenpolitischen Kampf," *Preussische Jahrbücher*, CCXXXV (1934), 131.

[10] W. von Schweinitz, ed., *Denkwürdigkeiten des Botschafters H. L. von Schweinitz* (Berlin, 1927), I, 242–43. See also Prince Kraft zu Hohenlohe-Ingelfingen, *Aus meinem Leben, 1848–1871* (4 vols.; Berlin, 1897–1907), III, 172.

was held in check by a deep religious sense and a complete devotion to the Prussian state. He lived—as Elisabeth Schmitz has written—in a world of the Kantian categorical imperative with its stern postulates which were so well adapted to the life of the Prussian officer.[11] Whatever his private dreams, the guiding passion of his life was duty to his God and his King.

Manteuffel's political philosophy was as simple as his fundamentalist religious faith. He was a dogmatic royalist who believed that the greatness of the Prussian state depended upon the strength of the Prussian crown that had created it.[12] Sovereignty was, he held, embodied in the person of the Prussian King and, if Prussia were to continue to survive, the unrestricted nature of this sovereignty must be maintained. This involved not only implacable hostility to any idea of popular sovereignty but also rejection of the theories of constitutional parliamentary government as practiced in England and Belgium. Above all, there must be no weakening of the royal *Kommandogewalt,* the King's absolute right of control over the army. In the last analysis, the state would be ruled by whoever controlled the military establishment. As a politician, Manteuffel always regarded the army issue as crucial and, throughout his career, was the indomitable defender of the military prerogative of the crown.

He had served in that capacity in 1848, when the King's power over the army had for the first time been seriously challenged. On 18 March 1848, when Berlin rose in revolt, Manteuffel, a relatively junior officer assigned as aide-de-camp to Prince Albrecht of Prussia, found himself in the royal palace. On his own responsibility, he elected to remain there, and, in the feverish and confused debates that took place among the royal advisers, he took a rather more prominent part than was justified by his rank. On 19 March, as the military situation in Berlin deteriorated and the troops began to withdraw from the city, he boldly urged the King to go with them and to continue the fight.[13] Frederick

11 Schmitz, *op. cit.,* pp. 73 ff. On Manteuffel's religion, see also his letters to his son Hans Karl in *Deutsche Revue,* XXXVIII (3) (1913).

12 Ludwig Dehio, "Edwin von Manteuffel und der Kaiser," *Deutsche Rundschau,* CCVI (1926), 42.

13 Felix Rachfahl, "König Friedrich Wilhelm IV und die Berliner Märzrevolution im Lichte neuer Quellen," *Preussische Jahrbücher,* CX (1902), 441. One of the senior officers present said: "Manteuffel, what responsibility are you taking on yourself?" He answered: "All responsibility before God and man, where no one else has any advice and it is a matter of the King's security." See also E. L. von Gerlach, *Aufzeichnungen aus seinem Leben and Wirken* (Schwerin, 1903), II, 240. On the previous day, Manteuffel had strongly opposed the King's withdrawal

William IV, however, hesitated to accept counsel that presupposed a continuation of the civil strife and, allowing the troops to withdraw from Berlin without him, threw himself upon the mercies of his subjects. Manteuffel wrote, years later, that this surrender of the King represented a dangerous abandonment of "the military principle" that was inherent in the Prussian system and an almost irreparable concession to the spirit of revolution.[14] Inevitably it encouraged the representatives of the Prussian people to try to consolidate their success by placing permanent limits on the King's military prerogatives.

Perhaps unfortunately for the cause of liberalism in Prussia, the subsequent attack upon royal control of the army, while fierce and sustained, was not systematic. In the second United Diet and later in the National Assembly, there was much talk of replacing the standing army with a genuinely popular militia; there were demands that the existing military establishment be liberalized by reform of military education, abolition of separate military courts of justice, the granting of full civil rights, including the right to vote, to all soldiers, and the dismissal of reactionary officers;[15] there were even attempts to interfere with the King's power of command and to veto his choice of commanding generals in the field.[16] Had these various demands been formulated as a constructive program and had the Assembly at the same time acted quickly to write them into a constitutional draft acceptable to the majority of its members, the royal *Kommandogewalt* might have been seriously restricted.[17] This, however, was not the case; and for a number of reasons—the growing split between liberals and democrats in the Assembly, the increasing desire of the middle classes for a termination of popular disorders, the unexpected stubbornness of the King when his

---

from the city. Rachfahl, *op. cit.*, pp. 302–3. This, however, was before it was clear that the troops would have to withdraw.

[14] Roon Papers: Manteuffel to Albrecht von Roon, 8 April 1862. These papers, formerly among the captured German documents in the National Archives, Washington, D.C., and now returned to Germany, include some 120 letters from Manteuffel to Roon, written during the years 1859–66. Many of these, but by no means all, have been published, but the collection remains a highly important source for students of the *Konfliktszeit*.

[15] Reinhard Höhn, *Verfassungskampf und Heereseid: Der Kampf des Bürgertums um das Heer, 1815–50* (Leipzig, 1938), especially pp. 145 ff.

[16] See Leopold von Gerlach, *Denkwürdigkeiten* (Berlin, 1892), I, 163–64; Karl Haenchen, *Revolutionsbriefe 1848* (Leipzig, 1930), pp. 97–101, and 101 n.

[17] See the criticism of the Assembly's tactics in Fritz Hartung, *Deutsche Verfassungsgeschichte vom 15. Jahrhundert bis zum Gegenwart* (2d ed.; Leipzig, 1922), pp. 152–53. See also Veit Valentin, *Geschichte der deutschen Revolution, 1848–49* (Berlin, 1931), II, 47 ff., 289–90.

own rights were involved,[18] and the general waning of revolutionary ardor[19]—the attack on the military prerogatives of the crown faltered and finally came to a halt. After November 1848, when Wrangel's troops re-entered Berlin without opposition, the liberals abandoned most of their demands and concentrated upon a campaign to force the army to take an oath to the constitution. Even this demand, however—although it enraged or frightened supporters of the crown[20]—was not realized. No army oath was provided for in the constitution promulgated on 5 December 1848, and, despite some rather ambiguous promises by the King, this omission was not made good in the revised constitution of 1850.[21]

The liberal failure in 1848 appears much more decisive to historians, however, than it did to contemporaries. Edwin von Manteuffel was certainly impressed less by the ultimate victory of the crown than he was by the narrow margin by which disaster had been avoided. How narrow it had been he had very good reason to know, for he was seldom very far from the center of power. In April 1848 he had been appointed *Flügeladjutant* to the King; at the same time, he became an increasingly active associate of Generals von Rauch and von Gerlach, the chiefs of the so-called *ministère occulte.*[22] In his later years, indeed, Manteuffel said that his period of greatest personal power was the period 1848–50, when it was his duty "to be a rock and to offer opposition to the party of movement," and when his name stood high on the proscription list of the revolutionary party.[23]

Allowing for an element of exaggeration that often crept into Manteuffel's judgments of his own past, there is a good deal of truth in this. It is clear that he played an important role in the abrupt dismissal of the Assembly in December 1848, which preceded the promulgation of the constitution.[24] More important, he had striven with some success to

18 R. Stadelmann, *Soziale und politische Geschichte der Revolution von 1848* (Munich, 1948), p. 63.

19 *Ibid.*, p. 97; Stephan Born, *Erinnerungen eines Acht-und-Vierziger* (Leipzig, 1898), p. 116.

20 Max Jähns, *Feldmarschall Moltke* (Berlin, 1900), p. 167; Höhn, *op. cit.*, pp. 343 ff. Hohenlohe-Ingelfingen wrote later that the imposition of a constitutional oath on the army "would have greatly contributed to undermining order in the armed establishment, forcing the troops into political activity, making it their duty to pass judgment on their officers, and thereby making anarchy permanent." Hohenlohe-Ingelfingen, *op. cit.*, I, 77.

21 Höhn, *op. cit.*, p. 358.

22 Gerlach, *Denkwürdigkeiten,* I, 150, 502.

23 R. Schmidt-Bückeburg, *Das Militärkabinett der preussischen Könige und deutschen Kaiser* (Berlin, 1933), p. 52.

24 Haenchen, *op. cit.*, pp. 247 ff.

keep that document as innocuous as possible. He later told Leopold von Gerlach that it was he who had persuaded the King to delete the army oath from the ministry's constitutional draft;[25] and he seems also to have been successful in placing restrictions upon the budgetary powers provided in the constitution for the lower house of the parliament.[26] All in all, if the Prussian constitution of 1848–50 was, as has been claimed, a mere *charte* which preserved the original nature of the divine-right monarchy,[27] Edwin von Manteuffel was at least partly responsible.

Yet the fact that Prussia now had a written constitution, and that the King was pledged to defend it, proved that the royal victory was by no means completely decisive.[28] By its recognition of the principle of ministerial responsibility and of parliamentary control over the budget, the constitution gave important powers to the liberal opposition, and powers which affected, or could affect, the army. Manteuffel, therefore, although he had cooperated in the drafting of the document, had done so very reluctantly, and he had bitterly, although vainly, opposed the idea of the King taking an oath to defend the constitution. He recognized that the liberal opposition had won a *point d'appui* that they had not had before 1848, and he looked to the future with gloomy anticipation, confidently expecting new political convulsions and hoping that, when they came, he would be privileged to stand at the King's side.

II

The second phase of the struggle begun in 1848 was not long delayed. The introduction of the army reform bill in 1860 brought differences between crown and parliament in its wake, and the state was soon involved in a constitutional conflict which, in duration and bitterness, transcended that of the earlier period.

Historians have long speculated whether the conflict of the 1860's was not avoidable. There seems no reason to doubt Erich Brandenburg's

25 Schmitz, *op. cit.*, p. 61; Höhn, *op. cit.*, pp. 347–48.

26 Schmitz, *op. cit.*, p. 61; Ranke, *Neue Briefe*, p. 561.

27 H. Ritter von Srbik, *Deutsche Einheit* (Munich, 1935 *et seq.*), I, 391–92; Fritz Hartung, *Volk und Staat in der deutschen Geschichte* (Leipzig, 1940), pp. 212–213; Kurt Kaminsky, *Verfassung und Verfassungskonflikt in Preussen, 1862–66* (Berlin, 1938), pp. 19 ff.; Valentin, *op. cit.*, II, 291 ff.; Stadelmann, *op. cit.*, pp. 149–50.

28 That the King himself sensed this is shown by his reluctance to take the oath to the constitution and his complaints after he had done so. See Gerlach, *Denkwürdigkeiten*, I, 391, 400 ff., 708; H. von Petersdorff, *König Friedrich Wilhelm der Vierte* (Stuttgart, 1900), pp. 165 ff.

judgment that the original motivation of the army reform was technical rather than political.[29] The new ruler—the Regent, Prince William, later King and Emperor—had long been conscious of the inadequacies of his army and was convinced that, unless they were corrected, Prussia could not hope to play a role in European politics commensurate with her position as a great power.[30] The liberals in the Landtag, critical of the weakness of Prussia's foreign policy in the last decade, had no objection in principle to the introduction of necessary reforms.[31] There was no apparent reason, therefore, why major disagreements should develop.

The political atmosphere in Prussia, however, was still poisoned by the memory of 1848, and objective consideration of the proposed reforms was almost impossible. If the liberals, in theory, believed that Prussia should have a stronger army, they nevertheless suspected that the crown had ulterior motives in demanding it and that the enlarged army would be used, not to strengthen Prussia's power position, but rather to suppress civil liberties at home. Their fear in this respect was reinforced by specific features of the proposed reform, notably the measure to increase the army of the line at the expense of the Landwehr, reducing the latter in size and relegating it to a subordinate position in the armed establishment, and the proposal to increase the term of military service from two to three years. To all liberals the Landwehr was a living reminder of the popular rising of 1813; and, since it was a civilian force led largely by officers elected from the ranks, it seemed a healthy counterbalance to the caste-dominated, ultraconservative line army.[32] "We cleave to the Landwehr," wrote one liberal, "with religious fa-

[29] Erich Brandenburg, *Die Reichsgründung* (Leipzig, 1916), I, 444. For opposing views, see Max Lenz, *Geschichte Bismarcks* (4th ed.; Munch, 1913), pp. 116 ff.; and E. R. Huber, *Heer und Staat* (2d ed.; Hamburg, 1943), pp. 242–43. In 1863, Albrecht von Roon wrote his friend Perthes that, at the time of the introduction of the army reform, he had no political designs and had been "guided solely by technical motives." See R. Hübner, *Albrecht von Roon: Preussens Heer im Kampf um das Reich* (Hamburg, 1933), p. 84.

[30] For Wilhelm's interest in reform, see Erich Marcks, *Kaiser Wilhelm I* (4th ed.; Leipzig, 1900), pp. 110–11; and Freiherr von Loë, *Erinnerungen aus meinem Berufsleben* (2d ed.; Stuttgart, 1906), pp. 26 ff. On the demonstrated weaknesses of the army during the mobilization of 1859, see F. Löwenthal, *Der preussische Verfassungsstreit, 1862–1866* (Altenburg, 1914), pp. 24 ff.; and Friedrich von Bernhardi, ed., *Aus dem Leben Theodor von Bernhardis* (Leipzig, 1893–1906), III, 243–44.

[31] Alfred Vagts, *A History of Militarism* (New York, 1937), p. 204.

[32] Egmont Zechlin, *Bismarck und die Grundlegung der deutschen Grossmacht* (Stuttgart, 1930), pp. 173–81.

naticism, with the whole weight of our youthful memories."[33] The liberal majority in the Prussian Chamber, therefore, opposed the reform bill of 1860 and finally forced the government to withdraw it.

While understandable, the liberal attitude was probably over-suspicious of royal intentions. It was certainly unfortunate in its results.[34] The military advisers of the Prince Regent began to sense some secret design behind the liberal objections. That indefatigable note-taker, Theodor von Bernhardi, talked with former War Minister von Stockhausen in March 1860 and found the general filled with dark forebodings. The opposition in the Chamber, he said, were seeking to replace the professional army with a people's militia, and their defense of the old Landwehr was a clear indication that they were planning another *Revolutiönchen*.[35] In the royal entourage, even men who were far from reactionary in their views began now to be oppressed by memories of 1848 and to suspect the liberals of deliberately precipitating a new fight for control of the state. As for the inveterate opponents of constitutionalism, they now saw their worst suspicions confirmed and raised their voices to demand a counteroffensive against the liberal conspiracy.

Chief among this last group was Edwin von Manteuffel, now *Generalmajor* and Chief of the Military Cabinet, a position of great power and one which gave him frequent access to the sovereign. For him, the liberal opposition to the army reform was clearly a resumption of the struggle of 1848; and he threw himself into the fight with vigor and with a kind of solemn joy. He felt that the decisive hour of the Prussian monarchy was approaching; and he saw himself as another Strafford, standing beside the sovereign in the great crisis and, if necessary, giving his life that the royal position might be maintained.[36]

Like Strafford also, Manteuffel called for the policy of Thorough; and it is this that makes his role in the constitutional struggle important. From 1860 to 1866, he was the leader of that party in the state which

[33] Eyck, *op. cit.,* I, 344.

[34] Heinrich von Sybel argued that the liberal position was also tactically unsound. Since the liberals had a majority in the Chamber, they had an opportunity to make the army reform their own, subsequently claiming credit for its passage and strengthening their position as the governmental party. Instead they were trying to act as both governmental party and opposition and were playing directly into the hands of the reaction. Bernhardi, *op. cit.,* III, 313–14.

[35] *Ibid.,* III, 279.

[36] "[Manteuffel's] ideal was Lord Strafford in prison, who, when he was condemned to death for his royalism, wrote to his King pleading that he confirm this death sentence, since his execution was at this moment the only possible salvation for the monarchy." Hohenlohe-Ingelfingen, *op. cit.,* III, 172.

rejected all idea of compromise with the opposition and called for an imposition of the royal will even at the cost of civil war. The policies he advocated, indeed, seemed at times designed to provoke revolution, on the assumption that the subsequent suppression of the rebels would enable the crown to dispense with the constitution and re-establish the pre-1848 political system.

Had he been called on to justify his position, Manteuffel would probably have maintained that the issues were too important for half measures. The habit of seeing your opponent's point of view and attempting to meet him half-way was disastrous when the very fate of the monarchical principle was at stake. Failure to be strong in 1848 had proved this point all too clearly. "I have always found in my twelve years of experience in revolutionary life," Manteuffel wrote to War Minister von Roon, "that when a question of principle rises, all the world counsels concession and compromise and advises against bringing matters to a head; and that when this or that minister has acted upon these rules of prudence and the momentary mood has passed, then everyone says, 'How could he have given in like that?' "[37] He was determined that no such question would be raised in his own case. If his advice were followed, there would be no surrenders to complain of.

Manteuffel's influence was clearly at work in the determination of the tactics followed by the crown after the withdrawal of the army reform bill in May 1860. At the beginning of the year, the Prince Regent had taken the first steps toward realizing his desired reform by authorizing the creation of certain new "combined regiments," designed to replace existing Landwehr units.[38] Once the government had been forced to withdraw its reform bill, however, the legality of the new formations was dubious; and it remained so even after the Chamber had, in May, 1860, made a provisional grant of funds for the army. This *provisorium* was voted on the understanding that it would be used only to strengthen existing army units and that it would not prejudice later parliamentary decisions with regard to the proposed reforms.[39] Strictly speaking, then, the new combined regiments should have been disbanded. The Regent hesitated, however, to give them up; and he was encouraged in this by his Chief of Military Cabinet. Manteuffel, indeed, urged that, despite the Chamber's action, the units should be organized definitively, commissioned, and entered into the line of battle. Either to disband them or to consider them provisional formations would be an

[37] Roon Papers: Manteuffel to Roon, 11 March 1860.
[38] Löwenthal, *op. cit.*, p. 44.
[39] *Ibid.*, pp. 41–44; Brandenburg, *op. cit.*, I, 422–23.

admission that the Chamber had the right to determine the strength and organization of the army. "I consider the state of army morale and its inner energy imperiled and the position of the Prince Regent compromised," he wrote to Roon, "if these regiments are not established definitively at once."[40] "Your Excellency said recently that to make the army really strong is the best and most influential measure against the attacks of the opposition—and I am also convinced of that. Reasoning helps little; facts convince."[41]

Manteuffel was using similar arguments in his talks with the Regent[42] and was apparently pleading his cause well, for, in the last months of 1860, William proceeded to issue the desired orders to the new regiments. Moreover, after the death of his brother and his own succession to the royal title, William went a step further. He announced that, on 18 January 1861, he would dedicate the standards of the new regiments at the tomb of Frederick the Great. A gesture so provocative was sure to cause a sharp deterioration of relations between crown and parliament, a prospect that did not please the more moderate members of the opposition. Accordingly they sent one of their number, Minister Auerswald, to Manteuffel, urging him to dissuade the King from proceeding with the ceremony. Auerswald found Manteuffel delighted with the royal announcement and in his most arrogant mood. Coldly he said:

> I do not understand what Your Excellency desires. His Majesty has ordered me to arrange a military ceremony. Am I to renounce this because there are a number of people sitting in a house in the Dönhoffplatz, who call themselves a Landtag and who may be displeased with this ceremony? I fail to see how these people concern me. As a general, I have never yet been ordered to take my instructions from these people.[43]

The dedication, then, took place as scheduled, and it has justly been considered the decisive event in securing the success of the military reforms.[44] The future organization of the army and the fate of the Landwehr had, in effect, been decided by a royal *fait accompli*. The action enraged liberal opinion; throughout the parliamentary session of 1861, there were heated attacks against the military caste and considerable talk about cutting the military budget.[45] But the moderate liberals still

40 Roon Papers: Manteuffel to Roon, 29 May 1860.
41 *Ibid.*, 26 June 1860.
42 *Ibid.*, 17 July 1860.
43 Hohenlohe-Ingelfingen, *op. cit.*, II, 255–56.
44 See, for instance, Zechlin, *op. cit.*, p. 183.
45 Löwenthal, *op. cit.*, pp. 49–50.

hesitated to take up the gage thrown down by the crown, and they ended the rhetorical exercises by making another provisional grant of funds to the government, insisting, however, that in the next session a comprehensive military service law be placed before the Chamber for consideration.

This timid action should have been enough to convince the King that Manteuffel's talk of a liberal conspiracy against the crown was, at the very least, exaggerated. But William was so irritated by attacks on his beloved army that his mind was closed to cooler calculations and, in any event, his attention was now diverted by another theatrical gesture on the part of his Chief of Military Cabinet. In the spring of 1861, an obscure city councilor named Carl Twesten wrote a brochure in favor of retention of the two-year-service law, in the course of which he accused the Military Cabinet, and Manteuffel personally, of seeking to divorce the army completely from the Prussian people and warned that this could easily "produce an atmosphere of distrust and hostility between the military and civil society such as existed in its fullest flower before 1806."[46] Manteuffel immediately confronted Twesten with the alternatives of withdrawing his views[47] or fighting a duel and, when Twesten chose the latter, shot him through the arm.

Before proceeding with this *opera bouffe* affair—which gave wide publicity to a pamphlet that would otherwise have dropped into obscurity—Manteuffel informed all of his associates that his action was necessitated by the fact that Twesten was a tool of the secret revolutionary party that was plotting to overthrow the state. He doubtless believed this himself,[48] and he certainly convinced the King that it was true; for William, far from being outraged by the presumption of his cabinet chief, wrung his hands in despair at the thought that he might be expected to punish Manteuffel for his courage. He wrote to his War Minister:

> At this moment, to be deprived of Manteuffel's services, to have him hunted out of my presence by the triumph of democracy—the bother that this event will cause in my intimate circle—these are things which can rob me of my senses because they impress yet another unhappy stamp upon my reign. *Wo will der Himmel mit mir hin!*[49]

46 *Was uns noch retten kann,* especially pp. 61, 77–82.

47 Manteuffel did not restrict his demand to a withdrawal by Twesten of personal remarks about him but demanded, in effect, that he renounce the entire contents of his pamphlet. This Theodor von Bernhardi, among others, found completely unjustifiable. Bernhardi, *op. cit.,* IV, 131–32.

48 Schmitz, *op. cit.,* pp. 42–43.

49 Albrecht Graf von Roon, *Denkwürdigkeiten* (Berlin, 1905), II, 21.

Manteuffel, characteristically, insisted upon being punished and spent some weeks in fortress detention at Magdeburg, playing the role of Strafford with great enjoyment. "The more severe the King seems to me here," he wrote Roon on 6 July, "the better position he and your Excellency will be in to be severe to the other side . . . Liberalism and Jacobinism and Parliamentarianism." He urged Roon to stiffen the King's resistance and to remind him of the words of Maria Stuart in Schiller's drama: *"Bleibt bei der Sache, Lord, und weicht nicht aus."*[50]

Such warnings, however, were now scarcely necessary. Events in the latter half of 1861 caused a virtual panic in royal circles and created precisely the emotional atmosphere which was most favorable to Manteuffel's plans. The principal cause of this was a marked shift to the left on the part of parliamentary liberalism, the foundation of the Deutsche Fortschrittspartei and the decisive victory of this party in the Landtag elections of 6 December. Now the strongest single party in the Chamber, the DFP called for a much more aggressive program than the moderate liberal groups that had dominated the Chamber since 1859: it was pledged to the progressive development of the constitutional system, the reform of the upper house and a more complete realization of the principle of ministerial responsibility; and, with respect to the army, it was insistent upon retention of the two-year service, maintenance of the Landwehr and close supervision of the military budget.[51]

The program and the electoral victory of the DFP caused consternation among the King's military advisers. In a conversation with Max Duncker at the beginning of January 1862, Colonel von Seidlitz said: "In high military circles, they are afraid of everything. They are talking of a *coup d'état;* they suspect a great revolution."[52] In this atmosphere, it was easy for Manteuffel to persuade the King to make military preparations against the time of trouble. In the course of 1861, his friend General Hiller von Gärtringen, who had carried the challenge to Twesten, had prepared an elaborate plan of campaign for the expected fight for Berlin. This involved the immediate strengthening of the Berlin garrisons; the placing of artillery in prepared trenches at Windmühlenberg and light mortars on the roof of the Castle; the withdrawal

[50] Roon Papers: Manteuffel to Roon, 6 July 1861.

[51] Kaminsky, *op. cit.*, pp. 60–61; Eyck, *op. cit.*, I, 370–71; Zechlin, *op. cit.*, pp. 201–2.

[52] Max Duncker, *Politischer Briefwechsel aus seinem Nachlass* (Vol. XII of *Deutsche Geschichtsquellen des 19. Jahrhunderts,* J. Schultze, ed.) (Stuttgart, 1923), p. 305.

of the royal family from Berlin at the first sign of disorder—obviously a reflection of Manteuffel's memories of March 1848; and a systematic and remorseless conquest of the city by the army.[53]

In the months preceding the elections this plan was discussed thoroughly in the Military Cabinet and in the presence of the King; and in January 1862 the King adopted a modification of the Hiller-Manteuffel plan. In the event of a rising in Berlin, this envisaged the employment against the rebels of 34,500 infantry and engineers, 16,000 horse and 100 field pieces, the local units operating outward from the area of the Castle and the provincial regiments enveloping and assaulting the city from without. Sealed orders were sent to the units which would be used in this campaign, with instructions that they were to be opened only upon telegraphic advice. These included explicit instructions that negotiations with the rebels would be considered a violation of military honor and that officers surrendering their posts to the rebels would be tried by military tribunal.[54]

This was, ostensibly, a defensive plan, a necessary precaution against the threat of revolution; but there is every reason to believe that the leading spirit behind it, Edwin von Manteuffel, was eager to have it put into effect, even if he had to provoke the Chamber into revolution. And Manteuffel's influence seemed never greater than it was during the first months of 1862, for both the King and Manteuffel's nominal superior, War Minister von Roon, were apparently completely under his spell. In March 1862—after the Chamber had refused the two-year-service law, rejected the government's request for funds, and demanded a complete itemization of the budget[55]—Manteuffel not only urged dissolution of the Chamber but insisted that, because of its inability to control the Chamber, the ministry should be purged of its liberal members and reformed in a conservative direction.[56] When both these measures were adopted, Bernhardi recognized them as a sign that Manteuffel had reached the goal toward which he had been working "with shrewd calculation."[57] There were, indeed, indications that strong action was not far off. On 23 March, Bernhardi spent the evening with Roon, and the

[53] Ludwig Dehio, "Die Pläne der Militärpartei und der Konflikt," *Deutsche Rundschau,* CCXIII (1927), 93–94.

[54] *Ibid.,* pp. 94 ff. These orders were not called back until after the end of the Danish War in 1864.

[55] On this, see Löwenthal, *op. cit.,* pp. 69 ff.; Kaminsky, *op. cit.,* pp. 61 ff.; Adalbert Wahl, *Beiträge zur Geschichte der Konfliktszeit* (Tübingen, 1914), pp. 13–14.

[56] Roon Papers: Manteuffel to Roon, 7 March 1862.

[57] Berhardi, *op. cit.* IV, 238.

War Minister expressed the opinion that, if the forthcoming elections were unfavorable to the government, it could hardly be expected "to sheathe its sword and retreat." Bernhardi said: "Then we may be in position in June in which a *coup d'état* is unavoidable"; and Roon answered: "On that I am determined."[58] Bernhardi was inclined to dismiss this as scare talk, but three days later General Peucker told him that the new ministry expected a rising before the May elections and was confident that it would be suppressed and would be followed by a thoroughgoing political reaction. Peucker added that troops in Berlin were restricted to their quarters and that live ammunition had already been distributed. Bernhardi wrote in his diary: "I am convinced that these things emanate not from Roon and the ministers but from a quite different source"[59]—presumably from Manteuffel.

In these weeks following the dissolution of the Landtag, the constitutional conflict came to full crisis. The military, in Max Duncker's phrase, were "panting after riots, like the hart after the waterbrooks"; and had there been even a minor outbreak of disorder in Berlin, it seems probable that the secret orders would have been put into effect. In that case, Manteuffel might very well have realized his dream of entering the pages of history as the great soldier-statesman in Prussia's critical hour. For the kind of warfare that would have ensued in Berlin he had a stronger will than Roon and more military ability than Wrangel;[60] and, once his plans had led to the complete suppression of the rebels, he would have earned the right to direct the backward revision of the constitution. Indeed, throughout the spring and summer of 1862, there was talk, at least in the reactionary group headed by the Gerlachs and Kleist-Retzow, of elevating Manteuffel to the position of Minister President.[61]

Manteuffel's great hour, however, never arrived. At this crucial moment in Prussian affairs, both the King and Roon began to entertain doubts concerning the advisability of bringing matters to a head. At the beginning of April, the King—in despair over the opposition of the Chamber—intimated that he was confronted with a choice between

[58] *Ibid.*, IV, 255–56.

[59] *Ibid.*, IV, 260.

[60] In the event of fighting in Berlin, Wrangel was to be over-all commander of the troops. See Dehio, "Die Pläne der Militärpartei und der Konflikt," p. 96. On Wrangel's talents, or lack of them, see Valentin, *op. cit.*, II, 246 ff. For a more favorable account, see F. von Meerheimb, "Graf von Wrangel," *Militärwochenblatt, Beihefte* (1877, No. 7), pp. 355–418.

[61] Gerhard Ritter, *Die preussischen Konservativen und Bismarcks deutsche Politik* (Heidelberg, 1913), p. 69.

concessions to the opposition or abdication. This horrified Manteuffel, and he pleaded with the King to stand firm. As he wrote later:

> I told the King that I had advised him four years ago that we were living in a revolution; but the question was whether he would act like Charles I and Louis XVI and allow power to be wrested from his hands before it came to an open fight. Today he still had power and had the army; if, however, he gave way at the expense of the army in order to secure favorable election results, he would still not secure that objective but would only shake the army's confidence in his firmness.[62]

Roon too was wavering and was beginning to think that it might be wise to surrender on the three-year-service term.[63] In a long letter of 3 April 1862, Manteufel tried to convince him that compromise at this stage of the conflict would be fatal. "I recognize no advances in the battle except with weapons in hand!" he wrote, "and we are in the middle of the battle." He pointed out that the King had identified himself with the three-year-term. "How can the three-year service be given up during his reign, without bringing shame upon the personal position of the All Highest? . . . The army will not understand it; its confidence in the King will be shaken; and the consequences for the internal condition of the army will be incalculable." The fight must go forward unless a Chamber favorable to the Crown is elected. If this does not happen, then "we shall see bloody heads, and *then* good election results will come. . . . The point of my long speech is this. The views of the King must be maintained; nothing must happen which compromises him; concessions lead to ruin; in firmness there is no danger."[64]

If these arguments were intended to persuade the King and Roon that the time for a *coup d'état* had arrived, they failed of their purpose. However much Manteuffel might yearn for bloody heads and the kind of open conflict that would justify an all-out assault upon the defenders of constitutionalism, he found that his superiors were afraid to take the responsibility for resort to the *ultima ratio*. And that meant, of course, that it would be impossible to put the plans of January 1862 into effect

[62] Dehio "Die Pläne der Militärpartei und der Konflikt," p. 99. Wrangel told the King that abdication would be desertion in the face of the enemy and threatened him with the mutiny of the whole army.

[63] On Roon's attitude during the constitutional conflict, see Andrea von Harbou, *Dienst und Glaube in der Staatsanschauung Albrecht von Roons* (Berlin, 1936), pp. 68, 73 ff. Erich Marcks, *Männer und Zeiten* (Leipzig, 1912), I, 317 ff., is also useful.

[64] Roon Papers: Manteuffel to Roon, 3 April 1862. See also the letter of 8 April, cited in footnote 14 above.

unless the opposition in the Chamber took the initiative and themselves precipitated a revolution. It became rapidly apparent that the liberals had no intention of doing that. Despite its aggressive program, the DFP did not want to fight a revolution to secure it. Predominantly drawn from the middle economic groups, its members remembered the disorders of 1848 with something less than pleasure; in any case—as Johannes Ziekursch has written—barristers and businessmen do not man barricades.[65] The DFP relied upon its parliamentary strength, which was further increased in the elections of May 1862, and believed that the Chamber's budgetary powers would be enough to break the royal will.[66]

With both sides refusing then to make the final resort to force, the conflict became purely parliamentary in nature. In such a contest, Manteuffel could not hope to play a dominant role; decisions on questions of principle and tactics would be made, in the last analysis, by the King's ministers who had to face the opposition in parliament. Nevertheless, his influence, even if necessarily indirect, was far from negligible, thanks to his intimacy with the King and the War Minister. The friendship with Roon was, it is true, subject to considerable strain, for the choleric War Minister was increasingly irritated by the vanity and arrogance of the cabinet chief.[67] But the King retained his confidence in Manteuffel's counsels and often preferred them to those of his ministers. That fact rapidly became apparent as Bismarck entered upon the stage and assumed the direction of the fight to maintain the royal prerogative.

Even before Bismarck had been seriously considered as potential Minister President, there had been a perceptible coolness between him and Manteuffel. During his term as envoy to the German Confederation at Frankfurt, Bismarck had complained to Leopold von Gerlach that Manteuffel seemed suspicious of him and was always passing sentence on him "like a High Tribunal." However, he added cheerfully, "we can both live without loving one another, he in his assassins' den behind the *Marstall,* I at the fountain of the Danaides in the Eschenheimer Gasse."[68] Now, however, this mutual forbearance was bound to

[65] Johannes Ziekursch, *Politische Geschichte des neuen deutschen Kaiserreiches* (Frankfurt, 1925 *et seq.*), I, 64–65. See also Hartung, *op. cit.,* pp. 214–15; Bernhardi, *op. cit.,* IV, 328.

[66] See Löwenthal, *op. cit.,* pp. 76–87; Zechlin, *op. cit.,* pp. 275–276.

[67] See Roon Papers: Manteuffel to Roon, 19 February 1862. As early as October 1859, writing of Manteuffel to his wife, Roon had said: "What frightful vanity there is in this man!" Roon, *Denkwürdigkeiten,* I, 392.

[68] Horst Kohl, ed., *Bismarcks Briefe an General Leopold von Gerlach* (Berlin, 1896), p. 338.

disappear; and in September 1862, when Roon persuaded the King to call Bismarck to power, a rivalry began which ended only with Manteuffel's death.[69]

Bismarck's advent was hailed by the reactionary press and regarded, on the liberal side, as a sign that a *coup d'état* was imminent.[70] In reality, however, the new Minister President did not wish to deliver himself into the hands of the reactionaries, who were unsympathetic to his ambitious foreign plans; and he was well aware that that would be the inevitable result of a royal *Putsch*.[71] He realized, moreover, that sooner or later he would have to reach some kind of reconciliation with the liberals, if his national program was to be carried out. Thus, while he was determined firmly to establish the royal *Kommandogewalt* and to set definite limits to parliamentary power, he had no desire to smash parliament and return to the pre-1848 system. On the contrary, he was perfectly willing to make reasonable concessions to the opposition in order to bring the domestic conflict to a close. Even after his first attempts to reach an understanding with the opposition had failed[72] and he had raised reactionary hopes by defying parliament and ruling without a budget, he kept the possibility of a deal with the liberals in mind and exploited every opportunity to make one.

Manteuffel, always fearful of compromise with the enemy, was fully aware that Bismarck could not be trusted to defend the principles in which he himself believed. As early as 4 October—within two weeks of Bismarck's assumption of office—he wrote Roon that certain recent

[69] On the latter stages of this rivalry, see especially Dehio, "Edwin von Manteuffel und der Kaiser," pp. 40 ff. Throughout the 1870's, Manteuffel was frequently mentioned as a possible successor to Bismarck and was believed by many to be plotting against the chancellor. See, *inter alia,* Eyck, *op. cit.,* III, 68–75, 246–47, 324–25; Priesdorff, *op. cit.,* p. 165; Ulrich von Stosch, ed., *Denkwürdigkeiten des Generals und Admirals Albrecht von Stosch* (Stuttgart, 1904), pp. 247–48; Julius Heyderhoff, ed., *Im Ring der Gegner Bismarcks: Denkschriften und politisches Briefwechsel Franz von Roggenbachs* (Vol. XXXV of *Deutsche Geschichtsquellen des 19. Jahrhunderts* (2d ed.; Leipzig, 1943), p. 168 n.; Bogdan Graf Hutten-Czapski, *Sechzig Jahre Politik und Gesellschaft* (Berlin, 1935), I, 113–29. See also Manteuffel's letter of 11 August 1873 to Bismarck, disclaiming any desire for the chancellorship. Horst Kohl, ed., *Bismarck-Jahrbuch* (Berlin, 1894), IV, 113 ff.

[70] O. Nirrnheim, *Das erste Jahr des Ministeriums Bismarcks* (Heidelberg, 1908), pp. 58 ff.

[71] Huber, *op. cit.,* pp. 228–29. See also Ritter, *op. cit.,* pp. 69–70; Kaminsky, *op. cit.,* pp. 72 ff. Zechlin (*op. cit.,* pp. 342–43) feels that Bismarck almost certainly knew of the military plans of January 1862 but was determined to use them only as a last resort.

[72] Zechlin, *op. cit.,* pp. 324–29.

statements by the Minister President smelled of concession and, as usual, cited the history of the Stuarts to show the folly of dealing with the opposition.[73]

The Chief of the Military Cabinet was correct at least in his suspicion that Bismarck's policy would be a tortuous one. In October, the Minister President and his friend Roon conceived an entirely new approach to the army dispute.[74] They drafted for submission to the Chamber an army service bill which provided, first, that the size of the army would henceforth be fixed at a given percentage of the population —probably 1 per cent. This army would consist of two elements: long-term volunteers (*Capitulanten*) comprising one-third of the total force; and conscripts who would serve for only two years. To support the volunteer formations—the existence of which would presumably reduce the number of conscripts called annually—all eligible males who were placed in the *Ersatzreserve* instead of being called up, and all actual conscripts who wished to be sure that their term of service would not exceed two years, would pay a special tax (*Einstandsgeld*). Finally, instead of having to pore over the complicated details of a military budget, the Chamber would henceforth automatically grant a fixed annual sum (*Pauschquantum*) per soldier in the army.

This plan could not help but be attractive to elements of the opposition, and therein lay its shrewdness. The provision for two-year service for conscripts would satisfy one of the liberals' most important demands, while the introduction of volunteer contingents and the elaborate scheme of taxes for their support seemed to promise that well-to-do young men might be exempted from active service in peacetime. Behind these concessions to the opposition, however, lay very tangible advantages for the crown: the *Pauschquantum* scheme was a clever blow at the budgetary rights of the Chamber; and the royal *Kommandogewalt* would certainly be strengthened by the proposed removal of the questions of army strength and finance from the arena of parliamentary discussion.

It is impossible to say what effect this plan would have had if submitted to the Chamber. It seems likely that if it had not won the opposition, it might have split it. It never had a chance to do either, for it was effectively sabotaged by Edwin von Manteuffel. Doubtless moved in part by growing jealousy of Bismarck but certainly more by his

[73] Roon Papers: Manteuffel to Roon, 4 October 1862.

[74] Ludwig Dehio, "Bismarck und die Heeresvorlagen der Konfliktszeit," *Historische Zeitschrift*, CXLIV (1931), 31 ff. The plan was drafted by Roon, but Dehio's argument that Bismarck was the moving spirit behind it is convincing.

hatred of concession in any form, he argued that the prospective advantages to the crown were outweighed by the moral victory which the admission of the two-year service would give to the opposition. Moreover, to allow the peacetime strength of the army to be fixed by a law, however permanent, was to weaken the whole constitutional position of the crown. The King had always insisted that, in military affairs, the Chamber had only a budgetary right; decisions on size, organizations and command of the army were made by the King alone.[75] These arguments were perhaps not convincing to Bismarck; but they were to the King. Overborne by the eloquence of his Chief of Military Cabinet, he refused to countenance the plan.[76]

Manteuffel's intervention and the King's stubbornness made it inevitable that the constitutional conflict would drag on, as it did for four years until the impact of the Danish and Austrian Wars destroyed the position of the parliamentary opposition and led it, in 1866, to sue for peace. Bismarck's conduct of the fight against the Chamber is too well known to need recapitulation here. It may be noted, however, that, as he pursued his objectives, he did not forgive Manteuffel for his part in the defeat of the *Pauschquantum* plan. Writing in September 1862, Albrecht von Stosch had confided to his diary: "Manteuffel must fall. Then Bismarck will persuade the King to accept the two-year service for the infantry and we will have peace."[77] After December 1862, Bismarck would have agreed with the first sentence of that entry. Manteuffel's regard for principle was an awkward thing, and persuading the King to any course of action was difficult when the cabinet chief was at William's elbow.

Bismarck was too shrewd, however, to attempt to force the expulsion of his powerful adversary,[78] and Manteuffel remained as Chief of Military Cabinet and self-appointed conscience of the King until 1865. Those years brought no alteration in his principles. In February 1863, when the Chamber dared send a special message to the King, he expressed the opinion that, if he were minister, he would have the leaders of the opposition jailed for breach of the constitution.[79] In April

[75] Roon Papers: Manteuffel to Roon, 5 December 1862.

[76] Dehio, "Bismarck und die Heeresvorlagen der Konfliktszeit," pp. 37–41.

[77] Stosch, *op. cit.*, p. 52.

[78] Manteuffel had his uses as far as Bismarck was concerned. During the storm of indignation over Bismarck's secret agreement with Russia in early 1863, the Minister President appears to have spread the story that it was really Manteuffel who inspired it. Bernhardi, *op. cit.*, V, 37.

[79] Roon Papers: Manteuffel to Roon, 2 February 1863.

he was detecting new ministerial attempts to resort to compromise;[80] and in October he was arguing against Bismarck's German policy.[81] Throughout most of 1864, the Danish War absorbed his energies, but in 1865 his influence in the constitutional struggle was once more perceptible. Indeed, in May 1865, when the Chamber itself took the initiative in seeking a reconciliation and produced a plan that met the approval of Bismarck and all the ministers, it was Manteuffel once more who prevented its realization. On 2 May 1865, he wrote to the King:

> Who rules and decides in Prussia, the King or the ministers? . . . Your Majesty's ministers are loyal and devoted, but they live now only in the atmosphere of the Chamber. If I may express my opinion, it is this: Your Majesty should hold no council but should write to Minister Bismarck saying: "Now that I have read the proposal, I have decided that the government will not agree to it."[82]

The King followed this counsel.

After this blow Bismarck was determined to secure Manteuffel's removal from Berlin, and he was seconded by Roon, whose personal and administrative differences with Manteuffel had now become insupportable. They found their opportunity when it became necessary to appoint a man of personal stature and diplomatic skill to the difficult and important post of Governor of Schleswig; and although it was not easy, they finally persuaded the King that Manteuffel was the indispensable man for that assignment.[83] Thus, the powerful cabinet chief moved on to a new phase in his crowded career;[84] and before he returned to Berlin the Austrian War had been fought and the constitutional conflict brought finally to a close.

The conflict was liquidated by the so-called Indemnity Law of September 1866. This has quite rightly been described as a defeat for Prussian liberalism,[85] but it was far from the kind of defeat that Man-

[80] *Ibid.*, 21 April 1863.

[81] *Ibid.*, 9 October 1863.

[82] Rudolf Stadelmann, *Das Jahr 1865 und das Problem von Bismarcks deutscher Politik* (Munich, 1933), pp. 31 ff.; Bernhardi, *op. cit.*, VI, 200.

[83] Roon Papers: Note by Roon, 13 May 1865; Manteuffel to Roon, 29 June 1865. Bernhardi, *op. cit.*, VI, 211; Erich Brandenburg, Hermann Oncken, *et al.*, eds., *Auswärtige Politik Preussens (1858–71)* (Oldenburg, 1932 *et seq.*), VI, 140–41.

[84] On his policy in Schleswig and his differences with Bismarck, see especially Clark, *op. cit.*

[85] See Ziekursch, *op. cit.*, pp. 197 ff., Huber, *op. cit.*, pp. 234–35; Kaminsky, *op. cit.*, pp. 116 ff.

teuffel had worked for. His objective had been a definitive victory over parliamentary pretensions, followed by a constitutional revision that would make the King's power over the army complete and indisputable for all time. The distinctive feature of the settlement of September 1866 was that it settled nothing definitively. Both parties agreed to remain silent about the issue that had been the original cause of the dispute—the army reform. The reconciliation was confined to a royal declaration that the government had violated the law in proceeding without a budget (an admission that must have wounded Manteuffel deeply) and an agreement by the Chamber to vote retroactively all of the funds withheld. Tacitly, of course, the liberals, in voting the indemnity, accepted the army reform; nor was there much hope that organized liberalism would ever again effectively oppose the King's will in military matters. But legally there had been no clarification of the basic issue—whether the Chamber could use its budgetary powers to reject or modify government plans for the organization of the army[86]—and the legal powers of the Chamber were no weaker after the conflict than they had been at the beginning. This being so, it was likely that new opposition groups would arise in time to contest the absolute supremacy of the crown in military affairs, and the history of the later century was to give abundant proof of this. Such an indefinite result could scarcely meet the approval of Edwin von Manteuffel, who was no believer in truces and who had always held that "the game must be played to the end!"[87]

III

For all his criticism of the inadequacies of the settlement of 1866, Manteuffel must have derived considerable satisfaction from one thing. Though his political principles had been flouted in the parliamentary truce, he had been able to work quietly behind the scenes and to effect changes that made the army a much more reliable instrument of royal power than it had ever been before. This achievement came as a result of his rejuvenation of the officer corps, his influence upon army education, and his expansion of the power of the Military Cabinet.

[86] See the views of Carl Schmitt in *Staatsgefüge und Zusammenbruch des zweiten Reiches: Der Sieg des Bürgers über den Soldaten* (Hamburg, 1934), pp. 11 ff.; and Löwenthal, *op. cit.*, pp. 296–97. On the disappointment of the conservatives in the settlement, see Ritter, *op. cit.*, pp. 173–74.

[87] Roon Papers: Manteuffel to Roon, 5 December 1862.

"My captain," says Baron Osten in Fontane's *Irrungen, Wirrungen,* "was Manteuffel, he to whom we are all grateful for having made the army and, with the army, the victory." The praise is not entirely unjustified. When Manteuffel became Chief of the Military Cabinet in 1857, he began immediately to weed out incompetents and to eliminate from the officer corps commanders whose age seemed to impair their efficiency. The ruthless way in which he pursued this objective caused consternation in the army. Schweinitz, the future ambassador to Russia, tells us that, when he was a major, he was warned by his commanding officer to dye his hair lest his premature grayness cause his severance from the service.[88] Manteuffel's own letters in the early 1860's reflect his preoccupation with the necessity of "rejuvenating the army in the higher commands and in general";[89] later in his life he was often to say: "That was my greatest political accomplishment; without this cleansing, the victories of 1864, 1866, and 1870 would not have been won. The officer corps at the beginning of the 1850's was far worse than in 1806."[90]

There is reason to suspect, however, that the cleansing went far beyond the elimination of the unfit and that it was, in part at least, a political purge as well. Certainly officers who entertained advanced opinions found their progress in the service slowed up, and by 1863 liberal officers were complaining of the arrogance of their comrades and the spirit of espionage and thought-control that was spreading in the regiments.[91] In December 1862, Theodor von Bernhardi had warned the Crown Prince that these activities would have a deleterious effect upon army morale and had received the resigned answer: "If the affair stems from Manteuffel, there is nothing that can be done."[92] That the Chief of the Military Cabinet kept a weather eye out for potential dissidents seems clear. When he learned that the Commandant at Cologne, Dresler von Scharffenstein, was on good terms with several of the local merchants, he called in one of Dresler's friends and questioned him. The friend vouched for Dresler's reliability. "But he goes around with civilians!" said Manteuffel. The friend repeated his assurances. "Very well," said the Chief of the Military Cabinet, "then we can count on him if the shooting begins?"[93]

88 Schweinitz, *op. cit.*, I, 88.

89 Roon Papers: Manteuffel to Roon, 2 May 1860. See also the letters of 25 February and 11 June 1860.

90 Karl Demeter, *Das deutsche Heer and seine Offiziere* (Berlin, 1930), p. 20.

91 Lenz, *op. cit.*, pp. 179–80.

92 Bernhardi, *op. cit.*, IV, 338.

93 *Ibid.*, V, 30–31.

If the officers with progressive political ideas found the officer corps uncomfortable during Manteuffel's regime, those who had the misfortune to have middle-class origins found it even more so. To Manteuffel, middle-class officers were objectionable not only because of the likelihood that they were contaminated by liberal opinions but also because he felt that their social class lacked the military spirit.[94] As early as March 1860, the military commission of the Prussian Chamber was objecting to the systematic elimination of bourgeois officers from the army,[95] and these complaints were repeated year after year.[96] The Chamber had an understandable fear that an army that was headed by an officer corps predominantly anti-bourgeois in its opinions would be a standing threat to constitutional liberties; this fear was heightened when, in 1865, an army representative admitted that of 8,169 officers, 4,172 were nobles.[97] One could not, of course, dispense entirely with middle-class officers. They were apt to possess an embarrassingly useful technical and mathematical proficiency. But Manteuffel's housecleaning saw to it that they were relegated to the artillery and engineer formations, while the crack (and socially correct) infantry and cavalry regiments remained aristocratic preserves. Moreover, it is worth noting that in the highest ranks in the whole army—the generals and the colonels—well over 80 per cent of the officers were of noble origin.[98]

Manteuffel's prejudice against middle-class officers was so deep that it permitted him to flout the principle laid down by Scharnhorst in the reform period—namely, that admission to the officer corps should be conditional upon demonstration of educational qualification. He tried to justify his evasion of existing rules by arguing that it was unwise "to require erudition from all officers," since "the great majority . . . will consist always of qualified front officers, and for them scholarly training is not necessary in such a high degree."[99] In reality, his objection stemmed from the fact that the tightening of educational requirements represented a threat to the social cohesiveness and, hence, the political

[94] This was a belief shared by Moltke, who said in 1861: "We have to turn away a lot of the bourgeoisie, partly because they are useless young people who turn to military service because they can't get on in other careers, partly because they don't have the *Gesinnung* which must be preserved in the army." *Ibid.*, IV, 166.

[95] *Ibid.*, III, 284.

[96] See, for instance, Twesten's *Was uns noch retten kann,* p. 8.

[97] Löwenthal, *op. cit.*, pp. 247 ff.

[98] Demeter, *op. cit.*, pp. 34–35; Vagts, *op. cit.*, pp. 200–201.

[99] Manteuffel to his son, 16 September 1864. *Deutsche Revue,* XXXVIII, No. 3 (1913), 198.

ʼeliability of the officer corps. In October 1861 a royal order stipulated :hat henceforth candidates for commissions would be required to present ı certificate showing that they had reached the *Prima* in a *Gymnasium* ɔr *Realschule* and could pass examinations in subjects required in the ɹpper grades of such institutions. The order caused a storm of fury in :he old officer class, who protested hotly that it marked the beginning ɔf a thorough bourgeoisification of the army. In an anonymous letter to Manteuffel, a group of officers asked plaintively: "Instead of Dönhoffs, Dohnas, etc., will not the sons of rich bankers capture the places in the Garde du Corps? Would an officer corps thus altered show the same attitude as it did in 1848? . . . Would it not be dangerous to offend the nobility so seriously?"[100]

Manteuffel thought that it would be. Without consulting the War Minister,[101] he waged a determined battle against the order of October, persuading the King, first, to remind regimental commanders that character requirements were to be weighed equally with education and, later, to delay application of the order for three years.[102] In effect, the order was never applied in the spirit in which it was written. If, as Meinecke has pointed out,[103] the modern German officer corps was dominated by the spirit of the professional and was dangerously naïve in political and nontechnical matters, the responsibility is partly due to the attitude taken by Manteuffel in the 1860's.

The continued success of Manteuffel's policies required, of course, that the selection and advancement of officers remain completely free from parliamentary influence of any kind. To secure this freedom, Manteuffel worked implacably from 1857 to 1865 to remove selection policy from the control of the War Ministry.

His policy here was not motivated by personal vanity or even by the tendency to "empire-building" that is common to bureaucrats the world over. In Manteuffel's eyes the most important question of the future was whether the army was to be dependent upon a constitutional minister who was responsible to parliament or one bound to the King in a feudal relationship of personal loyalty. If the answer was to be the former, then the power and authority of the War Minister must of necessity be limited; for, since he was responsible to parliament, the wider

100 Demeter, *op. cit.*, pp. 88–89, 260–61.

101 That is clearly the conclusion to be drawn from his letter of 19 February 1862 to Roon (Roon Papers).

102 Demeter, *op. cit.*, pp. 90–91.

103 Friedrich Meinecke, *Die deutsche Katastrophe: Betrachtungen und Erinnerungen* (Wiesbaden, 1946), chapter 5.

his powers the greater the potential control of parliament over the army.

During the Scharnhorst-Boyen era at the beginning of the century, the army organization had been unified by subordinating all of its administrative units directly to the authority of the War Minister. After Boyen's fall in 1819, however, this tendency was reversed. In particular, the third division of the War Ministry, the Division of Personal Affairs, tended to assume an ambiguous position. This division operated primarily as the unit that handled selection procedure, promotions, and similar matters, but it served also as a private bureau or cabinet of the King, responsible directly to him for matters assigned to it. In time, the second function began to usurp the first. The Division of Personal Affairs became known commonly as the Military Cabinet and was listed as such in the *Staatskalendar*. Its chief, in his capacity as division head, was still responsible to the War Minister; in his capacity as Chief of the Military Cabinet, however, this was not true.[104]

During the revolution of 1848, the Military Cabinet, long suspected in the eyes of liberals as a center of reaction, was deleted from the *Staatskalendar* and lost most of its authority. It was never, however, despite the desire of War Minister von Reyher, actually abolished;[105] nor was the administrative confusion caused by its dual function corrected. This was the situation in 1857 when Edwin von Manteuffel became Chief of the Division of Personal Affairs and of the Military Cabinet.

From the outset, Manteuffel was determined not only to maintain the independence of the Military Cabinet *qua* Cabinet, but also to free the functions of the Division of Personal Affairs from the control of the War Minister as well. Within a year of his appointment he was engaged in a furious dispute with War Minister von Bonin, who objected strenuously to Manteuffel's habit of making decisions on matters of appointment and promotion and of communicating directly with the commanding generals without consulting the War Minister. With a characteristic gesture, Manteuffel, at the height of this dispute, submitted his resignation to the Prince Regent, saying that, in view of Bonin's attitude, it was impossible to maintain "the military principle in its full purity, as I understand it."[106] The Regent did not accept

104 The authoritative work on the development of the Military Cabinet is Schmidt-Bückeburg, *op. cit.* For additional details, see H. O. Meisner, "Militärkabinett, Kriegsminister und Reichskanzler zur Zeit Wilhelms I," *Forschungen zur brandenburgischen und preussischen Geschichte*, L (1918), and especially *Der Kriegsminister, 1814–1914* (Berlin, 1940).

105 Schmidt-Bückeburg, *op. cit.*, pp. 38, 47–48.

106 Meisner, *Der Kriegsminister*, pp. 105 ff.

Manteuffel's resignation, and the question of principle was postponed; but it is significant that a year later Bonin was forced out of office, in part at least because of Manteuffel's growing influence.

Once Roon had succeeded Bonin, it might have been supposed that differences between the War Ministry and the Military Cabinet would cease, for Roon was as fully opposed to parliamentary control over the army as Manteuffel was. As minister, however, Roon quickly developed a jealous regard for the prerogatives of his office, and, like Bonin, he was soon irritated by Manteuffel's habit of informing him of actions only after they had been taken. In the course of 1860 he complained repeatedly of Manteuffel's conduct,[107] with little success, since Manteuffel either excused himself by saying that he was acting on royal instructions or explained that he could not communicate to the Ministry matters that concerned the Military Cabinet more than they did the Division of Personal Affairs.[108] This quibbling, however justified by the curious complexities of Prussian military administration, infuriated Roon, who was a man of forthright mind.

Manteuffel's long-run objectives were perceptibly advanced in January 1861, when he persuaded the King to issue a notable, if momentarily unappreciated, cabinet order. The document, dated 18 January 1861, stipulated that henceforth army orders dealing with personnel, service details or matters of command would not require ministerial countersignature before becoming valid; and that only purely administrative orders, and orders which affected the budget or required legislation, need be signed in the future by the War Minister.[109] The order was a tremendously important landmark in the freeing of the army from parliamentary control,[110] for at a stroke it removed the most vital military matters from the final jurisdiction of the only person whom parliament could hold accountable for military matters—the War Minister. Inevitably, in doing this, it greatly increased the authority of the Military Cabinet, for the matters withdrawn from ministerial countersignature were now handled with growing independence by that office.

107 Roon Papers: Manteuffel to Roon, 8 March, 10 March, 20 June, 10 October, 6 November 1860—all of which seem to be written in response to, or in order to forestall, complaints from Roon.

108 Roon Papers: Manteuffel to Roon, 8 March 1860. See also the letter of 10 March in which Manteuffel says he regards "the unconditional maintenance of the Military Cabinet, particularly at the present moment, as a necessity."

109 For fuller details, see Schmidt-Bückeburg, *op. cit.*, pp. 73 ff.

110 See the comments in Meisner, *Der Kriegsminister*, pp. 24–25; Huber, *op. cit.*, p. 198; Kaminsky, *op. cit.*, p. 53; Srbik, *op. cit.*, III, 31.

There was little doubt, after the signing of the order of 18 January 1861, that the Military Cabinet was in the ascendant.[111]

Roon did not immediately perceive the consequences of all this for his own position. He welcomed the order of 18 January because it virtually destroyed the principle of ministerial responsibility and struck a direct blow at parliamentary pretensions.[112] He seems even to have supported the increased independence of the Military Cabinet. In October 1862, in a speech in the Chamber, he rejected parliamentary demands that it be controlled by saying that the Military Cabinet was a part of the War Ministry only when it was handling personnel matters.[113]

The War Minister soon discovered, however, that, even in personnel matters, Manteuffel paid little attention to his technical subordination to the War Ministry and that in other matters—especially the relationship between the King and the commanding generals—he consulted the War Minister as little as possible. From the beginning of 1862 on, there were sharp clashes between Manteuffel and Roon, and the former was not able completely to appease the War Minister by appealing to their common principles or reminding him that he was acting only as "an organ of the King."[114] Relations between them were already so strained by the end of 1862 that Manteuffel was suggesting that it might be better if he resigned, since "with my philosophy and my individuality I must always work against the views of the [War] Minister."[115]

Roon's feeling that he was being left out of important decisions reached its height during the Danish campaign of 1864, when, in a stormy scene at Karlsbad, he accused Manteuffel of deliberately withholding from him action reports sent from the commanding generals to the King. In a prolix letter written a few days later, Manteuffel pointed out that Roon had a right to see only such reports or portions of reports as the King authorized for transmission to him, and that, however unpleasant this might be personally, it was fully in accord with the principle that "the King personally holds the command of the army, without the mediation of a third and without any bureaucratic authority intervening in the direct relationship of the army to its warlord." The implication here was that to give the War Minister an auto-

111 See Auerswald's remarks in September 1861, Duncker, *op. cit.*, p. 297.

112 Schmidt-Bückeburg, *op. cit.*, p. 78; Zechlin, *op. cit.*, pp. 210–11.

113 W. von Roon, ed., *Kriegsminister von Roon als Redner* (Breslau, 1895–96), I, 339.

114 See Roon Papers: Manteuffel to Roon, 19 February, 5 March 1862.

115 Roon Papers: Manteuffel to Roon, 8 December 1862.

matic right to review matters of command or even to see action reports would give dangerous encouragement to the principle of ministerial responsibility.[116]

After this incident, relations between Manteuffel and Roon were never completely cordial again. There was another brush in 1865 when Manteuffel intervened in a dispute between Roon and General von Steinmetz in such a way as to contest the War Minister's authority over the commanding generals.[117] This helped precipitate Manteuffel's fall, for Roon now worked with Bismarck, who had his own reasons for wishing to see Manteuffel removed from Berlin, and the Chief of the Military Cabinet was in the same year sent to Schleswig as Governor.

Manteuffel's principles, however, were completely victorious. When Roon sought a clarification of his rights in relation to the commanding generals, the King rejected his request on the grounds that any directive on the subject "could easily lead to the formation of a court of appeal in matters of command between the commanding generals and myself."[118] After this, the War Minister was virtually excluded from all matters relating to the command of the army, and questions of this nature were handled directly by the King through the Military Cabinet.

Manteuffel's desire to free all personnel matters—selection, promotion, decorations and the like—from the War Ministry was not fully realized. But the first steps toward this had been taken when the War Minister's right of countersignature had been restricted in 1861, and Manteuffel's successors in the Military Cabinet pushed this policy to its logical conclusion. Albedyll, Chief of the Military Cabinet from 1871 to 1887, not only took Manteuffel as his model but consulted him frequently;[119] it was with Manteuffel's full approval that he succeeded, first, in greatly increasing the number and variety of orders that could be excluded from ministerial countersignature, and finally, in 1883, in freeing the Military Cabinet itself and all personnel matters from the last vestiges of ministerial control. After this victory, Manteuffel—now very close to death—wrote to Albedyll to congratulate him on his consolidation of the *Kommandogewalt,* an event which, he said, effectively destroyed the pernicious French theory "that the War Minister is *quasi*

[116] *Ibid.,* 8 July 1864. The letter includes a survey of the history of the War Ministry since 1848.

[117] Schmidt-Bückeburg, *op. cit.,* pp. 89 ff.

[118] Meisner, *Der Kriegsminister,* p. 12.

[119] *Ibid.,* p. 30; Schmidt-Bückeburg, *op. cit.,* pp. 124 ff.

chief of the army."[120] It is doubtful whether congratulations were really in order. The policy inaugurated by Manteuffel in 1857 led to the destruction of the administrative unity which the army had enjoyed in the days of Scharnhorst and Boyen, and this had highly unfortunate results in the war of 1914–18.

Manteuffel was not interested, however, in the maintenance of unity under a minister who might be held to accountability by parliament. In the struggle between crown and Landtag in the 1860's, he had seen a threat to the very existence of the state. Balked of his desire to eliminate that danger once and for all by resort to force, he undertook to make the army completely immune to liberal influence. His rejuvenation and educational policies were designed to secure the predominance in the officer corps of those classes most devoted to the maintenance of unrestricted royal power. His deliberate campaign to weaken the authority of the War Minister was motivated by the fear that parliament might take advantage of the responsibility of that minister to meddle in army affairs. There can be little doubt that these policies succeeded in making the army a reliable instrument in the hands of the King; but it is clear that the transformation of the army into a praetorian guard that had no essential connection with the society in which it lived worked in the end to the tragic disadvantage of Germany.

[120] Meisner, "Militärkabinett, Kriegsminister und Reichskanzler," pp. 102–3.

6. Relations Between Civilian and Military Authorities in the Second German Empire: Chancellor and Chief of Staff, 1871-1918

Alfred Vagts has written that "the natural tendency of armies is not only toward a self-government brooking no outside influences, but also toward the extension of their power beyond their own circles."[1] Whatever may be said of this as a general rule, it certainly applies with telling force to the army of the second German Empire. A large part of the energies of military administrators during the imperial period was devoted to the task of protecting the military establishment from any effective measure of civilian control—of maintaining the army, in the words of one of its leaders, as "an insulated body into which no one dare peer with critical eyes."[2] But at least as much effort was spent on attempts to extend military influence into spheres that are normally reserved, in western society at least, to civilian direction; and it was this activity that was the principal source of the frequent disputes between civilian and military authorities that characterized the history of the second Reich.

Behind this military aggrandizement was the unwritten assumption that the army, because it had won the victories which established the

"Relations Between Civilian and Military Authorities in the Second German Empire" was first read at the annual meeting of the American Historical Association, Chicago, December 1953.

[1] Alfred Vagts, *A History of Militarism* (New York, 1937), p. 320.

[2] Chief of Military Cabinet von Hahnke in 1895. See Fürst Chlodwig zu Hohenlohe-Schillingsfürst, *Denkwürdigkeiten der Reichskanzlerzeit* (Stuttgart, 1931), p. 116.

Empire, was the true embodiment of the national interest and that, consequently, soldiers were better qualified than civilians to determine what was good for the nation, not only in the military sphere proper, but in the field of domestic and foreign affairs as well. This assumption the civilian ministers of the period 1871–1918 opposed, but with steadily diminishing vigor and determination. The result was that the military establishment succeeded in subordinating all civilian policy-making agencies to its control, a process that was completed during the First World War.

That this victory was won by the soldiers is well known. The way in which it was achieved, the important contribution that even such a decided opponent of "political generals" as Bismarck made to the success of the military, and the constitutional issues raised in the civil-military conflict of the war years are perhaps less familiar. These things cannot be treated exhaustively in a short paper, but they can at least be illustrated by a consideration of the relations between the Chancellor and the Chief of the General Staff of the Army during the imperial period.

Even before the unification of Germany had been completed, there had been serious disputes between Chancellor and Chief of Staff over matters of competence and responsibility in policy matters; and Bismarck's clashes with Moltke during the wars of 1866 and 1870 have been the subject of an extensive literature.[3] At the risk of oversimplification, we can say that these differences stemmed from Moltke's insistence that, once mobilization for war had begun, "neither diplomatic negotiations nor political considerations should impede . . . military progress."[4] The Chief of Staff was capable of interpreting this to mean that such things as the determination of the scope of a war, the decision as to when it was advisable to treat with the enemy, and the formulation of peace terms were matters in which the soldiers should have the decisive voice. Bismarck, on the other hand, regarded these as essentially political questions that could not be decided by people like Moltke, whom he described, in a moment of irritation, as a "*verknöcherte Generalstabsmensch* who doesn't understand anything about politics."[5] "It is exactly as if I gave a lecture about placing a battery in this or that place," he

[3] See, for instance, Anneliese Klein-Wuttig, *Politik und Kriegführung in den deutschen Einigungskriegen* (*Abhandlungen zur mittleren und neueren Geschichte*, LXXV) (Berlin, 1934).

[4] Helmuth von Moltke, *Militärische Korrespondenz,* 1864, p. 16.

[5] Ernst Feder, ed., *Bismarcks grosses Spiel. Die geheimen Tagebücher Ludwig Bambergers* (Frankfurt-am-Main, 1932), p. 207.

said on another occasion;[6] and he complained to his wife that, "the military gentlemen make my work terrifically difficult for me. They lay their hands on it, and I have to bear the responsibility."[7]

Here, of course, was the nub of Bismarck's opposition. He insisted that he was the King's chief adviser and the man ultimately responsible for the success or failure of governmental action; therefore, as long as he was in office, his advice in political matters must be paramount. This was a constitutional theory which Moltke was not prepared to accept. When his differences with Bismarck came to a head in the acrimonious dispute over the nature of terms for the surrender of Paris in 1870, and when the King admitted that this was a matter in which Bismarck's views should prevail, the Chief of Staff sent a memorandum to the King:

> I believe [he wrote] that it would be a good thing to settle my relationship with the Federal Chancellor definitively. Up till now I have assumed that, especially in time of war, the Chief of the General Staff and the Federal Chancellor are equally competent and mutually independent agencies under the direct command of Your Royal Majesty.[8]

When one remembers that the General Staff was still, in 1870, a subordinate department of the Ministry of War, this is a remarkable statement. Even the grudging parenthetical modification "especially in time of war" does not weaken its force. It was a claim, in fact, to equality with the Chancellor in decisions of high policy; and, although the King apparently decided to disregard it,[9] the subsequent course of German history was to show that the General Staff was not convinced that he was right in doing so or that Moltke's claim was invalid.

In the long period of peace that followed the French war, for instance, the General Staff repeatedly challenged the Chancellor's authority in the field of foreign policy. The most notable examples of this occurred after 1890, and, because of this, it is sometimes assumed that the growth of military influence is attributable to the weakness of Bismarck's successors at the *Reichskanzlei* and the Foreign Office. There is, of course, some truth in this; but it should nevertheless be noted that, despite his clear record of opposition to military pretensions in the political sphere,

[6] Moritz Busch, *Tagebuchblätter* (Leipzig, 1899), I, 298.

[7] Bismarck, *Briefe an seine Gattin aus dem Kriege 1870/71* (Stuttgart, 1903), p. 54.

[8] Rudolf Stadelmann, *Moltke und der Staat* (Krefeld, 1950), pp. 434–38.

[9] The draft of the royal reply, which is in the files of the Military Cabinet, does not touch on the constitutional issue raised by Moltke. *Ibid.*, p. 505.

Bismarck himself must bear a major share of the responsibility for putting the General Staff in a position that would enable it to exert continuous influence in foreign policy. In the year 1883, the Chancellor actively supported an important reorganization of the army administration, which freed the General Staff from War Ministry control and, for the first time, granted its chief the privilege of having regular audiences with the Emperor in time of peace.

Considering the fact that Bismarck knew perfectly well that he was not loved in the *"Rote Bude"* on the Königsplatz, his assent to this important increase in the Chief of Staff's authority seems curious. It is, however, easily explicable, for it was a by-product of his growing concern over the course of events in the Reichstag.

Starting with the debate on the army budget in 1874, the opposition parties in the Reichstag had begun to indulge in attacks upon the military establishment that were unpleasantly reminiscent of the kind of thing that had gone on in the Prussian Chamber in the 1860's. The passage of the first Septennat bill was achieved with the greatest difficulty; before it was finally approved, the bill was angrily described by the Progressive leader Eugen Richter as "a restriction placed by absolutism on the parliamentary system" and "a bit of absolutism that will eat its way forward like a cancer."[10] At the beginning of the 1880's, assaults of this kind increased in number and violence. In January 1883, for instance, Richter, Ludwig Windthorst of the Center, the Socialist Georg Vollmar, and other deputies criticized the army command in scathing terms for excessive and unwise expenditure of public funds, citing such things as the outlay for cavalry regiments, the amount of money spent on military bands, and the pensioning off of officers at the so-called "majors' corner." Richter distinguished himself by a sarcastic fling at the Guard Regiments, which he described as "parade troops," unsuited to the conditions of modern war; and he and others raised the old issue of the three-year-service law, insisting that the stipulated term should be reduced.[11]

These attacks—concerned more with matters of command relationships, personnel policy, and the internal administration of the army than with strictly financial questions—struck Bismarck as an unwarranted interference with the royal power of command and as the beginning of a systematic attempt to widen the Reichstag's competence in military matters. The Chancellor was himself capable, when involved

[10] See Adalbert Wahl, *Deutsche Geschichte* (Stuttgart, 1928–36), I, 114; Erich Eyck, *Bismarck, Leben und Werk* (Zurich, 1943–44), III, 76.

[11] *Stenographische Berichte des Reichstages,* 1882–1883, III, 990 ff., 1016.

in dispute with army leaders, of threatening to join the parliamentary opposition and to impose effective controls on the army, but he never, of course, meant this seriously. As his conduct during the constitutional conflict of the 1860's showed, Bismarck was fully committed to the principle that the maintenance of monarchical government in Germany depended on the royal power of command being kept free of important restrictions, and he was always on the watch for new parliamentary attempts to accomplish what the Prussian liberals had failed to accomplish in the 1860's. The Chancellor, therefore—already worried by the growth of the opposition parties and the rise of socialism, and beginning, perhaps, to doubt the wisdom of the constitutional arrangements made in 1871—took the gravest possible view of the Reichstag outburst in 1883.

It is understandable, therefore, that he should have responded favorably when he was approached by General von Albedyll, the Chief of the Military Cabinet, with a proposal for relieving the parliamentary situation. The Albedyll plan involved, first, the dismissal of the present Minister of War, General von Kameke, an officer suspected by his professional colleagues and by the Chancellor of having liberal leanings. Bismarck had once said, with reference to Kameke, "A parliamentary general on active service is always a disagreeable phenomenon, but one as War Minister is dangerous";[12] and he readily agreed to use his influence to secure Kameke's dismissal. Albedyll suggested further that, before a new War Minister was appointed, the functions of the office be greatly reduced;[13] that all matters of personnel and officer selection be removed from the minister's supervision and vested in the Military Cabinet; and that the General Staff be freed completely from War Ministry control and made an independent agency immediately responsible to the Emperor. The justification given for the change was that it would remove from the sphere of parliamentary discussion all important matters of internal military administration and policy. Once he was shorn of his powers, the Minister of War—the only officer who regularly appeared before the Reichstag—could simply brush aside awkward parliamentary questions concerning personnel and command matters by stating that they lay outside his own field of competence. To all of this

[12] H. O. Meisner, "Militärkabinett, Kriegsminister und Reichskanzler zur Zeit Wilhelms I," *Forschungen zur brandenburgischen und preussischen Geschichte,* L (1938), 95.

[13] Albedyll had been trying to have this done since 1874. See R. Schmidt-Bückeburg, *Das Militärkabinett der preussischen Könige und deutschen Kaiser* (Berlin, 1933), p. 128.

Bismarck agreed—primarily, we must assume, because he believed it would hamper effective parliamentary debate of military matters and, to that extent at least, buttress the royal power of command.[14] The administrative reorganization, therefore, was effected in accordance with Albedyll's plan.

The fact that the reorganization of 1883 did not produce the parliamentary results expected by its authors need not concern us here; nor need we dwell on the unfortunate military results of a plan that represented, after all, a disruption of the administrative unity which the army had enjoyed since the days of Scharnhorst and Boyen. In the context of the present discussion, the importance of the change of 1883 was that it greatly increased the prestige and influence of the Chief of the General Staff and, by granting him the privilege of immediate access to the Emperor in peacetime, made him a potential competitor of the Chancellor in policy matters.

It is certainly more than coincidence that, within four years of the reorganization, Bismarck himself was faced with a very dangerous example of such competition in the field of foreign policy. In 1887, when the Chancellor was seeking a solution for the thorny Bulgarian crisis and was trying to avoid the possibility of an Austro-Russian war that would almost certainly involve Germany, he discovered that his efforts were being deliberately undercut by the military. At the height of the crisis, Alfred von Waldersee, Moltke's principal aide in the General Staff, sought to use his chief's influence to convince the Emperor of the necessity of war against Russia and, simultaneously, made indiscreet and provocative suggestions to the Austrian ambassador in Berlin. At the same time, the German military attaché in Vienna—presumably on Waldersee's advice—gave the Austrians the impression that a joint war against Russia was desired in Berlin and that his government would waive the restrictions on the *casus foederis* of the Dual Alliance of 1879 if the Austrians should decide to launch an attack. By prompt action, Bismarck was able to prevent these military plans from succeeding and to impress upon the Austrians that the treaty of 1879 was, and would remain, a strictly defensive engagement; but he was seriously disturbed by the meddling of the soldiers. In one of his notes to Vienna, he included a warning that may be taken as an indication of his awareness of the effects of the recent increase of the Chief of Staff's authority. "We must both take care," he wrote, "that the privilege of giving

[14] On Bismarck's motives, see H. O. Meisner, *Der Kriegsminister, 1814–1914* (Berlin, 1940), pp. 30–37, 64 ff., 93–104; and Schmidt-Bückeburg, *op. cit.*, pp. 129–30, 154–55.

political advice to our monarchs does not in fact slip out of our hands and pass over to the General Staffs."[15]

But power was in fact slipping out of the Chancellor's hands. The chief conclusion the soldiers drew from the crisis of 1887 seems to have been that the Chancellor had lost his ability to understand the realities of the European situation and that it would be better if they themselves were now permitted to decide what were the requirements of national interest. It was this that inspired Waldersee's ambitious attempts, especially after he had succeeded to Moltke's post in 1888, to free the military attachés in all capitals from their subordination to the civilian chiefs of mission and to transform them, in effect, into an independent diplomatic corps reporting directly to the Chief of Staff and the Emperor. This grandiose scheme also failed, thanks to the spirited opposition of Bismarck and his successor Caprivi; but it is nevertheless true that, in the subsequent period, staff officers serving as attachés abroad were encouraged to express political judgments and that these were often used to refute the opinions of the professionals in the diplomatic service and the Foreign Office.[16]

The Chiefs of Staff who followed Waldersee were neither as personally ambitious nor as willing to accept complete responsibility for the direction of German foreign policy as that officer had been. Yet—quite apart from the important fact, which cannot be elaborated here, that their activities in the field of operational planning had serious political repercussions and, by imposing a rigid war plan on the nation, limited the government's freedom of diplomatic action—both Schlieffen and the younger Moltke were capable of astonishing personal sallies into the domain of the Chancellor and the Foreign Minister. In 1905, for instance, Schlieffen persuaded himself that it was to the national interest to seize the opportunity offered by Russia's defeat at the hands of Japan to force war on France; and during the first Moroccan crisis, he and his intimate friend Holstein pursued that objective tenaciously, to the dismay of the Chancellor and the Emperor when they discovered, belatedly, the dangerous pass to which they had been brought.[17] The Chief of Staff's role in this affair seems, incidentally, to have been the primary cause of his fall in January 1906, and it is significant that the

[15] *Die Grosse Politik der Europäischen Kabinette,* 1871–1914, VI, 67.

[16] Gordon A. Craig, "Military Diplomats in the Prussian and German Service: The Attachés, 1816–1914," *Political Science Quarterly,* LXIV (1949), 82–93.

[17] See, *inter alia,* Peter Rassow, "Schlieffen und Holstein," *Historische Zeitschrift,* CLXXIII (1952), 302 ff., and Gordon A. Craig, *From Bismarck to Adenauer: Aspects of German Statecraft* (rev. ed.; New York, 1965), pp. 31–32.

Emperor, in announcing Schlieffen's retirement to his generals, went out of his way to add, "The Moroccan question has aroused the greatest tension in Germany and also in the army. I tell you here, however, that I shall never fight a war for the sake of Morocco."[18]

It would be going too far to interpret these words as a warning that politics was the domain of the Chancellor and the Foreign Minister. Even if they were intended as such, however, they had no effect. Schlieffen's successor, the younger Moltke, never doubted for a moment that in the major questions of foreign policy, he was a better judge of the national interest than the Chancellor or the other ministers; and, in 1909, he succeeded, where Waldersee had failed in 1887, in effecting a fundamental change in the treaty of 1879 by promising to support Austria in a war against Russia, even if it were caused by Austrian aggressive action. This commitment was made in a letter from Moltke to the Austrian Chief of Staff, Conrad von Hötzendorf; and, before sending it, Moltke showed it to the Emperor and the Chancellor. It is perhaps significant of the changed relationship between the Chancellor and the Chief of Staff that Bethmann-Hollweg was satisfied by this purely formal recognition of his authority and raised—as far as we can tell—no objections to the action itself or to the arguments of military expediency upon which it was based.[19]

In the final crisis of July 1914, Moltke dispensed even with the formalities he had observed in 1909. His famous telegram to Conrad on 30 July,[20] urging the Austrians to mobilize against Russia immediately, was dispatched without any attempt being made to inform the Chancellor, and it cut directly across Bethmann's efforts to hold the Austrians back. In the circumstances, Count Berchtold's startled query, "Who rules in Berlin, the Chancellor or the General Staff?" is understandable,[21] and it too may be taken as a commentary on the growing subordination of the Chancellor to the military leadership.

With the coming of the war, the claim that Moltke had made in 1870 —that the Chancellor and the Chief of Staff were equals—was simply taken for granted by the soldiers. In his memoirs, Ludendorff expresses it in somewhat different terms. With the outbreak of hostilities, he

[18] Generaloberst von Einem, *Erinnerungen* (Leipzig, 1933), p. 114.

[19] For the exchange of letters between Moltke and Conrad, see Feldmarschall Conrad, *Aus meiner Dienstzeit* (5 vols., Vienna, Berlin, 1921), I, 380–84, 631–34. On the significance of the commitment, see Bernadotte Schmitt, *The Coming of the War, 1914* (New York, 1930), I, 13–18; and, more recently, Luigi Albertini, *Le origini de la guerra del 1914,* I (Milan, 1942), 287–88.

[20] Conrad, *op. cit.,* IV, 152.

[21] *Ibid.,* IV, p. 153.

writes, "the Supreme Command became an agency which *shared responsibility* with the Chancellor [italics added]."[22] The first wartime Chancellor never consistently contested this claim. On occasion—in the submarine controversy, for instance—Bethmann could say: "This is a political matter for which I alone am constitutionally responsible, and I cannot hand it over to anyone else."[23] But he never backed this up with a willingness to resign if his responsibility were not recognized. Gradually, Bethmann drifted into the acceptance of a constitutional theory that would have been rejected out of hand by Bismarck: namely, that, even in political matters, the Supreme Command's views must be considered on the same level as his own and that, if there was a difference of opinion, the Emperor must decide. Given the character of the Emperor and his inclination to the military point of view, this meant that in crucial questions arguments of military expediency were generally given more weight than political considerations. Apart from that, it represented a complete surrender to the Moltke theory of 1870.

But Chief of Staff von Hindenburg and his aide Ludendorff were not content to stop there. In the July crisis of 1917, they claimed the right to demand the resignation of Chancellor Bethmann-Hollweg because of his views on policy matters—specifically, questions of war aims and internal political reform[24]—that, in Bismarck's time, were clearly recognized as lying within the Chancellor's sphere of competence; and, once Bethmann had fallen, they subsequently made good their right to nominate his successor.[25] This went far beyond anything the elder Moltke had claimed, and it amounted to an assertion of the army's right of final decision in all matters of policy. It altered fundamentally the relationship between the civilian military leadership of the state and, by its implicit limitation of the Emperor's right to choose and dismiss his ministers freely, struck a blow at the very foundations of the monarchical system.

One man at least recognized the seriousness of the issue raised by the July crisis. Arnold Wahnschaffe, Under Secretary of State in the *Reichskanzlei*, tried to persuade Ludendorff to deny publicly that he and Hindenberg had had anything to do with Bethmann-Hollweg's dismissal

[22] Erich Ludendorff, *Meine Kriegserinnerungen* (Berlin, 1920), p. 5.

[23] R. von Valentini, *Kaiser und Kabinettschef* (Oldenburg, 1931), p. 243.

[24] The interrelationship of these two questions, and the part they played in influencing the soldiers to force the dismissal of Bethmann-Hollweg, are discussed in Hans Gatzke, *Germany's Drive to the West* (Baltimore, Md., 1950).

[25] William II had never met Michaelis, who took Bethmann's place, and yielded to Hindenburg's recommendation. See Richard von Kühlmann, *Erinnerungen* (Heidelberg, 1948), pp. 501–2.

—a declaration he said was needed to counteract widespread rumors to the effect that the supreme command had made the Chancellor's position untenable by informing the party leaders that the war would be lost if he remained in office. Wahnschaffe insisted, somewhat disingenuously perhaps, that he himself did not believe the current rumors but that they would have the gravest possible consequences if they went unchecked. "Their effect continues and is growing," he wrote, "and it is a dangerous effect, seriously damaging the authority of the government and, indeed, threatening the stability of the state structure." Ludendorff refused to issue the desired *démenti* and, when Wahnschaffe proved persistent, turned the correspondence over to the new Chancellor. Michaelis, who was heart and soul on the side of the military, simply informed the Under Secretary that it would be unseemly for him to pursue the matter further.[26]

Thus, the constitutional issue was buried. Indeed, from this time until the end of the war, there was only one occasion when it was even dimly recognized that there was a constitutional question involved. In January 1918, disgusted by the moderate territorial demands made by the Foreign Minister, Kühlmann, in the negotiations at Brest-Litovsk, Hindenburg and Ludendorff resorted once more to the tactics they had employed successfully in July 1917. In letters to the Emperor and the Chancellor, Hindenburg intimated that Ludendorff and he were prepared to resign unless Kühlmann were dismissed and unless the position he had adopted at Brest-Litovsk were abandoned. In his memoirs, Kühlmann tells us that he and the current Chancellor, Hertling, decided that the time had come to make a stand against the soldiers. They persuaded the Emperor to write a letter to the Chief of Staff pointing out that he had overstepped the bounds of constitutional propriety, and enclosing a memorandum drafted by the two civilian leaders that discussed the relative responsibility of the civil and military leadership in political matters, stressing the final responsibility of the Chancellor.[27]

Kühlmann would have us believe that this was a victory for the principle of civilian dominance in politics. This is surely an exaggeration. It is true that the Foreign Minister was not dismissed; but, on the important issue concerning the terms to be offered to the Russians, the Chancellor and he were forced to yield to the supreme command's views,

[26] This episode is discussed, and the correspondence reproduced, in *Das Werk des Untersuchungsausschusses der Deutschen Verfassunggebenden Nationalversammlung und des Deutschen Reichstages 1919–1926. Die Ursachen des Deutschen Zusammenbruches im Jahre 1918,* Series Four, II, 34–38.

[27] Kühlmann, *op. cit.,* pp. 538–42.

as the provisions of the Treaty of Brest-Litovsk showed clearly. Moreover, Kühlmann himself gained only a momentary respite. Five months later, when he made remarks in the Reichstag in opposition to the soldiers' views on how the war was to be ended, the supreme command demanded his head by flatly refusing to have any further communication with him; and this time, neither the Chancellor nor the Emperor could save him.

So much for the Emperor's constitutional lecture to the soldiers. If it has any importance, that document can be considered as a very belated attempt to clarify the relationship between the civilian and military leadership of the state—a relationship that had never been made clear at the time of the foundation of the Empire[28] and had become even less so as a result of the administrative arrangements of 1883 and the increasingly successful intervention of military authorities in the field of policy formulation in the prewar years. There was no possibility that such a clarification would be successful at this late date in persuading the General Staff to change its ways, certainly not after so many concessions had been made by the civilians to the philosophy that the army was the best judge of the national interest.

[28] See Gerhard Ritter, "Das Problem des Militarismus in Deutschland," *Historische Zeitschrift,* CLXXVI (1954), 19.

7. The Impact of the German Military on the Political and Social Life of Germany During World War II

If one compares the position of the German military during the First World War with that which it occupied during the Second, it is readily apparent that so marked a diminution of influence had taken place in the latter case that it is virtually impossible to speak of the military having an appreciable "impact" on the political and social life of Germany during the years 1939–45. During the first world conflict, the projection of military authority into nonmilitary spheres was remarkable. Not only did the high command assume the power of decision-making on the national level, virtually ending the normal functioning of cabinet and Reichstag, but it took on extensive powers of local government as well, administering the German states through the *Generalkommandos* and other army headquarters. In addition, as Albrecht Mendelssohn Bartholdy has pointed out,[1] the military controlled other areas that profoundly affected the social activity and attitudes of the German people—economic production, allocation of strategic materials and staples, food distribution, labor policy, public information, censorship, to mention only the most important. Wilhelm Groener, who was later head of the all-embracing *Kriegsamt,* wrote in 1916: "The uniform counts more among us now than the black coat of the civilian, and the cry of dictatorship by the military is raised on every side."

In the war of 1939–45, the picture was markedly different. Instead of

"The Impact of the German Military" was read at the Twelfth International Congress of Historical Sciences, Vienna, September 1965. It is reprinted from Comité International des Sciences Historiques, XIIe Congrès International des Sciences Historiques, *Rapports–IV. Méthodologie et Histoire Contemporaine.*

[1] Albrecht Mendelssohn Bartholdy, *The War and German Society* (New Haven, 1937), p. 111.

the military assuming civilian functions at the outset of the war, the reverse occurred, and the administration of the home front passed under the control of the *Gauleiter* of the Nazi Party, who—with the imposing title of *Reichsverteidigungskommissaren*—arrogated to themselves responsibilities normally reserved in wartime for soldiers, including the raising, training, and even (in the case of the *Volkssturm* in 1945) the command of reserves. Instead of controlling war production and armaments—as Defense Minister von Blomberg had, in the first years of the National Socialist regime, hoped might be possible through the agency of a centralized *Reichsverteidigungsrat* under military supervision—the soldiers were gradually deprived of even advisory functions in the field of economic mobilization and were forced to look on while responsibility for arms production was vested first in the Todt organization and later in that of Albert Speer. Instead of having the kind of social influence that results from the exercise of wartime police powers, manpower controls, and propaganda direction, the army leadership was incapable of retaining control over these activities even within the areas in which the armed forces conducted their operations and, in the end, even within the ranks of the armed forces themselves. Increasingly as the war went on, police and security functions, manpower allocation, psychological mobilization and ideological indoctrination, at home and at the front, in civilian society and in the army itself, were taken over by Party organizations. In September 1943, Josef Goebbels wrote: "The Führer is totally opposed to the Wehrmacht engaging in tasks that are not germane to it. . . . He wants not only to make changes in propaganda [management] but also to take from the Wehrmacht all economic, legal, and social-security questions. The Wehrmacht is to limit itself to conducting the war in a military sense and to leave everything else to civilians."[2] Long before those words were written, the sovereignty of the military even in the strictly operational sphere had been severely diminished; and, within the year that followed that entry in Goebbels' diary, Heinrich Himmler was telling an assembly of *Gauleiter* that the last vestiges of the authority of the old military leadership was about to be destroyed and that a new National Socialist *Volksarmee* under Party command was in the making. "The task which the Führer has given me is to reorganize the army from the ground up, and he intends to place it bit by bit in my hands!"[3]

[2] *The Goebbels Diaries, 1942–1943,* edited, translated, and with an introduction by Louis P. Lochner (New York, 1948), p. 476.

[3] Heinrich Himmler, speech of 3 August 1944, in *Vierteljahrshefte für Zeitgeschichte,* III (1953), 363 ff.

The process by which the army—which had always been as much an *Ordnungsfaktor,* a shaping and stabilizing force in political and social life, as it had been a purely military instrument—was brought to this sorry pass has been analyzed by a number of scholars, notably Gerhard Ritter, Wolfgang Sauer, and Thilo Vogelsang, and it is reasonably well known. Briefly speaking, the military—that is, the upper leadership of the army, which recognized and sought to maintain what they considered to be the traditional and legitimate prerogatives and responsibilities of their service—were the victims of their own fears and frustrations and of the political skill (or what Rauschning called the "tactical virtuosity") of the man who became Reich Chancellor on 30 January 1933.

By the beginning of the 1930's, the military—perhaps more subconsciously than explicitly—were longing for a return to the security of an earlier age in which military organization, military techniques of leadership and military thinking had served more or less as models for political life. In addition, as leaders of an establishment charged with the national security, they quite openly yearned for a regime that would give political stability to a nation that had long been deprived of it and would be able to mobilize the national energies in such a way that the country would no longer be vulnerable to external pressure or attack. Such a regime would hopefully close the gap that presently yawned between the German people and its armed establishment. It would also, the military hoped, obviate the necessity of a continuation of the active part played by soldiers in German politics since the days of Hans von Seeckt. This dabbling in politics, described most recently and most satisfactorily by Francis L. Carsten,[4] had gone so far by the early 1930's that Wilhelm Groener could say, apparently with satisfaction, that no political decision could now be made in Germany without the army being consulted. Unfortunately, the kind of political intervention professed by Generals Groener and Schleicher neither brought viable solutions to Germany's problems nor contributed to the domestic peace; it merely involved the military in a frustrating and apparently endless process of party manipulation and intrigue. By 1933 they wished at almost any cost to escape from this involvement.

It was the intensity of this desire that accounted for their uncritical acceptance of Hitler's promises in 1933 and their willing collaboration with him until at least 1938. In different circumstances, one might have expected some of them at least to have been suspicious of the alacrity with which the new Chancellor—in his first programmatic statement to

[4] Francis L. Carsten, *Reichswehr und Politik, 1918–1933* (Cologne, 1964).

his army commanders—took them at their word and the firmness with which he asserted that they would indeed be as completely excluded from politics as they seemed to desire. The Wehrmacht, Hitler said on 3 February 1933, was to remain "unpolitical and above party. The fight on the home front was not their affair, but that of the Nazi organizations."[5] The military's tacit acceptance of this denial of the army's traditional role as *Ordnungsfaktor* (which is to be explained perhaps by the fact that they were distracted by Hitler's promise in the same speech to restore universal military service and to inspire the nation's youth and the people as a whole with a will to defend their country) implied a willingness to remain passive while Hitler established a personal dictatorship by whatever means he chose. And, indeed, the army did stand *Gewehr bei Fuss* during the creation of the totalitarian state in 1933 and during the purge of June 1934; and, in the subsequent period, its leaders allowed themselves to become so absorbed in the labors incidental to the implementation of the service law of March 1935 that they could claim that they had no time for political and social problems. The result of their attitude was that Hitler was enabled to secure his own position and to prepare the way for the *Gleichschaltung* of the army that was inaugurated with the Blomberg-Fritsch affair in 1938 and completed during the war years.

All of this, as noted above, has been frequently described and presents no serious problems for the historian. What has attracted less attention and analysis is the precise nature of the dilemma that confronted the military when the scales fell from their eyes in 1938 and that continued to confound them when their country went to war in the following year. One way of describing this would be to say that the most reflective of the army leaders belatedly admitted the irresponsibility of their collaboration with Hitler and realized that they were now caught between a total mobilization of society, which went beyond the limits of anything they had ever considered desirable and which they regarded as potentially disastrous for Germany, and a progressive diminution of their own actual or potential ability either to control it or to oppose it effectively.

Even soldiers who in 1933 had favored a mobilization of the vital forces of the nation and a re-awakening of its *Wehrwille* were appalled by the forms assumed by Hitler's brand of total mobilization, and their objections were of three kinds. In the first place, it was clear by 1938 that *totale Mobilmachung* was motivated not by a desire to strengthen

[5] A précis of the statement is to be found in *Vierteljahrshefte für Zeitgeschichte*, II (1954), 434–36.

the defenses of the country but actually by a determination to go to war; and, after hostilities began in 1939, the absence of a rational war plan or of clearly defined political objectives indicated that Germany had been led into an ever-expanding total conflict fought for the sake of war itself. In the second place, it was a mobilization that even before 1939 strained Germany's economic resources and that, once war began and the strain increased, came to rest on the fallacy, described by Wolfgang Sauer, of believing that material deficiencies in wartime could be offset indefinitely by psychological means and efforts of the will.[6] Finally, the most thoughtful of the military leaders saw that it was a form of mobilization that pandered to the worst instincts of the German people, awakened their basest ambitions, and tended to stultify their critical capacity and brutalize their behavior. It was a policy designed to do precisely what General Adam had warned against as early as 1933, "to make the people drunk with fanfares."[7] For all these reasons it promised to be a disastrous policy and must be stopped. We must, argued General Ludwig Beck before the war and in talks to private groups after it had begun, resist theories of total mobilization and total war which will inevitably involve us in "wars of long duration, of expanding scope, of increasing lack of scruple in the choice of means, of self-intensifying feelings of hatred and revenge—in short, the degeneration of warfare into a condition of ever increasing human misery . . . destruction and barbarity."[8]

But could the military, particularly after 1939, hope to check the headlong course of the man who had long since consolidated his position as dictator of the country and supreme commander of its armed forces?

In the discussions of this question of military resistance to Hitler that have taken place in Germany since 1945, the emphasis has usually been placed on the legal and moral issues involved and upon such problems as the responsibility of military commanders to civil authority and to their own troops, the soldiers' right to resistance, and the much controverted question of the validity of the officers' oath of allegiance to the Führer. Recently, however, the American scholar George Romoser has rightfully insisted that there is another dimension to the question

[6] Karl Dietrich Bracher, Wolfgang Sauer, and Gerhard Schulz, *Die nationalsozialistische Machtergreifung* (Cologne, 1960), p. 808.

[7] Gerhard Meinck, *Hitler und die deutsche Aufrüstung* (Wiesbaden, 1959), p. 8.

[8] "Die Lehre vom totalen Krieg," in Ludwig Beck, *Studien* (Hans Speidel, ed.) (Stuttgart, 1955).

and that the dilemma of the military was essentially political in nature. The question was less whether they had the right to oppose the Führer than whether they had the power, and this in turn depended upon the degree of popular support they could count on if and when they struck. The military's doubts about this had a profound influence on the history and the tactics of the resistance movement.[9]

Hitler's military opponents, and the civilian leaders who felt as they did, might seek to convince themselves that the *militärfrommes Volk* would not merely support an attempt on their part to stop Hitler's disastrous course but would *expect* them to make such an attempt—this was Beck's argument in 1937, and Carl Goerdeler was repeating it as late as 1943[10]—but they never really believed it, especially after the war had started. The impact they had once been able to make on German political life and attitudes and their own institutional prestige had suffered from their long collaboration with the dictator and from their failure on many critical occasions to protest against his actions. They had been associated with Hitler too long to expect that a break with him now would be understood by the mass of the people. This was particularly true in wartime, for the German people had succumbed to the kind of drunkenness that General Adam had feared. In June 1940, Fritz Lehmann wrote in his diary that, if the people had been thoughtful and worried in September 1939, "the fanfares of victory are now drowning out every word of criticism and any thought of concern over the future."[11] As long as this mood lasted, resistance by the military could not hope for popular backing.

But there was no indication that this mood would change significantly as the war proceeded, even when the first victories were followed by defeats in Africa and Russia; and, in any event, the increasingly effective control of the *Gauleiter* over the civil sector prevented any real communication between the military and the masses. On those rare occasions when differences between the military and the Führer became public property, the propaganda ministry was skillful in intimating to the public that these signs of opposition were the result of defeatism, aristocratic reaction, and inability on the part of the military leaders to understand

[9] George K. Romoser, "The Politics of Uncertainty," *Social Research,* XXXI (1964), 73 ff.

[10] Wolfgang Förster, *Ein General kämpft gegen den Krieg: Aus nachgelassene Papiere des Generalstabschefs Ludwig Beck* (Munich, 1949), p. 103; Gerhard Ritter, *Carl Goerdeler und die deutsche Widerstandsbewegung* (Stuttgart, 1955), p. 353.

[11] Fritz Lehmann, *1939–1945: Beobachtungen und Bekenntnisse* (Hamburg, 1946), p. 40.

the revolutionary dynamism of the National Socialist movement. Goebbels' agency succeeded to a surprising extent in turning military doubts into Party assets. In May 1943, Hans-Georg von Studnitz confided to his diary that the waning of military influence had been promoted by the contrast between the skepticism of the professional soldiers and the confidence of the Party leaders at the outset of war in 1939. "The *Blitzkriege* and *Blitzsiege* seemed to prove that the Party was right in contrast to the army. . . . When the military picture changed during the two eastern-war winters, the position of the Party was already so strong that the idea could be spread among the people that it was the army that had failed. The army's prestige began to sink. The same Party that had known how to profit from the lightening victories of the first years now knew how to distance itself from the defeats."[12]

The doubts and hesitations that affected the military conspirators in 1944 were attributable in large part to the realization that they had so far lost contact with the German people that they could not hope for popular understanding and must expect to be regarded as traitors, as defeatists, and as men who had lost all contact with the political and social aspirations of the German people. That they were correct in their prognosis was shown after 20 July 1944 by the readiness with which the official Party explanation of the events of that day was accepted by the common people. "Hitler is all of a sudden the man of the people again," wrote one contemporary observer, "for whom even former . . . Marxists discovered some sympathy at the moment when he was on the point of being liquidated by 'generals and monarchists,' by 'aristocrats' as they are now called. 'An attack on the Führer is a scoundrelly act . . . naturally, the aristocrats . . . they want to have the monarchy back again!' "[13]

A month before the attempt on Hitler's life, Major General Henning von Tresckow said to Count Stauffenberg: "The *attentat* must succeed, *coûte que coûte*. . . . It is no longer a matter of its practicality, but a matter of demonstrating to the world and before history that the resistance movement dared the decisive gamble. Beside that, everything else is a matter of indifference."[14] This appeal to posterity, born of resignation, tempts one to raise a final point here. If it is true that the impact of the military upon the political and social life of Germany in the Second World War was, for the reasons given above, minimal, it may

[12] Hans-Georg von Studnitz, *Als Berlin brannte* (Stuttgart, 1963), p. 71.

[13] Joachim Günther, *Das letzte Jahr: Mein Tagebuch, 1944/45* (Hamburg, 1948), p. 203.

[14] Ritter, *op. cit.*, p. 390.

be equally true that—thanks to their action on 20 July 1944—they have had, and are having, a delayed but beneficial impact on the political and social life of the Federal Republic of our own day. But that is a complex and still open question and one which, in any case, lies within the province of the contemporary political analyst rather than that of the historian.

PART THREE

DIPLOMACY

8. Neutrality in the Nineteenth Century

I

In April 1630, at the height of the Thirty Years' War, the Swedish King Gustavus Adolphus landed with his armies on the shores of Pomerania and prepared to march in the direction of the Elbe to meet and attack the imperial forces of Ferdinand II of Austria. Desiring to preserve his lines of communication and to assure himself of a certain means of withdrawal to the coast, Gustavus was anxious to persuade the Kurfürst of Brandenburg to enter the war on his side. The Kurfürst, however, wanted to remain neutral and sent envoys to Gustavus' headquarters to explain this to him. The Swedish King attempted to reason with them, pointing out, among other things, that the conflict presently raging was one of conflicting religious faiths, that unless the Emperor were checked he might extirpate the Protestant religion in all northern Germany, and that this design could be thwarted only by armed cooperation against him. The Brandenburg envoys listened but remained true to their instructions and repeated their prince's desire to remain uninvolved in the war.

The Swedish King's patience was finally exhausted and he gave way to a characteristic explosion of wrath. "For God's sake," he cried, "think things over a bit and fasten upon *mascula consilia*. . . . I for my part cannot turn back, *jacta est alea, transivimus Rubiconem*. One thing I tell you plainly: I don't want to know or hear anything about any neutrality. His Highness must be either friend or foe. When I come to the border, he is going to have to blow hot or cold. God and the Devil are fighting here. If His Highness wants to stand on God's side, good!

"Neutrality in the Nineteenth Century" was first read at a Princeton University Conference on Neutralism and Neutrality in March 1959.

Then let him join me. If he prefers to stand by the Devil, then, in truth, he is going to have to fight with me. *Tertium non dabitur,* that is certain."

At this point, one of the Brandenburgers interjected the suggestion that there were certain advantages to having a few neutrals around; they were useful in ending conflicts by mediation. This increased the King's fury. "Such a thing is nothing but pure *Quisquiliae,* which the wind lifts and blows away. *Was ist doch das für ein Ding: Neutralität?* I don't understand it."[1]

These words are interesting not only because they are a fine example of the tumultuous style of Sweden's greatest king. In them we find, although very compressed, some of the criticisms of neutrality made most frequently by belligerent powers: namely, that the neutral attitude is unmanly and disqualifies the state adopting it for serious consideration as a power of substance; that neutrality is militarily inconvenient for those who have crossed Rubicons and hence cannot be tolerated by them; that it is immoral for failing to recognize the religious and ideological issues at stake in whatever war is going on at the moment; and that, for reasons unnecessary to explain, it makes no sense.

Throughout the course of western history, these sentiments have been expressed by many persons who found themselves in Gustavus' position. Something like them is to be found on the lips of the Athenian commissioners to Melos of whom Thucydides tells, who were so exasperated by the Melians' desire to "be friends to you and foes to neither party" that "they betook themselves to hostilities" and "put to death all the grown men whom they took, and sold the women and children for slaves." Many years later, Napoleon Bonaparte was making Gustavian speeches to representatives of the Republic of Venice, when they were seeking—timorously and, as events showed, fruitlessly—to remain neutral in the war between France and the Austrian Empire, and was telling the Swiss, as his Swedish predecessor had told the Brandenburgers, that their neutrality was something he could not understand.[2] Some of Gustavus' arguments may have stirred in the mind of Horatio Nelson when he took his ships into the harbor of Copenhagen in 1801 and destroyed a neutral fleet that was proving to be an inconvenience to

[1] Johannes Paul, *Gustav Adolf* (Leipzig, 1930), II, 180–81.

[2] In 1809, when the Swiss wanted an explicit recognition of their neutrality from him, Napoleon is reported to have said: "Vis-à vis de moi, cette neutralité est un mot vide de sens qui ne vous sert qu'autant que je le veux." Edgar Bonjour, *Swiss Neutrality: Its History and Meaning* (trans. Mary Hottinger) (London, 1946), p. 47.

his country; and Gustavus' fury at the idea of a neutral intervening to adjudicate conflicts and end war was shared completely by Adolf Hitler, who told his generals in August 1939 that the only thing he feared was that some *Schweinehund* might try to mediate the pending conflict.[3] In our own day and our own country, some of Gustavus' arguments have been found useful by high administration spokesmen, when they have been asked to comment on the role of neutrals in the cold war.

But more important than these individual repetitions is the fact that the reprobation of neutrals which inspired Gustavus' statement has enjoyed the general approval of society (or at least that part of organized society which thinks about politics) from the Middle Ages until very recent times, with the exception of one interesting interval; and that this highly critical view of neutrals has come once more, in our own day, to represent the thinking of a great many people. It is precisely because so many people today seem to believe that international politics should be conducted according to the principle of Falstaff's friend the Ancient Pistol—who cried "Under which king, Bezonian? Speak or die!"—that it may be well to remind ourselves that there was a time, and not so very long ago, when this was not so. The nineteenth century was an age in which neutrality was regarded as a status that any country had a right to claim when other states went to war, and the wartime rights of those who did so received better protection in the nineteenth century than in earlier periods.[4] Moreover, the existence of nations which were *permanently* aloof from foreign combinations and conflicts—which were, if you will, neutralist, as the United States and Sweden were, for instance, by choice, and Switzerland and Belgium, by treaty stipulation—was not necessarily so offensive in the eyes of other powers as it sometimes seems to be, in certain quarters, today.

II

There were a number of reasons why this was so, but I shall mention only four, and the first of them has to do with the nature of Great Power politics in the nineteenth century. During the greater part of the period that stretched from the fall of Napoleon to the beginning of the First World War, Europe was still—in Mazzini's phrase—the lever that moved the world; the five Great European Powers held the center of the world's stage; and the interests, rights, and even liberties of other

[3] See Alan Bullock, *Hitler, A Study in Tyranny* (New York, 1953), p. 483.
[4] J. L. Brierly, *The Outlook for International Law* (Oxford, 1944), p. 25.

states and peoples, inside Europe and out, were necessarily affected by, and dependent on, the actions of their more powerful neighbors. It was fortunate for those interests, rights, and liberties that the relations of the Great Powers with each other were characterized neither by unity of view on basic issues nor by the kind of divisiveness that leads to the formation of permanent and monolithic leagues of powers. After 1815, there was nothing resembling an effective system of collective security among the Great Powers (although something of the sort was tried); nor was there anything like the contraposition of the NATO and Warsaw pacts of our own time (at least, not until the century was drawing to its end).[5] For lesser states in general, and for those who professed the neutral attitude in particular, this was fortunate.

Probably the closest the Great Powers ever came to complete harmony was in the days of the Holy Alliance, immediately after 1815, when the Russian Tsar, supported by Prince Metternich of Austria, was attempting to establish a kind of Great Power collective-security system directed against the forces of revolution. That this never materialized was largely due to the attitude of Great Britain, whose government made it clear that a country with representative institutions could not permit its future policy to be determined by abstract principles derived from current ideological struggles.[6] If Britain had not taken that stand, and if the Holy Alliance had become an effective combination, the outlook would have been dark for any country that desired to remain neutral, let us say, in a conflict between a deputized force of that Alliance and another suspected of harboring revolutionary movements. How true this is is shown by the fact that, in the years before Britain had made her position clear, the neutrality of Switzerland was repeatedly violated by the Austrian Government in the name of the Great Powers, on the grounds that the Swiss were giving aid and comfort to subversive movements in the German states and that their press was showing sympathy for Italian patriots in Austrian jails. A Swiss historian has written that, while it lasted, "the Holy Alliance led to infringements of Swiss sovereignty and a disregard of Swiss neutrality such as had only been experienced under [Napoleon]."[7]

[5] One cannot speak of a Triple Entente opposing a Triple Alliance until 1907, when the Anglo-Russian agreement was concluded, and the Triple Entente was anything but monolithic.

[6] See Castlereagh's State Paper of 5 May 1820 in H. W. V. Temperley and Lilian M. Penson, eds., *Foundations of British Foreign Policy, 1792–1902* (Cambridge, 1938), pp. 60–61.

[7] Bonjour, *op. cit.,* p. 20.

When Great Britain finally withdrew from her association with the states of the Holy Alliance in the early 1820's, George Canning said jubilantly, "The time for Areopagus and the like of that is gone by. . . . Every nation for itself and God for us all."[8] While not entirely accurate, this is not a bad description of the way the Great Power system worked for the greater part of the century. The Great Powers pursued their interests, sometimes alone, sometimes in combination, competing, balancing, finding and changing partners. The combinations formed were generally adventitious; the explicit long-term alliance was not sought after until the 1870's, and there was no real tendency on the part of the Great Powers to divide into permanent coalitions until even later. What seemed to be a clear-cut division of Europe in the 1830's between the three reactionary powers (Russia, Prussia, and Austria) and the two liberal powers (Britain and France) was more apparent than real—Russia and Britain, for instance, finding it quite possible, despite their different political philosophies, to cooperate effectively in the 1830's and 1840's.[9] The absence of real blocs meant that there was no competition for new adherents to them, with the danger that such competition necessarily brings to states of neutral inclination.

In general, then, it may be said that the rivalry of the Great Powers, and the constantly changing pattern of their relations with each other, worked to the advantage of neutral states, making a combined Great Power assault upon their liberties unlikely and rendering even unilateral infringements a matter of calculation and risk for the violator.

A second reason for the relatively strong position of neutrals in the nineteenth century was a new acceptance of war as a natural and legitimate activity of the state, a political act rather than one vested with theological significance. The old distinction between the just and the unjust war, which had been dominant among theorists until the eighteenth century and which influenced political thought on many levels, now gave way to the idea that the justice of a war, if not irrelevant, was certainly incapable of easy determination by others than the one precipitating it, and that wars are better viewed as natural methods of pursuing state interest.

If all nations are free, independent, and equal, wrote Emerich de Vattel, an eighteenth-century theorist much admired and much quoted in

[8] Walter Alison Phillips, *The Confederation of Europe* (2d ed.; London, 1920), p. 264.

[9] Gordon A. Craig, "The System of Alliances and the Balance of Power," *The New Cambridge Modern History*, X (Cambridge, 1960), 246 ff.

the nineteenth, then they have "the same right to the pursuit of their pretensions, without regard to the intrinsic justice of their conduct, of which others have no right to form a definitive judgement."[10] If a nation resorts to war in pursuit of its interests, "we are not entitled to complain of it as a violator of the law of nations." *"Regular war, as to its effects, is to be accounted just on both sides."*[11] Canning's "Every nation for itself and God for us all" seems only a gloss on Vattel; and the Darwinians, later in the century, did little but put this idea in less inhibited and more popular language.

This change of view had both theoretical and practical consequences. Theoretically, it strengthened the legal case for the protection of neutral rights in wartime; for if states can resort to force without worrying about the justice or injustice of their cause, it must be recognized that third powers have an absolute right to remain aloof and to refuse to declare themselves one way or another on the issues involved in the dispute.[12] Practically, it will be clear that statesmen who thought about war as Vattel did were not likely to conduct the wars they engaged in as crusades and to regard neutrals as criminals, but to fight for definite objectives, hoping meanwhile to limit the conflict in duration and scope. All of Bismarck's wars were limited wars, in which he tried not to bring the neutrals in but to keep them out; and most of the long list of nineteenth-century wars were localized conflicts in which the neutrals, by and large, fared well.

A third reason for the strengthening of neutral rights in the nineteenth century was the great influence that the doctrines of classical liberalism exerted on the thinking of the time. The almost mystical reverence which liberals had for the flow of commerce, as well as their insistence that government should not be permitted to smother the individualism of its citizens, undoubtedly contributed to the clarification and the observance of the rights of neutrals in maritime war. Charles de Visscher has pointed out that it was the liberal traditions of individualism and *laissez-faire* that made possible the famous distinction, or double distinction, in the so-called Rules of Washington of 1871—first, between the acts of a government and those of its nationals, and second, between the private acts a neutral government must forbid and those in relation to which it need only withdraw its diplomatic protection from their

[10] Vattel, *Le Droit de gens,* Prél., § 21.
[11] *Ibid.,* Book. III, chapter 12, § 190.
[12] Nicolas Politis, *Neutrality and Peace* (trans. Francis Crane Macken) (Washington, D.C., 1935), p. 14.

authors.[13] In its time, this distinction was celebrated for bringing a new precision and authority to neutral rights and—until the coming of the First World War—it was generally respected.

Finally, the whole conception of neutrality was profoundly influenced by the existence outside of the European system of powers of a young but vigorous nation, free from the weight of European traditions, with ideas and interests of its own, and with a firm determination to protect its recently won independence from the dangers of involvement in European wars. This was the United States, the greatest of the nineteenth-century neutrals.

Nicolas Politis has written that "in its final form, neutrality [that is, the theory of law and neutrality] bears very clearly the American imprint."[14] From the Napoleonic period—when, conscious of the dangers of her position, the United States took an almost exaggerated view of the duties of neutrals[15]—until the coming of the First World War, American thinking about neutrality advanced along two lines: first, that neutral states were to be unmolested by belligerents, provided they stood absolutely aloof, acted impartially, and gave military aid to neither side; and, second, that neutral *individuals* were to be interfered with by belligerents as little as possible and to be allowed maximum possible freedom to maintain relations with both sides.[16] The United States' known willingness to fight for these rights as they applied to herself (and perhaps her possession of a hostage from the world's greatest naval power, in the shape of Canada) enabled her to win recognition of these rights in the nineteenth century; and this helped consolidate the laws of neutrality generally. The American Neutrality Act of 1794 served as a model for the English Foreign Enlistment Acts of 1819 and 1870 as well as for other national legislation; American views of the rights of neutral nationals were enshrined in the Rules of Washington; and American influence was pronounced in the general codification of the law of neutrality at the Second Hague Peace Conference of 1907.[17]

In this listing of the factors that worked to the advantage of neutral states in the nineteenth century, there should be no suggestion that neutrality or neutralism was without risk or that it did not have to be

[13] Charles de Visscher, *Theory and Reality in Public International Law* (trans. P. E. Corbett) (Princeton, N.J., 1957), p. 48. See also Politis, *op. cit.*, p. 20.

[14] *Ibid.*, p. 19.

[15] André Fugier, *La révolution française et l'empire napoléonienne* (Paris, 1954), p. 364.

[16] Brierly, *op. cit.*, p. 27.

[17] Politis, *op. cit.*, pp. 19, 27.

paid for, one way or another. The most reliable protection of neutral status, then as now, was, not the codification of laws or the influence of liberalism or even the way the balance of power worked, but rather strength and geographical isolation.[18] Nor were these by themselves always enough, for neutrality or neutralism could prove dangerous even to Great Powers. The classical example is Austria, which was made to pay for an ill-conducted neutrality during the Crimean War with the loss of all international sympathy or support when she was at war with France and Piedmont three years later.[19] The example of Great Britain might also be cited, for when she adopted a policy of aloofness from European entanglements in 1864 and subsequently remained neutral in the wars of 1866 and 1870, she was forced to watch the destruction of the territorial balance her statesmen had helped devise and Russia's unilateral repudiation of a treaty which British soldiers had fought and died to establish only fifteen years earlier.

Permanent neutrality, legal or voluntary, was, moreover, bought with a price. This price varied, but at the minimum, it was a somewhat reduced status in the eyes of more active powers. One could be safe and prosperous and happy as a Sweden or a United States, but one could not, at the same time, expect to be treated as a Great Power. One could not demand respect and deference and the right to be consulted on all major decisions of the European Concert, if it were known that one would not accept or share the responsibility of seeing that those decisions were carried out, by force if necessary. That is why some Europeans found President Theodore Roosevelt's intervention in the negotiations that resolved the first Moroccan crisis so comic and so irritating.[20] The neutral attitude, in short, did not give a nation a claim to very extravagant influence in the chancellories of the world.

As long as it recognized these things, however, a state had an absolute right to choose neutrality for itself, and there was no moral reprobation attached to its doing so. When Austria won the universal disapprobation of the other powers in the years 1854–56, it was not because she did not fight on either side but because she was never properly neutral. The Russians were alienated by Austrian troop dispositions that were clearly directed against them, and the western Allies were estranged by the fact that the Austrians had promised to enter the war on their side, and had actually signed a treaty to that effect, but had

[18] Hans Morgenthau, *Dilemmas of Politics* (Chicago, 1958), p. 191.

[19] See Josef Redlich, *Emperor Francis Joseph* (New York, 1929), pp. 161 ff.

[20] Harold Nicolson, *Portrait of a Diplomatist* (new ed.; New York, 1939), pp. 142–43.

never made the pledge good. Far from being considered immoral, neutrals were often, for some reason—Brierly suggests because of American propaganda[21]—regarded as of finer clay than belligerents, nobler, more worthy of protection.

III

None of this, of course, was destined to last, and the very years in which the laws of neutrality were being consolidated and codified, the last quarter of the century, were years in which the forces were gathering that were to change the picture completely. The flexibility and variability that characterized Great Power relations in the first part of the century disappeared. The 1880's saw the beginning of the competition for allies; in the 1890's, two coalitions were already formed; and by the first decade of the new century those leagues, now embracing all of the Great Powers, were beginning to exert pressure on the neutrals to declare themselves one way or another.

This development was prompted by the greater anxieties of international relations and especially by the greater speed of military operations, which made permanent combinations seem necessary.[22] This latter factor also promised an ill future for neutrals. When the German General Staff perfected its plans for a possible war against France (the so-called Schlieffen Plan, 1905 version), it decided that, because of the premium that must be placed on proper deployment and speed of advance, Germany could no longer have "blind trust in the sacredness of neutrality" but must violate Belgium's neutral status "in accordance with the law of necessity."[23] This decision, implemented in 1914, marked the beginning of a new sacrifice of neutral rights to military expediency.

Simultaneously, the much discussed, defined, and codified neutral right to trade in wartime had been undermined in the last years of the century by the waning of economic liberalism, the growth of neo-mercantilism, and the consequent blurring of the distinction between state and individual action in the economic sphere. The expansion of war in the direction of totality and the increased attention it was to pay to the economic supply lines of the enemy were soon to complete the

21 Brierly, *op. cit.*, p. 28.

22 See William L. Langer, *European Alliances and Alignments, 1871–90* (2d ed.; New York, 1950), pp. 5–6.

23 Gerhard Ritter, *Der Schlieffenplan: Kritik eines Mythos* (Munich, 1956), pp. 81–82.

process of making neutral trading rights unreal and insistence upon them dangerous.[24]

Finally, the exaggerated nationalism of the last quarter-century, often encouraged by governments anxious to divert the attention of their peoples from pressing but embarrassing domestic problems, inculcated by state systems of education and by a new sensational popular newspaper press, and encouraged by the sharp diplomatic crises that occurred with such frequency after 1900, destroyed the relatively reasonable atmosphere in which the problems of neutrals had been discussed for decades. The fact that even international lawyers could now talk about neutrality as "rubbish wormy with selfish maxims" and as the consecration "of egoism and cowardice"[25] showed that moral judgments of neutrality were coming back into vogue. When war came now, thanks to these new tendencies, it would tend very quickly to become theological; and the belligerents would once more be saying, like Gustavus Adolphus: "*Was ist doch das für ein Ding: Neutralität*? I don't understand it."

[24] See W. P. J. A. Van Royen, *Analyse du problème de la neutralité* (The Hague, 1938), pp. 89 ff.

[25] Heffter and Lorimer, cited in Politis, *op. cit.*, p. 27.

9. A Study in the Application of Nonintervention: Great Britain and the Belgian Railways Dispute of 1869

In the year 1864, Great Britain's continental policy underwent one of those abrupt changes which, on so many occasions, have caused misunderstanding and bewilderment in Europe. After five years of spirited meddling in continental affairs, Britain withdrew to a position of almost complete isolation, and for the next seven years, years of revolutionary importance in Europe, her influence was almost negligible.

Ever since the Crimean War, the desire for abstention from continental troubles had been growing in the country. The Radicals, led by Cobden and Bright, had long urged the application of the *laissez-faire* principle to foreign as well as commercial policy; and the Derby wing of the Tory party was already beginning to argue that the national interest lay not in Europe but overseas.[1] But the growing desire for isolation was given a great stimulus in the years 1863–64 as a result of the anger and humiliation caused by the policy pursued by Palmerston and Russell in the Polish and Danish crises. The swashbuckling manner in which the two elder statesmen had rushed to the aid of the Poles and the Danes, only to abandon them in the face of Russian and Prussian resistance, was galling to Englishmen of both parties. Irritated at the weakening of British prestige, they criticized the policy which

"Great Britain and the Belgian Railways Dispute" is reprinted from *The American Historical Review,* L, No. 4 (July, 1945), with the permission of the American Historical Association.

[1] Robert W. Seton-Watson, *Britain in Europe, 1789–1914* (Cambridge, 1937), p. 465.

had been followed since 1859 as lacking in consistency and basic principle and demanded a thorough reform.

In the great debate on foreign policy that was held in the House of Commons in July 1864, it was made apparent that the days of Palmerstonian diplomacy were past and those of isolation were at hand. The keynote was struck by one of the Radicals, when he announced that it was time "for replacing the muddling, dishonest system of apparent intervention . . . by an honest, dignified and plainspoken system of nonintervention";[2] and repeatedly, as the debate went on, speakers on both sides of the House returned to that phrase, describing nonintervention as the traditional policy of Great Britain and the one to which the nation must now return. By the fourth night of the debate, it was clear that Britain was about to enter a period in which nonintervention would be the shibboleth of both parties. What did not emerge from the discussion, however, was either an exact definition of the word nonintervention or an explanation of the manner in which a policy based on it would affect England's treaty obligations and her interest in the European balance of power. And it was precisely this lack of definition that was to cause confusion in the years 1864–71 and thus to effect a further diminution of Britain's continental prestige.

In its original interpretation, nonintervention was the rule that forbade the intervention, forcible or supported by force, of one independent state in the internal affairs of another.[3] It was in this sense that Castlereagh had used the term, when, in his state paper of 5 May 1820, he had announced that Britain would not support the Holy Alliance's policy of interference in the affairs of small states.[4] This was also the interpretation placed upon it by his successor Canning, who made the principle of nonintervention the basis of his "system of policy."[5] But neither Castlereagh nor Canning had ever interpreted nonintervention as a policy of complete withdrawal from European affairs. In the same note in which he announced the principle, Castlereagh had proclaimed Britain's cardinal interest in the European balance of power; and his successor, while opposing "restless and meddling activity in the concerns of the nations which surround us," had added that Britain's

[2] *Hansard,* 3d series, CLXXVI, 859.

[3] Mountague Bernard, *On the Principle of Non-Intervention* (Oxford, 1860), p. 1.

[4] H. W. V. Temperley and Lilian M. Penson, eds., *Foundations of British Foreign Policy, 1792–1902* (Cambridge, 1938), p. 61.

[5] Augustus G. Stapleton, *George Canning and His Times* (London, 1859), p. 368.

position forbade "an exclusive selfishness."[6] Indeed, Canning made the principle of nonintervention a positive affirmation of British interests, maintaining always that abstention from needless activity would strengthen Britain's hand on those occasions when she was called upon to mediate between powers that threatened the general peace. He argued further that Britain's constant duty must be "to keep treaties, whatever the cost, for thus alone could confidence in their sanctity or in the public law of Europe be justified";[7] and he did not hesitate to depart from nonintervention when Britain's treaty obligations required that he do so.[8]

In the debate of July 1864, the principle of nonintervention was given a much narrower interpretation than it had been by its early advocates. Certainly the followers of Cobden and Bright were not thinking in terms of Canningite doctrine. Cobden wished England, in a very real sense, to withdraw from the continent and its troubles, for he had no faith in diplomatic correspondence, concerts of Europe, or theories of the balance of power. By nonintervention, he and his followers meant "no foreign politics."[9] Nor were many of the Tories far removed from these opinions. Although Conservative speakers quoted Canning in their speeches, there was a strong feeling in their ranks that Britain had "scarcely any geographical interests on the Continent which might not be covered by Lord Russell's capacious hat."[10] Canning had never forgotten the importance of the balance of power; but Disraeli himself, in the debate of 1864, struck out at the theory of the balance of power as being "founded on the obsolete traditions of an antiquated system."[11] Canning had always insisted upon Britain's respect for treaty obligations; but, in one of the most warmly received speeches of the debate, General Peel stated that he was "opposed to all treaties and guarantees which render it necessary to interfere with the affairs of others."[12] These were, of course, mere random assertions in a very long debate, but they were important, for in the next seven years the governments that ruled England were, in their pursuit of nonintervention, to neglect both the balance of power and their treaty obligations.

6 Seton-Watson, *op. cit.*, p. 119.

7 H. W. V. Temperley, *The Foreign Policy of Canning* (London, 1925), p. 466.

8 Thus Canning departed from a strict policy of nonintervention in Spanish affairs in 1823 and in Portuguese affairs in 1825. See *ibid.*, p. 459.

9 Richard Cobden, *Political Writings* (London, 1878), I, 22, 43.

10 *Saturday Review*, XIX (January 28, 1865), 96–97.

11 *Hansard*, 3d series, CLXXVI, 731.

12 *Ibid.*, 800.

The change in Britain's continental policy after the debate of 1864 was immediate and complete. For the remainder of their term in office, the Liberals pursued a policy of extreme caution with regard to Europe. When Lord Clarendon became Foreign Secretary after Palmerston's death in 1865, he not only abstained from the partisan tactics of the past but regarded with almost complete indifference the growing threat of war on the continent. To the Queen, who insisted that England should intervene between Austria and Prussia to preserve the general peace, Clarendon wrote that such intervention was inadvisable since "neither English honour nor English interests are involved" in the dispute between those powers.[13] The possibility of England's mediating in the German conflict was removed when the Liberal ministry fell from office in June 1866, and, by the time the Conservative government had been formed, the Seven Weeks' War had been fought and won by Prussia. But even if there had been no cabinet crisis, it is doubtful whether Britain would have intervened effectively. Clarendon had already set the tone of Britain's new policy. As Eugène Forcade said of the English, *"Il y a eu des temps où ils se mêlaient de tout, et ils sont fini par ne plus vouloir mêler de rien."*[14]

The Derby-Disraeli ministry came to office in 1866 committed, both by their criticism of Palmerston's diplomacy and by the declarations of their leaders, to the policy of nonintervention. The Foreign Office was assigned to Lord Stanley, the eldest son of the Prime Minister. Shortly after the latter's accession to power, the Austrian ambassador wrote of him:

> [Lord Stanley] belongs to that school of statesmen who make a dogma of the most complete non-intervention and the most absolute abstention of Great Britain from the affairs and quarrels of Europe. According to Lord Stanley, the only great interest of this country consists in the pacific development of its prosperity and its colonial and commercial power, and, as England could not attain this goal and at the same time interfere actively and influentially in the affairs of Europe, she ought not to hesitate between the two courses.[15]

In his three years of office, Stanley showed that this was an accurate forecast. His one adventure in foreign politics came in 1867 when the complicated question of the Grand Duchy of Luxembourg threatened to precipitate a Franco-Prussian war. On that occasion Stanley did

[13] Seton-Watson, *op. cit.*, p. 468.
[14] *Revue des deux mondes*, LXIV (July 1, 1866), 248.
[15] Temperley and Penson, *op. cit.*, p. 306.

intervene to find a peaceful solution, and Britain joined in that collective guarantee of Luxembourg's neutrality which was designed to prevent similar disputes in the future. But what credit Britain gained on the continent by her intervention in this affair was offset by the extreme reluctance with which Stanley had moved and by his subsequent declaration that Britain was not called on to protect the neutrality of Luxembourg by force of arms if any of the other guarantors should violate their pledge.[16] To the House of Commons Stanley made it clear that the Luxembourg adventure was an exception to his general line of policy and that England was not going to be drawn into new European complications. Indeed, in April 1868, the government emphasized its withdrawal from Europe even further, when, in the debate on the Mutiny Bill, it acquiesced in the deletion of that part of the preamble of the bill which referred to England's traditional interest in the preservation of the European balance of power.[17]

The policy of nonintervention was applied not only in western Europe but in Near Eastern affairs as well. Since 1866, the island of Crete had been in revolt against its Turkish overlord, and, as the revolt continued, unrest and disorder spread through Turkey's European provinces.[18] Yet, although these disturbances were a constant preoccupation for three years, Stanley steadily refused to join in any collective

[16] The best monograph on the Luxembourg affair is Gaspard Wampach, *Le Luxembourg neutre: Etude d'histoire diplomatique* (Paris, 1900), although the literature on the subject is voluminous. The parliamentary debates on the Luxembourg guarantee and the interpretations made by Stanley and Lord Derby are to be found in *Hansard,* 3d series, CLXXXVII, 148 ff., 1910 ff.; CLXXXVIII, 967 ff. Discussions of their interpretation are found in Temperley and Penson, *op. cit.,* pp. 309–12; Horst Michael, *Bismarck, England und Europa (vorwiegend von 1866–70)* (Munich, 1930), p. 66; and Charles P. Sanger and Henry T. Norton, *England's Guarantee to Belgium and Luxemburg* (London, 1915).

[17] *Great Britain: Statutes,* 31 Victoria chap. xiv (April 3, 1868). Robert C. Binkley, *Realism and Nationalism, 1852–1871* (New York and London, 1935), pp. 283–84, mentions the change in the preamble of the act but ascribes it erroneously to the Gladstone ministry in 1869. It is true that the Gladstone government accepted the change, and in the Mutiny Acts the offending phrase was omitted. For the circumstances of the revision, see *Hansard,* 3d series, CXCI, 326, 556–57.

[18] The most complete account of the Cretan situation is Edouard Driault and Michel Lhéritier, *Histoire diplomatique de la Grèce* (Paris, 1925), III, book 2. For British policy throughout the revolt, see "Correspondence respecting the Disturbances in Crete," *Great Britain: Accounts and Papers (1867),* LXXIV (3771), L/C, February 7, 1867; "Further Correspondence," *Accounts and Papers (1867–68),* LXXIII (3965–11), L/C, December 2, 1867–May 21, 1868; "Correspondence respecting the Rupture of Diplomatic Relations between Turkey and Greece," *Accounts and Papers (1868–69),* LXIV (4116), L/C, March 2, 1869.

action of the powers to restore peace in the Near East. This application of the nonintervention principle was, in the light of the ambitions of some of the other powers, not entirely unjustifiable. But Britain's adherence to what Gorchakov called a policy of "political nihilism"[19] could not help having unfortunate effects. It not only prolonged the dangerous situation in the Near East but very effectively destroyed the settlement of 1856. The Treaty of Paris had attempted to substitute collective action in the Near East for the separate action of single powers. English nonintervention destroyed the organic reality of such collective action and removed the one check on the ambitions of the separate states.[20] When, however, Stanley was warned of this probable result of his attitude, and when he was reminded of Britain's guarantee of Turkey, he bluntly stated that "it seemed certain to him, in the light of his knowledge of the feelings animating England at present that the Government of the Queen will not take it upon themselves to defend in another time, except perhaps in the case of the possession of Constantinople itself being put in question."[21] This was an implied repudiation of the guarantee of 15 April 1856, and its inevitable consequence, as Rheindorf has suggested, was Russia's violation of the Black Sea

By the end of 1868, when the Derby-Disraeli ministry fell from

clauses in 1871.[22]

the integrity of the Ottoman Empire by force, as they would have done office, the systematic application of nonintervention had led to an almost complete withdrawal from European affairs. In the revision of the Mutiny Act, Britain had disclaimed any interest in alterations of the

[19] E. Charles-Roux, *Alexander II, Gortchakoff, et Napoleon III* (Paris, 1913), p. 453.

[20] The return to separate action on the part of the powers was clearly forecast when the Russian Government, supported by Prussia, France, and Italy, announced that, in view of the failure of the Turkish Government to liquidate the disorders in Crete and in view of its failure to follow the advice of the powers, the Porte must accept responsibility for all future consequences of its policy. See Driault and Lhéritier, *op. cit.*, III, 219; *Great Britain: Accounts and Papers (1867–68)*, LXXIII, nos. 282, 283; *Les Origines diplomatiques de la Guerre de 1870–71*, XVIII, nos. 5770, 5771 (hereinafter cited as *Origines*).

[21] Kurt Rheindorf, *Die Schwarze-Meer-(Pontus-) Frage* (Berlin, 1925), pp. 62 ff.

[22] In this connection it is interesting to note that, as early as January 1868, there was a feeling in the Russian Foreign Office that Britain, at least as long as Lord Stanley was in office, would accept a *fait accompli* in the Near East. See Reuss to Bismarck, January 17, 1868, in *Die Auswärtige Politik Preussens, 1858–1871; Diplomatische Aktenstücke,* hrsgb. von der Historischen Reichskommission unter Leitung von Erich Brandenburg, Otto Hoetzsch, Hermann Oncken (Oldenburg, 1932–), IX, No. 515; and Rheindorf, *op. cit.*, p. 63.

balance of power. In the Luxembourg affair, the government had shown an extreme reluctance to assume new treaty obligations and a more extreme reluctance to honor them when assumed. In its conduct of eastern affairs, it had cast grave doubt upon its willingness to uphold obligations already undertaken. All of this could not but damage Britain's prestige in Europe. But it remained for the new Liberal ministry to carry this policy of retreat even farther, by showing that not even Britain's long-standing guarantee of Belgium was safe in the new age of nonintervention. England's desire to escape from the continent was never more clearly illustrated than in an incident that has never been fully treated from English sources—namely, the curious episode of the Belgian railways in 1869.

The affair which Emile Ollivier later called *"l'hallucination des chemins de fer belges"* was, like the crisis over Luxembourg in 1867, a tempest in a teapot caused by the desire of France to strengthen her eastern frontiers. Unlike the earlier crisis, however, it was not initiated by the French but had its inception in certain financial plans of Belgian railway speculators.

The Belgian railway system in 1868 represented a curious mixture of private and state ownership. The government had built many of the lines and operated them as state enterprises. There were, however, other lines which had been ceded to private firms. This was especially true of the eastern part of the country, the chief railroads of which were owned by two companies. The first of these, the Compagnie du Grand Luxembourg, operated the line which ran from Luxembourg north to Marloie and there split into two branches, one of which went to Brussels, the other to Liège. A second private corporation, the Compagnie du Liègeois-Limbourgeois, controlled the railway that ran from Liège, by way of Limbourg, to the border of the Netherlands.

In 1868, both these private companies were heavily in debt. Because of financial mismanagement, unwise speculation, and excessive jobbing, their income barely exceeded their operating costs. In the case of the Grand Luxembourg line, it was estimated that 30 per cent of the original capital had been squandered. The company had no funds to make necessary improvements, and since 1866 its dividend payments had been highly irregular.[23] The financial status of the company was so bad that, in March 1868, its board of directors had urged the Belgian Govern-

[23] "Memorandum on the Attempted Transfer to the French Société de l'Est of the Belgian Grand Luxemburg and Liège-Limburg Railways. Printed solely for the use of the Cabinet, 12 March 1869." FO France/1383; to Lyons, no. 274, confidential, 16 March 1869, enc. (Public Record Office, London).

ment to repurchase the line.[24] They had received no encouragement and were forced to turn elsewhere in their search for financial salvation. In October 1868, company representatives arrived in Paris to propose that their road be taken over by the French Compagnie de l'Est.[25] At the same time, a certain Baron Hirsch, leading stockholder in the Liège-Limbourg Company, opened negotiations with the Compagnie de l'Est for the purchase of his line.[26]

The interest shown by the French company in these proposals is easily explained. In January 1868, the Compagnie de l'Est had concluded a railway convention with a private corporation operating in the Grand Duchy of Luxembourg. By this agreement, the French company had taken over the operation of all lines controlled by the Compagnie Guillaume-Luxembourg for a period of forty-five years and agreed to pay a fixed annuity for this privilege. The Compagnie Guillaume-Luxembourg ceded to the French society the railway running from the Swiss border to the city of Luxembourg and, in addition, a line that crossed the Belgian frontier and ran to the environs of Liège. It was apparent that, if new arrangements were made with the two Belgian companies, their railways would serve as an extension of this system and the Compagnie de l'Est would dominate the stretch of territory that flanked the Rhine from Switzerland to the Dutch frontier.[27]

The French company did not possess the resources to enable it to take over the Belgian railways unassisted. But behind the Compagnie de l'Est stood the French Government. It had already promised to indemnify the company for any losses sustained in the operation of the Guillaume-Luxembourg lines. In view of the economic and strategic advantages promised from the possession of the Belgian roads,[28] it could be expected to do the same again.

[24] The best account of the financial difficulties of the companies and their plans to escape them is in Paul Hyams, *Frère-Orban* (Brussels, 1905), II, 155 ff.

[25] FO Belgium/293; from Lumley, no. 100, March 12, 1869.

[26] Hymans, *op. cit.*, II, 163 ff.

[27] The British minister in Brussels reported that "by means of an apparently simple Railway speculation, the French Govt., without appearing in the matter, would for all strategic purposes have held within its grasp the Kingdoms of Belgium and the Netherlands." FO Belgium/294; from Lumley, no. 120, confidential, March 21, 1869.

[28] The economic advantages of the system planned were as important as the strategic. Belgian iron works at Liège and Charleroi depended to a large extent on ore shipments from Luxembourg. Once the French company controlled the sole system of transportation, rates could be manipulated in such a way as to benefit the iron works in northeastern France which were competing with the Belgian firms. FO Belgium/298; from Lumley, no. 1, commercial, January 1, 1869; no. 2, commercial, January 2, 1869; no. 6, commercial, January 10, 1869.

The Belgian Government was well informed as to the course of the negotiations in Paris. The chief representative of the Compagnie du Grand Luxembourg was M. Tesch, former Belgian minister of justice. It is interesting to note that, in advising the government of the company's intentions, he pointed out that several of the company directors were Englishmen, and he intimated that the British Government would frown upon any governmental interference with the excellent bargain that was being arranged.[29] It is doubtful whether the Belgian Government was convinced of the truth of this argument, but it is strange that it should have done nothing to block the negotiations in their early stages. It was not until 12 December that M. Jamar, the Minister of Public Works, announced publicly that the proposed cession could not take place without the consent of the government and that such consent would never be given.[30] By that time, the preliminary arrangements for the cession of the two Belgian roads to the Compagnie de l'Est had been made in Paris.

The Belgian Government had assumed that Jamar's proclamation would end all talk of cession. In this, it was mistaken. The company representatives in Paris assured the French that their government would give way as soon as the agreements were ratified. This view was echoed by La Guéronnière, the French minister in Brussels, an ardent advocate of French absorption of Belgium. La Guéronnière informed the Quai d'Orsay that Belgian consent was inevitable, first, because the Belgian Government had no legal right to block the cession and, second, because "men of affairs" in Belgium would not suffer interference with their material interests.[31] In Paris, the Belgian minister, Baron de Beyens, worked hard to convince the directors of the Compagnie de l'Est of the

[29] The Foreign Office papers show that the English directors of the Compagnie due Grand-Luxembourg did attempt to persuade Lord Clarendon, the British Foreign Secretary, to intercede in their behalf. On March 11, 1869, they sent a report to the Foreign Office, arguing their legal right to cede their line to the Compagnie de l'Est. In the event that the Belgian Government should persist in its opposition, they requested that Clarendon should persuade that government to purchase the line in question. In the accompanying letter, Mr. W. Fenton, the chairman of the board of directors, wrote, "I feel confident that my own interests and the interests of my company are safe in your Lordship's hands and that you will not willingly see a great injustice committed upon British subjects. I would not for the world that France should touch Belgium with its little finger; but I *do* object to our property being offered up on the altar of Belgian patriotism." Clarendon politely refused to intercede. FO France/1384; to Lyons, no. 298, March 23, 1869, enc.

[30] Emile Banning, *Les Origines et les phases de la neutralité belge* (Brussels, 1927), p. 225.

[31] *Origines,* XXII, no. 7072: from La Guéronnière, December 17, 1868.

resoluteness of his government's opposition but found all of his efforts unavailing.

Beyens discovered also that, whenever the French company showed the slightest hesitation, it was prodded on by officials of the French Government, especially by Rouher, the "vice-emperor," and Gressier, the imperial Minister of Works.[32] Indeed, thanks to La Guéronnière's enthusiastic reports from Brussels, the French Government had decided to make the railway cession an objective of official policy. Despite Beyens' remonstrances, the Compagnie de l'Est, on 30 January 1869, concluded agreements with both the Grand Luxembourg and the Liège-Limbourg companies, assuming the exploitation of their lines for a period of forty-three years. The agreements were to be submitted for the approval of the French and Belgian governments *"en tant que de besoin."*[33]

The forcing play in Paris strengthened rather than weakened Belgium's resistance to the railway project and led the government to translate its feeling into legal terms. At the beginning of February, Frère-Orban, the leader of the government, summoned a ministerial council and proceeded to draw up a *projet du loi* for submission to the Chambers. The *projet* stated simply that private railroad societies in Belgium could cede the lines for which they were concessionaires only with the consent of the government. In cases of infraction of this rule, the government would take over the lines, although the companies would be allowed recourse to the courts for the recovery of losses.

This law, at once a warning to the *actionnaires* in Paris and a measure of security for the future, was introduced in the lower Chamber on 6 February. In his argument for passage, on 13 February, Frère-Orban was careful to avoid making any allusions to the political significance of the pending action of the Belgian railway companies. He stressed only the economic issues involved, and his case was stated so clearly that the bill passed with little debate.[34] A week later, the *projet* was passed by the Senate and became the law of the land.

With the passage of the law, this petty dispute over railway rights, like so many relatively insignificant questions in this period, was transported to the higher ground of diplomatic controversy. The French Government could no longer hide behind the Compagnie de l'Est. Indeed, before the *projet* had moved up to the Senate, La Guéronnière had warned Frère-Orban that France found Belgium's conduct inexplicable and insulting. To Frère's insistence that he had no intention

32 Hymans, *op. cit.*, II, 175–78.
33 *Ibid*, II, 177.
34 A full discussion of the debate is given in *ibid.*, II, 185 ff.

of insulting France and that newspaper reports had given the *projet "une apparence trompeuse,"* the French minister replied that that in itself was sufficient cause for complaint. "A great nation like France," he said, "must not be wounded. Not only that, but people must not be given the impression that she can be wounded."[35] In Paris, the semi-official press was unleashed, and, with one accord, these journals announced that there was but one possible explanation for the Belgian position, namely, that it was the result of a Prussian plot.[36] This theory, so readily adapted to all causes of French irritation in this period, was taken up by the Emperor himself. On 16 February Napoleon told the Belgian minister that he must not underestimate the gravity of the railway question. "The truth is," he said, "that M. Frère-Orban has premeditated all of this, that he went expressly to Berlin, and that the matter was concerted with Bismarck. . . . I shall insist that the law be repealed."[37]

Ollivier has printed a very interesting dispatch that leaves no doubt as to the Emperor's intentions. Writing to Marshal Niel on 19 February, Napoleon spoke plainly of the possibility of war and annexation:

> A government, like a man, must accept the challenge when it is provoked and, when the occasion presents itself, must seize it in order to prove its virility. What is the question posed today? The Belgian Government is demonstrating its ill will toward France, and public opinion is convinced, rightly or wrongly, that Belgium would not be so arrogant were not Prussia behind her. In these circumstances, to be conciliatory and to retreat in the face of a proceeding which injures us would be to surrender, before the face of Europe, all our legitimate influence. Must war arise out of this conflict? I do not know. But it is necessary to act as if it will arise.[38]

The Emperor then discussed the great advantages that would result from a war with Belgium at this time. He raised the question of Prussia's position in such an eventuality and concluded that, although Bismarck might interfere, he would probably adopt the more prudent course of using the occasion to annex the South German states. But the most interesting feature of the letter is to be found in its omissions rather than in its content. It contains not a single reference to England.

[35] *Origines,* XXIII, no. 7237; from La Guéronnière, February 16, 1869.

[36] See the report of the Paris correspondent in *The Times,* February 22, 1869. It points out that the only *independent* newspaper that joined this campaign was *Liberté,* whose editor, Emile Girardin, was an ardent advocate of Belgian annexation. See also *Origines,* XXXIII, no. 7245 and notes.

[37] *Ibid.,* XXIII, no. 7249, note.

[38] Emile Ollivier, *L'Empire libéral* (Paris, 1895), XI, 375 f.

There can perhaps be found no better illustration of the complete disregard in which England was held at this time. For the neutrality and independence of Belgium was protected by an English guarantee, and the security of Belgium had long been regarded as a vital British interest. Since 1831, when Palmerston had threatened war "in a given number of days" unless French troops were withdrawn from the country,[39] no one had doubted England's willingness to stand by Belgium. There was good reason to doubt it in 1869. Though the railway question had been public property for more than two months, the British Foreign Office had maintained an almost complete, even if uneasy, silence.

In England, Queen Victoria had been the first to see danger for Belgium in the railway cession. In January 1869, aroused by a series of worried letters from King Leopold of Belgium, she had expressed her concern to the Foreign Office and insisted that the government make clear its willingness to uphold the Belgian guarantee.[40] Lord Clarendon had, however, no desire to make such a statement. Intervention in the railway dispute, he felt, might very well involve Great Britain in the slowly evolving duel between France and Prussia. Such involvement could be not only embarrassing but, in view of the tense relations between Britain and the United States at this time, actually dangerous. Despite the advice of the Queen, therefore, Clarendon not only refused to act but, with an impulsive irritability, blamed the Brussels Government for having allowed the railway question to become one of European interest. Gladstone, although the responsible head of the cabinet, seems not to have interfered directly. He defended Clarendon to the Queen and in general left the matter in the Foreign Secretary's hands.

When the Belgian Government first brought the railway question to his attention, Clarendon had urged it "to put a stop to the sale, not by a veto, but by a purchase of the railways."[41] The Belgian Government had answered that for financial and political reasons this was impossible and that, among other things, such purchase would cause every bankrupt railway company in Belgium to demand the same treatment.[42] The British Foreign Secretary showed a tendency to regard this decision as the root of the trouble which ensued.

Thus, when in February 1869 the policy of the French Government led people to expect English intervention, Clarendon was fully as critical

[39] Sir Henry Bulwer, *Life of Viscount Palmerston* (London, 1870–76), II, 108.

[40] Lord Newton, *Lord Lyons, a Record of British Diplomacy* (London, 1913), I, 212.

[41] FO Belgium/122; to Lumley, no. 6, January 16, 1869.

[42] FO Belgium/292; from Lumley, no. 36, confidential, January 30, 1869.

of Belgian policy as he was of French, and this fact prevented his advice from having any deterrent effect in Paris. On 18 February he instructed Lyons to point out at the Quai d'Orsay that Belgium had every right to pass legislation affecting her own railway system and that he had reason to believe that there was no justification for the claims that the Belgian actions were inspired in Berlin.[43] But in communicating these opinions to the French ambassador in London, Clarendon moderated his tone considerably and spent a good part of the interview expressing regret at the *maladresse* of the Belgians. Prince La Tour d'Auvergne placed considerable emphasis on this fact in his report,[44] which naturally weakened the effect of Lyons' communication. For the French Government was not contesting Belgium's right to pass railway legislation but was accusing the Brussels government of insulting France without warning before the eyes of Europe.[45]

The French Government must have been equally encouraged by the attitude taken by *The Times*. The erstwhile *Thunderer* confessed that its sympathies were "in favor of unrestricted commercial enterprise, and particularly of such amalgamations or working conventions between the Continental railroad lines as shall facilitate traffic and give the greatest advantages to the public."[46] It absolved the French Government from all suspicion and maintained that Belgium's caution was "in this instance overstrained. An agreement that the French 'Est' should manage and work the Arlon line can no more threaten the independence of Belgium than an agreement that the French 'Nord' should work the London, Chatham and Dover would facilitate the invasion of England."[47]

[43] FO France/1383; to Lyons, no. 195, confidential, February 18, 1869.

[44] *Origines,* XXIII, no. 7248; from La Tour d'Auvergne, confidential, February 18, 1869.

[45] In his instructions to La Guéronnière, La Valette stressed the fact that the Belgian Government had introduced the railway law without making any attempt to inform the French Government officially of its opposition to the project. *Origines,* XXIII, no. 7242. La Tour indicated that Clarendon shared the opinion that this conduct had been ill-advised.

[46] *Times,* February 19, 1869. *The Economist* went farther in stressing the economic issues involved and wrote (no. 1331, February 27): "Whatever may be the result of the controversy, it is hoped that, the Great-Luxemburg line having been constructed in a great degree by means of English capital, the interests of the proprietors will not be sacrificed to political considerations."

[47] *The Times,* February 23, 1869. This attitude was strongly criticized by the *Pall Mall Budget* (February 27, 1869), while the *Saturday Review* (XXVII [February 20, 1869], 232) said of an earlier and similar editorial that "such writing as this can only be characterized as a disgrace to the nation."

It soon became apparent that Napoleon III did not deserve this confidence and was bent upon gaining satisfaction from Belgium. The British ambassador in Paris reported on 4 March that the irritation in Paris had not subsided. There was a prevalent notion, he added, that, if France attempted to annex Belgium, Prussia would raise no objections, and "it is doubted whether, if Prussia connived at the spoliation, England would be willing, or indeed able, to make any effectual resistance to it."[48] Two days later, Lumley, the minister in Brussels, reported that France was demanding the appointment of a mixed commission that would examine the question of the railway contracts and "the questions attached to it." In case of a Belgian refusal, La Guéronnière was to be recalled from Brussels.[49]

Even after the receipt of this news, Clarendon was reluctant to exert any pressure in Paris. He sent a mild dispatch to Lord Lyons, the ambassador in Paris, suggesting that France should call in a third party to mediate in the dispute rather than break off diplomatic relations.[50] Lyons, who was quite as prudent as his chief, did not communicate even this suggestion. He reported on 8 March that he was confident that Napoleon's ambitions would be checked by the natural caution of La Valette, the Foreign Minister, and that, under the circumstances, it might be well to persuade Belgium to agree to the plan of a mixed commission.[51]

The Belgian Government, which considered the railway question closed, had not the slightest inclination to give way to such a plan. It was, indeed, the extreme resistance of the government that made Clarendon amenable to Lyons' suggestion, for it revived his former belief that the railway incident was a plot to involve England in the continent. He was, for instance, extremely startled by a telegram from Lumley which read, "The King is confident that Your Lordship will let him know whether and when you think he should commence military preparations."[52] Clarendon telegraphed immediately that any military proceedings were out of the question and instructed his minister to urge the Belgian Government to agree to the French plan.[53] After some

48 FO France/1749; from Lyons, no. 249, very confidential, March 4, 1869.

49 FO Belgium/293; from Lumley, no. 87, March 6, 1869.

50 FO France/1383; to Lyons, no. 241, confidential, March 6.

51 FO France/1750; from Lyons, no. 268, very confidential, March 8.

52 FO Belgium/293; from Lumley, telegram, March 9.

53 In an instruction to Lyons on March 17, Clarendon wrote that the Belgians were trying to make the English Government "co-partners in any responsibility they may incur in dealing with the French proposals; but Her Majesty's Government can not allow this to be so assumed by the Belgian Government." FO France/1383; to Lyons, no. 284.

hesitation the Belgians agreed to send a delegate to Paris, as *"un témoignage de déférence pour les conseils du gouvernement anglais."*[54]

Once the Belgian Government had made this concession to France, it fully expected British support in the ensuing negotiations. In England, too, there was a strong feeling in influential quarters that the Foreign Office should make a declaration that would restrain France during the Paris talks, and this became so insistent that Clarendon was forced to make certain concessions to it.

He did so, however, in characteristic fashion. On 16 March he addressed a long dispatch to Lyons. He spoke of "the value and importance attached not only by Her Majesty's Government but by the people of England also to the alliance with France." The intimacy between the two governments made it possible for him to express, without fear of misunderstanding, "apprehensions respecting eventualities which appear to be possible." This clumsy phrase apparently referred to the Belgian difficulty, for the Foreign Secretary spoke at length of the great sympathy the English people felt for Belgium and of England's position as one of the guarantors of that state. He then alluded cautiously to the possibility of a French attack on Belgium. This, he said, would have very grave consequences for the Emperor, for Belgium was protected by the guarantee of 1839 and "an engagement so solemn and for so many years religiously respected could hardly remain a dead letter now." Clarendon did not say directly that England would be prepared or willing to act. He contented himself with saying that "in view of the armaments and the rivalries *in Europe,* Her Majesty's Government think that they cannot be taxed with exaggeration when they declare their apprehension that war would ensue [italics added]." In such an event "the interruption of cordial relations with France" would be inevitable.[55]

Although neither a menacing nor an unequivocal dispatch, this document did include a warning that could not be without effect in Paris. But the warning was never delivered. The Foreign Secretary, in his concluding paragraph, gave Lyons no instructions for its use but indicated that the manner and the time of its delivery would be left to the discretion of the ambassador.

This expression of confidence was not entirely pleasing to Lord Lyons. On 17 March, he wrote, "The language of the Despatch is very guarded and very friendly towards France; but without reference to the

[54] Baron Beyens, *Le Second Empire, vu par un diplomate belge* (Paris, 1924), II, 347.

[55] FO France/1383; to Lyons, no. 266, very confidential, March 16, 1869.

particular language used, the French Government will certainly consider the step taken—the 'démarche' as they will term it—as equivalent to a serious warning or, to speak plainly, to a threat." If England wished to threaten France, he pointed out, the dispatch would be most effective if it included a definite statement authorizing Lyons to read it to M. La Valette at a given time. He preferred, accordingly, to await such specific instructions. In his personal opinion, however, any such threat might have an effect contrary to that hoped. The Emperor "may feel, or in all events declare, that the intervention of Her Majesty's Government has made it impossible for him to deal with the Belgian Question in the conciliatory manner he intended." In that case, war would ensue.[56]

The responsibility for the *démarche*, if there was to be one, reverted to the Foreign Secretary, and, after reading Lyons' dispatch, he decided that silence was the more prudent counsel. Accordingly, he wrote on 18 March that he had decided to await the outcome of Frère-Orban's visit to Paris before taking the step suggested in his dispatch of 16 March.[57]

This was curious conduct for a nation supposed to be vitally interested in Belgian security. But Clarendon and Lyons were operating upon the assumption that time and English silence would solve the dispute. In Belgium's agreement to enter discussions in Paris, they saw hope for a solution, and Lyons believed that this had removed the question "from the dangerous ground of international dignity on which it had been placed."[58]

In Brussels, Frère-Orban hoped that this was true. He was quite willing, he told the English minister, to discuss in Paris means of improving the commercial relations between France and Belgium. He had little confidence, however, in the Emperor's willingness to limit the talks to that subject. He suspected that the French "would try to extort from the Belgian Government its consent to the draft contracts," and he pointed out that "any minister who would consent to them would sign the death

[56] FO France/1750; from Lyons, no. 297, March 17, 1869.

[57] FO France/1383; to Lyons, no. 287, March 18. The writers of the two most complete discussions of the Belgian railways dispute, Rheindorf (*Deutsche Rundschau*, CXCV, 118) and Michael (*op. cit.*, p. 228), give the impression that the English *démarche* was made, despite Lyons' dispatch, "a few days later." This view is certainly mistaken and seems to be based upon an undated private letter, reproduced in Newton (*op. cit.*, I, 216), in which Clarendon expressed the belief that the warning *might* have to be sent to Paris. No English pressure, however, was brought to bear in Paris at this time.

[58] FO France/1751; from Lyons, no. 314, March 23, 1869.

warrant of the independence of Belgium."[59] To safeguard Belgium's interests, the minister president decided to go to Paris himself.

Frère-Orban's fears were strengthened by the conduct of the French minister in Brussels. La Guéronnière had been delighted by the Belgian acceptance of a mixed commission, which he interpreted as a complete surrender to France.[60] Before Frère left for Paris, the French minister made it his duty to advise him to accept the railway conventions without hesitation. He pointed out that the position of Europe made Belgian neutrality impossible. Treaties, he said, had an ideal value, but they no longer protected small states. In the circumstances, *"la Belgique doit dorénavant pencher vers la France."*[61] Nor were the apprehensions aroused by this advice completely removed by Frère's first conversation with Napoleon III after reaching Paris. For the Emperor, in a long and rambling conversation, expressed regret that Louis Philippe had not succeeded in uniting France and Belgium and said that, although such union was, perhaps, unnecessary now, it should be the task of today's statesmen to remove all barriers between the two countries.[62]

The commissioners appointed to deal with Frère-Orban were La Valette, Rouher, and Gressier. They gave concrete expression to the Emperor's hopes by demanding outright that Belgium assent to the conclusion of the conventions between the Compagnie de l'Est and the Belgian roads. Frère was able to delay his decision until 12 April by securing permission to make alternative proposals. He had determined, however, to concede to the French company only certain tariff adjustments and rights of way and to insist that the railways in question remain under Belgian control.[63] He embodied this decision in a memorandum submitted to the French representatives.

When discussions reopened on 16 April, it became apparent that a rupture between the two parties was almost inevitable. The French commissioners declared flatly that the counterproposals were inadequate and used every argument in their power to make Frère give way. This he refused to do, insisting that "for Belgium to accept the treaties, even with some modifications, would be to admit that the independence of

59 FO Belgium/294; from Lumley, no. 125, confidential, March 23, 1869.

60 See his very interesting report of March 28, *Origines,* XXIV, no. 7358.

61 This advice was not conveyed directly to Frère-Orban but to the Secretary General of the Foreign Ministry. A memorandum, written by the latter, appears in Hymans, *op. cit.,* II, 232 f.

62 *Ibid.,* II, 240. Lumley found the King of the Belgians extremely agitated by the news of this conversation. FO Belgium/294; from Lumley, no. 152, private and confidential, April 11.

63 Banning, *op. cit.,* p. 228.

the country was an empty word."[64] There was a memorable incident on 20 April, when Frère threatened to appeal to the powers that had guaranteed Belgian independence in 1839. At this suggestion, Rouher rose abruptly from the conference table and, striding into the anteroom, cried, "It is evident that Prussia is behind all this. But—sooner war then surrender! In any event, sooner or later, that war is inevitable. The Prince Imperial will never reign unless Sadowa is wiped out. *Eh bien!* If they want it, let there be war!"[65]

The threatening attitude of the French made some action on the part of England imperative. Clarendon was still reluctant to apply pressure to France, and he had used his influence in newspaper circles to restrict public discussion of the railway dispute as much as possible.[66] He had no such means, however, of restraining his sovereign. In a letter to her Foreign Secretary of 15 April, Queen Victoria raised once more the question of England's guarantee to Belgium, insisting that "if it were to be generally understood that we could not any longer be relied upon, except for moral support, England would soon lose her position in Europe."[67]

The Foreign Secretary's answer to this letter showed not only that he was still irritated at Belgium but that his conception of England's obligation to that country was far different from the Queen's. He accused Belgium of holding out England's material force as a menace to her "real or supposed enemies" and added:

> It is the duty, as Lord Clarendon humbly conceives, of your Majesty's Government to consider the interests of England, and not to disguise from themselves the many difficulties of our position and the exceeding delicacy of calling upon Parliament to give effect to Treaties which, if public opinion years ago had been what it now is, would not have been sanctioned. It seems to be the duty of your Majesty's Government to bear in mind how widely different are the circumstances of this country now to when those Treaties were concluded and that, if their execution were to lead us into war in Europe, we should find ourselves immediately called upon to defend Canada from American invasion.[68]

The Foreign Secretary tried to sugar this pill by adding that he hoped England would always fulfill her obligations when "rightfully called

64 Hymans, *op. cit.*, II, 261.

65 Ollivier, *op. cit.*, XI, 384; Beyens, *op. cit.*, II, 350–51.

66 *Origines*, XXIV, no. 7339; from La Tour d'Auvergne, confidential, March 19, 1869.

67 *Letters of Queen Victoria*, 2d series, I, 589.

68 *Ibid.*, I, 590.

upon" to do so. The Queen, however, was deeply distressed. There was, she pointed out, "a disposition on the Continent to believe that England is not to be moved, either by interest, or the obligations of Treaties, into giving more than *moral* support in any complications that may arise, and that the aggressive Power may dismiss all fears of finding 'England across its path.'"[69] This feeling endangered the cause of peace. England must make clear her willingness to stand by her pledges on the continent. An expression of the Queen's concern was also transmitted to Mr. Gladstone, with the remark that Clarendon's conduct was "so *very* curiously guarded, as to be hardly *straightforward.*"[70]

The Queen's demand for more vigorous action coincided with the reports of increasing friction in Paris. Clarendon was losing what confidence he had had in the French Government, and he wrote sadly to Lyons, "I did not think they would have exposed the cloven foot so soon and completely as they have done."[71] On 21 April, he made the *démarche* he had withdrawn a month earlier. His language was still not wholly straightforward, nor did he make England's position entirely clear, but he indicated that the English Government saw no reason for France's demand for the ratification of the railway contracts. Persistence in this course would cause the public opinion of Europe to "lean to the belief that the independence of Belgium was menaced by France." If this were true, the cordial relations between England and France would of necessity be interrupted, an eventuality that could not appear desirable to the French Government.[72]

The reaction of the French Foreign Minister to this communication was primarily one of surprise. His rejoinder, sent to La Tour d'Auvergne in London on 25 April, is a curious blend of injured innocence and incredulity. He insisted—and this was perhaps only natural—that France had not the slightest intention of violating the neutrality and independence of Belgium. But implicit in La Valette's dispatch is an admission that the French Government had expected no English intervention. After all, the Foreign Minister seemed to say, England had known about the dispute from the beginning; she had actually supported the French demand for a mixed commission; and it was surely illogical for her now to make scarcely veiled accusations against France.[73]

[69] *Ibid.*, I, 592.
[70] *Ibid.*, I, 593.
[71] Newton, *op. cit.*, I, 217.
[72] FO France/1386; to Lyons, no. 428, April 22, 1869. *Origines,* XXIV, no. 7404; from La Tour d'Auvergne, confidential, April 22.
[73] *Ibid.*, XXIV, no. 7415; La Valette to La Tour d'Auvergne, minute, April 25.

Nevertheless, the French gave way very soon after the communication of Clarendon's dispatch. On 27 April, their commissioners surrendered completely to Frère-Orban's terms. In the protocol signed on that date, they admitted that they would forego the execution of the railway contracts that had been concluded with the Compagnie de l'Est. They saved face by appointing a new commission to draw up service conventions between the French and Belgian roads, but they guaranteed the incontestable right of Belgium to control and regulate the lines within her borders.[74]

On the surface, this withdrawal on the part of France represented a diplomatic victory for England. There is reason to doubt, however, whether Clarendon's dispatch of 22 April had exercised in itself a decisive influence in Paris. The French Government was fully cognizant of England's reluctance to become involved in continental struggles, and it was well aware of England's transatlantic difficulties.[75] Lyons had reported that there was a feeling in Paris that England would do nothing to prevent an attack on Belgium, especially if Prussia remained neutral.[76] But in April, the French Government had begun to suspect not only that Prussia would no longer remain indifferent but that she was urging England to act and promising support if she should do so. This suspicion was borne out, at the very moment when La Valette was pondering Clarendon's note, by a dispatch from the French ambassador in London. La Tour reported a confidential conversation with Clarendon on 23 April in which the latter had intimated that Bismarck "was in entire agreement with the views of England and was ready, if it were possible, to enter into *pourparlers* with her on the subject of this affair."[77]

Reviewing the railways dispute at a later date, Bismarck claimed that Great Britain had prevented French absorption of Belgium in 1869, not by making manifest her own determination to prevent such an event, but, rather, by bringing Prussia into the dispute without specific authori-

[74] *Ibid.*, XXIV, no. 7424, note.

[75] Michael, *op. cit.*, p. 249, n. 43.

[76] FO France/1749; from Lyons, no. 249, very confidential, March 4, 1869.

[77] *Origines*, XXIV, no. 7412. According to Newton (*op. cit.*, I, 218), Clarendon advised Lyons on 19 April that "we might tomorrow, if we pleased, enter into a coalition with Prussia against France for the protection of Belgian independence." There is nothing in the Foreign Office documents to show that Lyons ever used that information in his conversations with the French Foreign Minister, although it has been assumed that he did. (See, for instance, Michael, *op. cit.*, p. 248.) The dispatch, quoted above, proves beyond doubt that Clarendon himself warned the French of the possibility of an Anglo-Prussian understanding.

zation from Berlin.[78] A brief consideration of the relations between England and Prussia during the railway dispute will show perhaps what justification there was for that charge.

The Prussian Government had maintained a very reserved attitude throughout the early stages of the affair. At the beginning of the French agitation against Belgium, there had been considerable expression of sympathy for Belgium in the press and an occasional hint that Prussia should protect her.[79] Bismarck, however, who had been extremely irritated by the hesitant policy followed by England during the eastern crisis, was determined to take no initiative in the matter. Belgium, he maintained, was the special charge of Great Britain. If Britain was ever to abandon the sterile policy of nonintervention that had of late years ruled her counsels, she would do so in the present crisis. But she would have to take the first step herself.

Count Bernstorff, the Prussian ambassador in London, was instructed, then, to refrain from committing his government in any way but, at the same time, to discover, as quietly as possible, how far England was prepared to go in defense of Belgium. At the beginning of March, Bernstorff was forced to report that he could get nothing but commonplaces from government spokesmen and that not one of them was prepared to state whether England would honor her pledge to Belgium. When King William had read Bernstorff's reports, he wrote to Bismarck, "It seems to me that we must go along with England in the Belgian affair; and yet, in doing so, let us not pull any chestnuts out of the fire, for I firmly refuse to believe that England will set a single man or a single dollar in motion if it comes to blows!"[80]

Bismarck was apparently of the same opinion, and, in a long conversation with Lord Loftus on 12 March, he made the Prussian position clear. On the basis of Bismarck's declaration, the British ambassador formed the opinion "that the Question of the Independence of Belgium was especially one of importance and interest to Great Britain: that if that Independence were to be attacked, Prussia could not be expected to defend it alone and that consequently the course which Prussia might eventually take would depend entirely on the Policy of Great Britain."

[78] Bismarck, *Gesammelte Werke,* VIb, no. 1383; intro.

[79] "The *Cross Gazette* [*Kreuzzeitung,* Berlin] of this evening, in a leading article headed 'The Future of Belgium,' declares that it is to the interest of all the Great Powers that the independence and neutrality of that country should be preserved, adding that if, contrary to expectation, she should be threatened from any other quarter, Allied Germany must vigorously undertake her defence." "Latest Intelligence," *The Times,* February 4, 1869.

[80] Bismarck, VIb, no. 1344, intro.

Everything rested, in short, on "whether the Policy of non-intervention would still be maintained." If it were, Loftus received the impression that Bismarck would make the sacrifice of Belgium the basis of an understanding with France. If, on the other hand, England declared that she would resist any attack on Belgium by force, Loftus thought Bismarck would try to secure the alliance of Great Britain.[81]

Bismarck intended to go even farther than this in his attempt to dislodge England from her position of abstention. On 16 March he prepared a long dispatch for communication to Bernstorff, which opened with a significant declaration: "The impossibility of being able to take into account England's influence in the political affairs of the continent is felt by us not only as a loss but indeed as a danger to peace, the more so because we are convinced that the weight of that influence will never fall into the scale on the side of wanton disturbances of European peace." Bismarck recognized that England's close connection with Belgium had led her to entertain lively apprehensions as to the future security of that state. But what of the future security of Europe? French agitations against Belgium were insignificant in comparison with France's constantly threatening attitude toward Germany. Prussia could not be expected to show an interest in Belgium until England became aware of the importance of the larger question. Specifically, England's willingness to assume some continental obligations would best be expressed, and her interests best protected, by concluding "a firm and intimate alliance . . . with Germany for the preservation of the peace and for protection against every disturber of that peace and every act of aggression from without."[82]

Before Bismarck could send off this dispatch, he received another note from King William. The King had been reading the Belgian press and he had found indications there "that England was already *cooling off* in the Belgian question!" William, always impressed by questions of military importance, did not relish the prospect of Belgium becoming a French sphere of occupation or influence. Bismarck's professed indifference for Belgium, he said, might hasten such an eventuality, for it might easily make England "cool off entirely." Rather than run the risk of frightening the British Government, the King instructed Bismarck to withhold the dispatch.[83]

[81] FO Prussia/661; from Loftus, no. 131, most confidential, March 13, 1869. This dispatch and that of April 17 are printed in the appendix to Veit Valentin, *Bismarcks Reichsgründung im Urteil englischer Diplomaten* (Amsterdam, 1937).

[82] Bismarck, VIb, no. 1344; Bismarck to Bernstorff, March 16, 1869, *reserviert.*

[83] *Ibid.,* VIb, no. 1345, intro.

The King, in this instance, seems to have had a better understanding of the position of the English Government than his chief minister. Bernstorff reported on 17 March that Clarendon was becoming more cautious every day. The Prussian ambassador had asked him whether England would offer to "mediate" between France and Belgium in the event of a breakdown of the mixed commission in Paris. The Foreign Secretary had answered vaguely that he would be glad to "suggest" the mediation of a third power but that he had to consider the delicate sensibilities of the French Emperor. The Emperor might be insulted, Clarendon said, if England should mediate between France and such a small state as Belgium.[84]

More evidence of England's "cooling off" came from Florence. Arnim, the Prussian minister there, reported on 1 April that his English colleague, Lord Odo Russell, had, in an indiscreet moment, shown him some private letters he had received from Clarendon. In one of these, the British Foreign Secretary had written, "Bismarck pretends that he will support Belgium in common with England, if England will determine to take the initiative. But I believe that he tries only to lurch us into a mess and that it is he who is supporting Napoleon in his *politique de brigandage*. . . . Above all, then, it is necessary to patch this business up in any way."[85] What sacrifices this patching-up process might entail for Belgium the dispatch does not make clear, but it throws more light upon Clarendon's suspicion that everyone was trying to involve England in continental difficulties. It was that feeling on his part which weakened his determination to make any declarations with regard to the Belgian guarantee.

It is interesting to note that the two persons most eager to support Belgium were the reigning sovereigns of England and Prussia. King William was anxious to act with England in defense of Belgian independence, although he agreed with Bismarck that the first overtures must come from London. When Loftus came into the chancellery on 12 April, it appeared that the long awaited news of England's position had come. To Bismarck's surprise, however, the English ambassador read a lengthy communication the burden of which was that any Prussian move in the direction of southern Germany would be unwise at present and would have a very bad effect on Franco-Prussian relations.

The Prussian minister, somewhat taken aback, pointed out that there had been no question of such a step and that, surely, the Belgian ques-

84 *Ibid.*, VIb, no. 1351, intro.
85 *Ibid.*, VIb, no. 1363, intro.

tion was the one that should be occupying their attention. Loftus immediately indicated that he had no instructions on this matter. But Bismarck had now made up his mind to apply the pressure he had withheld at the King's command. He repeated his arguments of 1[illegible] March and, using the King's phrase, said that if England was not ready to declare her willingness to support Belgium, *"ce n'est pas à nous de tirer les marrons du feu."* England professed to be worried about the South German question. She would have more reason for this fear if France were allowed to annex Belgium, for Prussia would look elsewhere for compensation. This startled the English ambassador, and he protested that this would be a "policy of robbers." But the policy of great states had always been governed by such considerations, Bismarck answered. If England disapproved of this tendency and wished to check it, she could easily do so. "If," said Count Bismarck, "you would only declare that whatever Power should wilfully break the Peace of Europe would be looked upon by you as a common enemy—we will readily adhere to, and join you in that declaration—and such a course, if supported by the other Powers, would be the surest guarantee for the Peace of Europe."[86]

The report of this conversation—Clarendon referred to it as "a curious despatch from Loftus"[87]—arrived in London when the Paris talks were on the verge of breaking off and at a time when the Queen's insistence upon English action had reached its height. Without making an official answer to the Prussian proposal,[88] Clarendon, as has already been indicated, intimated to the French ambassador that an agreement with Prussia was possible. The solution of the crisis was in part due to that declaration. Once the French had given way, the Foreign Secretary conveyed to Bismarck an expression of his gratitude for the conduct of Prussia throughout the dispute.[89] But he made no mention whatsoever of the Prussian plan for securing the peace of Europe.

King William was delighted with this new check to French ambitions and expressed satisfaction at the *bonne entente* between England and

[86] FO Prussia/662; from Loftus, no. 198, most confidential, April 17, 1869. In his dispatch informing Bernstorff of this conversation, Bismarck used the words, *"eine gegenseitige Assekuranz aller Mächte gegen jeden Friedenstörer."* Bismarck, VIb, no. 1368.

[87] Newton, *op. cit.*, I, 218.

[88] In a private letter to Lyons on 19 April, Clarendon referred to the Prussian proposal as "a ruse to detach us from France" and added, "I did not choose that Bernstorff should have to report the slightest encouragement to the suggestion, but it may come to that after all." Newton, *loc. cit.*

[89] FO Prussia/663; from Loftus, no. 235, confidential, May 8, 1869.

Prussia.[90] Bismarck was not so well pleased. He had deliberately held Prussia aloof from the Belgian difficulty, making her potential intervention contingent upon either an English declaration of willingness to support Belgium by force, or an expression of her readiness to join Prussia in a common agreement against peacebreakers. The British Government had satisfied neither condition, had pursued no straightforward and independent policy, and had finally projected Prussia into a conflict which, as Bismarck had insisted, was of no immediate concern to her. As a result, Bismarck felt, any irritation caused in France by this new disappointment would be directed, not against England, but against Prussia. After Loftus had expressed England's thanks for Prussia's aid, Bismarck wrote:

> The Ambassador indicated that the knowledge of the existing *Fühlung* with Prussia made it possible for the English Cabinet to exercise a firm pressure in Paris. In consequence, I am led to believe that, in Paris, they alluded more plainly to a coalition than can be to our interest. France's conduct in the future will certainly make clear to us to what extent England used her knowledge of our views in Paris, in order to impress the Emperor.[91]

To Bismarck, the conduct of the British Government in the Belgian affair proved the stubbornness of its adhesion to the principle of nonintervention. England had been embarrassed by the threat to Belgian independence; she had been able to escape from that embarrassment by using the influence of Prussia.[92] But Prussia would scarcely be justified in expecting reciprocal services if she herself were threatened.[93] England's statesmen were still bereft of what Gladstone was fond of referring to as a "sense of Europe,"[94] and abstention from continental disputes was still their guiding principle.

In England, the conduct of the government during the railways dispute was attacked by a few isolated critics. The *Saturday Review,* for instance, was annoyed because Belgium, so clearly in the right, had been forced to negotiate in Paris. Why, it asked, had not government spokesmen in Parliament put an end to the dispute at the outset by declaring their readiness to act, if necessary alone, upon the treaty which guaranteed Belgian neutrality?[95] Did not Britain's appeal to the forbearance of

90 Bismarck, VIb, no. 1383, intro.

91 *Ibid.*, VIb, no. 1383; to Bernstorff, *ganz vertraulich,* May 4, 1869.

92 See above, p. 172 and n. 77.

93 Bismarck, VIb, no. 1385; to Reuss, *vertraulich,* May 7, 1869.

94 John Morley, *Life of Gladstone* (London, 1904), II, 337.

95 *Saturday Review,* XXVII (March 20, 1869), 371.

the aggressive power give color to the notion that the efficacy of the guarantee had been impaired?[96]

The answer to the latter question may be found in a letter that the Prime Minister wrote at the height of the crisis. Referring specifically to the Belgian guarantee, Mr. Gladstone had asserted that "England should keep entire in her own hands the means of estimating her own obligations upon the various states of facts as they arise . . . that it is dangerous for her to assume alone an advanced, and therefore an isolated position in regard to European controversies; that come what may, it is better for her to promise too little than too much."[97] Believing as he did that Britain must not be involved in continental disputes, Gladstone was suspicious of all obligations undertaken by previous British governments. He feared that unequivocal recognition of such obligations might be the means of breaking down the isolation he desired for England. Clarendon's refusal to admit that England would uphold the Belgian guarantee in 1869 therefore received the complete approval of the Prime Minister, who later declared that in any event, "a guarantee gave the right of interference [but] it did not constitute of itself an obligation to interfere."[98]

Such an interpretation could not but gravely weaken the legal validity of the Belgian guarantee of 1839. To the extent that it did so, it weakened also the whole body of European public law, the maintenance of which George Canning, an advocate of nonintervention in an earlier age, had declared to be the first responsibility of Great Britain.

[96] *Ibid.*, XXVII (April 24, 1869), 539.
[97] Morley, *op. cit.*, II, 318.
[98] *Hansard*, 3d series, CCX, 1178.

10. Bismarck and His Ambassadors: The Problem of Discipline

In a famous eighteenth-century treatise on the art of diplomacy, the French writer Callières tells the story of a Grand Duke of Tuscany who complained to a citizen of Venice that the Venetian government had sent as minister resident to his court a man of limited talent, low intelligence, and offensive personality. "I am not surprised," said the Venetian finally. "We have many fools in Venice." "We also have fools in Tuscany," rejoined the Duke, "but we take care not to export them."[1]

Any government that takes its foreign policy seriously and hopes that it will be effective must be able to make the same boast as Callières' duke. Other things being equal, the success of a nation's policy will depend on the quality of its diplomatic corps, which must execute it. A good diplomatic corps is one in which a high percentage of the officers in the senior grades are men who, when they are in residence abroad, perform their duties of representation with distinction, carry out their instructions with loyalty and accuracy, report on all matters of importance to their home office with clarity, perception, and judgment, and —in the varied tasks of negotiation that fall to them—show initiative, tact, and intelligence.

To maintain a diplomatic service of this quality will obviously be a difficult task. It is apt to be achieved most easily by nations in which foreign policy is generally acknowledged to be important, where the prestige of the foreign service is sufficiently high, and the material condi-

"Bismarck and His Ambassadors" is reprinted from *The Foreign Service Journal* (Washington), XXXIII (June, 1956), with the permission of the American Foreign Service Association.

1 *The Practice of Diplomacy*, being an English rendering of François de Callières' *De la manière de négocier avec les souverains*, presented with an introduction by A. F. Whyte (London, 1919), p. 59.

tions of foreign service are sufficiently attractive, to persuade young men of talent to enter the diplomatic corps, and where those new recruits are aided, during their years of training, by the existence of an established diplomatic tradition or a body of received doctrine concerning procedure, discipline and other aspects of the diplomatic art. It is apt to be achieved less easily by nations where none of those conditions exists.

The dazzling successes achieved by the foreign policy of Prussia and Germany under the leadership of Otto von Bismarck rather obscure the fact that in the Bismarckian state conditions were not favorable for the creation of the kind of diplomatic corps described here. This was, indeed, one of Bismarck's greatest problems after he became Minister President and Foreign Minister of Prussia in 1862. It may be of interest to consider how he sought to solve that problem, for the methods he employed, the standards he sought to establish, and the difficulties he encountered in his efforts to create and maintain a competent and disciplined diplomatic service can tell us a good deal about the strength and weakness of German diplomacy in the years before the First World War.

I

The fact that Bismarck was the first professional diplomat in Prussian history to rise to the highest position in the state is enough in itself to throw into relief the problem that confronted him when he assumed the direction of foreign affairs in 1862. Prussia was a state that had been created by soldiers and internal administrators; in the eighteenth century, the talented young men of the gentry had been selected and trained for the army and the civil service rather than for diplomacy. A foreign service had, indeed, been established by Frederick William I, but it enjoyed little prestige. During the reign of Frederick the Great, for instance, a good many foreign posts had to be filled with Huguenots and Italians because there were not enough native candidates with the linguistic ability, social versatility, and other gifts necessary to qualify them for service abroad; and, although this situation was gradually corrected, Bismarck tells us in his memoirs that, when he entered the service in 1850, "foreign names were at a premium: Brassier, Perponcher, Savigny, Oriola."[2] For the most important tasks of negotiation, Prussian kings relied on civil administrators or soldiers. At the Congress

[2] Otto von Bismarck, *Gesammelte Werke* (15 vols. in 19; Berlin, 1924 *et seq.*), XV, 7–8.

of Vienna, for instance, Prussia's leading negotiators were Hardenberg and Wilhelm von Humboldt, neither of whom was a professional diplomat, although both proved to be very capable negotiators, and the latter an indefatigable and efficient organizer of Congress business.

When, in addition to these facts, one remembers the timid and vacillating nature of Prussian foreign policy during the first sixty years of the nineteenth century, it is easy to understand why able young men were not attracted to the foreign service and why Prussia, in contrast to France and Austria, was not able to develop a diplomatic tradition that could serve to school the diplomats she had. In this latter connection, it is fair to say that the Prussian foreign service before 1862 was disorganized to the point of chaos. Methods and procedures differed from post to post. The level of reporting was most uneven, and despatches from abroad were apt to be tendentious rather than informative. Channels of communication between the field and Berlin were not clearly laid down; and legations and embassies did not always recognize that they were in any sense subordinate to the Foreign Office. There were times, indeed, when Prussian missions abroad seemed to be carrying out different and mutually contradictory policies.

All of these conditions Bismarck managed to correct in the course of his long tenure of office, partly by deliberate indoctrination, in part simply by the force of his own example. With respect to personnel, for instance, it is probably true that the new spirit and energy that Bismark brought to Prussian foreign policy was more successful in attracting outstanding talent to the foreign service than a deliberate recruiting campaign or any other artificial means could have been. The success of Bismarck's methods in transforming what had been a relatively backward state into the leading continental power invested diplomacy with a new prestige; while, at the same time, it became obvious that career opportunities in the foreign service of the new Reich were more promising than they had ever been in the diplomatic corps of Prussia or the other German states. Being a member of the diplomatic corps never, perhaps, became as much of a distinction as being a member of the general staff corps of the army; but it became infinitely more glamorous than being in the Ministry of the Interior or any other branch of the civil service. This was reflected in the increased number and improved quality of candidates for the service.

In the selection and advancement of the candidates, Bismarck always played the leading role; this is shown, for instance, by the care he took to bring the brightest of the young men to the Foreign Office where they worked under his personal supervision before being sent to important posts in the field. In filling foreign posts, he had strong prejudices, but on the whole they were not unreasonable ones. Despite his criticism of the number of foreign names in the old Prussian service, he did not make the mistake of giving preference to native Prussians in the new. He was aware that the Prussian temperament was marked by inflexibility and excessive sensitivity, and that these are handicaps in the profession of diplomacy. He knew also the importance of avoiding giving the impression, either at home or abroad, that the new imperial service was to be dominated by Prussians. Bavarians, Swabians, Hanoverians did not, therefore, find themselves at a disadvantage in applying for appointments or in rising in the service; and the Bismarckian diplomatic corps was truly German in character.[3]

Men with extreme political views, democrats, socialists, and Jews were not welcome in the diplomatic service; in general Bismarck insisted upon complete political orthodoxy. He was not, however, so rigid in his attitude toward the social background of his diplomats. While it is true that the most important foreign posts were always filled by men of noble lineage, this was probably the result more of the prejudices of the Emperor and of the courts with which Bismarck had to deal than of strong feelings on his part; and, in any case, the aristocratic preponderance in the field was leavened to some extent by the employment of middle-class talent in the Foreign Office, where men like Bucher, Stumm, Brauer, and Raschdau had long and distinguished careers. On the other hand, Bismarck did feel that the possession of a private income was a prerequisite to a career in the political side of the diplomatic service as distinct from the consular service or the legal and technical sections of the Foreign Office. He wanted his country to be represented at foreign courts with dignity and style, and, although he was willing to fight in the Reichstag for living allowances that would make this possible, he recognized the need for a greater outlay than the state was likely to provide. Nobody, therefore, was accepted in the political diplomatic service who did not have a private income equal to a high official's salary.[4]

As far as personal traits were concerned, Bismarck had a partiality for men who had had some military service, for he believed that they were more likely to understand the importance of discipline, upon which, as we shall see, he placed a high valuation. He was suspicious of candidates from other government services, because of his scorn for

[3] A. von Brauer, "Die deutsche Diplomatie unter Bismarck," *Deutsche Revue*, XXXI (1906), 71–72.

[4] *Ibid.*

the rigidity of the bureaucratic mind. Finally, he distrusted academic learning and preferred practical men to men who were, or fancied themselves to be, scholars. In a speech in the Reichstag in 1877, he said:

> The work of the diplomat . . . consists of practical intercourse with men, of judging accurately what other people are likely to do in given circumstances, of appreciating accurately the views of others, of presenting accurately his own. I might say that personal attractiveness and knowledge of mankind often accomplish more [than learning]. We have had a good many unlearned diplomats, who were nevertheless in fact the ones who achieved most.[5]

This preference—and Bismarck's well-known tendency to overlook the past failures and indiscretions of young men who entered the service—led some people to say: "The Prince thinks that anyone who has failed his exams or run through all his property is a genius."[6] There may be something in this. Bismarck's memory of his own flaming youth made him very charitable toward the peccadilloes of the young, provided they weren't perpetuated into the years of maturity. Especially when a man had proven talent, Bismarck was capable of putting up with personal delinquencies that might have given pause to more cautious administrators. Hatzfeldt, for instance, led a most disorderly existence and was always in debt; yet Bismarck bore with him, and on occasion even persuaded his private banker to help him out of his difficulties. Hatzfeldt, Bismarck often said, was "the best horse in his stable," and he felt that the service needed him.[7]

Whatever one may think of Bismarck's personnel policies, they seem to have worked. It is difficult to call to mind quickly the names of many pre-Bismarckian Prussian diplomats. When, on the other hand, one thinks of the late Bismarck period one is likely to remember at least the so-called "great prophets":[8] Hatzfeldt, Hohenlohe, Schweinitz, Reuss, Münster, and Radowitz. These men would have graced any diplomatic service in the world; and, in addition to them, in the junior posts, there were many other competent, reliable, industrious representatives. Even

[5] Bismarck, XI, 515.

[6] Brauer, *op. cit.*, 75.

[7] On Hatzfeldt, see J. M. von Radowitz, *Aufzeichnungen und Erinnerungen* (Hajo Holborn, ed.) (2 vols.; Stuttgart, 1925), I, 255; Moritz Busch, *Tagebuchblätter* (2 vols.; Leipzig, 1899), II, 191; Hans Goldschmidt, "Mitarbeiter Bismarcks im aussenpolitischen Kampf," *Preussische Jahrbücher*, CCXXXVI (1934), 31.

[8] Hajo Holborn, "Bismarck und Werthern," *Archiv für Politik und Geschichte*, V (1925–26), 469.

so critical a judge as Harold Nicolson has written that, from the standpoint of talent and efficiency, the German diplomatic service compared favorably with any in Europe.[9]

Bismarck was very conscious of his responsibility as the founder of the German diplomatic service and took endless pains to help its members perfect their performance. German diplomats were constantly receiving advice from Berlin, not only with respect to special problems of negotiation with other powers, but also on how they should carry out the normal, daily functions of diplomacy. On the question of reporting, for instance, Bismarck was very hard to please. He insisted that reports from the embassies were meant to convey information and not to be essays in *belles lettres,* disquisitions on history, or collections of anecdotes. Accuracy and conciseness were qualities that he insisted upon; he once told Goltz, his ambassador in Paris in the 1860's, that his reports were so long that he could read them "only on the diagonal."[10] He distrusted styles of reporting that were too deliberately graceful; and, for this reason, in 1866, he did away with the standing order that despatches from abroad be written in French. "I have known many of our older ambassadors," he wrote in his memoirs, "to step into the highest positions simply on account of their proficiency in French, without any knowledge of politics; they only included in their despatches, too, what they could put fluently into French."[11] In doing away with the language requirement, Bismarck was, in effect, telling his service that content was more important than style.

From advice which Bernhard von Bülow, Bismarck's Secretary of State for Foreign Affairs from 1873 to 1880, gave to his son when the latter entered the service, we learn something more of Bismarck's standards with respect to reporting. Report only what is certain and nothing that may turn out to be unfounded later on, Bülow advised. Don't report gossip, exaggeration, overstatement; don't overcolor. *Point de fantaisie.* Don't compromise others in your reports. Don't write *ab irato.* Seldom prophesy, in any case not in official reports, and at the very utmost in private letters.[12]

This last point was one that Bismarck took very seriously indeed.

[9] Harold Nicolson, *Diplomacy* (2nd ed.; London, 1950), pp. 148–49.

[10] Radowitz, *op. cit.,* I, 35. See also H. L. von Schweinitz, *Denkwürdigkeiten* (W. von Schweinitz, ed.) (2 vols.; Berlin, 1927), II, 289.

[11] Bismarck, XV, 7–8.

[12] Bernhard Fürst von Bülow, *Denkwürdigkeiten* (4 vols.; Berlin, 1930–31), IV, 289–90.

In an instruction to Werthern, his minister in Munich, he wrote in 1869:

> Your Excellency's report no. 16 of the 14th of this month moves me to express the wish that henceforth you will make general and theoretical conjectures about the future, especially when they open up a gloomy prospect, as at the end of your despatch, the subject of *separate* reports. The conclusions which you reach about the future . . . have a great value for me personally; but, when they are put together with factual information, they make the official handling of your reports more difficult.

He couldn't take the time, Bismarck continued, to express in writing his disagreement with Werthern's prophecies before circulating the despatches in the Foreign Office and transmitting them to the Emperor and the Crown Prince; and he couldn't circulate them safely unless he did so.[13] In short, despite the charitable, but disingenuous, reference to the value of Werthern's crystal-gazing, Bismarck was saying, in effect, that he expected his diplomats to send home facts and to leave the speculation to him.

Bismarck's instructions to the field are filled with advice and admonitions with respect to other functions besides that of reporting. He had, for instance, a good deal to say about the correct relationship between his ambassadors and the courts to which they were accredited. He expected them to be sympathetic toward the wishes of those courts, but he was always warning them against the sin of becoming too closely identified with the interests of the state that was their temporary place of residence. He reminded his diplomats that it was their job to get on a good footing with the statesmen with whom they would have to deal, but that they should not try to improve their position by doing favors for them. Above all, it was not their function to forward to Berlin the embarrassing requests of foreign rulers or governments. If such requests had to be made, they should be made in Berlin by the diplomatic representative of the power in question, for it was easier, in those circumstances, to reject them.[14]

No one knew better than Bismarck that diplomacy was often an unpleasant business and that the envoy was frequently put in the position of having to disappoint the wishes and to defeat the designs of others. He should cultivate the ability to do this with firmness and courtesy and to do so, moreover, without becoming personally and emotionally involved, even to the extent of passing judgment upon the persons or

[13] Holborn, "Bismarck und Werthern," pp. 478–79.
[14] Bülow, *op. cit.*, pp. 290–91.

powers who wished to win his support. Irritation and touchiness, indignation and rancour were qualities that should not characterize the working diplomat; Bülow tells us that Bismarck always held that the envoy was meant to be "neither a preacher of penitence, nor a judge in a criminal court, nor a philosopher. His sole and exclusive interest must be the real and downright interest of his country," and he could not advance that interest if he allowed himself to be swayed by his personal feelings.[15]

Finally, with respect to their general conduct at their posts, Bismarck always cautioned his representatives against excessive zeal. They should not, of course, immure themselves in their embassies; but neither should they be too active. They should not want things to be happening all the time; and they should not, out of some misguided respect for action, try to force the pace of events. Patience was a great diplomatic virtue. "We can set our watches," Bismarck once reminded one of his ministers, "but time doesn't pass the more quickly because of that, and the ability to wait while conditions mature is a prerequisite of practical politics."[16]

II

It can be imagined that Bismarck's diplomats were not always happy about the streams of advice, rules of conduct, general observations about human nature and caustic reproaches that flowed from Berlin. Not all of them were as thick-skinned as Count Münster in London who accepted even gratuitous advice with tolerance and was unruffled by the not infrequent outbursts of Bismarckian rage. "How angry he must have been when he dictated that!" Münster would say, gazing ruefully at a rocket from Berlin.[17] Less phlegmatic representatives were doubtless often irritated and sometimes angered by the nagging to which they were subjected. Even so, it is probably true that most of Bismarck's ambassadors realized that the job he had set himself—that of doing away with the free and easy procedures of the earlier period and improving the standards of the service—was an important one and, furthermore, that there were, after all, few people as well qualified to advise them about diplomacy as their chief in Berlin. "When one has to deal with such

[15] *Ibid.*

[16] Holborn, "Bismarck and Werthern," p. 482.

[17] Bülow, *Denkwürdigkeiten,* IV, 524–25. On Münster, see also Trützschler von Falkenstein, "Kontroversen über die Politik Bismarcks im Jahre 1887," *Archiv für Politik und Geschichte,* VI (1926), 276–77.

outstanding persons as Bismarck," Werthern wrote, "and when one can never hope to equal them, then one must subordinate himself—even sacrifice himself—to them."[18]

This sentiment would doubtless have gratified Bismarck. He believed in the subordination of his ambassadors to his own wishes; indeed, he believed that discipline was the most desirable quality a diplomat could possess. And here we come to what is perhaps the central problem in Bismarck's administration of the German foreign service.

In a speech in the Reichstag in May 1872, Bismarck said: "An envoy is only a vessel, which attains its true value when it is filled with the instructions of the sovereign."[19] This remark was made incidentally, in the course of a speech on Germany's relations with the Vatican, and it is perhaps unwise to place too much weight upon it. We need not assume, for instance, that Bismarck meant that an ambassador existed *only* to carry out instructions. But it is perfectly clear, on the other hand, that he believed that an ambassador who would not carry out his instructions, who resisted them and quarreled over them and proposed alternative courses of action, could not be allowed to continue in the service.

The years in which Bismarck was charged with the administration of German foreign affairs provide enough examples to show how firmly he believed this and to what lengths he was prepared to go to break representatives who were hopelessly refractory. The two most famous cases, perhaps, are those of Usedom and Harry Arnim. Usedom had been one of Bismarck's rivals for political power before 1862 and had been employed in the diplomatic service since that date. He had a long record of opposition to Bismarck's policies, and, in 1868, when he was minister to Florence, this record caught up with him. For Bismarck took advantage of an awkward situation in which Usedom had become involved —not wholly through his own fault, but partly, as a matter of fact, through the intricacies of Bismarck's own diplomatic course—to persuade the King to dismiss him from the service.[20] Arnim, the ambassador to Paris in the 1870's, was deliberately seeking to defeat Bismarck's French policy; and Bismarck hounded him out of the service and, by instituting

[18] Holborn, "Bismarck und Werthern," p. 495.

[19] Bismarck, XI, 271.

[20] On the Usedom case, see Max Duncker, *Politische Briefwechsel aus seinem Nachlass,* herausgegeben von J. Schultze (Stuttgart, 1923), pp. 444 ff; Albrecht von Stosch, *Denkwürdigkeiten* (Ulrich von Stosch, ed.) (Stuttgart, 1904), p. 152; "Freytags Briefe an Stosch," *Deutsche Revue,* XXXVII (3) (1912), 146–47; Erich Eyck, *Bismarck: Leben und Werk* (3 vols.; Zurich, 1941–44), II, 209–10.

legal action against him for misuse of government documents, actually drove him into permanent exile.

So much has been made of Bismarck's lack of complete good faith in the first of these cases and his brutality in the second that a word or two must be said in explanation, if not in exculpation, of his conduct. In the first place, opposition on the part of ambassadors to their instructions did not always lead to such summary action. At least in the first stages of such disputes, Bismarck usually tried to convince his agents that their judgments were based on an inadequate appreciation of the over-all diplomatic situation and that the policy he was proposing was justified by sound reasons. He was apt also to appeal to the ambassador's professional sense, by pointing out that it was proper that the direction of foreign policy should lie in Berlin rather than in the field. In 1863, for instance, Count Robert von der Goltz, the ambassador in Paris, objected violently to the policy that Bismarck was following with respect to the situation in Schleswig and Holstein. Goltz urged that Prussia should take up arms, in collaboration with the other states of the Germanic Confederation, in order to free the duchies from the control of Denmark. Bismarck reasoned with his ambassador, pointing out that Prussia was a Great Power that could not subordinate her policy to the wishes of the lesser German states, outlining the advantages of playing a waiting game until the situation in the duchies was clarified, and giving other reasons for the devious course he was following. Then, passing on to professional considerations, he reminded Goltz that Prussia could, after all, have only one foreign policy at a time and added: "It must be the one on which the Ministry and the King are agreed. If you want to overthrow it, and thereby to overthrow the Ministry, then you will have to undertake that here in Berlin, by means of the Chamber and the press, and at the head of an opposition party."[21] Goltz, although not without misgivings, yielded; and it can be said generally that this kind of Bismarckian argument—coupled as it usually was with a systematic refutation of an ambassador's views—was enough to restore unity of policy, except in the most stubborn cases.

In the second place, it must be remembered that Bismarck was handicapped by some awkward constitutional circumstances. He did not have the power simply to command his ambassadors to obey him. The theory that an ambassador was an agent of the prince—a theory that in the constitutional states of the west was becoming a kind of legal fiction—retained its force in Germany. The ambassadors had the privilege of

[21] Bismarck, XIV/2, 660.

reporting directly to the Emperor; and Prussian tradition held that their primary allegiance was to the sovereign rather than to the Foreign Minister or the Chancellor. If, therefore, an ambassador refused to be swayed by Bismarck's arguments and persisted in his insubordination, Bismarck was forced—in defense of his own position—to resort to extreme measures against him. The Arnim case is a case in point.[22]

Arnim, while ambassador in Paris, believed that his mission lay in helping to restore monarchical government in France. This directly contradicted Bismarck's own policy, which was based upon the premise that the maintenance of republican institutions in France was to Germany's direct interest, since a republican France, in a Europe that was predominantly monarchical, would presumably find it difficult to secure allies. When he discovered that his ambassador had ideas of his own, Bismarck explained his policy very carefully to Arnim, and, as usual in such cases, he added the argument that the efficiency of German policy depended upon unity and discipline, just as, in a military campaign, success depends on cooperation between the divisional commander and his brigadiers. Arnim—an ambitious man who hoped to supplant Bismarck as Chancellor of the Reich—remained obdurate. He carried his fight directly to the Emperor, arguing his case in letters and in personal interviews, and he urged his friends in Berlin to use their influence at the court to undermine Bismarck's position.

Unable to dismiss Arnim without the Emperor's assent, and having discovered that the ruler was disinclined to give this, Bismarck adopted the only means he thought were left to him. He set spies on Arnim so as to be fully informed of his activities. Through the French ambassador in Berlin, he intimated to the French Foreign Office that Arnim was unreliable and should, as far as possible, be bypassed in all official business between the two governments. He spread rumors (perhaps not entirely unjustified) of financial manipulation on Arnim's part. He found fault with everything Arnim did. And, by all these means, he sought to weaken the Emperor's confidence in the ambassador and, simultaneously, to goad him into an indiscretion so outrageous that he would not merely be recalled (he was too dangerous a man to be allowed to join the anti-Bismarck *fronde* in Berlin) but utterly destroyed. In the end, Bismarck succeeded.

The Arnim case was the high point in Bismarck's campaign to

[22] On the Arnim case, see E. von Wertheimer, "Bismarck und Arnim," *Preussische Jahrbücher*, CCXXII (1930); Fritz Hartung, "Der Prozess Arnim," *Historische Zeitschrift*, CLXXI (1951); Norman Rich, "Holstein and the Arnim Affair," *Journal of Modern History*, XXVIII (1956).

discipline the German foreign service. There were no cases like it after 1875. The chaotic conditions that had characterized the older system disappeared; the position and authority of the Foreign Office as the central policy-making agency was strengthened; attempts to circumvent the Chancellor in matters of policy became unthinkable. And all of this doubtless increased the efficiency with which German foreign policy was executed.

Whether the results were all good is nevertheless doubtful. A nation's ambassadors are not, after all, meant to be merely yes-men. They are expected to show initiative of their own, and to have a sense of responsibility that will lead them, if not to oppose, at least to question Foreign Office policy when they think it is misguided. Were Bismarck's envoys likely to display those qualities after the Arnim case? Common sense would lead us to suspect that the kind of ministerial terrorism (to use one of Goltz's phrases) the Chancellor used could not help but discourage initiative and responsibility.

The story is told of a German envoy who, upon submitting a request to a foreign court and being rebuffed, cried in consternation: "But it is Prince Bismarck who desires this!"[23] The tale is probably apocryphal but but it might as well be true. After the Arnim case, there must—especially among the men at lesser posts—have been some who were terrified at the thought of Bismarck's disapprobation and more who were disinclined to risk becoming its targets by gestures of independence. Even Radowitz, one of Bismarck's most gifted juniors, says in his memoirs: "To oppose the Bismarck of the 1870's and the 1880's in any matter would have been unthinkable to me!"[24] Diplomatic representatives ambitious to rise higher in the service must also have suffered from—and, perhaps more often than we know, yielded to—the temptation to report to the Foreign Office, not what they knew to be true about the situation at their posts, but what they thought would please their chief.

It is possible that the "great ambassadors" did not give way to these weaknesses; but, even in their case, there is some evidence of a shrivelling of initiative. The shadow of their chief hung over them constantly; their subordination to him seems to have drained them of independent will. It was said of Hatzfeldt, for instance, that this brilliant diplomat was never quite the same after 1890, when he could no longer feel Bismarck behind him.

Moreover, Bismarck's successful imposition of discipline upon the German service played into the hands of his enemies in the military

[23] Brauer, *op. cit.*, 77.
[24] Radowitz, *op. cit.*, I, 266.

establishment who, in the last years of the Bismarck period, were seeking to increase military influence in the sphere of foreign policy.[25]

After 1883 especially, when the General Staff became an independent agency and when its administrative chief, General Count von Waldersee, began to interest himself in foreign policy, the military attachés began to send political despatches directly to the General Staff and, with Waldersee's connivance, to the Emperor. Since these reports were often sharply critical of the Foreign Office and its policy, Bismarck sought to put an end to this practice. He was never completely successful, partly because the soldiers very shrewdly argued that the attachés were technicians who understood the realities of foreign politics better than their civilian colleagues and that, moreover, in reporting to Berlin, they had the courage of their convictions, whereas Bismarck's diplomats reported only what the Chancellor wanted to hear.

These were plausible arguments, and they were not without effect upon William II, after he assumed the throne in 1888. The preference which William gave to military advice in foreign affairs, his frequent criticism of the Foreign Office and such actions as his dismissal of Count Metternich from his post in London for being "too flabby"[26] are all attributable, in part at least, to the results of Bismarck's disciplinary methods.

There is another aspect of this question which demands some attention. Goltz once accused Bismarck of seeking to establish a dictatorship of the Foreign Office over the embassies by a process of withholding necessary information from the ambassadors and even keeping them in the dark concerning the real purposes of his policy. There is a good deal of truth in this charge. Schweinitz, the long-term ambassador in St. Petersburg, says in his memoirs that "in critical situations Bismarck loved to leave the chiefs of mission who were not directly involved without information. Then they could compromise themselves but not him."[27] Bismarck doubtless also found this practice a useful means of keeping ambassadorial objections to his policy at a minimum and defeating them when they arose by demonstrating that the criticisms were incompetent because they weren't based on all the available facts.

But foreign services are not supposed to be run for the personal convenience of foreign ministers, and this Bismarckian practice had deplorable results. Ambassadors were likely to pursue a course of nego-

[25] See above, Chapter 6, pp. 126–27.

[26] See Gordon A. Craig, *The Politics of the Prussian Army, 1640–1945* (new ed.; Oxford, 1964), pp. 297–98.

[27] Schweinitz, *op. cit.*, I, 200.

tiation with energy and perseverance only to learn in the end—as Goltz did on one occasion in the 1860's—that Bismarck had never intended the negotiations to succeed, but had deliberately neglected to tell them so.[28] Again, ambassadors sometimes received stinging reprimands for failure to carry out instructions that were, in fact, so cryptic as to be misleading. Much of the confusion that characterized Anglo-German negotiations with respect to Angra Pequena in 1884 was the result of Bismarck's failure to take his ambassador in London, Count Münster, completely into his confidence; and this was no inadvertence on his part, for when his Secretary of State suggested that Münster be fully informed of Germany's intentions, Bismarck curtly rejected this as unnecessary.[29] In such circumstances, it was easy for envoys to make mistakes. Even such an experienced hand as Prince Reuss, the ambassador in Vienna, proved capable in 1887 of flying in the face of one of the fundamental axioms of Bismarckian policy: the insistence that the Austro-German Treaty of 1879 was a strictly defensive instrument. Inadequately informed, and bewildered by the tactical improvisions of Bismarck's diplomacy, Reuss made the mistake of intimating to the Austrians that, if they precipitated a conflict with Russia, Germany would support them. The Austrian Foreign Minister refused to believe this, and he was right, as Reuss discovered from later instructions.[30]

The results of Bismarck's refusal to introduce his ambassadors into the secrets of his over-all policy were shown in a most striking way in the debate over the renewal of the Reinsurance Treaty in 1890. One might have thought that the "great ambassadors" at least would have put up a spirited defense of the tie with Russia, which was so indispensable a feature of the Bismarck system. They did not do so; they seem, indeed, not even to have appreciated what was at stake. Familiar only with the problems of their own special posts, they were incompetent to judge in matters of high policy.

As organizer and educator of the German foreign service, Bismarck's achievement was a notable one. The importance he attributed to discipline, however, and the methods he used to achieve it, had less fortunate results. Discipline is doubtless important in any career service, and,

[28] See, for instance, the documents on Goltz's negotiations with Napoleon III in 1867 in *Auswärtige Politik Preussens: Diplomatische Aktenstücke,* herausgegeben von der Historische Reichskommission (Oldenburg, 1931 ff.), VIII, *passim.*

[29] On this incident, see the materials cited in Gordon A. Craig, *From Bismarck to Adenauer: Aspects of German Statecraft* (rev. ed.; New York, 1965), p. 77, n. 22.

[30] H. Krausnick, *Holsteins Geheimpolitik in der Aera Bismarck* (2d ed.; Hamburg, 1942), p. 155.

in view of the conditions that Bismarck inherited in 1862, he had good reason to desire it. But discipline can surely be achieved without destroying, or even weakening, the initiative and sense of responsibility that a nation's foreign representatives should possess. Even while admitting the special constitutional problems that confronted Bismarck, one finds it very difficult to justify the means he used to impose his personal authority over his ambassadors. One suspects also that Baron Holstein, who later—in the words of Harold Nicolson—"entangled the whole German foreign service in a spider's web of suspicion, jealousy and intrigue,"[31] was merely improving on the Bismarckian example.

Finally, however technically competent a diplomatic corps may be, it cannot operate with true efficiency unless it is kept fully informed. The relationship between the Foreign Office on the one hand and the foreign missions on the other should be one of mutual confidence. Under Bismarck this was not true; and this is one reason why his task of educating the foreign service remained incomplete. None of his ambassadors was trained to succeed him. The Bismarckian diplomatic tradition came to an end with Bismarck's fall.

[31] Nicolson, *op. cit.*, p. 149.

11. The Revolution in War and Diplomacy, 1914-39

A COMMEMORATION OF THE outbreak of the First World War cannot but be a melancholy affair. Few wars in history are capable of arousing such poignancy as this tragic conflict, perhaps because we have so much testimony to the mood of enthusiasm and hope and idealism with which it was entered into, and so many staggering statistics about the losses of those who shared those feelings. In 1939 soldiers went off to the front soberly, fatalistically, stoically, sometimes cynically: they had an awareness of what lay ahead. The recruits of 1914 rushed into conflict as if it were a feast or a frolic—"War is like Christmas!" said one young German with delight as he received his uniform and side arms[1]—or they embraced it as a vital experience that would change and improve the world.

> Now [sang Rupert Brooke], God be thanked who has matched us
> with His hour,
> And caught our youth and waken'd us from sleeping,
> With hand made sure, clear eye, and sharpened power,
> To turn, as swimmers into cleanness leaping,
> Glad from a world grown old and cold and weary.[2]

"The Revolution in War and Diplomacy" was delivered at Roosevelt University, Chicago, in April 1964, as the opening lecture in a series on "The First World War as Turning Point, 1914–64."

[1] Siegfried A. Kaehler to Friedrich Meinecke, 28 August 1914, in Friedrich Meinecke, *Ausgewählte Briefwechsel* (Ludwig Dehio and Peter Classen, eds.) (Stuttgart, 1962), p. 326.

[2] *The Collected Poems of Rupert Brooke*, with an introduction by George Edward Woodberry and a biographical note by Margaret Lavington (New York, 1915).

The same note was struck by young poets in other countries. In Germany, for instance, Bruno Frank wrote ecstatically:

> Rejoice, friends! that we are alive
> And that we're young and vigorous.
> Never has there been a year like this,
> And never has youth been so blessed.
>
> For we can stand and we can march
> Where the morning dawns and the evening
> sinks.
> The greatest of all epochs
> Puts its mark upon our young hearts.
> . . . .
>
> [And no matter what may befall any one of us]
> He shall have seen this proud year.[3]

How brutally those fine hopes were disappointed we all know. The war which these young men expected never materialized. Instead, they had to experience what one of the characters in F. Scott Fitzgerald's novel *Tender is the Night* described to some friends as they made a visit to the Somme valley after the war. "See that little stream," he said, "we could walk to it in two minutes. It took the British a whole month to walk to it—a whole empire walking very slowly, dying in front and pushing forward behind. And another empire walked very slowly backward a few inches a day, leaving the dead like a million bloody rugs."[4] Among those dead were many of the young idealists of 1914, whose vigor and intelligence might have helped change the world in many useful ways if they had been allowed to survive. In the Great War of 1914–18, the good died young and quickly. Alfred Duff Cooper tells us in his memoirs how he sat in the Foreign Office in London during the first year of the war and learned in despair of the death, one after another, of all of his closest Oxford friends.[5] In her study of the Marne campaign, Barbara Tuchman tells the story of a

[3] Bruno Frank, "1914," in *Das ewige Brunnen* (Ludwig Reiners, ed.) (Munich, 1955), p. 440.

[4] F. Scott Fitzgerald, *Tender is the Night: A Romance,* with the Author's Final Revisions, preface by Malcolm Cowley (New York, 1948), p. 117.

[5] *Old Men Forget.* The Autobiography of Duff Cooper (Viscount Norwich) (London, 1953), pp. 49 ff.

young Frenchman who, because of illness, was unable to report to his unit for duty in August 1914. As a result he was the only one from his *lycée* class of twenty-seven boys who was still alive by Christmas.[6] It is stories like these, and their implications of dreadful waste, that make any commemoration of the Great War a somber and dispiriting business.

Even so, it is important that we do not avoid it. Before it was over, the war had wrought changes in almost every aspect of western society —its structure, its institutions, its values—and it is possible that, if we look at those changes with the benefit of fifty years of hindsight, we may succeed in throwing a little light upon some of our present perplexities, many of which are rooted in the past. In these pages, I shall attempt to deal with the effects that the 1914 conflict had upon two of the most important institutions of the western world—War itself, and Diplomacy.

It is appropriate that we consider these two together, for they belong together. Classically, diplomacy was—in Sir Ernest Satow's definition[7]—the process of employing tact and intelligence in the adjustment of the relations and the interests of independent states, and war was the means used for the same purpose when tact and intelligence failed. As the great German military theorist Clausewitz once explained, war was not an independent and self-sufficient agency, but merely a continuation of policy by other means.[8] It was an instrument of statecraft, its ends and even its means determined by the requirements of policy, and its results defined and legalized by diplomatic negotiation. The greatest statesmen of the nineteenth century understood this intimate relationship. At the time of Prussia's mobilization against France in July 1870, for example, Bismarck read and underscored the phrase "Blessed are the peacemakers!" on his devotional wall calendar.[9] This has sometimes been taken as a proof of the Chancellor's essential cynicism; it might more properly be interpreted as a sign of determination on his part that the impending war would be kept within its political bounds and would be ended by diplomatic means as quickly as was expedient, once the state's political objectives had been secured. This kind of politico-military coordination was not always easy to achieve, and Bismarck himself had serious difficulties with the Prussian Chief of Staff during the last phase

[6] Barbara W. Tuchman, *The Guns of August* (New York, 1962), p. 439 n.

[7] Sir Ernest Satow, *A Guide to Diplomatic Practice* (3rd ed.; London, 1932), I, 1.

[8] Karl von Clausewitz, *Vom Kriege* (ed., Werner Hahlweg) (16th ed.; Bonn, 1952), p. 77.

[9] Arnold Oskar Meyer, *Bismarck, der Mensch und der Staatsmann* (Stuttgart, 1949), pp. 412–13.

of the French war.[10] But even so, despite the friction that occurred in concrete cases, there was, until 1914, fairly general agreement that the tasks of the soldier and the statesman (or diplomat) were complementary.

Perhaps the most fateful change effected by the First World War was the destruction of this relationship. Warfare was revolutionized in a way that made it increasingly difficult for civilian authorities to control. Simultaneously, the expanding violence of the conflict smashed the very framework of traditional diplomacy and released forces which, in the subsequent period, militated against the kind of consensus necessary to effective international collaboration, and undermined the authority and prestige of professional diplomats in their own countries.

I

When we talk of the revolution that has taken place in warfare in our time, we think in the first instance of all of the frightening ways in which science and technology have enhanced its potential for destruction. This process, which culminated (or perhaps merely reached its penultimate stage of dreadfulness) during the Second World War, began during the First, and did so with a suddenness that startled the soldiers themselves. After one of the first British attacks in Flanders, a young subaltern said to Lieutenant General Sir Douglas Haig, "Sorry, sir. We didn't know it would be like that. We'll do better next time." The remark was prompted by the ghastly experience of learning for the first time what the combination of well-placed machine guns and barbed wire could do to massed attacks across an open field. Similar excuses must have been made on other occasions by regular officers of the armed forces—by Austrian commanders on the Drina and Galician fronts in 1914, for example, or by Russian officers on the Gorlice-Tarnow line in 1915—for those who had made a career of soldiering before 1914 always seemed to be more surprised than the nonprofessionals by the forms their vocation took during the First World War, as conventional assumptions about strategy and tactics were repeatedly shattered by the appearance of new weapons, or combinations of weapons, or techniques of combat. Neither the machine gun nor the use of wire was new in 1914, but their combination in articulated defensive systems and scientifically devised patterns of fire was new enough to have escaped

[10] See Gordon A. Craig, *The Politics of the Prussian Army, 1640–1945* (new ed.; Oxford, 1964), pp. 204–15.

the attention of those who made war plans, and this had a decisive effect upon the tactics of the war. Nor was this combination the only innovation. Others were the Big Bertha gun, the use of the submarine on a massive scale, the employment of smoke and poison gas to screen infantry attacks, the use of manned aircraft for reconnaissance, for anti-troop and anti-air combat, and for the bombing of installations, and the introduction of the tank.[11] And this list is not exhaustive.

In the employment of these weapons the armies of 1914–18 were not always expert, and the results were sometimes modest. Only about 1,400 Englishmen and 750 Germans lost their lives as a result of air raids between 1914 and 1918[12] (a far cry from the 75,358 homes and residential buildings that were totally destroyed and the 135,000 persons who were killed in the fourteen hours of aerial bombardment of Dresden in 1945[13]). Poison gas proved an unpredictable weapon that was likely to kill as many friends as foes; and the tank was misused in its first appearance in the field and played no important role until the war was almost over. But, even so, the new weapons had come to stay; as time passed, they would be improved; and eventually they would be superseded by even more effective ones. There were people in the period after 1918 who tried to pretend that this was not so, and who sought to block new expenditure on armor or new experimentation with air power;[14] but these were people who failed to draw the proper conclusions from the first world conflict.

In a technical sense, the First World War, as Hanson Baldwin has written, "provided a preview of the Pandora's box of evils that the linkage of science with industry in the service of war was to mean."[15] It started that *Technisierung* of war which engrosses so much of the energies and resources of modern nations and makes the average citizen so apprehensive of "missile gaps" and "technological breakthroughs" and

[11] See the discussion in Herman Kahn, *On Thermonuclear War* (Princeton, 1960), pp. 350–57.

[12] Hanson W. Baldwin, *World War I: An Outline History* (New York, 1962), p. 159. See also Cyril Falls, *The Great War, 1914–1918* (New York, 1959), pp. 365–66.

[13] See David Irving, *The Destruction of Dresden* (New York, 1963), pp. 11, 237–38.

[14] For illustrations, see Irving M. Gibson (pseud.), "Maginot and Liddell Hart," in Edward Mead Earle, ed., *Makers of Modern Strategy: Military Thought from Machiavelli to Hitler* (Princeton, 1943), pp. 376–77; Andrew Boyle, *Trenchard, Man of Vision* (New York, 1962), pp. 354 ff.; Robert Graves and Alan Hodge, *The Long Weekend* (New York, 1941), pp. 261–62; Alfred F. Hurley, *Billy Mitchell, Crusader for Air Power* (New York, 1964), *passim.*

[15] Baldwin, *op. cit.*, p. 159.

other presumed threats to his security that he is apt to give uncritical support to his nation's armed establishment.

Important as this change in the nature of warfare was, it was less revolutionary than another: the extent to which war now absorbed the full energies of the societies that engaged in it. The war of 1914 was the first total war in history, in the sense that very few people living in the belligerent countries were permitted to remain unaffected by it during its course. This had not been true in the past. Even during the great wars against Napoleon many people could go on living as if the world were at peace. All of Jane Austen's characters did so; none of them ever mentions the campaigns on the continent at all. It is said that on the evening of the allied disaster at Austerlitz, there was great excitement in London, but this was caused not by the military defeat but rather by a boxing match between two well-known champions. This kind of detachment, which was true also of the wars in Central Europe in the 1860's, was wholly impossible during the First World War. This was, for one thing, the first war in which the distinction between soldier and civilian broke down, a development that was partly due to the expansion of warfare made possible by those technological innovations which have already been mentioned. When dirigibles began to drop bombs over London and submarines began to sink merchant ships, war had invaded the civilian sphere, and the battle line was everywhere.

But this relative universalizing of the possibility of death in battle was not the only thing that made war total. Even when the dirigibles did not come, the civilian was caught up in the war, and all of his activities were geared to its requirements. Once it had been discovered, in the winter of 1914, that the war was not going to be over by Christmas, that it was not going to be a short war like those of 1866 and 1870, and that it was not going to be won by military means alone but by the effective mobilization of the total resources of the nation and its allies, every mature citizen became an active participant in the war effort. He was subjected to disciplines and deprivations similar to those binding on the soldiers at the front, and restrictions upon his freedom which varied with the fortunes of war and the distance of his country from the theater of operations. The energy and morale of the civilian now became just as important a resource as the spirit and determination of the man in the trenches—which, of course, is why the enemy tried to drop bombs on him or starve him into compliance with its will.

Moreover—and here we come to the most fateful aspect of these changes—precisely because war became so total and was prolonged so long, it also became ideological, taking on a religious cast that had not characterized warfare in the west since the Thirty Years War. Front-line soldiers could feel sympathy for fighting men on the other side, who had to put up with the same dangers and miseries that they bore themselves; on feast days, they could even declare private armistices with them and exchange presents. Aviators, with a chivalry that belonged to olders forms of war, were known to drop wreaths on the graves of enemy fliers or—as in the case of the German ace Richthofen, who was shot down behind French lines—to give them elaborate funerals. The civilian was not prone to this kind of behavior. He could not look the enemy in the face and recognize him as another man; he knew only that it was the Enemy, an impersonal, generalized concept, that was depriving him of the pleasures of peace. As his own discomfort grew, his irritation hardened into a hatred that was often encouraged by government propagandists who believed that this was the best way of maintaining civilian morale. Before long, therefore, the enemy was considered to be capable of any enormity and any idea of compromise with him became intolerable. The foe must be beaten to his knees, no matter what this might cost in effort and blood; he must be made to surrender unconditionally; he must be punished with peace terms that would keep him in permanent subjection.

The result of this was that the cautionary precept of Clausewitz was ignored and that rational calculation of risk versus gain, of compromise through negotiation versus *guerre à outrance,* became virtually impossible for the belligerent governments. There were soldiers and statesmen during the First World War who understood the truth later expressed by Professor Herbert Butterfield, when he wrote, after the second world conflict,

> If you possess an international order, or if it is your desire to assert the existence or the authority of such an order, you are the party which must refrain from conceiving the ends of war as though you were fighting barbarian hordes entirely outside the system. . . . So long as an international order exists, or so long as we may desire one to exist, wars must come short of the last degree of irreconcilability and must retain some of the characteristics of a conflict between potential allies, some trace of the fact that they are quarrels between friends.[16]

Unfortunately, those who felt this way were few and ineffective. As the war expanded in scope and violence, the masses who had to bear its rigors closed their minds to reason and called for a war of extermination.

It is sometimes pointed out, as a proof of the power of special interest

[16] Herbert Butterfield, *Christianity, Diplomacy and War* (New York, n.d.), pp. 96–97.

groups in the determination of Germany's wartime policy, that both Chancellor Theobald von Bethmann-Hollweg and Foreign Minister Richard von Kühlmann were forced out of office because they advocated a peace short of total victory. It is true that these officials were the victims of a military–big business cabal that wanted no negotiated settlement,[17] but it is surely worth noting that their dismissal elicited not the slightest evidence of any popular indignation over the treatment accorded them. Nor should it be forgotten that, when the former Foreign Secretary Lord Lansdowne, sickened by the slaughter in the trenches, wrote a letter to the *Daily Telegraph* in November 1917 in which he urged that a negotiated peace be arranged while there was still something of European civilization to save, he was viciously attacked by the Northcliffe and Rothermere press, was denounced by politicians who described his letter as "craven" and "inept," and—in the words of his biographer—was subjected to "a flood of invective and an incredible mass of abusive correspondence which, though largely incoherent, was marked by a violence rare in English political life."[18] In the First World War, popular passion was probably more responsible than governmental obtuseness, not only for the prolongation of the war to the point where the old framework of Europe was smashed beyond repair, but also for the worst of the mistakes made at the Peace Conference as well. It is easy to understand why Jan Smuts of South Africa, watching war-induced hatreds prevail over reason at Paris, should have been moved to tell his friend John Maynard Keynes the story of the old Griqua chief who, in perilous times, prayed: "Lord, save Thy people. Lord, we are lost unless Thou savest us. Lord, this is no work for children. It is not enough this time to send Thy son. Lord, Thou must come Thyself."[19]

As a result of the First World War, therefore, the art of warfare had been revolutionized by technological innovation, extended in scope, and given a pseudo-religious cast—and for all of these reasons it had become more dangerous, more destructive, and much more difficult to get back under control once it had been loosed.

II

The changes wrought by the war in diplomacy were equally profound and were rooted in the tendency of warfare to assume its absolute and most unrestrained forms by 1917 and 1918.

[17] Gerhard Ritter, *Staatskunst und Kriegshandwerk, III* (Munich, 1964), 536 ff.
[18] Lord Newton, *Lord Lansdowne: A Biography* (London, 1929), pp. 468–69.
[19] W. K. Hancock, *Smuts:* Vol. 1: *The Sanguine Years, 1870–1919* (Cambridge, 1962), p. 521.

In the first place, as has already been indicated, the very context within which diplomats had operated in the past was altered out of recognition by the prolongation of the war. The nineteenth-century diplomatic system—Europe-centered and dominated by five self-confident and, for the most part, monarchical powers—dissolved in a holocaust unparalleled in history. The Habsburgs, the Hohenzollerns, and the Romanovs now left the stage of history, and out of their empires the peacemakers in Paris fashioned new states which entered the diplomatic community without either tradition or experience to guide them. The war also loosened the ties of empire, inspiring the British dominions to demand a stronger voice in the determination of imperial policy and arousing a desire for full sovereignty and independence in foreign affairs among the dependencies and protectorates of Great Britain and other colonial powers. Even during the course of the war, it had become apparent—with the intervention of Japan and the United States—that Mazzini's description of Europe as the lever that moved the world was no longer a true one, and that the course of world affairs could no longer be determined by congresses or ambassadorial conferences like those of Berlin and Algeciras. With the sharp increase in the number of states participating in world affairs and in their geographical diversity—both tendencies that were to be accelerated by the Second World War—new forms of diplomatic organization had to be found; and the League of Nations was only the first of attempts made to cope with this problem.

The expansion of the diplomatic community was not the only change. Equally disturbing in its effects was the breakdown of the internal homogeneity of the diplomatic system. Before 1914, the states that were active in international affairs were in general agreement about basic things. Charles Burton Marshall has written recently:

> Their regimes drew on a generally common fund of history. The frame of discourse among them was unified to a degree permitting any government participating significantly in world affairs to be confident of having its utterances understood by others in the sense intended. None was a revolutionary power. Ideologies were "a minor theme" through most of the period. . . . The basis of general order was not at issue. A common notion of legitimacy prevailed.[20]

After 1918, all that had been changed. The nations no longer accepted the same norms of international behavior, and it was often true that their representatives used the same words in quite different ways.

[20] Charles Burton Marshall, "The Golden Age in Perspective," *Journal of International Affairs* (Special Issue: "Diplomacy in Transition"), XVII, No. 1 (1963), 11.

The fact that the war ended on the one hand in revolution and on the other with a punitive peace settlement made this almost inevitable. In the first flush of their victory, the new regime in Russia, for example, made their rejection of all of the principles of the old diplomacy explicit, and Lenin and Trotsky made an earnest attempt to abolish what they considered a wicked bourgeois institution that was wholly inappropriate for a proletarian state. When this attempt failed and they were forced in self-defense to cultivate contacts with other powers through traditional channels, and even to seek admittance to organizations like the League of Nations, they practiced diplomacy in what they considered to be the true bourgeois spirit—with as much disingenuousness, duplicity, and cynicism as they could get away with. Secretary of State Bainbridge Colby wrote indignantly in 1920 that the Government of the United States had become convinced, against its will, that "the existing regime in Russia is based upon the negation of every principle of honor and good faith, and every usage and convention, underlying the whole structure of international law; the negation, in short, of every principle upon which it is possible to base harmonious and trustful relations, whether of nations or of individuals." How could there be any common ground, he asked, upon which the western powers could stand with a government whose conceptions of international relations were so entirely alien to their own?[21] This was a question that must often have been in the minds of diplomats whose governments could not, like the United States Government, simply ignore the Soviet Union and who, therefore, had to go on trying to adjust their traditional concepts of diplomatic practice to Soviet wrecking tactics.

Nor did they have to concern themselves only with Lenin and his successors. Governments that resented the treatment they had received at Paris were not disinclined to follow the Soviet example, and some of them found leaders whose virtuosity matched that of the men sent forth from the Kremlin. Mussolini built a career upon his discovery that a flagrant breach of custom sometimes elicited more consternation than effective resistance; and Hitler won his early successes by means of outrageous falsehoods that were accepted by western statesmen schooled in the tradition that diplomats were gentlemen and gentlemen did not lie to each other. In a sense, the whole period between the two world wars was a *dialogue des sourds* between those governments which were attempting to construct a genuine comity of nations on the ruins left by the war and were seeking new rules that would be accepted by all its

[21] *Foreign Relations of the United States,* 1920, III, 460 ff.

members, and those revolutionary powers which preferred to recognize no rules at all or desired to retain the freedom to determine when they would obey rules and when they would break them.

The degeneration of accepted standards of international intercourse and the confusion of the intellectual atmosphere in which diplomacy had to be conducted was further increased by the fact that the newly created or recently liberated nations were also likely to show a disinclination to accept traditional restraints. Their late arrival on the scene and their relative lack of status was often in itself a goad to defiance of the restrictions that a genuine community of nations requires; in some cases resentments inherited from a colonial past inspired a rejection of legal arrangements, diplomatic principles, or methods of procedure simply because they were western in origin or character. The behavior of the new nations—regarded from the standpoint of self-interest—was often illogical and self-defeating; but their leaders ignored this in their gratification over the confusion they proved capable of creating, and contributed powerfully to the complexities and the failures of communication of the new diplomacy.

Finally, it should be noted that, in those countries which had the greatest interest in maintaining the public law and creating an effective international system after 1919, the ability of professional diplomats to cope with the problems caused by the war was seriously diminished by the loss of their former prestige and public support. In Great Britain and the United States in particular, it was widely believed that the diplomats had caused the war, because they had been the authors of what Woodrow Wilson called that "concatenation of alliances and treaties, [that] complicated network of intrigue and espionage which unerringly caught the entire family in its meshes."[22] As if intent on sharing Lenin's prejudices, politicians in both countries demanded that foreign policy be removed from the hands of the professionals and turned over to the people and were roundly applauded for doing so. There was little objection (except among officials of the Foreign Office and the State Department) when heads of state began to use persons with no special qualification in foreign affairs as their diplomatic advisers, or to send politicians and businessmen abroad as envoys extraordinary in time of crisis, or even to go to foreign capitals themselves and to supersede their own ambassadors in negotiations.

George Kennan has written that summit diplomacy, a method of negotiation that has brought much imprecision and many unreasonable

[22] Wilson on 16 October 1916, quoted in Bernadotte Schmitt, *Triple Alliance and Triple Entente* (New York, 1931), p. 1.

expectations into international intercourse since 1945, had its start during the Paris Conference of 1919, where the Council of Four was a permanent summit conference in which heads of state, often without the assistance of professional diplomatic aides, sought to plaster loose formulae over intractable problems.[23] Despite its indifferent success at Paris, the experiment was carried further by the statesmen of the interwar period, the British being particularly prone to what came to be called "open diplomacy." Lloyd George, Ramsay MacDonald, and Neville Chamberlain all found it impossible to delegate the execution of policy and the delicate tasks of negotiation to professionals, of whom, indeed, they had an opinion bordering on contempt and whose methods—the time-tested procedures of negotiation on the basis of written documents—they considered ill suited to the conditions of the new age.[24]

These tendencies, which had unfortunate results in English practice, were not confined to Britain. In France, when Briand and Laval were prime ministers, the Foreign Office was less than perfectly informed of the nature of their conversations with, and the extent of their commitments to, foreign statesmen like Stresemann and Mussolini. Nor would anyone deny that the distrust of professional diplomacy that was inspired by the First World War caused dislocation, imprecision, and confusion in the administration of foreign affairs in the United States. Wilson was not alone in his distrust of the techniques of the old diplomacy.[25] The history of the London Economic Conference of 1933 and the elaborate methods employed subsequently by Franklin Roosevelt to bypass the State Department (methods commented upon most recently by Robert Murphy in his memoirs[26]) were in full accord with the kind of pattern set by the Council of Four in 1919 and Lloyd George's personal diplomacy in the years that followed.

III

In the middle of the nineteenth century, Sir Robert Peel defined diplomacy as the great machine whose primary purpose was the preservation of peace. The revolutionary impact of the First World War upon the size and homogeneity of the diplomatic community and upon the

[23] George F. Kennan, *Russia and the West under Lenin and Stalin* (Boston, 1960), p. 129.

[24] See below, Chapter 12, pp. 212 ff.

[25] For an amusing picture of how far Wilson could carry this distrust, see Sir Charles Webster, *The Art and Practice of Diplomacy* (New York, 1962), p. 28.

[26] Robert Murphy, *Diplomat among Warriors* (New York, 1964), p. 70.

nature of diplomatic practice was admirably designed to make the fulfillment of that purpose impossible and to release the expanding energies of war upon the world once more. How could the newer and smaller powers learn to cultivate restraint, responsibility, and recognition of collective values when older and stronger powers so conspicuously lacked those qualities? How could the *velléités* of Ramsay MacDonald or the arrogant amateurishness of Neville Chamberlain cope with the brutal forthrightness and lack of scruple of Mussolini or the deliberate obstructionism of the Soviet Union? Or, for that matter, with the ambitions of Adolf Hitler, who regarded diplomacy not as a machine for peace but as a means of preparing the way for the destructive war after which he lusted?

The Second World War was, to a very large degree, the direct result of the revolution in diplomacy that had been set in train in the years between 1914 and 1918. At the same time, the second global conflict demonstrated that the technological and psychological changes that had begun to affect warfare in 1914 had been raised to a new and frightening dimension. The war that began with Stukas diving on Warsaw ended with the mushroom cloud over Hiroshima and Nagasaki, and, in the interval, any shadow of a line between soldier and civilian disappeared forever. The war became total to an extent that could not be exceeded; and it was fought with unimaginable bitterness to a point beyond all reason, until the destruction of the last vestiges of the system so badly shaken a quarter of a century before had been completed and the world had been handed over to the uncertainties of the cold war.

12. The Professional Diplomat and His Problems, 1919-39

One of the recurring themes in those books on the diplomatic prehistory of the Second World War which have come to us from the former enemy countries is the plight of the professional diplomat, whose training and knowledge convinced him that the policy of his government was leading straight to disaster but whose advice was seldom solicited and never followed. The memoirs of Erich Kordt, of Herbert von Dirksen, and of Rudolf Rahn, the books of Elisabetta Cerruti, Mario Donosti, and Filippo Anfuso[1] include abundant and circumstantial evidence of the lack of influence exercised in matters of high policy by the permanent staffs of the foreign offices of Germany and Italy and by their agents in the field. In his study of the origins of the Pact of Steel, Mario Toscano has described the desperate efforts made by Attolico, the Italian ambassador in Berlin, to convince his political superiors in Rome of the inadequacies and dangers of the projected alliance with Germany.[2] Those efforts failed; and they were certainly resented by the "realists" in Rome, who had long since reached the conclusion that foreign policy was too important to be left in the hands of professional diplomats. The same conclusion had been reached in Germany; and it was persisted in until the collapse of 1945. As early as 1936, the German

"The Professional Diplomat and His Problems" is reprinted from *World Politics*, IV, No. 1 (January, 1952), with the permission of the editors.

[1] Erich Kordt, *Nicht aus den Akten* (Stuttgart, 1950); Herbert von Dirksen, *Moskau, Tokio, London: Erinnerungen und Betrachtungen zu 20 Jahren deutscher Aussenpolitik, 1919–39* (Stuttgart, 1950); Rudolf Rahn, *Ruheloses Leben* (Düsseldorf, 1950); Elisabetta Cerruti, *Visti da vicino* (Milan, 1951); Mario Donosti, *Mussolini e l'Europa: la politica estera fascista* (Milan, 1945); Filippo Anfuso, *Roma Berlino Salò* (Milan, 1950).

[2] Mario Toscano, *Le origini del Patto d'Acciaio* (Florence, 1948), especially pp. 170–80.

foreign service had been deprived of most of its former prerogatives in the processes of policy formulation and execution. Ernst von Weizsäcker, the State Secretary for Foreign Affairs from 1938 until 1944, says in his memoirs: "Amateurish and irregular reports were often preferred to the official ones. Decisions were taken without the Foreign Minister or the Foreign Office having had a say in the framing of them. The carrying out of the decisions was entrusted to the most various quarters. . . . The foreign service had been degraded to the level of a mere technical apparatus."[3]

We could dismiss all of this evidence of the diminution of the influence of expert advice in modern diplomacy as being nothing more than an interesting sidelight on the nature of totalitarian regimes if it were not for one thing that is sometimes forgotten. And that is that the experience of the professional diplomat in Germany and Italy finds striking parallels in the diplomatic practice of the democratic states of Europe in the interwar period. In both Great Britain and France especially, the neglect and abuse of the resources of expert diplomacy was a recurrent phenomenon in the years 1919–39; and, when the new Fay or Schmitt or Seymour appears to write a comprehensive history of the origins of the Second World War, he will have to compose at least a lengthy footnote on the subject. The political scientist who is willing to relate the experience of history to current problems will probably wish to do more than that, for some of the more unhappy features of prewar British and French practice are recognizable—in somewhat exaggerated forms—in the conduct of foreign relations in our own country at the present time.

I

"The art of diplomacy," Harold Nicolson has written, "as that of water-colours, has suffered much from the fascination which it exercises upon the amateur."[4] The years after 1919 were years in which the political leaders of the Western states found that fascination irresistible and in which, undeterred by their lack of previous experience in the arts of diplomacy, they took into their hands "delicate work for which a life's training is no sure guarantee of success, and for which sciolism is an almost certain presage of failure."[5] Their successful penetration into

[3] *The Memoirs of Ernst von Weizsäcker* (Chicago, 1951), p. 106.

[4] Harold Nicolson, *Curzon: The Last Phase, 1919–1925* (New York, 1939), p. 54.

[5] A. L. Kennedy, *Old Diplomacy and New* (London, 1922), pp. 363–64.

what had formerly been the preserve of diplomats of career is, of course, easily explained. Even in normal times, career diplomats are not beloved in democratic states, where foreign affairs seem, at the very least, to be a distraction from the true business of the nation and, at the worst, a source of constant trouble and danger, and where men who make a career of dealing with foreign affairs are apt to be viewed with grave suspicion. "On n'aime pas," Jules Cambon has said, "ces porteurs de secrets que sont les ambassadeurs."[6] In 1919 this vague suspicion had been greatly strengthened by the prevailing conviction that the secret diplomacy which was their stock in trade had been the principal cause of the recent war. When Woodrow Wilson announced in the Fourteen Points that "diplomacy shall proceed always frankly and in the public view," his demand was accorded widespread approval; in March 1918, a speaker in the House of Commons proclaimed the doom of the professional caste when he declared: "The old ambassadorial system has failed and is discredited in the eyes of most people. After the war, the old diplomacy of Court and upper classes will be, in the eyes of most people, obsolete and inadequate. . . . Difficulties between nations should no longer be settled in conclaves of Ambassadors."[7]

The cry of the times, then, seemed to be for new diplomatic methods and new diplomatic personnel, and the political leaders of the western states were quick to respond to what they considered to be the popular desire. Conclaves of ambassadors at the Quai d'Orsay, the Wilhelmstrasse, and the Ballplatz—names now of sinister connotation—gave way to "frank and friendly conversations" in such charmingly unconventional places as the golf course at Cannes, the bosom of the Lago Maggiore, the mountain tavern at Thoiry, and a certain mossy log on the banks of the Potomac. The correctly dressed and distressingly uniform diplomats, who had until now held the center of the stage, ceded their places to a succession of politician-diplomats with such striking and memorable characteristics as plus-fours, Scots brogues, shaggy coiffures, white linen neckties, underslung pipes, and various kinds of umbrellas. The new dispensation was dignified by the name "diplomacy by conference" and was celebrated in a much-read essay by Sir Maurice Hankey, who in the early years served as impresario for the entertainment.[8]

If we consider the case of Britain alone, it is easy to demonstrate that

[6] Jules Cambon, *Le diplomate* (Paris, 1926), pp. 10–11.

[7] *Parliamentary Debates:* Commons, CIV (1918), 846.

[8] Sir Maurice Hankey, "Diplomacy by Conference," *The Round Table,* XI (1920–21), 287–311.

the new diplomacy created serious problems for the Foreign Office, the agency constitutionally charged with the conduct of Britain's foreign relations, and made its position embarrassing and at times almost insupportable. Think, for instance, of the four long years of insult and injury suffered by it at the hands of Lloyd George. Lloyd George's contempt for the diplomatic profession and its conventions was well known, for he made little attempt to conceal it. "I want no diplomats," he said during the course of the war. "Diplomats were invented simply to waste time. . . . It is simply a waste of time to let [important matters] be discussed by men who are not authorized to speak for their countries."[9] He showed that he meant this during the Paris Peace Conference. He went to that gathering, it is true, surrounded by clouds of experts from the Foreign Office and from other government departments; but he made singularly little use of them. He seems to have been irritated by their habit, when consulted, of producing closely argued analyses bristling with statistics. In any event, he soon relegated the Foreign Secretary and his staff to the limbo already tenanted by Mr. Lansing and his,[10] while he himself retired with Wilson, Clemenceau, and Orlando to see what intuition could do to solve the intricate problems of the peace.

When it appeared subsequently that intuition had not been enough and that the formulae devised by the Council of Four had postponed, and minimized, but certainly not solved, acute differences of opinion between the European Powers,[11] Lloyd George was not dismayed, nor was his faith in his own diplomatic talents shaken. He set out bravely to solve all the problems created by the Treaty of Versailles. That this should be done by methods tested by experience—by careful soundings of opinion in other capitals, by the tedious, but always useful, exchange of formal correspondence—does not seem to have occurred to him. "I

[9] Kennedy, *op. cit.*, pp. 364–65.

[10] If this seems an exaggeration, it should be remembered that, even in such an important matter as the treaty in which Great Britain and the United States guaranteed to come to France's aid in the event of future German aggression, the Foreign Secretary was not consulted. Only after the Treaty of Guarantee had been drafted in accordance with Lloyd George's personal instructions and had been approved by Wilson and Clemenceau was Balfour informed of it. Lord Hardinge of Penshurst, *Old Diplomacy* (London, 1947), p. 241.

[11] See, for instance, "Is There a New Diplomacy?", *Fortnightly Review* (1922), CXI, 711. Formula-making became a characteristic feature of Lloyd George's diplomacy. One of his biographers says: "Failure to reach agreement or to do no more than expose divergencies to the world could, as a rule and for the moment, be veiled in intentional obscurity by drafting a dexterous formula, an art in which his secretaries became proficient." Thomas Jones, *Lloyd George* (Cambridge, Mass., 1951), p. 180.

wish the French and ourselves never wrote letters to each other," he said in 1920. "Letters are the very devil. They ought to be abolished altogether. . . . If you want to settle a thing, you see your opponent and talk it over with him. The last thing you do is write him a letter."[12] According to this prescription Lloyd George acted in the years 1919–22, meeting his opponents at San Remo and Spa and Cannes and Genoa and, when the occasion demanded greater intimacy, at his breakfast table at 10 Downing Street. At these meetings, without prior or even subsequent consultation with the Foreign Office, he decided policy, negotiated claims, and made commitments to foreign governments. At the Spa Conference, for instance, he gave promises of protection to the Polish Government which had not been authorized by the Cabinet and of which the Foreign Office and His Majesty's representative in Warsaw were given no intimation until after they had been discussed in the popular press.[13] The Foreign Office, with reason, came to expect the worst of the Prime Minister's peripatetic activities; and Curzon said sadly at the time of the Genoa Conference, "When I reflect that the P.M. is alone at Genoa with no F.O. to guide him . . . and when I recall the whole trend of his policy for the past three years—I can feel no certainty that we may not find ourselves committed to something pregnant with political disaster here."[14] The results of Genoa were startling, but not as calamitous as Curzon feared; but the apprehension of the Foreign Secretary was nevertheless justified. A year later, indeed, disaster was very narrowly averted, as Lloyd George's stubborn refusal to listen to Foreign Office advice in eastern affairs and his unfortunate habit of encouraging the Greeks by winks and nods brought Britain to the verge of war at Chanak.

It is not intended to suggest here that the eclipse of the Foreign Office in the Lloyd George period was permanent. Indeed, in Curzon's last years in that office and in the years when Austen Chamberlain was Foreign Secretary, the Foreign Office resumed its normal position in the conduct of British policy. It cannot, however, be denied that Lloyd George's methods had created unfortunate precedents. The Prime Minister cannot be expected to stay out of foreign affairs, for he is ultimately responsible for policy. But perhaps never before Lloyd George had the Prime Minister interfered so directly, so frequently and so secretly with the actual day-by-day business of foreign relations—that is,

[12] Lord Riddell, *Intimate Diary of the Peace Conference and After* (London, 1933), p. 206.
[13] Kennedy, *op. cit.*, p. 337.
[14] Nicolson, *op. cit.*, p. 245.

with the implementation of formulated policy and with the varied tasks of negotiation. And this kind of interference was repeated sporadically, and generally with unfortunate effects, in the years that followed, reaching its highest point in the years 1937–39. Here we need cite only a few examples. During the crisis created by the French occupation of the Ruhr in 1923, when the Foreign Office was maintaining a position of studied neutrality in the double hope of restraining the French and preventing the victory of extremism in Germany, an ill-timed visit of Mr. Baldwin to Paris and an injudicious *communiqué* issued without Foreign Office knowledge created the impression that Britain was supporting French policy without reservation. This debacle led the British ambassador in Berlin to suggest that "it might be wise to apply to British Prime Ministers the rule governing the peregrinations of a Lord Chancellor and forbid their leaving England."[15] The rule, of course, was not invoked, as the subsequent wanderings of Ramsay MacDonald attest. Concerning these, we need note only that Mr. MacDonald, like other amateur diplomats, was apt to make imprecise but enthusiastic promises to his opposite numbers abroad and then to forget to tell the Foreign Office about them. There was an embarrassing business, for instance, in 1932, when MacDonald had talks at Bessinge with Tardieu, Bruening, and Stimson concerning the policy to be followed at the Lausanne Conference. The Germans argued later that the Prime Minister had promised to support their claim to equality of treatment in armaments. Mr. MacDonald didn't think he had said that at all. The Foreign Office had no way of telling whether he had or not, for they had received no record of the talks.[16]

The Foreign Office was never, perhaps, reduced to the "mere technical apparatus" that the German Foreign Office became under Hitler. But throughout the period it was subjected to more interference than any other service department;[17] it was often bypassed; periodically it was inadequately informed of meetings between economic experts, military advisers, and labor officials, and deprived of any opportunity of evaluating the findings of such meetings; and, with distressing frequency, the right of its permanent staff to be considered as *the* expert advisers on foreign policy was contested or ignored. There was a recurring tendency on the part of the political leaders of the state, when matters of high moment were pending, to believe that the professionals in the Foreign

[15] *An Ambassador of Peace: Lord d'Abernon's Diary* (London, 1929), II, 285.

[16] Rohan D. Butler and E. L. Woodward, eds., *Documents on British Foreign Policy, 1919–1939* (London, 1949, *et seq.*), second series, III, 123, 517 n.

[17] See, for instance, Curzon's views on this in Nicolson, *op. cit.*, p. 60 n.

Office were incompetent to deal with them because of narrowness of view, dependence upon traditional concepts, or lack of "realism." Lloyd George believed this; Ramsay MacDonald believed it; and it became dogma with Neville Chamberlain.[18] Mr. Chamberlain, indeed, revived some of the more unfortunate methods of Lloyd George and carried them further—for, in justice to Lloyd George, it must be admitted that he never contested the views of his Foreign Secretary in the presence of a foreign ambassador, as Chamberlain did in a meeting with Eden and Grandi in 1938.[19] Like Lloyd George, Chamberlain preferred to find his advisers on foreign policy outside the Foreign Office[20]; and it is perhaps fitting that he should have included among them Lord Lothian, who, as Lloyd George's secretary in an earlier period, had announced that the Foreign Office "had no conception of policy in its wider sense."[21] It is doubtless fitting also that, in pursuance of such wider policy, Chamberlain should have tried his hand at "diplomacy by conference," although his travels, it is true, were restricted by circumstances to Germany, and although the fractiousness of his host rendered them less pleasant than the junkets of his predecessors.

18 The word "realism," with all its variants, was used with remarkable frequency by Chamberlain and by other British officials who associated themselves with his policy, often to differentiate their views and objectives from those of Eden, Vansittart, and others who had no faith in the policy of appeasement. The Germans and Italians were quick to realize that the word possessed persuasive, if not magic, qualities when introduced into conversations with the British, and they came to rely upon it heavily, as the diplomatic correspondence of the period shows. See, for instance, *Documents on British Foreign Policy,* third series, I, 22, 28, 49, 109, 257, 273, 307, 345, II, 133, 385; *Documents on German Foreign Policy, 1918–1945: From the Archives of the German Foreign Ministry* (Washington, 1949 *et seq.*), series D, I, 221, 264. See also Chamberlain's letter of 16 January 1938 to Mrs. Morton Price in which he says: "As a realist, I must do what I can to make this country safe." Keith Feiling, *Life of Neville Chamberlain* (London, 1946), p. 323. The German ambassador in Paris spoke in July 1938 of French anxiety over "the dreaded realism of the British." *Documents on German Foreign Policy,* series D, I, 1168.

19 See Galeazzo Ciano, *L'Europa verso la catastrofe* (Verona, 1948), 249 ff.

20 Feiling, *op. cit.*, p. 327. According to a German memorandum of 11 October 1938, a "confidential agent of Neville Chamberlain" informed a member of the Dienststelle Ribbentrop in London that "in all future moves [i.e., negotiations between Britain and Germany] it was important that all major questions be dealt with directly, thus bypassing the Foreign Office." *Documents on German Foreign Policy,* series D, IV, 306. After February 1938, Lord Vansittart, formerly permanent Under-Secretary for Foreign Affairs, held the office of Diplomatic Adviser to His Majesty's Government. The title had little meaning, and Vansittart once said, in a private interview: "Nobody asks my advice and, when it is tendered, it is ignored."

21 Riddell, *op. cit.*, p. 219.

The emphasis placed here on the British experience should not leave the impression that the French were unaffected by these developments. After the Second World War, a commission was established by the French Constituent Assembly to investigate the "political, economic, diplomatic, and military events" that contributed to the collapse of 1940. The first summary report of that commission makes specific reference to the personal diplomacy of heads of states and political ministers:

> After the conclusion of the treaties of 1919, ministers had the habit of multiplying their contacts with their colleagues in other countries. The abuse of direct conversations opens the door to numerous dangers. Engagements are taken too easily. They are often improvised. It is better to define the course of a negotiation by a note which has matured in the silence of the ministry than by chance exchanges which are likely to be imprecise.[22]

This passage doubtless has reference to the kind of improvisation that took place at Geneva, where—after Germany's entrance into the League—the foreign ministers of the Great Powers met four times a year. The unnecessary frequency of these meetings had a stultifying effect on normal diplomatic work, since the Foreign Office was placed in the position of waiting anxiously to see what decisions were made by the ministers. The ministers themselves, being politicians, were always anxious to reach decisions, since it seemed important to be able to record some success before they went home; they were likely, in consequence, to "pluck the fruit before it was ripe."[23] Nor was it only the Geneva activities that gave concern to the permanent staff at home. There were other and more dangerous *tête-à-têtes.* Philippe Berthelot, the Secretary General of the Quai d'Orsay, was never, for instance, able to learn from Briand precisely what the latter had promised to Stresemann at Thoiry in 1926.[24] And no one has ever been able to discover what Laval did, or did not, promise Mussolini in January 1935, although that mystery had an undoubted effect in disrupting the coordination of Anglo-French policy in the Stresa period.[25]

[22] Commission d'Enquête parlementaire sur les événements survenus en France de 1933 à 1945: *Rapport de M. Charles Serre, député au nom de la Commission d'Enquête parlementaire* (Paris, 1951), p. 86.

[23] Weizsäcker, *op. cit.,* p. 69.

[24] André Géraud, "Diplomacy, Old and New," *Foreign Affairs,* XXIII (1944–45), 267.

[25] L. B. Namier, *Europe in Decay: A Study in Disintegration, 1936–1940* (London, 1950), p. 17. See also Joseph Paul-Boncour, *Entre les deux guerres: souvenirs sur la IIIe république* (Paris, 1945–46), III, 14–16.

II

The French report cited above dwells on one other development that demands at least brief consideration in any discussion of the diplomatic methods of this period—and that is the decline of the position and the authority of the ambassador. Traditionally, the ambassador—apart from what are known as his duties of representation—had a twofold function. He was supposed in the first place to communicate the wishes of his own government to that court at which he was resident and to use his trained judgment and experience in negotiation to secure their fulfillment. He was expected in the second place to send home objective reports on the political, economic, and social conditions of the country in which he was stationed. With the invention of the telegraph, and later of the telephone, the importance of the ambassador as a negotiator declined;[26] and it has been reduced even more by the recent tendency of governments to send special missions and "men of confidence" to foreign capitals to hold conversations that could often be conducted quite effectively by the resident diplomatic agents. The ambassador's importance as a trained observer of foreign conditions has diminished also, although for reasons that are more difficult to explain. In view of the issues at stake in the 1930's, for instance, it might be supposed that the situation reports of ambassadors and other agents abroad would have been read with interest in London and Paris and weighed carefully when policy had to be defined. This does not always seem to have been the case.

Two examples may be cited to illustrate this. As early as the fall of 1935, the French consul general in Cologne and other French agents in Germany were sending circumstantial reports to Paris with evidence that clearly pointed to an imminent German reoccupation of the Rhineland.[27] French governmental circles nevertheless expressed surprise and consternation when Hitler actually did send troops into that area in March of the following year. Again, when Robert Coulondre, the French ambassador in Moscow, visited the Commissariat for Foreign Affairs immediately after the Munich settlement, Potemkin, the Vice-

[26] Sir Horace Rumbold speaks of "this age of rapid communication, of what I would call the telegraphic demoralization of those who formerly had to act for themselves and are now content to be at the end of a wire." *Recollections of a Diplomatist* (London, 1902), I, 111–12. See also Cambon, *op. cit.*, pp. 13, 118–19.

[27] Commission d'Enquête parlementaire: *Rapport,* pp. 86–87. See also the testimony of Jean Dobler, *ibid.*, II: *Témoignages et documents recueillis.*

Commissar, said to him: "My poor friend, what have you done? For us I see no other way out but a fourth partition of Poland." On the basis of this warning, Coulondre reported to Paris on 4 October 1938 that a Russian *rapprochement* with Germany could now be expected.[28] There was, however, no indication in the long months that followed that anyone in Paris was concerned about, or even envisaged, any such possibility. Coulondre's message had as little effect as Attolico's warnings to Rome a year later.

The failure to pay proper attention to reports from missions abroad can be explained in several ways. The tremendous increase of incoming correspondence in all foreign offices in the 1930's[29] probably forced overworked departmental staffs to give priority to cables that required action and to defer the analysis of situation reports to a later time which sometimes never came. The commission appointed by the French Assembly has suggested also that, in the period under review, the rapid increase of a departmental staff composed largely of men who had never served in the field tended to raise an "impassable barrier" between France's agents abroad and those charged with the formulation of her policy. "Too often," their report reads, "the ministers were informed of events abroad only through the medium of established functionaries of the ministry . . . functionaries who made their career almost exclusively in the offices of the Quai d'Orsay"[30] and who, in consequence, lacked knowledge and judgment to appreciate the reports reaching their desks.

However valid these two explanations may be, they should not lead us to exclude a third. In any country and at any time, political ministers have a tendency to seek to impose their preconceived notions of foreign affairs upon the agents in the field; they are apt, moreover, to place greatest confidence in those representatives abroad whose reports confirm their own views. German diplomats in the nineteenth century frequently complained that they were expected only to tell Bismarck that he was right; Hitler's ambassadors learned that it was dangerous to depart from the line established in the *Reichskanzlei;* and this sort of thing was certainly neither unknown nor unimportant in British and French diplomacy between the wars. The difficulty, in short, was not always that reports were not read, but that they were read and

[28] Robert Coulondre, *De Staline à Hitler* (Paris, 1950), p. 165.

[29] "In 1913, the number of dispatches &c. received at the Foreign Office was 68,119. The figures for the years 1935–38 were 169,248 in 1935, 187,878 in 1936, 201,323 in 1937, 223,879 in 1938." *Documents on British Foreign Policy,* first series, I, iii.

[30] Commission d'Enquête parlementaire: *Rapport,* pp. 86–87.

rejected, sometimes with intimations of punishment for future nonconformity. In 1922, a high official in England—and one attached to neither the Foreign Office nor the War Office—sought to effect the recall of Brigadier General J. H. Morgan from the Inter-Allied Control Commission in Germany because he persisted in reporting, in the teeth of denials from England, that the Germans were defying the disarmament provisions of the Versailles Treaty.[31] In 1938, a member of the French embassy staff in Moscow received a stinging reprimand from Paris because he had reported, with statistics to support his opinion, that the Russian army was stronger than it was the fashion in Paris to believe and was well equipped with tanks and aircraft.[32]

It is worth remembering that, if some British and French ambassadors of this period were men of mediocre attainments, independence of judgment and clarity of view were not always expected or rewarded. In the 1920's, Jules Cambon said to his brother Paul: "Are you aware that nowadays we could not serve as ambassadors?"[33] In the late 1930's, the Cambons would have been very rare birds indeed, for the approved diplomats were men like Perth in Rome and Henderson in Berlin, the latter of whom especially never reported anything that did not echo and reinforce the opinions and policies of Neville Chamberlain and who was probably kept in Berlin because he followed that practice.[34]

III

If we relate the deficiencies of British and French diplomatic practice to the known results of the policies of the two governments—and surely there is a logical relationship—it is difficult to avoid the conclusion that they were ill advised in their cavalier treatment of professional diplomacy after 1919. Yet these by-products of the so-called "new diplomacy" —the practice of bypassing the Foreign Office, of failing to consult it or to keep it informed in important matters, and of giving preconceived ideas priority over intelligence from the field—have attracted little criticism and attract little today, although they are still very much a part of democratic practice in foreign affairs.

A brief reference may be permitted here to current American experi-

[31] J. H. Morgan, *Assize of Arms: The Disarmament of Germany and Her Rearmament, 1919–1939* (New York, 1946), pp. xvi-xvii.

[32] Coulondre, *op. cit.*, pp. 126–27, 129.

[33] Géraud, *op. cit.*, 267.

[34] "The Makers of Munich," *Times Literary Supplement* (London), 29 September 1950, p. 607.

ence. In this country the word "diplomat" is even more a reproach than it was in Britain immediately after the First World War; the average citizen seems willing and eager to believe the worst of the foreign service. In this atmosphere of popular antipathy, the State Department has lost much of its former authority as the central agency for the administration of foreign affairs in this country. Functions formerly reserved to it have been farmed out all over the government, to the Pentagon, the CIA, and the Treasury, to the Secretaries of Commerce and the Interior and to the Attorney General, to the Bureau of the Budget and the Export-Import Bank and other agencies. Some of this delegation of authority can be justified by the specialized nature of problems that have arisen since the end of the war; but the coordination of the activities of multiple agencies is always difficult and in this case leaves much to be desired. The State Department is often placed in the awkward position of having to assume responsibility for actions taken without its knowledge.

In addition to this, in the field of political negotiation, this country has not escaped the evils of abrupt and inexpert intervention by officials whose experience has been confined to the domestic field; and—in view of President Truman's expressed wish not so long ago, to send Fred Vinson to Moscow—we cannot be sure that we shall not see more of this in the future. Finally, it would be difficult to contend that we are sufficiently conscious of the importance of encouraging integrity on the part of our foreign service officers in the field. Who today can say how many of our representatives abroad feel compelled to adjust their judgments to preconceived notions at home or to the vagaries of Congressional opinion? In 1951, fragmented and unrelated passages from a diplomatic report written from China in 1944 were read before a Congressional committee in an apparent attempt to prove their author sympathetic to Communism;[35] and other examples could be cited of the unfortunate tendency to force diplomats to explain and justify their past judgments before ill informed, and essentially irresponsible, committees. This, at least, is something that the British and French never came to; and in 1918, when popular criticism of professional diplomacy was at its height, a British Foreign Secretary expressed very clearly the dangers of such procedure.

> If [said A. J. Balfour in the House of Commons] you are going to ask Foreign Office officials . . . to expend some of their energy in getting

[35] John S. Service, "'. . . pertinent excerpts . . .'," *Foreign Service Journal* (October 1951).

ready for cross-examination, you will really be destroying the public service. . . . They are not accustomed to it and they ought not to be accustomed to it. They are not trained for it, and they ought not to be trained for it. . . . I beg the House to remember that any system that keeps constantly before the eyes of the civil servants of this country the fear of examination, cross-examination and re-examination by gentlemen who may be described as professional politicians, would be most disastrous in the public interest.[36]

It is possible, of course, that the professional diplomat is an anomaly in democratic society and that we must seek new forms and procedures of foreign relations which are more fitting to this type of political community. That is a subject upon which a historian would be reluctant to embark. He can only suggest, on the basis of the interwar experience of the two great democracies of western Europe, that flagrant neglect of the resources and conventions of professional diplomacy have in the past had unfortunate results.

36 *Parliamentary Debates:* Commons, CIV (1918), 876.

13. Totalitarian Approaches to Diplomatic Negotiation

IN A TREATISE that is justly admired by students of diplomacy, François de Callières wrote in 1716:

> The art of negotiation . . . is so important that the fate of the greatest states often depends upon the good and bad conduct of negotiations and upon the degree of capacity in the negotiators employed. . . . It is not necessary to turn far back into the past to understand what can be achieved by negotiation. We see daily around us its definite effects in sudden revolutions favorable to this great design of state or that, in the use of sedition in fermenting hatreds between nations, in causing jealous rivals to arm against each other so that the *tertius gaudens* may profit, in the formation of leagues and other treaties of various kinds between monarchs whose interests might otherwise clash, in the dissolution by crafty means of the closest unions between states: in a word, one may say that the art of negotiation, according as its conduct is good or evil, gives form to great affairs and may turn a host of lesser events into a useful influence upon the course of the greater.[1]

Since these words were written, changes in methods of communication, in the nature of international society, and in the distribution of

The introduction and sections I, II, V, and VI of "Totalitarian Approaches to Diplomatic Negotiation" are reprinted with permission from my article of the same title in A. O. Sarkissian, ed., *Studies in Diplomatic History and Historiography* (London: Longmans, Green and Co., Ltd., 1961), and sections III and IV from my article "Techniques of Negotiation" in Ivo J. Lederer, ed., *Russian Foreign Policy: Essays in Historical Perspective* (New Haven, Conn.: Yale University Press, 1962).

[1] *The Practice of Diplomacy*, being an English rendering of François de Callières' *De la manière de négocier avec les souverains*, presented with an introduction by A. F. Whyte (London, 1919), pp. 7, 16.

political power within the states that it comprises have profoundly affected the forms and techniques of diplomatic negotiation; but its importance as an instrument of national power has in no way been diminished. There is no easier way to demonstrate this than to consider the role of negotiation in the history of the totalitarian states of the first half of the twentieth century. The failure of the Fascist and National Socialist governments to understand or take advantage of the uses of negotiation was not the least important cause of the difficulties that in the end overwhelmed Italy and Germany; whereas the Soviet regime's ability to devise new techniques of negotiation and to adapt traditional ones to its own purposes carried it through the hazards of the interwar period and, after the Second World War, consolidated and expanded the position won by Soviet arms.

I

The deficiencies of Fascist diplomacy and the amateurishness of its leader's ventures into negotiation may be explained, in part at least, by the fact that the first years of Mussolini's political life were spent as a journalist. The talents that are required to make a man a good newspaperman are different from those one expects to find in a competent diplomat. Cavour is one of the rare individuals who have possessed both kinds, and Mussolini, in this and other respects, was no Cavour. The Duce's newspaper experience left him with a tendency to be preoccupied with style rather than substance, with a hankering after sensational strokes and dramatic coups that would look good in headlines, and—although this hardly accords with that cynicism which newspapermen are traditionally supposed to possess—with an excessive regard for newspaper opinion and a dangerous sensitiveness to newspaper criticism.

Mussolini's fundamental attitude toward diplomacy, and the attention he paid to its purely verbal aspects, were bound up, in a curious way, with his editorial policy for *Il Popolo d'Italia.* He once explained how he had impressed upon that journal, "in thousands of articles, headlines, drawings and sketches inspired by me, a polemical and aggressive character, one of continual battle";[2] after he became chief of state, he seemed to feel that it was only fitting that this should become the characteristic mark of every aspect of Fascist policy, including foreign policy. He was forever talking about the "Fascist style," which he equated with

[2] Herman Ellwanger, *Sulla lingua di Mussolini* (Verona, 1941), p. 22.

courage, resolution, action, forcefulness, dynamism. "Note that I do not love the hesitant and conventional form," he said in December 1925. "I affirm."[3]

This dislike of the hesitant and the conventional extended to those forms of diplomacy which sought, with a minimum of public display and a maximum of deliberation and reflection, to solve European problems in the first postwar decade, as well as to the frequent attempts made, at Geneva and elsewhere, to reach collective agreements by means of multilateral negotiation. All of these were, in a phrase frequently used by the Duce's son-in-law, "contrary to our diplomatic style."[4] Mussolini's prejudice against multilateral negotiation can probably be traced back to the chastening experience of his first diplomatic venture, when, at the Lausanne Conference of November 1922, his *gaucheries* were received by the other delegates with an amusement that bordered on scorn.[5] But there can be little doubt that it was rooted also in his belief that the satisfactions to be gained from collaborative diplomacy in the interest of general appeasement were not worthy of Fascist Italy, which must dazzle the world with spectacular triumphs of its own.

During the first decade of his regime, however, Mussolini could not afford, and did not attempt, to base his policy upon these prejudices. The defiant, and only partly successful, stroke at Corfu in August 1923[6] was not imitated in the years that followed; and, if Mussolini was prone to ringing declarations of imminent action, he generally allowed the word to stand for the deed. Thus, in February 1926, when he electrified Europe by a clear threat of military action north of the Brenner unless an end was made to criticism of his policy in the South Tyrol by the Austrian and German parliaments, he backed down quickly when the Austrians proposed to bring the matter before the League of Nations, delivering a second speech in which, behind "a characteristic parade of truculence," he converted his earlier menaces into "an inoffensive intimation that he would defend himself if attacked by others."[7]

Throughout these early years, the exigencies of domestic policy reduced Mussolini's dynamism to what has been called a "random and uncoordinated striking-out in all directions in the hope of scoring points

[3] Benito Mussolini, *Scritti e discorsi* (Milano, 1934–39), V, 321 ff.

[4] Galeazzo Ciano, *L'Europa verso la catastrofe* (Verona, 1948), p. 338.

[5] See Harold Nicolson, *Curzon: The Last Phase* (New York, 1939), pp. 288 ff.

[6] See Gaetano Salvemini, *Prelude to World War II* (New York, 1954), pp. 44 ff.

[7] A. J. Toynbee, ed., *Survey of International Affairs, 1927* (Oxford, 1929), p. 199.

on the cheap."[8] The best that can be said of it is that it did no real harm to Italy's basic interests, since Mussolini was content to leave the bulk of the diplomatic business of the state, which was, as elsewhere, carried on by the continuous negotiations that go on in embassies and foreign offices, in the hands of the professional foreign service and the permanent officials in the Palazzo Chigi. By making concessions to their leader's vanity, these officials were able to moderate his outbursts and control his ambitions, while cementing relations with those powers, like Great Britain, which were willing to respect Italy's traditional interests and even to assent to modest increases in her influence in Africa and eastern Europe.[9]

All of this changed when the deterioration of economic conditions in the early 1930's, and the consequent disruption of European power relationships, opened new vistas to Mussolini's eyes and made him impatient with old restraints. The dismissal of Grandi as Foreign Minister in July 1932 marked the inauguration of a new policy of all-out revisionism and, simultaneously, the beginning of that decline of the influence of the professionals in Italian diplomacy which was to reach its nadir in the Foreign Ministry of Galeazzo Ciano.[10] As their role diminished, negotiation became almost a forgotten art in the Italian service, a tendency encouraged by the belief that the goals Italy now sought must be attained not by diplomacy but by heroism.

Even the atmosphere of conventional courtesy that customarily reigns in the diplomatic corps and is conducive to the useful exchange of views was dispelled by Ciano. Once he had become Foreign Minister, he seems to have determined to realize his father-in-law's stylistic ideals and insisted that Italian diplomats must henceforth make their behavior reflect the approved *tono fascista*.[11] The meaning of this phrase is elusive; it seems to have meant a proud and militant bearing that would impress the foreigner with the dignity and strength of the new Italy. Its practical effect was to make ambassadors dispense with traditional forms and usages of polite intercourse (Ciano insisted on the deletion of even the most conventional expressions of good will from ambassadorial declarations[12]), to be constantly on the alert for slights to Italy's honor,

[8] H. Stuart Hughes, "The Early Diplomacy of Italian Fascism," in Gordon A. Craig and Felix Gilbert, eds., *The Diplomats, 1919–1939* (Princeton, 1953), pp. 224 ff.

[9] *Ibid.*, pp. 216 ff.

[10] See especially Felix Gilbert, "Ciano and his Ambassadors," in *ibid.*, pp. 512 ff.

[11] Raffaele Guariglia, *Ricordi, 1922–1946* (Naples, 1950), p. 193.

[12] *Ibid.*, pp. 255 ff.

to adopt a hectoring tone in delivering communications and complaints to the governments to which they were accredited, and, in general, to conduct themselves, especially in countries that were not bound by ideological or more formal ties to Italy, as if they were in an enemy camp.

This made it virtually impossible for envoys abroad to perform effectively their duties of representation, reporting, and negotiation. Representing Italian interests seemed now to consist for the most part of continual protestation against criticisms of Fascism, even when they were made by private citizens; and this, as one Italian diplomat noted, was ludicrous, when one remembered that Fascist Italy was "all too prone to criticize, injure, jeer at, and menace all the peoples of the world, and not in private conversations, but in manifestations of an official character and in articles in a press which the whole world knew was rigidly controlled by the government."[13] Ambassadorial reporting degenerated into demonstrations of conformity to Fascist style; and the reports from posts like Belgrade, Sofia, and Bucharest in the last years of the peace contained little of interest except descriptions of the ambassadors' success in bullying their hosts.[14] Finally, the possibilities of ambassadorial negotiation of any kind were handicapped, not only by this new cult of bad manners, but also by the apparent belief in the Palazzo Chigi that, in certain capitals—Paris, for example—an attitude of disdainful reserve was all that should be expected of a Fascist diplomat. "What ought I try to accomplish in Paris?" asked Guariglia as he left for his post in November 1938. "Nothing," answered Ciano. "It will be difficult," the ambassador replied, "but I will do my best."[15]

The subordination of diplomacy to the *tono fascista* was even more patent in the negotiations that Ciano carried on personally at Mussolini's orders. In these he appears to have been more interested in the speed with which an agreement could be reached and the publicity that could be garnered from it than in anything else. In general, his negotiations were amateurish in technique and dangerous in result.

The best illustration of these failings is to be seen in the negotiations for the Pact of Steel of May 1939—"this fatal error," as Guariglia calls it, "of inauspicious memory."[16] The reasons for seeking a military alliance with Germany were in themselves hardly compelling. There is

[13] Emanuele Grazzi, *Il principio della fine* (Rome, 1945), p. 13.

[14] *Documenti diplomatici italiani* (Rome, 1952 *et seq.*), eighth series, XII, 100, 177, 672, 819.

[15] Guariglia, *op. cit.*, p. 357.

[16] *Ibid.*, p. 395.

strong reason to believe that Mussolini was goaded into abandoning his earlier reserve by scornful articles in the French press about Italo-German friction,[17] although he may have been moved also, as Italian and British diplomats have argued, by a desire to replace the loose Axis tie, which gave Italy no control over her German associate and no right to be consulted by her, by a formal treaty that gave her both these things.[18] However that may be, the way in which the pact was negotiated on the Italian side was nothing short of slipshod. Mario Toscano has pointed out that the most inexcusable aspects of Ciano's conduct were his willingness to leave the actual drafting of the treaty of alliance entirely to the Germans and his failure, during the talks with Ribbentrop in Milan, "to discuss or even to set limits on the general nature of its contents."[19] As for Mussolini, while his Foreign Minister was placing this dangerous degree of trust in German intentions, his sole interest was apparently to have the pact proclaimed in the press even before its terms were worked out, presumably to put an end to the gibes in Paris.

Some time later, when he handed the draft treaty to Ambassador Attolico in Berlin, the Director of the Legal Department of the German Foreign Ministry told him that "the Foreign Minister [Ribbentrop] considered that the draft corresponded completely with what he and Count Ciano had recently agreed and that, therefore, it presumably did not require any more negotiations on the final version."[20] Since there was no clear definition, in either the Italian or the German record of the Milan talks, of what had been agreed upon there, it was difficult to contest this;[21] in any case, the Italian government seemed too eager for ratification to haggle over amendments. When Ciano and General Pariani came to Berlin at the end of May, some minor changes, based on suggestions of Attolico, were made;[22] but the final document was nevertheless dangerously imprecise.[23]

17 Mario Toscano, *Le origini del Patto d'Acciaio* (2d ed.; Florence, 1956), p. 308.

18 Massimo Magistrati, *L'Italia a Berlino, 1937–1939* (Verona, 1956), pp. 348 ff.; Rohan D. Butler and E. L. Woodward, eds., *Documents on British Foreign Policy, 1919–1939,* third series, V, 598. ("Mussolini has bought the right to be consulted by Hitler, and the price is the pact."—Sir Percy Loraine.)

19 Toscano, *op. cit.,* pp. 318 ff.

20 *Documents on German Foreign Policy 1918–1945: From the Archives of the German Foreign Ministry* (Washington, 1949 *et seq.*), series D, VI, 371.

21 Toscano, *op. cit.,* p. 339.

22 Magistrati, *op. cit.,* pp. 344 ff.

23 See the text in *Documents on German Foreign Policy,* series D, VI, 426. Ferdinand Siebert has written: "Seldom indeed in history has an alliance been concluded which, despite all its fine talk about cohesion, ideological kinship, and

Unlike most treaties of military alliance, the Pact of Steel included no definition of the *casus foederis,* no escape clauses, no stipulation of necessary consultation. There was not even a secret protocol defining German intentions; and the promise that no war was contemplated for three years, which had been requested by the Italians, was purely verbal and was not intended to be kept, as Ciano was to discover in his talks with Hitler and Ribbentrop at Salzburg in August 1939. On the other hand, the treaty so precipitately negotiated by Ciano was, as far as Italy's obligations were concerned, rigid and unconditional; and, unless Mussolini was prepared to repudiate his pledge, in case of German action of which he disapproved, Italy was bound to fight at a time of Germany's choosing. Moreover, the Germans were protected against any real possibility of Italian withdrawal by Mussolini's concern over what the newspapers wrote about him. Events were to show that, even when Hitler agreed in August 1939 to Italy's abstention from immediate hostilities—an agreement won in part by the skillful way in which Attolico presented Italy's deficiencies in materials and weapons[24]—the Duce was not content. Smarting under charges that he had broken his word, he led his country into a war for which she was neither materially nor psychologically prepared.

Given Mussolini's temperament, this might have been impossible to prevent in any case; but it was facilitated by the nature of, and the obligations imposed by, the Pact of Steel. All in all, it can hardly be denied that the neglect and misuse of negotiation deprived those Italians who desired peace in 1939 and 1940 of weapons with which to combat the vanity and impulsiveness of their leaders.

II

In retrospect, it would seem that the weakness of Italian diplomacy arose from the essential frivolity of the officials charged with the task of conducting it. Behind Ciano's shocked protest, upon learning in August 1939 of Hitler's intention of going to war, that "no indication had been given by Germany, either in the conversations at Milan, or

solidarity, was based—thanks to the levity of one partner and the disingenuousness of the other—on so many ambiguities and imprecisions as the German-Italian Pact of Friendship and Alliance of May 1939." "Das deutsch-italienische Stahlpakt," *Vierteljahrshefte für Zeitgeschichte,* VII (1959), 390.

[24] *Documenti diplomatici italiana,* eighth series, XIII, 293, 298, 304, 307; Magistrati, *op. cit.,* pp. 432 ff.; Galeazzo Ciano, *Diario* (Rome, 1946), I, 150; *Documents on German Foreign Policy,* series D, VII, 307, 308, 317.

in the talks during his visit to Berlin, that the situation in respect of Poland was so grave,"[25] lies a pathetic admission that he had not mastered the art of negotiating even with his own allies.

Adolf Hitler can hardly be accused of Ciano's kind of *leggerezza*. He both understood what could be gained by negotiation and, at various times in his career, demonstrated his ability to use it, in ways of which Callières would have approved, "in the dissolution . . . of the closest unions between states" and "in the formation of leagues . . . between monarchs whose interests might otherwise clash." His faults as a statesman are, therefore, of a different order from Mussolini's. He is to be criticized, not for lack of diplomatic proficiency, but rather for the fact that he refused to be content with the great gains that negotiation could bring to his country, and sought greater ones in war.

Despite the suspicion with which he was viewed by professional diplomats when he came to power, Hitler showed considerable facility in the use of diplomatic means during his first years. In the unfolding of his policy, there was, for one thing, little of the incoherence that had characterized Italian policy in the 1920's. Hitler was aware that the revisionism and expansion upon which his heart was set could be pursued only after the home front had been stabilized and Germany's armed forces built up. While the *Gleichschaltung* was being carried out, therefore, and the Versailles Treaty undermined, the Führer encouraged foreign states to believe that his government would effect no radical break with the policy of the past. This he did, in the first place, by retaining the existing Foreign Ministry staff and by relying on diplomats who were known abroad and whose continued employment would have a reassuring effect.[26]

In the second place, unlike Mussolini, Hitler was not given to complicating the work of his diplomats in the field (whose task, essentially, was to explain away the brutalities of his domestic program and to portray him as a force for European order) by inveighing against the international *status quo*. His public pronouncements at this stage were pacific, disarming, even ingratiating, designed to divert foreign attention from his real intentions and to blunt criticism of, or split possible opposition to, his policies, by promising concessions or hinting at willingness to make agreements desired abroad.[27] Hitler realized that the

[25] *Ibid.*, series D, VI, 43.

[26] Karl Dietrich Bracher, "Das Anfangsstadium der Hitlerischen Aussenpolitik," *Vierteljahrshefte für Zeitgeschichte*, V (1957), 69–70.

[27] A good example is Hitler's speech of 17 May 1933 concerning Germany's stand on disarmament. See Norman H. Baynes, ed., *The Speeches of Adolf Hitler* (Oxford, 1942), II, 1041–58.

public statements of heads of government were not the least important of modern channels of negotiation, and he showed great skill in using this means of advancing his purposes and supporting the efforts of his envoys at Geneva and foreign posts. It was by this means that he was able, after his withdrawal from the Disarmament Conference and the League of Nations in October 1933, to mislead the other powers by his professed willingness to consider any schemes of arms limitation they might propose; and this channel was also used with effect in persuading states that criticized his withdrawal from the collective-security system to enter bilateral negotiations with him.

In the last-mentioned area of negotiation, Hitler's first years were marked by two successes that were admirably designed to protect him from collective counteraction as his policy evolved. These were the pact with Poland, which drove a wedge into France's eastern alliance system,[28] and the Anglo-German naval agreement of June 1935, which split the Stresa Front and destroyed the last possibility of reprisals for Hitler's violations of the arms clauses of the Versailles Treaty.[29] The notable feature of these examples of "dynamic" diplomacy is that there was nothing impulsive about them. The possibility of a treaty with Poland seems to have been in Hitler's mind as early as April, 1933;[30] in September he instructed his Foreign Minister to talk with his Polish opposite number about "the best means of creating a better atmosphere in the relations between the two states"; and in November he authorized the formal negotiations that eventuated in the treaty of 26 January 1934.[31] The idea of a pact with Britain had interested Hitler for an even longer period, stretching back before his coming to power; after he became Chancellor, he took it up and played an important role in pushing the naval negotiations to a successful issue. His private talks with Lord Allen of Hurtwood in January 1935, with the British Ambassador in February, and with Sir John Simon in March, and his public address of 21 May 1935 certainly made a more important contribution to the

[28] Richard Breyer, *Das Deutsche Reich und Polen, 1932–1937* (Würzburg, 1955), pp. 106 ff., 113.

[29] See, for instance, the speech of 21 May 1935 in Baynes, *op. cit.*, II, 1218–46.

[30] Herbert von Dirksen, *Moskau, Tokio, London: Erinnerungen und Betrachtungen zu 20 Jahren deutscher Aussenpolitik, 1919–39* (Stuttgart, 1950), p. 123.

[31] Republic of Poland, Ministry for Foreign Affairs, *Official Documents concerning Polish-German and Polish-Soviet Relations, 1933–39* (London, 1940), pp. 11–24; *Documents on German Foreign Policy*, series C, II, 84, 87, 88, 217, 218, 219.

pact's conclusion than the tactics used by Ribbentrop when he led the German delegation to London in June.[32]

After the middle of 1935, when Germany's growing military might supplied an authoritative backing for her diplomacy, Hitler was never again as dependent upon negotiation as he was in his first years; and, after 1936, when he was given his first proofs of the weakness and indecision of the western democracies, his tendency was to rely more upon military pressure than upon negotiating skill and persuasiveness. The tone of German diplomacy now began to change; Hitler's public statements on foreign policy became menacing; and, especially after Ribbentrop became Foreign Minister in February 1938, the style of Foreign Ministry communications became peremptory and sometimes arrogant.[33] Ribbentrop himself had such an exalted conception of his role that he was led to indulge in astonishing displays of bad manners when he felt that his dignity had been hurt.[34] Aside from this, he had no real sympathy for genuine negotiation. As Attolico once said, he could see nothing but his own version of the facts;[35] he had no patience with lengthy deliberations, being desirous of headlong decisions;[36] and he was interested, not in agreements of mutual advantage, but only in settlements that were imposed upon his *vis-à-vis,* or treaties of alliance directed against third powers.

These traits were not considered as weaknesses by Ribbentrop's master, who had now lost his own interest in negotiation and the benefits it might bring. By the end of 1937, as the minutes of his conference with his generals on 5 November reveal,[37] he was thinking of triumphs that could be won only by the sword; negotiation had become the handmaiden to war. The change of attitude is clearly seen in the instructions given to Konrad Henlein, leader of the Sudeten German party,

32 See W. Malanowski, "Das deutsch-englische Flottenabkommen vom 18. Juni 1935 als Ausgangspunkt für Hitlers doktrinäre Bündnispolitik," *Wehrwissenschaftliche Rundschau,* 1955, p. 416; D. C. Watt, "The Anglo-German Naval Agreement of 1935: an Interim Report," *Journal of Modern History,* XXVIII (1956), 157, 159 ff.

33 This change was apparent even in the language of professionals like Ernst von Weizsäcker, the Under Secretary. See the language in which he "categorically refused" to accept a French protest after the Prague coup of March 1939. *Documents on German Foreign Policy,* series D, VI, 20.

34 See Paul Schmidt, *Statist auf diplomatischer Bühne, 1923–1945* (Bonn, 1949), pp. 457 ff.

35 *Documenti diplomatici italiani,* eighth series, XII, 503.

36 Ernst L. Presseisen, *Germany and Japan: A Study in Totalitarian Diplomacy 1933–1941* (The Hague, 1958), pp. 198, 208.

37 *Documents on German Foreign Policy,* series D, I, 19.

who was ordered, as he pursued his negotiations with the Czech government, to set his claims so high that the Czechs would rather fight than accept them.[38] The same point of view determined Hitler's own tactics as the Polish dispute came to a head a year later. The Führer seems to have been genuinely concerned lest the Poles decide to accept the terms that they had rejected in March 1939 or lest they, or someone else, submit counterproposals that might compel him to accept a compromise short of war. To prevent this, he not only declined the good offices of third powers,[39] but refused to allow his ambassadors to Poland and Great Britain, who were on leave in Germany, to return to their posts.[40] On 22 August 1939, Hitler openly admitted his preference for violent solutions by saying to his generals: "Now Poland is in the position in which I wanted her. . . . I am only afraid that at the last moment some swine or other will yet submit to me a plan for mediation."[41]

The irrationality that prompted this insistent refusal of present advantage and this fateful trust in the uncertain promises of war was to recur in June 1941, when Hitler declared war on the Soviet Union. The declaration followed a period of twenty-two months in which the Nazi had won tremendous concessions from Moscow by a combination of negotiation and subtle menace, and during which the Soviet Union had yielded on every contested point of the partition of eastern Europe that had been stipulated in Hitler's most spectacular diplomatic stroke, the agreement with Russia in August 1939. It has been said that in those twenty-two months "the Soviet Union had gone to greater lengths in appeasing Germany than the British and French governments had gone during the period between Hitler's advent to power and 15 March 1939";[42] and it was not certain that the limits of that appeasement had yet been reached.[43] Yet Hitler the warrior had superseded Hitler the negotiator; and even the knowledge that Great Britain was still un-

[38] *Ibid.*, series D, II, 107.

[39] Arnold Toynbee and Veronica M. Toynbee, eds., *Survey of International Affairs, 1939–1946: The Eve of War 1939* (London, 1958), pp. 342 ff. and 377.

[40] *Documents on German Foreign Policy*, series D, VI, 674; VII, 2, 32, 82; Carl W. Schorske, "Two German Ambassadors," in Craig and Gilbert, *op. cit.*, pp. 509–10.

[41] *Documents on German Foreign Policy*, series D, VII, 192.

[42] Arnold Toynbee and Veronica M. Toynbee, eds., *Survey of International Affairs, 1939–1946: The Initial Triumph of the Axis* (London, 1958), p. 365.

[43] As late as 28 April 1941 the German ambassador in Moscow was sure that the Soviet Government was "prepared to make even further concessions." R. J. Sontag and James S. Beddie, eds., *Nazi-Soviet Relations, 1939–1941* (Washington, 1941), p. 332.

ubdued did not dissuade him now from transforming the conflict in vhich he was already engaged into a two-front struggle that would in he end destroy his country.

III

In sharp contrast to Hitler's approach to negotiation is that of the oviet Union. Far from preferring the arbitrament of war to decisions nade at the council table, the Soviets have generally valued diplomacy or its ability to win great triumphs at small risk and have shown irtuosity, not only in mastering its procedures and forms, but also in evising formidable negotiating techniques of their own. In doing so, hey have followed the example of their imperial predecessors who, lespite the relative lateness of their admission to the western diplomatic ommunity, were swift in appreciating the uses of diplomacy.

There is no entirely satisfactory history of the origins and early evoluion of Russian diplomacy, but it is clear from what accounts we possess hat an early stage the court of Muscovy carried on negotiations with he khans of Asia and the caliphs of Bagdad; and in the time of Ivan II, diplomacy was as frequently used as war in adjusting Russia's relaions with the Golden Horde and the Tatars of the Crimea. That prince vas, indeed, engaged throughout his reign in continuous negotiation, not only with his nearest neighbors but also with the papacy, the Habsurgs, the king of Bohemia, and the Danish court, and he was reputed o be skillful in negotiation with ambassadors from abroad, a reputaion supported by the successes of his diplomacy.[44]

Russian relations with the west in this early period were intermittent out of increasing scope; and by the middle of the sixteenth century the ourt of Moscow found it expedient to coordinate the activities of the nany Greek, Italian, and other agents working for it in the west by stablishing a primitive foreign office, the Bureau of Ambassadors. As he ambitions of the rulers grew, and as their eyes began to turn to reas dominated by the Turks and the Swedes, they availed themselves of those coalition-making capabilities of negotiation of which Callières vas later to write, and sent envoys to seek alliances and other forms of id in Vienna and Berlin, in Venice and Madrid, and in London, Paris, nd the Hague.[45] Before the seventeenth century was over, the obvious

[44] J. L. I. Fennell, "Russia, 1462–1583," *New Cambridge Modern History,* II Cambridge, 1958), 536 ff.

[45] V. P. Potemkin *et al., Histoire de la Diplomatie* (trans. from Russian, 3 vols.; aris, 1946–47), I, 220–21.

advantages of continuous contact with foreign courts had led to th establishment of the first permanent missions abroad,[46] and this proces was pushed further by Peter the Great and by Catherine, whose polic was oriented to the west and who participated actively and profitabl in the complex play of diplomatic maneuver that filled the eighteent century. Although Peter may have had some doubts about the permanence of Russia's western connection (Ostermann insisted that the Tsa had said: "For a few score more years only shall we need Europe. Ther we shall be able to turn our backs on her."[47]), after Catherine's tim Russia's membership in the western diplomatic community was continuous.

The characteristics and negotiating techniques of Russia's diplomatist in the early years of this association were a source of contempt, amusement, or exasperation to western statesmen. The first Russians wh visited western countries as special envoys struck at least one observe as very little more than "baptized bears."[48] Certainly they comporte themselves as something less than human, and they made Muscovit grossness proverbial in the west by ruining the apartments assigned t them, breaking the furniture, and "leaving behind them unsupportabl odors and indescribable filth."[49] When Peter the Great led his "Grea Embassy" to the west in 1697–98, his suite virtually destroyed the hous in which they were quartered in London. The floors were left covere with grease and ink; the curtains, quilts, and bed linen were torn t rags; fifty chairs were broken or had disappeared entirely; twenty fin pictures were slashed and the frames destroyed; and 300 window pane were broken.[50] Damage of this nature could not be attributed wholl to inadvertence or to lack of breeding. Much of it appeared to be deliberate flouting of western convention in order to demonstrate Russian superiority. It accorded with other unpleasing traits of these firs embassies: rudeness in matters of protocol, scornful disregard for th laws of the land to which they were accredited, and studied incivilitie in their relations with their opposite numbers.[51]

Negotiation with the Russians was always a difficult and indee

[46] Otto Krauske, *Die Entwicklung der ständigen Diplomatie vom 15. Jahrhundert bis zu den Beschlüssen vom 1815 und 1818* (Leipzig, 1885), p. 144.

[47] V. O. Kluchevsky [Kliuchevskii], *A History of Russia* (trans. C. J. Hogarth) (London, 1931), IV, 221.

[48] Ian Grey, *Peter the Great: Emperor of All Russia* (New York, 1960), p. 101

[49] P. Milioukov [Miliukov], Charles Seignobos, and L. Eisenmann, *Histoire de Russie* (Paris, 1932–33), I, 229.

[50] Grey, *op. cit.*, p. 117.

[51] Potemkin, *op cit.*, I, 226–27.

tedious business. Envoys sent abroad were provided with detailed instructions prescribing how they should act, what they should say, what tone they should use, what persons they were authorized to meet, and much more. They were never given full powers and could decide nothing without reference to higher authority. The introduction of new subjects into the course of a negotiation in train, or a suggestion that the discussion be turned to a different level, invariably led to interruptions while the Russian representative sought new instructions. Nor was the tempo of negotiation appreciably faster in Moscow on those occasions when foreign envoys were given an opportunity to deal with the tsar through his chief ministers. All too often the envoys would learn, after interminable delays, that they were expected merely to accept fiats from the tsar; and demurrers on their part were met with pressures, menaces, and expulsions that showed little respect for the accepted code of diplomatic etiquette.[52]

Finally, negotiation with the Russians was hampered by certain characteristics of Russian intercourse that always delayed and sometimes defeated understanding. Perhaps because they had gone to school in Byzantium before they established a firm relationship with the west,[53] the Russians retained eastern habits of thought and discourse that were irritating to western negotiators. What John Wheeler-Bennett has called "the incalculable capacity of the Slav for interminable conversation"[54] tried their patience to the utmost, while Russian arts of mystification often surrounded negotiations with impenetrable fogs of confusion. Even such a pronounced westerner as Peter believed that dust should be thrown in the eyes of his western rivals and that obfuscation should be considered an important instrument of Russian policy. Peter's servants followed this injunction. Of A. I. Ostermann it was said that foreign ministers could sometimes talk with him for two hours and, on leaving his cabinet, be no better informed than when they entered it. "Everything that he wrote, everything that he said, could have a double meaning. . . . He never looked anyone straight in the eye for fear his own eyes would betray him."[55] Kluchevsky, no admirer of his, has written that if in private life one asked Ostermann "whether it was, say, gout or biliousness that he was suffering from, he would at once tie himself up in such a mass of unintelligible verbiage as proved him

[52] *Ibid.*, I, 228; Wildner, *op. cit.*, pp. 29–30.

[53] Wildner, *op. cit.*, pp. 28–29.

[54] John W. Wheeler-Bennett, *Brest-Litovsk: The Forgotten Peace* (new ed.; London, 1956), pp. 138–39.

[55] Potemkin, *op. cit.*, I, 274.

beyond all doubt to be as stupid as he was treacherous, pusillanimous and evasive."[56]

Alexis Bestuzhev-Riumin, who served both Empress Elizabeth and the great Catherine, carried these arts so far that he became a legend in the diplomatic world. For his seventeen years of office he carried on an elaborate deception:

> In his conversations with foreign ambassadors, he babbled in such a way that he could not be understood; he also complained of being deaf and of not being able to comprehend all the fine points of the French language and had the same things repeated to him a thousand times. It was his habit to write diplomatic notes in his own hand in a completely illegible manner, so that they had to be sent back to him, and he would succeed sometimes in deciphering the meaning.

When he fell into disgrace, however, he recovered his speech, his hearing, and all his faculties.[57]

All of these negotiating traits, like other aspects of pre-nineteenth-century Russian diplomatic behavior, were doubtless understandable in view of the fact that Russia was a latecomer to the western diplomatic community, aware of the advantages of membership but suspicious of the price that might have to be paid for it, uncertain of its ability to live by the rules, therefore insistent upon the validity of its own, fearful of commitment and therefore taking refuge in confusion. More important than the existence of these traits was the fact that they were not lasting ones. With experience in the practices of western diplomacy came great sophistication in their use.

IV

In his short study of the art of diplomacy, Harold Nicolson, while analyzing the diplomatic behavior of Great Britain, France, Germany, and the United States and finding significant national differences in negotiating method, has nothing to say about Russian diplomacy. This omission was possibly caused by his feeling that separate treatment of the Russians was unnecessary, and if this is true it seems justifiable. Russian diplomacy in the nineteenth century was virtually indistinguishable in method and technique from that of the states with which

[56] Kluchevsky, *op. cit.*, IV, 262.

[57] J. Klaczko, *Deux Chanceliers: Gortchakof et Bismarck* (Paris, 1876), pp. 100–101; Kurd von Schlözer, *Briefe eines Diplomaten,* ausgewählt und herausgegeben von Heinz Flügel (Stuttgart, 1958), p. 130.

it dealt; and the outstanding Russian diplomats could have been put to work in other services without causing the slightest inconvenience or disruption and with no need for retraining in the instruments and techniques of their craft. Their values, their language, their methods, in a word, their style was that of western diplomats in general.

Nesselrode, the long-term Foreign Minister under Alexander I and Nicholas I, had so few conspicuously Russian traits that the official Soviet diplomatic history dismisses him contemptuously as "the faithful servant of Metternich."[58] This is unjust, for he served his country well; but his diplomatic behavior was certainly that of the international community in which Russia now moved and in which, indeed, it played a leading role. Even Nesselrode's occasional disingenuousness was western rather than Slavic or Bestuzhev-ian in nature. His *roueries* were those permitted by his *métier,* and they may even have been suggested by careful study of the classic European diplomatic texts.[59] Gorchakov, who succeeded Nesselrode in 1856 after spending years as minister in the German courts and ambassador in Vienna, always posed as a *Russian* minister for foreign affairs rather than as a foreign minister, but the emphasis here was a tactical one designed to advance Gorchakov's fortunes; in practice, as the years passed, his ideas, policies, and methods became increasingly those of his predecessor.[60]

Among the diplomats in the field, the same tendency was apparent. Apart from the relatively few Pan-Slavs in important posts—like Ignat'ev in the 1870's and Hartwig and Nekliudov on the eve of the First World War—Russia's leading diplomatic representatives were men of cosmopolitan culture who mastered their profession and were often taken as models by younger diplomats of other states. Such a man was Brunnow, who in 1840 was sent by Nicholas I to London, where his secret negotiations with Palmerston laid the basis for the settlement of the dangerous Egyptian crisis, and who remained there until 1854 and again from 1860 to 1874. Brunnow has been described as "a diplomat of the . . . old school, versed in all the fine points of the game—a good speaker, a subtle dialectician, an exquisite stylist."[61] He was considered to be an encyclopedia of diplomatic lore and enjoyed the respect of

58 Potemkin, *op. cit.,* I, 383.

59 Klaczko, *op. cit.,* p. 101; Wildner, *op. cit.,* pp. 46 f.

60 See especially B. H. Sumner, *Russia and the Balkans, 1870–1880* (Oxford, 1937), pp. 20 ff.; and C. Friese, *Russland und Preussen vom Krimkrieg bis zum Polnischen Aufstand* (Berlin, 1931), *passim.*

61 Franco Valsecchi, *Il Risorgimento e l'Europa: l'Alleanza di Crimea* (Verona, 1948), p. 211.

all his colleagues and the affection of the younger men in particular. In his leisure hours, he read Cicero.[62] Other leading diplomatic representatives—Saburov, Novikov, Rosen, Benckendorff—were as European as Brunnow.

It may be noted that in the latter half of the nineteenth century the Tsarist regime had every reason to put a higher valuation on negotiation than on such other instruments of foreign policy as war and propaganda. If in other countries the complaint was sometimes heard that the diplomats were always surrendering what the soldiers had won, in Russia it often appeared that the main function of diplomats was to make good the mistakes of their military colleagues. The skillful tactics of Orlov and Brunnow at the Paris conference of 1856 tempered the demands of the victors in the late war and freed Russia from a diplomatic isolation that might have been dangerous in the ensuing period. In 1878, the masterly diplomatic campaign conducted by Peter Shuvalov in London and Berlin extricated Russia from the insupportable position to which it had been brought by a Pan-Slav policy. And in 1906, in the Portsmouth conference that ended the Russo-Japanese War, Witte and Rosen won a success that few would have predicted before the negotiations began.

Brilliant as these triumphs were, however, they were accomplished by standard diplomatic techniques. At Paris in 1856 the Russians were confronted with the problem that faces any power defeated in war: how to keep the price of defeat as low as possible. Their solution, while effective, was not of startling originality. Aware of the divided counsels in the camp of their enemies at the end of the frustrating war in the Crimea, they decided to attempt to drive a wedge between the allies and, in particular, to attempt to draw the French to their side. The delegation was chosen with this purpose clearly in mind. Brunnow, the Russian ambassador in London, was selected to carry the brunt of the negotiations because of his known abilities in this direction and his experience in dealing with the English. But the chief of delegation and the man who made all the final decisions was Prince Orlov, a soldier and *grand seigneur* who could be counted upon to ingratiate himself with French soldiers and with their emperor. Orlov's specific instructions were "to show the Emperor sentiments of friendship, to confide Russian interests to his care, and to create for him the position of an arbiter." To advance his case with Napoleon III, Orlov made some carefully planned public appearances before the negotiations began and attracted enough public attention and popularity to impress

62 Wildner, *op. cit.*, p. 51.

the Emperor, who was always sensitive to popular moods. That done, Orlov flattered Napoleon into a state of sympathy which brought some diminution of the war costs and laid the basis for what was the chief diplomatic result of the conference, a Franco-Russian entente that lasted until 1863.[63]

In 1878 Russia was rescued from the difficulties created by Pan-Slav enthusiasm and the peace of San Stefano by the efforts of its ambassador in London, Peter Shuvalov. A charming and popular figure in London society, Shuvalov had always carefully followed the precepts laid down by Catherine the Great for her envoys, especially those that enjoined the acquisition of contacts with all significant political groups; he had also obeyed Callières' precept that if cultivated with caution the women of the court can be just as useful as sources of information as the men.[64] The excellence and accuracy of his reports to St. Petersburg were supposedly due to his friendship with Lady Derby, the wife of the Foreign Secretary, who kept him informed about the nature of all cabinet discussions on Near Eastern affairs during the dangerous year 1877.[65]

Shuvalov used this information well, especially after Russia had forced the Treaty of San Stefano on the Turks. He argued persuasively in his reports to the Foreign Ministry that any attempt to insist upon the ambitious terms of that treaty would precipitate a war with Britain and Austria-Hungary for which Russia was ill prepared, and he supported his arguments with what appeared to be convincing proofs of this. When his government—fearful of the humiliation that might await it—proved reluctant to commit itself to the most likely alternative to war, an international conference of the kind suggested by Bismarck in February 1878, Shuvalov fell back on a time-tested diplomatic device: that of using informal *pourparlers* for the purpose of attaining reasonable assurances with respect to the issue of a pending dispute before formal negotiations were undertaken. This useful procedure[66] (which

[63] The best account of the conference is François Charles-Roux, *Alexander II, Gortchakoff et Napoléon III* (Paris, 1913), pp. 81 ff. See also Potemkin, *op. cit.*, I, 452–53.

[64] Callières, *op. cit.*, p. 23.

[65] Potemkin, *op. cit.*, II, 53; W. F. Monypenny and G. E. Buckle, *The Life of Benjamin Disraeli* (rev. ed.; New York, 1929), II, 1081–83; A. L. Kennedy, *Salisbury, 1830–1903: Portrait of a Statesman* (London, 1953), p. 108.

[66] "It was reasonable too, as it always must be, not to go into Congress without some previous understanding with the Powers to be there assembled. Every man conversant with the conduct of affairs knows very well that public and formal discussions cannot be conducted with any hope of a successful issue unless such preliminary understandings have been arrived at." The Duke of Argyll, quoted in Sir Ernest Satow, *A Guide to Diplomatic Practice* (3rd ed.; London, 1932), I, 286.

has often been neglected, with unfortunate results, in the age of summitry) averted what had been a real possibility of war in 1878. Shuvalov's direct talks with Derby's successor, Salisbury, produced a formula that was amended in St. Petersburg and confirmed in London in May and which made it possible for the two powers to go into an international conference with their most dangerous differences resolved. The lesser issues were cleared up in the working sessions of the Berlin conference, in which, as one young English diplomat said, Shuvalov "gained immense prestige . . . for his ability and conciliatory manner. He has been indefatigable in Congress, Committee of Delimitations, Committee of Redaction, Private Conferences, etc. and he has also managed to pay his usual attentions to the women and the wine."[67]

Bismarck, always a good judge of diplomatic talent, told Blowitz that Disraeli and Shuvalov were the most important people at the Congress of Berlin and that it was a pleasure to watch them operate. Shuvalov, he added, was a model diplomatist—courteous, charming, always on watch, and, in difficult stages of negotiation, much "like a stag under pursuit that shows its horns when too hard pressed."[68] Thanks to his vigilance and his general ability, Russia, while forced to abandon its more excessive demands on Turkey (and that it would have to do so was known before the conference assembled), made tangible gains in Bessarabia, the Balkans, and Asia Minor.

At Portsmouth in 1906, Russian negotiators once more demonstrated an ability to play losing cards with skill and once more retrieved fortunes that had sunk very low because of military misadventure. The conduct of the negotiations by Witte and Rosen was marked by the same attention to public opinion that had guided Orlov's conduct in 1856; and, thanks to adroit management of the press, an initially pro-Japanese public sentiment in the United States had shifted so far by the end of the conference that the announcement by the Russian delegates that they had been absolved from payment of any indemnity was greeted with satisfaction by the crowd assembled outside the conference hall.[69] In the negotiations proper, the Russians made the most of the Japanese mistake of posing excessive demands and succeeded in making them appear greedy even to themselves, with results beneficial to Russia.[70]

[67] Sumner, *op. cit.*, p. 503 and, for the most satisfactory account of the conference, pp. 501 ff., 517–56.

[68] *The Blowitz Memoirs* (New York, 1903), pp. 164–65.

[69] See Henry F. Pringle, *Theodore Roosevelt: A Biography* (New York, 1931), p. 387.

[70] On the Portsmouth meeting, see Baron Rosen, *Forty Years of Diplomacy* (London, 1922), I, 265 ff.

All in all, the conduct of Russian diplomacy in the nineteenth century was marked by competence and occasionally by brilliance, and, especially in conference negotiation, Russian diplomatists showed a special talent for making the most of bad cases. There was, however, nothing particularly original or distinctive about Russian practice. It was reserved for the Soviet regime to devise new techniques of negotiation, while at the same time challenging the patience and ingenuity of the west by the way in which it adapted the traditional techniques to its own purposes.

V

The Bolshevik regime began its career by announcing, in effect, that it was withdrawing Russia from the western diplomatic community, that it intended to repudiate all legal ties made with other nations by the Tsarist government, and that it would refuse henceforth to conform to the rules and procedures that had obtained in international relations. All this was made clear to the world by the Bolshevik Decree on Peace, passed by the second All-Russian Congress of Soviets on 8 November 1917[71] and by Trotsky's statement two weeks later, at the time of the publication of the secret treaties, when he announced the abolition of the old diplomacy and "its intrigues, codes, and lies" and promised inauguration of an "honest, popular, truly democratic foreign policy."[72] From now on, the Peace Decree stated, negotiation would be conducted "absolutely openly before the entire people";[73] and it was implied that intergovernmental negotiation would be minimal, especially after the restoration of peace, and that the Bolshevik regime, as a people's government, would henceforth direct its appeals and its messages to peoples rather than to their rulers. This would presumably make even the old diplomatic apparatus unnecessary, which is probably what was in Trotsky's mind when he spoke of issuing "some revolutionary proclamations to the peoples and then [closing] up the joint [i.e., the Foreign Office]."[74] This mood soon passed, and, from the days when G. V. Chicherin led a top-hatted and striped-trousered delegation to the Genoa Conference of 1922, the Soviet Union has made full use of all the possible channels of diplomatic negotiation and shown complete command

[71] Jane Degras, ed., *Soviet Documents on Foreign Policy, I* (London, 1951), 1–3.

[72] *Ibid.*, I, 8–9.

[73] *Ibid.*, I, 2.

[74] Theodore H. von Laue, "Soviet Diplomacy: G. V. Chicherin, Peoples Commissar for Foreign Affairs," in Craig and Gilbert, *op. cit.*, p. 235.

of the time-tested methods of the profession.[75] The official Soviet history of diplomacy says proudly: "Soviet diplomacy is master of its technique. In its relations with foreign powers, it defends the interests of its country in the most worthy manner, and, with an incontestable authority and impeccable special skills, it conducts negotiations and concludes agreements advantageous to its country."[76]

One need only think of some of the diplomatic successes won at moments when the Soviet Union was vulnerable to outside pressure, or threatened by outside attack, to admit the justice of this. In the first ten years after the Bolshevik revolution, the Soviet Union often faced the possibility of complete diplomatic isolation. It escaped this by its success in persuading England and other countries to enter negotiations for trade agreements, by the subsequent treaties of recognition concluded with the major powers, by continuous negotiation in areas like Afghanistan, the Middle East, and Poland for protective or diversionary purposes, and by the masterful cultivation of the association with Germany that was inaugurated so sensationally at Rapallo in 1922 and confirmed by the Treaty of Berlin in 1926.[77] These successes were won for the most part by patient negotiation and the skillful use of the techniques of classical diplomacy, especially the art of playing upon the differences of other powers or appealing to their greed or their apprehensions. In the use of the traditional arts of bargaining, Soviet negotiators, in these early days and later, showed themselves the equals of their adversaries, sometimes to the surprise of the latter;[78] and in preparing their case be-

[75] A number of western studies of diplomacy, including Sir Ernest Satow's *A Guide to Diplomatic Practice* and Jules Cambon's *Le Diplomate,* were translated into Russian in the interwar years and used in training courses.

[76] Potemkin, *op. cit.,* III, 787.

[77] The latter treaty in particular played a part in the initiation of the negotiations that led to the Nazi-Soviet pact in August 1939. See *Documents on German Foreign Policy,* series D, VI, 406, 490, 579, 607.

[78] Thus, during the negotiations for American recognition of the Soviet Union in November 1933, the British ambassador in Washington could write: "M. Litvinov has proved somewhat of a surprise to the State Department. I learn on good authority that he has been showing himself the toughest of negotiators. He has evinced no trace of any ambition to achieve a personal success. He has had the blandest, but firmest, of retorts ready for any question, and has appeared quite ready to depart empty-handed at any moment." *Documents on British Foreign Policy,* second series, VII, 542. Speaking of Molotov's conversations in Berlin in November 1940, Paul Schmidt wrote: "Molotov had a certain mathematical precision and unerring logic in his way of speaking and presenting arguments. In his precise diplomacy he dispensed with flowery phrases and, as though he were teaching a class, gently rebuked the sweeping vague generalities of Ribbentrop and, later, even of Hitler." *Statist auf diplomatischer Bühne,* p. 516.

fore the opening of negotiations, in mastering the agenda and the technical aspects of items included on it, and in tactical adroitness in exploiting the legal aspects of existing agreements which bore on current negotiations, they sometimes showed an embarrassing superiority of performance, as the first meetings of the Foreign Ministers after the Second World War showed all too clearly.[79]

Despite the excellence of their training in the external forms of diplomacy and their skill in using it, Soviet negotiators have always had a fundamentally different approach toward diplomacy from that of their western colleagues. To them diplomacy is more than an instrument for protecting and advancing national interest; it is a weapon in the unremitting war against capitalist society. Diplomatic negotiations, therefore, cannot aim at real understanding and agreement; and this has profound effects upon their nature and techniques.[80]

For one thing, it means that not all of the negotiations entered into by the Soviet Government are intended to eventuate in settlements, a fact that irritates or baffles some western diplomats and seems to represent a complete denial of the purpose of diplomacy.[81] Negotiations may be begun, or agreed to, by the Soviets, not as a means of promoting agreement on an issue, but of delaying it, pending the clarification of problems in other areas or the successful completion of other talks. They may be started out of mere speculation, as a means of eliciting the views, defining the interests, or testing the tenacity of the parties on the other side. They may be designed for purely propaganda purposes, as "elaborate stage plays" to edify and win the sympathy of the uncommitted part of the world.[82] Because of this, as Philip Mosely has written, the first task of the diplomats who engage in talks with Soviet negotiators is to try to discover whether the latter have instructions to negotiate seriously or, indeed, have any instructions at all, beyond a general directive to make

79 Newspaper reports of the meeting of Foreign Ministers in London in 1945 would seem to bear this out. See, more recently, "Topics of the Times," *The New York Times,* 26 July 1959; and John Foster Dulles, *War and Peace* (New York, 1950), pp. 27 ff.

80 See Stephen D. Kertesz, "Diplomacy in the Atomic Age," *Review of Politics,* 1959, pp. 132 and 193, and "American and Soviet Negotiating Behavior" in Stephen D. Kertesz and M. A. Fitzsimons, eds., *Diplomacy in a Changing World* (South Bend, Ind., 1959), pp. 144 ff.

81 "I have 'done' many conferences in my life but never went into one without some hope of a fairly quick result. No one could say the same today. Results are often not expected, and often not even desirable." Lord Vansittart, "The Decline of Diplomacy," *Foreign Affairs,* 1950, p. 184.

82 Henry A. Kissinger, "Reflections on American Diplomacy," *Foreign Affairs,* 1956, p. 46.

propaganda for the Communist cause.[83] If they do not, the result is apt to be what a British Foreign Secretary has described, in a moment of exasperation, as "negotiation by equivocation."[84]

Even when Soviet diplomats have been instructed to seek a settlement, the subsequent negotiations are apt to diverge in marked respects from the rules that have traditionally guided diplomatic intercourse in the western world. Soviet diplomats do not subscribe to Callières' belief that there exists between negotiators a *commerce d'avis réciproque.*[85] Bound themselves by rigid directives that allow little flexibility, they cannot understand the freedom of maneuver permitted to western diplomats. Moreover, since they regard their opposite numbers as ideological enemies, they are bound to view all their moves, however trivial, with suspicion[86] and to regard any means that promise to win advantage over them as legitimate.

These things being so, negotiations with the Soviet Union have generally been marked by an almost automatic Soviet opposition at the outset to all proposals from the other side of the table, followed by persistent and uncompromising advocacy of the Soviet point of view. The tactic of initial rejection extends to the most innocuous suggestions made by the partner in negotiation, since the Soviets apparently believe that "the trivial is the first line of defense on which to meet the enemy assaults that always aim at the crucial."[87] In September 1929, when Arthur Henderson presented Dovgalevsky with a list of questions that he felt should be discussed and settled before the resumption of diplomatic relations between their two countries, the Soviet representative came to the second meeting with a list of his own, with the questions in quite a different order, and proceeded to fight, with a zeal out of all proportion to its object, for his arrangement.[88] This sort of thing has been normal practice and has come to be expected by western negotiators.

The stoutness with which the Soviets hold to their own proposals has

83 Philip E. Mosely, "Some Soviet Techniques of Negotiation," in Raymond Dennett and Joseph E. Johnson, eds., *Negotiating with the Russians* (New York, 1951), p. 274.

84 Selwyn Lloyd, describing Gromyko's tactics during the London talks of July 1959, *The New York Times,* 22 July 1959.

85 Callières, *op. cit.,* pp. 20–21.

86 Writing of Molotov's behavior at the London meeting of the Foreign Ministers in 1947, Herbert L. Matthews said: "He is innately suspicious. He seeks for hidden meanings and tricks where there are none. He takes it for granted that his opponents are trying to trick him and put over something nefarious." *The New York Times,* 7 December 1947.

87 Nathan Leites, *A Study of Bolshevism* (Glencoe, Ill., 1953), pp. 55 ff.

88 *Documents on British Foreign Policy,* second series, VII, 20.

become proverbial. "Anyone accustomed to dealing with M. Litvinov," Sir Esmond Ovey wrote from Moscow in December 1929, "will remember how he frequently appears to be on the point of agreeing to suggestions made to him, but in practice, when pressed for any definite statement, he invariably reverts to his original point of view."[89] Similar statements have been made in more recent times about the persistence of Molotov and Gromyko.[90] Nor has this inflexibility in negotiation been easily shaken by nondiplomatic means. It is true that in 1940 and 1941, during the almost continual Soviet-German negotiations about the disposition of eastern Europe, the Soviet Union was forced repeatedly to yield to German gains, in face of *faits accomplis* backed by the threat of force.[91] But in the interwar years and since 1945, other cases of this are hard to find; attempts to bring nondiplomatic pressure to bear on the Soviets, far from succeeding, have sometimes merely given them an opportunity to claim loudly and publicly that they were being threatened by imperialist powers. When the British Government sought in 1933 to intimate in private negotiations that they would break off economic relations unless the Soviet Union released British engineers who were accused of wrecking and espionage, the Soviet Government replied with press releases claiming "gross external pressure" and persisted in their course.[92]

The granting of concessions in the hope of eliciting concessions in return has had no more effect in persuading Soviet negotiators to modify their positions. In the fruitless Anglo-French negotiations with the Soviet Union in the summer of 1939, the western governments repeatedly conceded points described by the Soviet negotiators as being of fundamental importance, hoping that this would facilitate agreement, only to discover, once they had done so, that new points were now of fundamental importance to the Russians, whose intransigence was in no wise diminished. This led Lord Halifax to question the genuineness of the Russian desire for a treaty and to complain to the Soviet ambassador that "the Soviet Government had not budged a single inch, and we had made all the advances and concessions. Saying 'No' to everything was not my idea of negotiation."[93] In the years since 1939, other diplomats

[89] *Ibid.*, 43.

[90] See Sidney Gruson's remarks on Gromyko's negotiating style, in *The New York Times,* 26 July 1959.

[91] See Toynbee and Toynbee, *The Initial Triumph of the Axis,* pp. 319 ff., 364 ff.

[92] *Documents on British Foreign Policy,* second series, VII, 306.

[93] *Ibid,* third series, VI, 135; Toynbee and Toynbee, *The Eve of the War 1939,* p. 454.

have learned, as the British did then, that yielding points or even changing one's original position for reasons other than the presentation of new evidence, merely encourages the Soviets to hold fast.[94]

Soviet inflexibility is generally combined with the skillful use of tactics designed to wear out the patience or weaken the judgment of their adversaries. Among these tactics is the use of bad manners, not out of personal or ideological vanity, which was responsible for the discourtesies of Ribbentrop and Ciano, but with the calculated intention of disconcerting their partners in negotiation, throwing them off balance, and thus betraying them into ill-advised decisions. It was a convention of the old diplomacy that one pretended not to notice the artifices employed by one's adversary and accepted the verbal formulas with which he covered them.[95] The Soviets have no patience with this kind of tolerance. "I may be mistaken," said Sir Anthony Eden at the Moscow Conference of Foreign Ministers in 1943, "but. . . ." "You *are* mistaken," Molotov interrupted harshly, breaking the thread of Eden's argument and destroying its effect.[96] By this kind of crude attack on rules of elementary courtesy and by false accusations, name-calling, and the imputation of the worst possible motives to their adversaries, Soviet negotiators have been able on occasion to obscure the real issues at stake, to divert the course of discussion to subsidiary points, and even to bully a conference into accepting their point of view. Deliberate assault upon the values and forms of the old diplomacy is a means by which the Soviets seek to impose their views and their standards on the rest of the world, and they have not been entirely unsuccessful.[97]

The most successful Soviet tactic is their use of time. Kurt Schumacher once said to an American diplomat, "The day you Americans are as patient as the Russians, you will stop losing the cold war."[98] American negotiators, and western diplomats in general, have found it difficult to learn this lesson and have sometimes, in their anxiety for a happy conclusion to talks, seized upon illusory concessions or grasped at dangerous "agreements in principle" in order to be able to claim a success.[99] This weakness is something the Soviets are constantly watching

[94] John N. Hazard in Dennett and Johnson, *op. cit.*, p. 46.

[95] See François Walder, *Saint-Germain ou la négoçiation* (Paris, 1958), p. 110.

[96] Mosely, *op. cit.*, pp. 283 ff.

[97] See Lord Strang, *Home and Abroad* (London, 1956), p. 206.

[98] Charles W. Thayer, *Diplomat* (New York, 1959), p. 96.

[99] A good example is afforded by the attitude of the Labour Party during the Anglo-Soviet trade negotiations in 1924, when they were so eager for agreement that they forced the Foreign Office to accept an unworkable formula. See Philip

for; and, because they are free from parliamentary or public pressure, they are usually able to hold their ground calmly, while insinuating into the foreign press charges that their adversaries are needlessly protracting negotiations. Since they have often been dealing with democratic countries in which there are parties or pressure groups sympathetic to the Soviet Union, these tactics have frequently been effective.

The practice of prolonging negotiations for months and even years, coupled as it sometimes is with a shifting of the center of negotiation from the ambassadorial to the ministerial level and from there to the level of heads of state, often has the effect of blurring the outlines of the issues at stake and making less precise the original points of difference. The Soviets make the most of this by issuing press communiqués that are designed to confuse the general public and that often impute to their opponents views that weaken their position while strengthening the Soviet case. This kind of tactics was used with effect in the repeated and protracted negotiations in the 1920's over the question of the Russian debts and enabled the Soviet Union to avoid payment without penalty. A more recent example of their use was afforded when, at the end of his visit to the United States in 1959 and his talks with President Eisenhower about the Berlin problem, Premier Khrushchev informed the press that he was satisfied that the President recognized that the existing situation in Berlin was "abnormal."[100] The President may indeed have used this term, for the western powers have never denied the abnormality of the Berlin situation, while attributing it to the failure to unite Germany. He did not, however, mean to suggest that this abnormality could be corrected by withdrawing western troops from the city or altering its status to the advantage of the East German regime, although this was what Khrushchev implied. But so many talks had been held on the subject since the original Berlin note, and in so many different places and with so much publicity, that it was not easy for newspapermen to detect the distortion immediately; once it had been printed, it could be cited, and has since been cited, as a significant American admission of the fundamental weakness of the western position in Berlin. One of the main tasks of those engaged in negotiations with the Soviet Union consists in keeping the record straight, so that it can be revealed to the public at any time without tactical disadvantage

---

Viscount Snowden, *An Autobiography* (London, 1934), II, 680–86. See also remarks of John Foster Dulles before the National Press Club in January 1958, *Department of State Bulletin,* 3 February 1958.

[100] Max Frankel in *The New York Times,* 30 September 1959.

to them,[101] and so that their position will not be eroded by unwitting concessions imposed on them by imputation.

These techniques of negotiation helped to protect the Soviet Union in its most vulnerable years, defended its interests in the period before the outbreak of the Second World War, and won from its allies more than adequate compensation for the losses it suffered in that war. But these have not been the only effective weapons in the Soviet diplomatic armory; in a more thorough analysis of Soviet negotiating behavior, attention would have to be paid to other methods that have helped consolidate the wartime gains and now threaten to expand them. These would include the new methods of economic diplomacy, which have been used with undeniable success by Soviet negotiators of agreements for technical assistance and aid to underdeveloped countries,[102] and the various techniques of public negotiation, with particular reference to their use in the United Nations.[103] Even in a brief account it can be noted that the Soviet Union has effectively emulated Hitler's use of the public statement as a means of negotiation and has employed the exchange of letters between heads of state for the same purpose. Indeed, it might almost be said that by these means the Soviet Union has been able to be a party to negotiations to which she has not been invited, for, by timely use of threats against NATO members,[104] of proposals for disengagement of Soviet and Allied troops from central Europe,[105] or of invitations to summit conferences,[106] she has forced the periodic meetings of NATO Council to discuss *her* views, *her* policies, *her* proposals rather than their own, and to spend time and energy combating the divisiveness promoted within the alliance by her tactics.

VI

Some years ago, when Sir Harold Nicolson delivered his Chichele Lectures on the evolution of diplomatic method, he said: "I have not observed that . . . the Soviet diplomatists and commissars have evolved

[101] On this, see Thayer, *op. cit.*, p. 98.

[102] Klaus E. Knorr, *Ruble Diplomacy: Challenge to American Foreign Aid* (Memorandum of the Center of International Studies, Princeton University), Princeton, N.J., 1956.

[103] See Kertesz, *op. cit.*, p. 376.

[104] Editorial, "Soviet Atomic Diplomacy," *The New York Times*, 28 March 1957; editorial, "Soviet Campaign," *ibid.*, 13 December 1958.

[105] See Gordon A. Craig, "Germany and NATO," in Klaus Knorr, ed., *NATO and American Security* (Princeton, N.J., 1959), pp. 254 ff.

[106] *Department of State Bulletin*, 2 June 1958, pp. 906 ff.

any system of negotiation that might be called a diplomatic system. Their activity in foreign countries or at international conferences is formidable, disturbing, compulsive. I do not for one moment underestimate its potency or its danger. But it is not diplomacy: it is something else."[107]

There are doubtless many who would agree with Nicolson in lamenting the decline of the older diplomacy and in refusing to consider the Soviet Union's way of conducting international relations as diplomacy at all;[108] but the question of nomenclature need not be debated here. What is clear is that the Soviet approach to negotiation has been less impulsive, more systematic, and more effective in its results than that of either Italian Fascism or German National Socialism. In an age when war is no longer acceptable as a continuation of policy by other means, and when the importance of reaching settlements short of war is undeniable, Soviet methods of negotiation would appear to deserve as much study by western diplomats as their own diplomatic tradition has received from their professional colleagues within the Soviet Union.

107 Harold Nicolson, *The Evolution of Diplomatic Method* (London, 1954), p. 90.

108 "Diplomacy could flourish only so long as there was a loose, tacit and general agreement to behave *more or less* like gentlemen." Vansittart in *Foreign Affairs,* 1950, p. 185. It is interesting to note that Adolf Hitler, at least before he came to power, felt a fundamental incompatibility between Soviet and western diplomacy. In 1932 he wrote: "I look upon . . . Soviet diplomacy not only as being unreliable but, above all, as being incapable of being considered of the same nature as the foreign political activity of other nations, and, in consequence, as being something with which one cannot negotiate or conclude treaties." Thilo Vogelsang, ed., "Hitlers Brief an Reichenau vom 4. Dezember 1932," *Vierteljahrshefte für Zeitgeschichte,* VII (1959), 434.

14. The Diplomacy of New Nations

During the past fifty years, we have been passing through a diplomatic revolution, one feature of which has been a remarkable expansion of membership in the diplomatic community.[1] Before 1914, only about twenty states in the whole world had any serious and continuous interest in foreign affairs and all but two or three of these were European powers. In the period after the First World War, this picture began to change, partly because of the existence and influence of the League of Nations. But the expansion of the international community that took place between 1919 and 1939 seems almost negligible in comparison with what has been happening since 1945. The Second World War smashed what was left of European dominance in world affairs and simultaneously destroyed the ability of the former colonial powers to resist the demands of their subject peoples for independence. The result of this has been the creation of forty new states since 1945, most of them in Africa and Asia. When the United Nations was founded in 1945, it had fifty-nine members. At the end of 1960 there were ninety-nine member states, forty-six of which were members of the so-called Afro-Asian bloc. These new states are proud of their independence and insistent upon demonstrating this in their foreign policy, and their diplomatic behavior has become a matter of great importance and constant concern to the more established powers, and to the leaders of the western and totalitarian blocs in the great-power competition that is being waged in the world today.

"The Diplomacy of New Nations" was originally delivered as the last of three lectures on "The Diplomatic Revolution of Our Times," the Haynes Foundation Lectures, University of California, Riverside, April 1961, and was printed privately by the Haynes Foundation.

[1] See above, Chapter 11, p. 202.

I

It is safe to say that we have all at one time or another found ourselves being profoundly irritated by some aspect of the foreign policy or diplomatic behavior of these states. This is perhaps only natural. We are ourselves citizens of a powerful and established nation, and most of these new states are neither powerful nor established, and their conduct strikes us at times as being pretentious. When we feel this way we are, of course, reflecting what may almost be described as the traditional attitude of great powers toward lesser ones. In 1878, during the meetings of the Congress of Berlin, the British Foreign Secretary Lord Salisbury was given residential quarters in Potsdam; and, after he had been there a day or so, someone asked him how he liked them. Salisbury looked gloomily past his interrogator at a group of representatives from the Balkan states and said: "At Potsdam we have mosquitoes. Here we have minor powers. I don't know which is worse."[2] The standard attitude of great-power statesmen in the nineteenth century was that the small state, like the mosquito, was apt to be both irritating and irresponsible. After the First World War, when an organization was founded that gave the lesser states an assembly in which they were considered the equals of the great powers and where they could actually discuss and criticize the policies of their stronger neighbors, this resentment grew and was sometimes imperfectly concealed. When Sir Austen Chamberlain was Foreign Secretary of Great Britain, one of his critics said that, whenever he appeared at the League of Nations, his face betrayed his displeasure and he always seemed to be saying, "We are perfect. We are British. And yet you, you dagoes, dare to come here and criticize US!"[3] Some of this irritation has carried over to our own times and is all too often expressed in speeches in our representative chambers and in articles in our newspapers, which are always complaining because states which they claim are smaller than Texas have votes equal to that of the United States in the U.N. Assembly.

This sense of irritation has been enhanced by some special circumstances. Since 1948, we have been engaged in a great contest with the totalitarian bloc; and we have regarded this struggle as a war of ideas, a struggle between freedom and slavery, between good and evil, in which no right-thinking person should have any hesitation about declar-

[2] B. H. Sumner, *Russia and the Balkans, 1870–1880* (Oxford, 1937), p. 506.
[3] Wickham Steed, *The Real Stanley Baldwin* (London, 1930), p. 129.

ing himself on our side. But the new nations have for the most part refused to declare themselves to be on our side and have clung to the concept of neutrality. Neutrals have never been popular with belligerents, least of all in conflicts that appeared to the belligerents to be religious wars. The reluctance of the Kurfürst of Brandenburg to join Gustavus Adolphus of Sweden in the war against the Habsburgs in 1630 was regarded as an act of apostasy by the choleric champion of the Protestant faith,[4] and the refusal of Francis Joseph of Austria to aid Nicholas I of Russia in his war against the liberal west in 1854 led the Tsar to issue what sounded like a decree of excommunication from the conservative fold.[5] Similarly, in the cold war of our own time, American statesmen have echoed the sentiments of those earlier ideologues when referring to states that insisted on preserving their neutrality of attitude, a fact that becomes abundantly clear if one reads some of the speeches made by Vice President Nixon and Secretary of State Dulles in 1956.[6] Ordinary American citizens have been no less critical, particularly in those cases where the neutrality of the new states has seemed to be a rather inconsistent neutrality. It has sometimes seemed in debates in the Assembly of the U.N., for instance, that the new states have a special kind of neutrality that is reflected in abstention from all projects that might hurt the Soviet bloc and all projects that help the position of the western powers—a kind of "heads they're right, tails you're wrong" neutrality. Thus, in the late fall of 1956, the Afro-Asian bloc showed unanimity in condemning the action taken by Great Britain and France at Suez but showed no similar agreement when it was suggested that the Soviet action in Hungary merited the same kind of criticism.[7] Nor was this the only occasion on which what appeared to be a double

[4] See above, Chapter 8, pp. 143–44.

[5] Josef Redlich, *Emperor Francis Joseph* (New York, 1929), pp. 144–45.

[6] On 9 June 1956, Secretary of State Dulles, in a speech at Ames, Iowa, described neutrality as "an obsolete conception" and "except under very exceptional circumstances . . . an immoral and shortsighted conception." On 4 July 1956, in Manila, Vice President Nixon said that the United States had no sympathy "for the brand of neutralism that makes no moral distinction between the Communist world and the free world." See "Debating Neutralism," Editorial, *New York Herald Tribune,* 15 July 1956.

[7] Annette Baker Fox, "Small State Diplomacy," in Stephen D. Kertesz and M. A. Fitzsimons, eds., *Diplomacy in a Changing World,* (Notre Dame, Ind., 1959), p. 362. The speeches of Nasser, Sukarno, Nkrumah, and Nehru at the meeting of the General Assembly in September 1960 illustrated the same point. They all attacked western imperialism, but none of them referred to the unprovoked Soviet threat to Berlin. See Henry A. Kissinger, *The Necessity for Choice* (New York, 1960), p. 335.

standard was used; and this has caused understandable irritation in the west.

Finally, the diplomatic behavior of some of the new states has been accompanied by a tendency to moralize that is all the more irritating because it seems unjustified. During his labored explanations to the Indian parliament of his behavior in the Hungarian crisis of 1956,[8] Mr. Nehru so frequently disclaimed the idea that "we are nobler or higher or purer than other countries" that Western observers could not help but feel that so much protestation indicated a belief that India really was superior morally; and this impression has been strengthened by the lectures which Mr. Nehru and Mr. Menon have on occasion given other nations for their failure to do things which an examination of the record shows India also fails to do. India's unwillingness to submit the Kashmir dispute to arbitration would seem good reason for its government not to criticize other nations for failing to avail themselves of the instruments of judicial settlement; but it has not had that effect.

II

To be irritated at these characteristics of the diplomatic behavior of the new states is understandable, but a tendency to irritation is not in itself a very positive or productive quality. If our relations with these states are to be effective, we shall have to master our own feelings and see matters a bit more from their point of view than we are always ready to do.

In the first place, we should remember what is the most obvious thing about them—that most of them are new members of the international community—and we should remember the natural consequences of this. They lack the experience; they lack the assurance; in some cases they lack even the trained public servants a state needs if it is to conduct foreign relations. Their diplomats at the U.N. have sometimes arrived with only the most rudimentary knowledge of what their function is and how it is to be discharged. Like latecomers to any established society, they have an inferiority complex that is apt to express itself in assertiveness and even arrogance. They are suspicious of slights and are constantly expecting condescension. Their individual and collective feelings are oversensitive and betray them into gestures that are excessive and even unwise. Their attitude seems always to be on the verge of

8 On this, see Adda B. Bozeman, "India's Foreign Policy Today: Reflections upon its Sources," *World Politics*, X (1958), 257.

belligerence. The spirit with which they approach their task was perhaps most clearly and succinctly expressed by Jawaharlal Nehru in the first meeting of the Asian nations at Delhi in 1947, when he said, with no apparent provocation: "Far too long have we of Asia been petitioners in Western courts and chancellories. That story must now belong to the past. We propose to stand on our own feet. . . . We do not intend to be the playthings of others."[9] This kind of shrill protestation typified the general attitude of the new states when they first entered the diplomatic community.

In the second place, because they have recently won freedom, in some cases after long years of struggle, their chief objective in foreign affairs is to assert, to preserve, and to enhance their independence, which they see subject to a variety of threats: territorial, economic, ethnic, and cultural. Their desire to establish their independence sometimes takes relatively innocuous forms. In its first vote in the U.N. Assembly, for example, the new state of Nigeria voted to admit the question of Red China's membership in the world organization to the Assembly's agenda. This gesture led one Western diplomat to speak of "Nigeria whose name should be Unpredictability,"[10] and it was interpreted by others as a vote against the very powers which had supported Nigeria's preparation for statehood. It would have been more accurate to regard it merely as a demonstration by Nigeria that, now it was independent, it was determined to be truly so and that the western powers would be well advised not to take its support for granted on all questions.

In the case of the Afro-Asian states in general, it is safe to say that their burning desire to preserve their independence has in large part determined their adoption of a neutral position in the cold war. The wisest of their statesmen doubtless feel that a complete bipolarization of global politics would be the surest way, first, of restricting their freedom (by making them members of a political bloc whose leaders were great powers) and, second, of destroying their freedom in the war that such a complete bipolarization would, in their opinion, inevitably cause. In their neutrality, they see both a chance to remain free and an opportunity, by joint action with other states like themselves, to use their influence to prevent the coming of war. Other statesmen of new nations have resented what appears to be the attempt of the big powers to form them into leagues without having the courtesy even to consult

[9] W. Howard Wriggins, *Ceylon: Dilemmas of a New Nation* (Princeton, 1960), pp. 430 ff.

[10] Marguerite Higgins, "Africans Try to Avoid the Cold War," *New York Herald Tribune,* 29 December 1960.

them. Thus, at the time of the announcement of the plan to form the South East Asia Treaty Organization (SEATO), *The Times* of Ceylon wrote:

> Mr. Dulles does not trouble to find out how Asia's repugnance to communism might be utilized in the cause of world democracy, *with Asia's consent.* He is in a hurry and, with bland arrogance, imagines that, because Free Asia abhors communism, it will automatically embrace any made-in-Washington scheme for liberating the Asians in spite of the Asians.[11]

The West's perhaps overly anxious desire to have an unambiguous declaration of friendship in the form of membership in SEATO or in the abortive Middle East Defense Command or in the Baghdad Pact has stimulated neutralism simply because it has appeared to be an attempt to impose shackles upon states that have recently won their freedom.

That the neutrality of the new states would tend, at least for a time, to be somewhat inconsistent should not have been surprising. These were all states that not only were newly independent but possessed a long colonial past. They could not help but be more suspicious of their old masters than they were of other powers, and to be susceptible to slogans that echoed their own sentiments even when those slogans were used by powers they had good reason to distrust. Thus, at the Bandung Conference of 1955, when twenty-nine African and Asian states gathered together, Sukarno's keynote speech stressed their common opposition to colonialism, poverty, and involvement in international wars, and, when Chou En-lai, who was making his first international appearance, echoed those sentiments in a skillful and conciliatory address, there was general satisfaction. But when Sir John Kotewala of Ceylon said that, as long as they were all against colonialism, they ought to note the new colonialism of the Soviet Union in eastern Europe and ought "to declare openly [their] opposition to Soviet colonialism as much as to Western colonialism," he was upbraided by Nehru and criticized by several of the other members of the meeting, whose emotions proved to be stronger than their logic.[12] A year later, when Britain and France attacked Egypt, the critics of Sir John Kotewala found confirmation for their worst suspicions of the imperialist powers; and their feelings were so inflamed that many of them quite sincerely felt that the Hungarian blood-bath was a matter of an entirely different order.

[11] Wriggins, *op. cit.,* p. 438.
[12] *Ibid.,* pp. 442 ff.

In the third place, with respect to the tendency of these states to adopt a high-flown moral tone, this too, while irritating, is understandable. It is the result, in part at least, of an efflorescence of cultural nationalism that leads them to seek to assert the uniqueness and superiority of their approach, not only to matters of the spirit, but to political matters as well. Many of these nations had, at one time, their own distinctive traditions of life and thought. These had died out during the centuries of European supremacy or had been overlaid with occidental ideas and institutions. When the new nations began to take their place as modern political communities, however, they began in many cases to seek to free themselves from the western intellectual tradition and to search their past for values of their own. The years in which India, for instance, was fighting her long fight for freedom from British rule were also years in which every step forward was accompanied by warnings from her own greatest political thinkers that freedom would mean nothing if it merely led to a subordination to western ideas. Thus, at the turn of the century, Vivekananda was writing:[13]

> New India is saying, "If we only adopt Western ideas, Western food, Western dress and Western manners, we shall be as strong and powerful as the Western nations." . . . Old India is saying: "Fools! By imitation, others' ideas never become one's own—nothing unless earned is your own." . . . Oh India! This is your terrible danger. The spell of imitating the West is getting such a strong hold on you that what is good and what is bad is no longer decided by reference to the Shastras.

A little later Rabindranath Tagore echoed this thought:[14]

> Europe has her past. Europe's strength lies in her history. We in India must make up our minds that we cannot borrow other people's history and that, if we stifle our own, we are committing suicide. . . . It does India no good to compete with Western civilization in its own field.

This insistence upon remaining true to one's own past and following ideas that are unique to one's own culture is felt to some extent by all of the new nations that have anything resembling a real history or political past; and their leaders today pay obeisance to this idea. And they are not disinclined, in cases where a return to the past is impossible (and this of course is sometimes true), to claim a special virtue for their

[13] D. Mackenzie Brown, *The White Umbrella: Indian Political Thought from Manu to Gandhi* (Berkeley, Calif., 1958), pp. 101 ff.
[14] *Ibid.*, p. 113.

ideas anyway and to assert that they are unique to their own culture and superior to western ideas.

To give one example of this, much has been made since the Bandung Conference of 1955 of what has been called a characteristically Asian and morally superior set of principles for the governance of foreign relations. This is the so-called *panca-sila*—a set of five principles signed by Nehru and Chou En-lai at Bandung and since subscribed to by other eastern states. Supposedly based on the Buddhist code of ethics, the five principles of the *panca-sila* are: (1) mutual respect for each other's territorial integrity and sovereignty; (2) nonaggression; (3) noninterference in each other's internal affairs; (4) equality and mutual benefit in all dealings; and (5) peaceful coexistence and economic cooperation.[15] This code has been so highly vaunted by eastern writers that it does little good to point out—as Adda Bozeman has pointed out[16]—that, in the first place, Buddhism has long ceased to be a frame of reference for individual conduct in India and China and that neither Nehru nor Chou En-lai is much influenced by Buddhism in his thinking; or that, in the second place, the Buddhist origins of the five principles is spurious in any case. As principles of international action, these five ideas are the end result of the modern history of international organization as developed in the western world; and they are more honored in the west today than they are by Chou En-lai. Yet it would be idle to attempt to impress this upon ardent followers of Mr. Nehru; and in general it must be admitted that the force of cultural nationalism is so great that this kind of moral posturing is, for a time at least, inevitable.

Moreover, we would be well advised, in tolerating this and the other characteristics of new-state diplomacy, to remember that we ourselves were once a new and inexperienced nation and that throughout the whole of our early experience, we shared the very traits we find objectionable in these newer ones. We would do well to remember, for instance, a passage by Alexis de Tocqueville which sounds as if it might have been intended to describe a newcomer to an Assembly meeting in New York but is really about us in our youth:

> An American leaves his country with a heart swollen with pride; on arriving in Europe, he at once finds that we are not so engrossed by the United States and the great people who inhabit it as he had supposed, and this begins to annoy him. . . . [He is also ignorant of the place he occupies in European society.] He is afraid of ranking himself too high;

[15] Wriggins, *op. cit.*, pp. 442, 446.
[16] Bozeman, *op. cit.*, p. 266.

still more is he afraid of being ranked too low. This twofold peril keeps his mind constantly on the stretch and embarrasses all he says or does. . . . He is like a man surrounded by traps; society is not a recreation for him but a serious toil; he weighs your least actions, interrogates your looks, and scrutinizes all you say lest there should be some hidden allusion to affront him. . . . He is full of scruples and at the same time of pretensions; he wishes to do enough, but fears to do too much, and as he does not very well know the limits of the one or of the other, he keeps up a haughty and embarrassed air of reserve.[17]

Lo, the poor Indonesian or Nigerian! But so once were we.

Nor should we forget, when we are complaining about neutrals, that we were once the greatest and the noisiest of all neutrals, that by our efforts in the nineteenth century we promoted the general recognition of neutral rights, and that, in the opinion of a great international lawyer, J. L. Brierly, it was we who spread the notion, so prevalent in the nineteenth century (but now conveniently forgotten by us), that neutrals were rather more virtuous than other people.[18]

It need hardly be added that we have no right to forget our own fulminations about colonialism (and how we permitted them to influence our attitudes in foreign affairs in earlier days) and our habit of moralizing on every possible occasion. Charles Dickens was so affronted by our claims of superiority of culture, manner, dress, and thought that he devoted long stretches of *Martin Chuzzlewit* to this congenital weakness of ours. It is in *Chuzzlewit* that he introduces us to General Choke who asks: "What are these United States for, sir, if not for the regeneration of man? But it is nat'ral in you to make such an enquerry, for you come from England and you do not know my country." Nor have we even today brought this tendency to attribute superiority to ourselves under control. I seem to remember an article of Mr. Walter Lippmann's not so long ago, arguing that we would make more friends in the world if we did not always seem to claim that we were not only the strongest and richest nation in the world but the best too.[19] And I know I have seen recently a cartoon in *The New Yorker* purporting to show a worried conference on the world situation in what appears to be the National

[17] Alexis de Tocqueville, *Democracy in America,* the Henry Reeves text as revised by Francis Bowen and further corrected and edited by Phillips Bradley (2 vols.; New York, 1954), II, 183. ("Why the Americans Show So Little Sensitiveness in Their Own Country and Are So Sensitive in Europe.")

[18] See above, Chapter 8, p. 151.

[19] Walter Lippmann, "The Grace of Humility," *New York Herald Tribune,* 24 September 1957

Security Council with one brash young man saying: "I don't know what we're so worried about. I mean, we're the good guys and they're the bad guys, and the good guys always win, don't they?"

III

If we remember these things, we can perhaps, by a process of identification, get a little closer to the position of these new nations; and, if we do that, we can prevent ourselves from being annoyed by characteristics that were until recently our own. This does not mean that we have no reason to be concerned about the course that has been followed by these nations. It means only that we can turn our minds away from such superficial things as manners of speech and attitude and concentrate upon sources of more legitimate concern. And of these there are several.

Among those principles of the old diplomacy upon which nineteenth-century statesmen always put a high valuation were *objectivity* (which may be equated with freedom from illusions and the ability to assess a situation realistically), *patience* (the ability to wait upon events), and *proportion* and *restraint* (which may be defined as the ability to see one's own limitations). It can hardly be denied that all too often the new states have shown a conspicuous lack of these qualities and, because of this, have opened themselves to grave risks. This is true even of the strongest of them. In March 1956, Nehru said in an interview printed in *The New York Times,* "Geography made India in her long past a closed country. Surrounded by the seas and the mighty Himalayas, it was not easy of entry."[20] Even as history, this is inaccurate, in view of the number of times India has been invaded since antiquity; and, as a basis for a foreign policy in our own day, it is wholly inadequate. Yet in some ways Nehru's policy has been based precisely upon this illusion of inaccessibility, and to the extent that this has opened his country to risks, this is a matter that must affect us all. The degree of self-delusion in the foreign policy of Prime Minister Nasser of Egypt needs hardly be commented on. His dream of a North African empire is perhaps rooted in the memory of the great medieval Muslim empire that once ruled the Mediterranean world; and the re-establishment of that empire would, in almost any conceivable circumstances, be unrealistic. But Nasser has also demonstrated, on at least one occasion, that he is incapable even of estimating his own military capabilities;

[20] Louis Fischer, *Russia, America and the World* (New York, 1960), p. 170.

and it is this combination of grandiose ambition and illusion that could well, unless it is checked by his own friends and allies, touch off troubles in the Middle East from which the world might not recover. Of all the leading statesmen of the new nations, it is Nasser who comes closest to sharing some of the most dangerous characteristics of Mussolini.

Lack of objectivity and proportion and lack of patience have also led, in the case of some of the new nations, to vulnerability to Soviet economic and cultural diplomacy, and, unless corrected by caution, this could well lead to the very thing these nations fear most of all: the loss of their freedom. In trade and aid negotiations with the western powers, the new nations as a class have revealed a high degree of irritability and have given every evidence of resentment when conditions were placed upon loans to them or attempts were made to elicit assurances concerning the uses to which the loans would be put. The fact that Western queries have for the most part been prompted by a sincere desire to see that the economy of the borrower would receive maximum benefit has done nothing to appease their feelings; and they have sometimes seemed to derive malicious pleasure from comparisons between our conditional approach to foreign aid and the free-handed way in which the Soviets have given them economic and technical assistance. Yet they have not seen fit to remember or to ponder a statement made by Premier Khrushchev to a group of visiting U. S. Congressmen in 1955 when he said, "We value trade least for economic reasons and most for political purposes." Behind every generous agreement with the Soviet bloc lies the cold purpose of the Soviets to use economic entanglement as the first step toward domination; and the states who have gone blithely into these agreements are assuming grave risks.[21]

The new nations are similarly vulnerable to Soviet cultural diplomacy, and one cannot pick up a newspaper these days without finding an item reading something as follows:

> *Addis Ababa, Ethiopia* (AP).—The Soviet Union and Ethiopia have signed a cultural agreement described here as one of the most comprehensive Moscow has concluded with an African country. The Russians offered scholarships in agriculture, scientific training, and languages. Ethiopia agreed to accept Russian education officers for the study of African problems.

[21] On Soviet economic diplomacy, see Klaus E. Knorr, *Ruble Diplomacy: Challenge to American Foreign Aid,* Memorandum of the Center of International Studies, Princeton University (Princeton, 1956).

The desire for economic progress and technical education is characteristic of all of the new states. They are convinced that true equality in the international community will be theirs only when they are industrialized, and for that they need lots of help. They are not willing to wait or to weigh offers or to consider all the risks involved or, indeed, to probe the motives of the donors. And this impatience, combined with the lack of objectivity and proportion that comes from ambition and from old resentments, represents a grave threat to the new nations and, by extension, to the free world, which cannot help but be threatened by continued vulnerability to communism on the part of these nations.

One must hastily add, on the other side, that there are signs of growing sophistication on their part and some evidence that they are not so prone to taking Soviet-bloc assurances at their face value as they formerly were.

Nehru, it is safe to say, became far less sure of the inaccessibility and impregnability of his country after his co-signatory of the *panchashila* of Bandung attacked his northeastern frontiers and proved unamenable to reason or negotiation; and the Chinese depredations against Tibet have had widespread repercussions in the Afro-Asian bloc. During 1958 and 1959, a shift of mood was apparent among many of the neutralist countries. Burma, for instance, became much more anxious about the threat of China, as did statesmen in Indonesia. In the autumn of 1958, Burmese and Indonesian statesmen privately approved the U.S. attitude in the Formosa Straits, although publicly remaining true to the policy of nonalignment.[22] It is true that recently Prime Minister U Nu of Burma met with Chou En-lai, signed a new border treaty, and conferred on his guest the unprecedented rank of "Supreme Upholder of the Glory of the Great Love," awarding him a lavish gold and jade medal, and making many speeches about co-existence. But this does not necessarily weaken the point, for it was probably less a demonstration of faith in the old Chou En-lai of Bandung than an attempt to make another accommodation in the hope that it would postpone trouble.

There are other signs of growing sophistication among the new nations. The members of the Arab bloc, who used to respond eagerly and passionately to Nasser's evocation of the idea of Arab unity, have been more reluctant of late to subordinate their own policies to Nasser's. There has been a dawning realization that what Bismarck used to call sentimentality in foreign policy, and what we call ideological unity, does

[22] Wriggins, *op. cit.*, pp. 454–55.

not always promise well. When the Syrian constitution was first drawn up, it stated that Syria was an individual political unity, but said further that "our people constitute a part of the Arab nation in their history, their present, and their future, look forward to the day when our Arab nation is united as one state, and will tirelessly work to realize that sacred aspiration."[23] It is doubtful that Syria is quite as enthusiastic about that ideal today. It is known that Iraq and Jordan are less so, and that both states suspect that the fulfilment of Nasser's ambitions (especially with respect to Israel) might well be disastrous for them.

What we may be seeing here is the dawning in many of the new nations of a clearer appreciation of the realities of foreign policy in a divided world, and the beginning of a diplomacy based less on sentimentality or ideology or history than on state interest.

What can we do to promote this healthy development?

For one thing, we can continue to be tolerant of those actions of the new nations which are the natural expression of their youth and inexperience, and we can stop thinking that they have a duty to side with us on all issues in which we take an interest. To regard every abstention or deviation from the western line as a sign of communism and to say so publicly, as Secretary Herter did of Kwame Nkrumah at a press conference during a meeting of the General Assembly in 1960, is not only naïve but dangerous, since it is calculated to alienate peoples who should be our friends. The sooner we stop thinking of neutralism as a dirty word the better. The world perhaps needs more neutrals than fewer.

In the second place, we should try to promote the ability of these states to be truly independent by increasing the magnitude of our economic aid and technical-assistance programs (without becoming less circumspect about the conditions of aid) and by divesting them of military conditions, upon which we have sometimes insisted so vehemently that it used to be said wryly that, if you asked the United States for a tractor, you received a tank.[24] Along the same line, it is high time that we began to match the Soviet cultural offensive in scope and imagination, in order to combat the unfortunately widespread notion (sedulously cultivated by Soviet propagandists) that we are the twentieth-century barbarians with nothing to export to the outside world but plumbing fixtures, Coca Cola, and guns (the last of which are not so good as those manufactured in Czechoslovakia and the Soviet Union).

[23] Adda B. Bozeman, *Politics and Culture in International History* (Princeton, 1960), p. 361.

[24] See Kissinger, *op. cit.*, p. 325.

In the third place, we can explore areas in which representatives of the new nations can meet in fruitful collaboration with Americans. The Peace Corps is one encouraging example of this. So is the recently launched "Young Diplomats Program" for the Carnegie Endowment of International Peace, which brings promising young members of the diplomatic service or the foreign offices of the newer countries—men and women under 30 and with less than five years of service—to American universities for a year's work in fields of international relations, diplomacy, international economics and finance, and similar subjects, followed by three months' experience in U.N. headquarters or other international agencies located in this country. Such a program can hardly fail to be productive of many kinds of good.

Finally, the most important thing that Americans can do is to refrain from actions that obscure our position or our purpose in the world. It would be a tragic mistake if we should, by speech or posture or action, give the impression to the new states that we were beginning to adopt the methods and the principles of our totalitarian adversaries. When he gave the Stafford Little lectures at Princeton in 1961, Sir Hugh Foot, the former Governor of Cyprus, said that the fate of the world might well rest with the new states that have joined the United Nations since 1945. Whether this is true or not, it would be folly for the United States to forget the importance of those states and, by failure of understanding, lack of sympathy, or mere indifference to their views, make them turn toward our enemies because they feel they have no other place to go.

15. John Foster Dulles and American Statecraft

It may be that some of what follows will arouse disagreement, for my subject makes this almost inevitable. Let me begin, therefore, with a statement that would be hard to contest: namely, that John Foster Dulles was not a popular man. Indeed, it would be difficult to think of an American Secretary of State who was less beloved during his term of office than Dulles. In his own country he was detested by liberals in general and the Democratic Party in particular. Even in his own party he was the object of bitter criticism, which came not only from the extreme right wing but also from Republicans who occupied leading positions in the Department of State and the missions abroad. Finally, large sections of the populations of foreign lands regarded him with aversion, and these included the subjects of some of his country's closest allies. A lot of water will have to flow down the Spree before a John-Foster-Dulles-Allee[1] graces London or Paris, and I know of no such boulevard in Washington.[2] A movement to repair this omission is hardly to be expected as long as the Democrats remain in power or even

"John Foster Dulles und die amerikanische Staatskunst" was first delivered as a Public Lecture at the Otto Suhr Institute of the Free University of Berlin, 23 July 1964.

[1] The John-Foster-Dulles-Allee starts at Schloss Bellevue, the official Berlin residence of the Bundespräsident, runs in an easterly direction along the southern bank of the Spree, and then, turning southeast, goes past the Kongress-Halle, slips between the Platz der Republik and the Soviet War Memorial, and finally joins the Friedens-Allee and the Strasse des 17. Juni at the Platz vor der Brandenburger Tor.

[2] Washington does, however, have a Dulles Airport, which, in view of the Secretary's extensive travels while in office, is an entirely appropriate memorial.

—if I interpret Senator Goldwater's interview with *Der Spiegel* correctly[3] —in the event that that statesman should be elected in November.

Dislike of Dulles as a person has also characterized a good part of the literature about him and the events with which he dealt. Thus, his critics are generally not content to list what they consider to be his faulty judgments and his errors of commission or omission but seem to feel compelled to ascribe these to moral obliquity and weakness of character, the more violent of them charging that he was not only wrong but hypocritical, disingenuous, treacherous, and, under pressure, cowardly. Typical of this kind of writing is Herman Finer's book on the Suez crisis of 1956, in which the author scoffs at Dulles' religious faith (with ponderous asides about his pharisaism, his "Calvinistically zealous" behavior, his "religiosity," "sanctimoniousness," and "self-righteousness," and with low-burlesque passages like: "October 25 was a particularly glorious day in Dulles' office. . . . The Soviet Empire was on the decline. Faith had been justified. The sinners were being whipped at last. God was not mocked!") and accuses him of "open and disguised panic before Russian power," of being "intimidated by what Moscow *might* do," of "quailing" before the Russian specter, and of much else.[4] Finer is a liberal, but his kind of criticism is not restricted to the left; during Dulles' lifetime, similar charges, couched in ideological rather than biblical terminology, were made about him by people whose political position was close to that of the John Birch Society.

It is not my purpose here to defend John Foster Dulles, but rather to try to explain why his policy as Secretary of State made such extreme (and, all things considered, unjustified) criticisms credible to so many people; to show how his diplomatic style was determined not only by his own personality and character, but also by the domestic political situation in which he found himself; and, finally, to hazard a tentative appraisal of his accomplishment and his stature. I use the word tentative deliberately, for it is obviously impossible at this time to say anything that would be final. Not until the Dulles Papers, currently being assembled at Princeton University, are made available to scholars will a definitive judgment of the career of this extraordinarily difficult man be

[3] *Der Spiegel*, No. 28/1964 (8 July 1964). Without mentioning him by name, Senator Goldwater made remarks that could be considered critical of Dulles' policy, at least in 1956. He expressed the opinion that the United States should have sent troops into Hungary in that year and added: "If the United States had fulfilled its duty to Hungary in this way, Hungary would be a free country today."

[4] Herman Finer, *Dulles over Suez: The Theory and Practice of his Diplomacy* (Chicago, 1964), pp. 7, 16, 17, 21, 31, 60, 72, 76, 78, 172, 173, 258, 322, 347, 371.

feasible; and it is unlikely that those files will be opened for at least another decade.[5]

I

One of the crimes most frequently laid at Dulles' door by his critics is the fact that he had the temerity to want to be Secretary of State. Exactly why this should be considered reprehensible in a country in which every red-blooded American boy is, or was, supposed to want to grow up to be President is not at all clear. Part of the reason is doubtless that many Americans have always had a deep suspicion of the Department of State, because it deals with foreign affairs and, indeed, with foreigners, a dangerous and obviously un-American occupation.[6] But there is also a tendency among some writers to regard Dulles' ambition as both vain and presumptuous.

Yet it is easy to find a more generous explanation. If Dulles persisted in defying the parochialism of many of his countrymen, it was partly because the career of diplomacy was a kind of tradition in his family; and if he had confidence in his own abilities in the field of foreign affairs, he had good reason to do so, for he had a long and systematic apprenticeship in this calling before becoming Secretary. Both his grandfather on his mother's side, John Watson Foster, and one of his uncles by marriage, Robert Lansing, served as Secretaries of State, the first under President Benjamin Harrison and the second under Woodrow Wilson; and it would have been unnatural if this had had no effect upon the young Dulles in the formative stages of his career. He once said that, after the Bible and Shakespeare, his grandfather's memoirs was the work to which he most frequently returned;[7] and after he

[5] In turning over his papers to Princeton University, Dulles expressed the wish that access to them be granted as widely as possible, and become unlimited after the expiration of twenty-five years from the date of his death.

[6] "Somewhere along the line, perhaps deeply rooted in our history and character, there must have been implanted an attitude of mind toward diplomacy—which is to say the conduct of foreign affairs—that creates a combination of distrust and depreciation. The long history of isolationism has something to do with it. So has a sense of inferiority that made us believe the British and the French and other foreigners were more astute, more clever, more subtle, more experienced than our diplomats." "The Foreign Service," Editorial, *The New York Times,* 30 August 1957.

[7] Richard H. Rovere, *Affairs of State: The Eisenhower Years* (New York, 1956), p. 53. John W. Foster's term as Secretary lasted only eight months, but he had entered the diplomatic service in 1872 and had a long and rich experience in it. See John W. Foster, *Diplomatic Memoirs* (2 vols.; Boston, 1909).

became Secretary himself his desk at the Department was flanked by portraits of Foster and Lansing.[8]

His own practical experience in diplomacy had begun long years before those pictures were hung and, indeed, some years before his uncle had moved into the gray pile on Pennsylvania Avenue which used to be the heart of American statecraft. In 1907, while still an undergraduate at Princeton University, he accompanied John Watson Foster to the Second Hague Peace Conference, where his grandfather served as counsel to the Chinese delegation and he himself as its secretary. It was an unusual assignment for an American college student (although he apparently did not think so, writing of it quite matter-of-factly in the fifth reunion yearbook of his class[9]), but it was not an inappropriate one, for it began the preoccupation with the tangled problem of devising means for preserving international peace which he possessed for the rest of his life.

After graduating from Princeton in June 1908 as class valedictorian, Dulles studied for a time at the Sorbonne and then buckled down to the task of qualifying himself for the practice of the law. But the war in Europe soon drew him back into the world of diplomacy. In March 1917 he was selected by President Wilson and Robert Lansing for the job of special envoy of the Department of State to Panama, Costa Rica, and Nicaragua, apparently to make soundings concerning the possibilities of alliance in the event of American involvement in the European conflict, but also, by his own admission, to investigate rumors of German subversion in those countries.[10] After the United States became a belligerent, he was commissioned in the army and made head of the Economic Section of the Positive Military Intelligence Division of the General Staff. Six months later, he was seconded to the War Trade Board, where he not only served as liaison officer with the War Industries Board and the General Staff and coordinator of the joint planning of the three bodies but also carried on extensive negotiations with Dutch shipping firms and with trade delegations from Denmark, Switzerland, and Spain, with a view to limiting neutral exports to Germany by means of preemptive buying.

[8] Finer, *op. cit.*, p. 1.

[9] Class of 1908 Fifth Reunion Yearbook (Princeton, 1913).

[10] *Approaching the Fifteenth.* Class of 1908 Reunion Yearbook (Princeton, 1922), p. 87. He had some previous knowledge of Central America and had written a book, *The Panama Canal Controversy between Great Britain and the United States,* which the Princeton University Press published in 1913.

When the war ended, Dulles resigned his commission and was im mediately appointed to the United States delegation to the Paris Peac Conference as counsel on reparations matters. In this capacity he helpe formulate the American position, defended it in discussions with othe governments, and, once the principles had been agreed upon, helpe to draft the reparations sections of the treaty itself.[11] Nor did the signa ture of the Treaty of Versailles terminate his part in the Europea settlement. At the President's request, he remained in Paris to work ou the reparations and financial aspects of the treaties with Austria-Hungar and Bulgaria; he participated in the first negotiations with the German concerning deliveries of shipping and coal and was the American mem ber of the Inter-Allied Commission that established political authorit in the areas of occupation; and, in the first months of 1920, after brief period in the United States, he was back in Europe, studying th effects of the economic clauses of the treaty in Germany, Austria Hungary and Czechoslovakia. In March 1920 he witnessed the firs of the ominous convulsions that were in the end to destroy the Weima Republic—the Kapp *Putsch* in Berlin and the subsequent Communis disorders in the Rhineland.[12]

The years that followed were devoted for the most part to the law and in 1921, at the age of 32, Dulles became partner in the prominent New York firm of Sullivan and Cromwell. But this position too broad ened his acquaintance of foreign affairs, for Sullivan and Cromwell had many European interests, and Dulles traveled continually to the conti nent and took part in a series of important cases that involved dealings with international or foreign firms and banks. At the same time, he gave legal advice to the underwriters of the Dawes loans, cooperated in the formulation of the Young Plan, and collaborated with Jean Monnet in working out the Polish Stabilization Plan.[13] In this way, he came to know Europe well, particularly France and Germany. During these years he also visited China and Japan and methodically informed himself about those countries.

[11] He was partly responsible for that preamble to section 231 which came to be called "the war guilt clause" because it appeared to justify the exaction of reparations by attributing sole responsibility for the war to Germany and its allies. He was later to admit that it was the revulsion of the German people from this article of the treaty which, as much as any other factor and more than most, paved the way for Adolf Hitler's conquest of Germany.

[12] *Approaching the Fifteenth,* p. 88.

[13] J. F. Dulles, ed., *Poland, Plan of Financial Stabilization, 1927: Documents* (New York, 1928). Printed for private distribution by Messrs. Sullivan and Cromwell.

In the years before the outbreak of the Second World War, Dulles became concerned about the fragility of the world order and increasingly interested in the part that organized religion might play in building a better basis for security and international justice. It was logical, therefore, that in 1939 he should have taken a leading part in the foundation of the Commission for a Just and Durable Peace, whose parent body was the Federal Council of Churches, representing some 25 million Christians. The Commission was designed to work for an international comity of peaceful nations that would revise the international treaty structure once peace was restored, adjust the public law to changed world conditions, promote the liberation of colonial dependencies, and secure recognition of the right of all peoples to intellectual and religious liberty.

Dulles became so well known through his work for the Commission that, in 1944, when Thomas E. Dewey became Republican candidate for the Presidency, he asked him to serve as the party's chief spokesman on foreign policy. In the years that followed, he won equal recognition from the Democrats. In 1946, 1947, 1948, and 1950 he was invited to join the United States delegation to the U.N. General Assembly; and, as special adviser to Secretaries of State Byrnes, Marshall, and Acheson, he took part in the meetings of the Council of Foreign Ministers in London in 1945, in London and Moscow in 1947, and in Paris in 1949. In the course of these meetings, he acquired a first-hand knowledge of Soviet techniques of negotiation, which he later described in his book *War or Peace*[14] and which he put to good use in 1950, when he served as special adviser to the State Department and negotiator of the Peace Treaty in Japan. The manner in which Dulles carried out this difficult assignment, and particularly the adroitness with which he defeated Gromyko's attempt to vitiate the negotiations with Japan by means of the wrecking tactics that had frustrated the conclusion of a German treaty, won grudging admiration from some of his sharpest critics.[15]

In view of all this, Dulles was justified in believing that he was qualified to serve in the highest diplomatic post in the government of his country when the Republican Party came to power in 1952. He certainly possessed more experience in foreign affairs than any other member of his party, and it may indeed be true that he was better qualified in this

[14] John Foster Dulles, *War or Peace* (New York, 1950), especially pp. 27 ff.

[15] On the negotiation of the treaty, see especially Bernard C. Cohen, *The Political Process and Foreign Policy: The Making of the Japanese Peace Settlement* (Princeton, 1957), especially chapters 2 and 7.

respect than any previous Secretary of State. That he had the strongest claim to the office was recognized in both parties, and no one was surprised when President Eisenhower asked him to fill it. Whether this was a wise request, however, and whether Dulles' achievement in office measured up to his qualifications, is another question, and one that is not easy to answer.

II

If dedication to his country, knowledge of foreign parts, mastery of the mechanics of international discourse, and experience in negotiation were all that were needed to make a man a great statesman, Dulles' place in history would be unquestioned. But there are other talents that are required of the diplomat. Anyone who looks into the handbooks and treatises left to us by such past practitioners as Hotman, Wicquefort, Callières, Martens, and Satow[16] will not fail to note that they all emphasize the importance of such qualities as precision, due respect for the legitimate interests of other countries, patience, restraint, and tact. It is fair to say that Dulles was not richly endowed with these gifts.

It is possible that a legal education is not the best preparation for diplomacy, not only because lawyers are less willing to admit the possible intrusion of *imponderabilia* into matters of business than professional diplomats should be, but also because they use language differently than diplomats. Finley Peter Dunne once wrote that what seemed to the eye of the ordinary citizen to be a brick wall looked like a triumphal arch to the eye of a constitutional lawyer. These were words that might easily have dropped from the lips of Dulles' allies in 1956, who repeatedly grumbled that what had seemed to them to be clear promises of support were transformed out of all recognition once Dulles had interpreted them; all of his notes seemed to have hidden escape-hatches through which the Secretary of State disappeared when they called upon him for assistance.

"My difficulty in working with Mr. Dulles," Anthony Eden wrote sadly in his memoirs, "was to determine what he really meant and in

[16] See, *inter alia,* Jean Hotman de Villiers, *L'Ambassadeur* (Paris, 1604); Abraham de Wicquefort, *The Ambassador and His Functions* (trans. John Digby) (London, 1716); *The Practice of Diplomacy,* being an English rendering of François de Callières, *De la manière de négocier avec les souverains,* presented with an introduction by A. F. Whyte (London, 1919); Sir Ernest Satow, *A Guide to Diplomatic Practice* (3rd ed.; London, 1932); and Heinrich Wildner, *Die Technik der Diplomatie: L'art de négocier* (Vienna, 1959).

consequence the significance to be attached to his words and actions."[17] Part of the trouble was that Dulles sometimes used strong words for their own sake, with little reference to their precise meaning. Robert Murphy has noted in this regard:

> One never could be quite sure of the thoughts in the innermost recesses of the Dulles mind. He was entirely capable of suddenly ejaculating in the midst of a critical situation, "It's about time we started throwing bombs in the market place!" But that type of statement was a relief from the pressures and was to be taken with a warehouse full of salt.[18]

People close to Dulles might be aware of this tendency, but how were foreign statesmen to know when the words used were meant seriously and when not? In August 1956, when the Secretary of State told the British and French Foreign Secretaries that "a way must be found to make Nasser disgorge what he is attempting to swallow,"[19] it is understandable that Eden should have been impressed by the determination of this forthright utterance, and he can be forgiven for being aggrieved later on when he discovered that he had read too much into Dulles' words.

On those occasions when his allies were misled in this way, Dulles always found it possible to demonstrate that his language had not said what they thought it said—that, in fact, *he* was precise and *they* were muddled. He could never be convinced that there is a difference between the precision that one finds in a legal contract and the precision of expression which, in diplomatic discourse, conveys an intention. Paul Nitze once explained this distinction by telling a story of Henry L. Stimson when he was Secretary of War. Stimson objected to the lack of clarity of a statement drawn up by his staff and was told that "all of the points he had in mind were covered somewhere in the language they had prepared. His reply was that in the world of politics one should never forget that any public statement is to be judged as though it were a poster, not a photograph. The over-all impression, not just the detailed words, must correspond with the thought that is intended."[20]

Dulles' failure to appreciate this, and his proneness to the kind of indulgence Murphy has described, frequently confused and angered his allies, and, in one unhappy hour, it persuaded some of them to react

[17] *Full Circle: The Memoirs of Anthony Eden* (Boston, 1960), p. 71.
[18] Robert Murphy, *Diplomat among Warriors* (New York, 1964), p. 386.
[19] *Full Circle,* p. 487.
[20] Paul Nitze, "The Impossible Job of Secretary of State," *The New York Times Magazine,* 24 February 1957, pp. 9 ff.

violently and tragically against what they considered to be lack of honesty on his part.

It is possible that the Secretary might have corrected this failing if he had been able to see things from another vantage point than his own, but this always appeared to be difficult for him. It seemed, for instance, to puzzle him when his ambassadors resented being left in the dark concerning matters that affected their missions and about which the governments to which they were accredited were likely to ask questions; and, in dealing with his allies, he was rarely capable of that sympathetic penetration of the minds of others which makes for mutual confidence. Because of this, he was capable even of startling and dismaying the Germans, his most intimate associates within the NATO alliance. At the end of 1958, his sister had to explain patiently to him that certain of his statements concerning the feasibility of dealing with East German guards on the *Autobahn* to Berlin as agents of the Soviet Union and of achieving German reunification without free elections were doubtless legally sound, but that they could not but make informed Germans fear that the United States was considering a basic change in its German policy.[21] To the very end of his term of office, Dulles remained unaware of the effect of his words on others and incapable of putting himself, even momentarily, in their shoes.[22]

This insensitivity to the feelings of others—and Dulles' failure to live up to Satow's definition of diplomacy as the application of intelligence and tact to the regulation of relations among states—was apparent not only in his private communications to other statesmen and his remarks in press conferences concerning specific issues, like the ones just mentioned, but also in his more comprehensive public declarations of policy. In these he had a preference for the kind of idealistic rhetoric that had characterized the speeches of Woodrow Wilson, Dulles' teacher and first chief in foreign policy and a man whom he greatly admired. But, whereas Wilson's speeches had lifted the hearts and aspirations of his domestic and foreign auditors, Dulles often left his fellow Americans in embarrassment, while infuriating people abroad. Walter Lippmann once wrote that his public statements always seemed to say that the United States was not only the richest, most highly developed, and strongest

21 Eleanor Lansing Dulles, *John Foster Dulles: The Last Year* (New York, 1963), pp. 221, 224.

22 Sympathy, it may be noted, is less highly thought of in the practice of law, where identification with the thoughts and interests of others can have unfortunate results.

country in the world, but the best as well. He was "too noble about our ideals and never humble at all about our human, our very human, failures and faults. This alienates, indeed enrages, those who are by national interest our friends and allies. . . . For with great power, which is always suspect, there should go a decent humility." Mr. Dulles made all this worse, Mr. Lippmann continued, by threatening other countries with dreadful consequences whenever they failed to follow our advice, a habit doubly harmful since the implied threat never materialized.[23] The criticism was sound, but it was unfortunately lost on the Secretary, and his speeches continued to be arrogant, moralistic, and, not infrequently, threatening, to friends as well as to foes.

In justice to Dulles, however, it has to be said that he was in a sense compelled to adopt the kind of attitude and language which Mr. Lippmann and others found objectionable by the context in which he had to work and the state of American public opinion when he took office.

III

In a sense that is true to the same degree in no other great nation, American foreign policy has always been determined by the people. Dexter Perkins has written:

> There were debates on foreign policy in the first days of our national history. There have been such debates ever since. Uninstructed though the average citizen may be in the facts of international life, he still has an opinion with regard to them. If he does not know, he thinks he knows And this conviction on his part is one that cannot be disregarded.[24]

No one was more keenly aware of this than John Foster Dulles, for he had seen how the foreign policy of his idol Woodrow Wilson had been destroyed by a sudden swing in public opinion and by his loss of control over Congress. And no one knew better than Dulles how strong a possibility there was in 1952 that the pressures of public opinion would make a coherent and effective foreign policy impossible. For the public mood was both frustrated and inflamed. The long-drawn-out war in Korea, with its heavy casualties, had caused wide dissatisfaction with

[23] Walter Lippmann, "The Grace of Humility," *The New York Herald Tribune,* 24 September 1957.

[24] Dexter Perkins, "The Department of State and American Public Opinion," in Gordon A. Craig and Felix Gilbert, eds., *The Diplomats, 1919–1939* (Princeton, 1953), p. 282.

America's allies—because their contributions in manpower were small and they opposed expanding the war as General MacArthur and his followers desired—and with the Democratic administration that had tolerated this behavior. A morbid suspicion arose that the government—to say nothing of the governments of its allies—had been undermined by Communists. A vocal desire was heard for a thorough housecleaning in Washington and "a victory over international Communism," whatever that might mean. At the same time, it was demanded that our allies should pay more of the costs and, simultaneously, be more obedient to our orders.

It is no exaggeration to say that the national mood imposed upon Dulles a diplomatic style that could not but annoy and frighten our friends abroad, and one which, in the strictest sense of the word, was dishonest. When he became Secretary of State, he knew what he wanted to accomplish in foreign policy, and he knew that it did not differ essentially from what the Truman administration had been seeking to do. To one of his ambassadors, he said, "I believe in the policy of the previous administration, but more firmly than they did." On the other hand, he dared not admit this publicly. From his favorite sport he had learned to trim sail to prevailing winds, and he did that now. With respect to the Department of State, he bowed to the public demand for a shakeup that became so extensive that it came close to making a shambles of morale in the Department itself and in the foreign service.[25] He did so in the apparent belief that an attempt to combat McCarthyism openly would merely paralyze the administration of foreign policy and that concessions to it were, therefore, necessary. In the field of international politics in general, he yielded to the popular desire for a "new foreign policy" more positive than the containment policy of the Truman administration. In his first television appearance after his assumption of office, therefore, he announced that the Eisenhower government would follow a policy of "liberation of the captive peoples" and of "rolling back the Communist world empire." In subsequent speeches, he threatened to respond to new Communist attacks with "massive retaliation" and to meet any failure by his allies to show the same united will and determination as the United States with "an agonizing reapprasial" of the country's position.

The new aggressive tone of Dulles' foreign policy, which was supported by sudden and not always welcome lightning trips to capitals in

[25] This is admitted even in such a friendly biography as John Robinson Beal, *John Foster Dulles: A Biography* (New York, 1957), pp. 138 ff.

the spotlight[26]—(a bad American pun spoke of his "infinite capacity for taking planes")—aroused dismay and concern in friendly nations. Later, as it became apparent that "liberation of the captive peoples" did not exactly mean what the words implied (the American reaction, or lack of reaction, to the East German rising of 17 June 1953 made this clear, and it was underlined during the Hungarian revolution of 1956), as "massive retaliation" was defined and redefined to the point of meaninglessness, and as the "agonizing reappraisal" did not take place, even when the French Assembly failed to ratify the agreement for a European Defense Community, publicists had a field day writing pieces about Dulles' hypocrisy and dishonesty—and they are still doing so.

And yet it can be seen that, however devious and lacking in candor his tactics may have been, they had succeeded in bringing American foreign policy out of the paralysis into which it had fallen during Truman's last days. Even if it was only by means of verbal attitudinizing (and Americans are a people, but surely not the only people, who take big words seriously), a reasonably solid public support had been created for the same policy that had been threatened with repudiation before November 1952; and, even if it was only by means of spreading irritation and insecurity in allied capitals, the western governments had by his urgency been galvanized into renewed activity in the field of rearmament and European federation. The result was that, even when the long negotiations for EDC ended in the defeat in Paris, another solution was quickly found in the form of the West European Union and the admission of Federal Republic of Germany to NATO. The commonly accepted version of this story is that, when the French Assembly issued EDC's death certificate, Dulles succumbed to a fit of the sulks and Anthony Eden saved the day by promising a permanent British contribution to European defense, thus making possible both the creation of the WEU and the expansion of NATO's membership. When one remembers the British coolness toward EDC, however, it is difficult to account for this sudden generosity, and we should perhaps not assume that Dulles' role was wholly negative in the crisis. When the records are opened, it is not unlikely that they will show that American pressure in London played some part in its resolution.

While these matters were being straightened out, the stabilization of the situation in the Far East had also been proceeding. The Korean War had come to an end, not least of all because of Dulles' intimation

[26] "Mr. Dulles flies in for a few days, delivers a couple of dour Calvinist forecasts of doom and retribution, and then heads back out to Bangkok or Rio or wherever." Rovere, *op. cit.*, p. 267.

in New Delhi that further delays by North Korea in the negotiations would mean that the war would have to be carried north of the Yalu into Manchuria.[27] In the same way, the Communist thrust toward Indochina was stopped by a warning to the Chinese that, however many successes they might win in Vietnam, the United States would not tolerate a complete victory or anything like the absorption of Southeast Asia. It was this policy which—after an even stronger Dulles line had failed to win British support at the time of the Dienbienphu crisis—paved the way for the Geneva Conference of 1954. The British writer Richard Goold-Adams has written: "Without the American stand, the Conference could never have taken place on the basis that it did. And . . . neither Eden nor Bidault could have kept the Conference going without Dulles' shadow in the background."[28] His firmness had stopped the possibility of Chinese expansion and made possible treaty arrangements that were not seriously challenged until the re-opening of Communist pressure in Laos at the end of 1960.

These were undeniable achievements, and the momentary easing of tension in 1955 was so apparent that the view prevailed in liberal circles at home and abroad that it should be exploited by means of new conversations with the Russians aimed at resolving other outstanding questions. This was the mood that led to the Geneva Summit Conference, which awakened so many vain hopes. It is worth noting that Dulles was opposed to this meeting on the grounds that nothing good could come out of unstructured talks between heads of state unless there was some concrete proof ahead of time of a desire on the part of the Soviets to negotiate earnestly; he agreed to American participation only because refusal would have had unfortunate repercussions in countries to which the United States was allied. His worst presentiments were confirmed. The Summit Meeting of 1955 and the subsequent meeting of the Foreign Ministers contributed nothing to a solution of Europe's problems. On the other hand, they led to a relaxation of the rearmament efforts of NATO's members and to new differences of opinion concerning the attitude that should be adopted toward the Soviet Union. There followed agitated exchanges of notes among the United States and its allies with respect to force levels, and new public concern in America over European foot-dragging and unreliability.

In this atmosphere of less than complete harmony, the Suez crisis

[27] Beal, *op. cit.*, p. 182.

[28] Richard Goold-Adams, *John Foster Dulles: A Reappraisal* (New York, 1962), pp. 129–30.

threatened to destroy allied collaboration, and the NATO alliance that embodied it, completely. It would be idle to deny that the faults of Dulles' diplomatic style, which have been touched on above, played a significant role in this western débâcle. If it is unsound to blame the crisis on his abrupt withdrawal of his offer to finance the Aswan dam, it must be admitted that it was sharpened by it. In the subsequent period, the Secretary of State was determined that the differences between Britain and France on the one hand and the Egyptian leader Nasser on the other should not be allowed to lead to hostilities. It is unfortunate that he never succeeded in making this entirely clear to his allies, who thought that he had broken promises to them and gradually came to the conclusion that he was being dishonest in his communications to them.[29] In this lack of mutual understanding, an important part was played by personal differences between Dulles and Eden, which had their origins in the days of the negotiation of the Japanese Peace Settlement[30] and had been complicated by Eden's refusal to supply troops for the defense of Dienbienphu in 1954. In 1956 the two statesmen were not speaking the same language, and out of this incompatibility, and the French intrigue with Israel into which Eden allowed himself to be drawn, much evil came. The Israeli aggression, and the Anglo-French support given it, enraged Dulles, because hostilities were begun before he had exhausted his efforts to find a peaceful solution and, above all, because the events in the Near East destroyed the moral advantage the western alliance possessed when Hungary revolted against Soviet domination, an advantage Dulles doubtless hoped to exploit in a general and a specific sense. As far as the Near East was concerned, that was now impossible. The west had been brought down to the same level as the Soviet Union.

Even if he had been able to overcome his own indignation, it is doubtful whether Dulles could have controlled public opinion, which was shocked by the allied action, to say nothing of the feelings of the President. It has become fashionable to regard President Eisenhower as a political Trilby under the influence of a Svengali-like Dulles, but the President had a will of his own, and it was he, in the last analysis, who made American policy. In November 1956 he regarded the Anglo-French action as a personal affront and a blow against that policy of preserving the peace to which he had dedicated himself. Robert Murphy has indicated that it was Eisenhower rather than Dulles who determined the American course after the attack took place and that it was he also

[29] See *Full Circle,* pp. 540–41, 557, 634.
[30] *Ibid.,* pp. 21–22.

who insisted that his allies should be censured in the General Assembly of the U.N.[31]

It is clear today that blame cannot be attributed exclusively to any of the participants in the Suez muddle, and it is ludicrous to write as if Dulles were the villain of the piece, motivated by a desire "to indulge his own conceit as a potent maestro of world political *savoir-faire* and to secure leverage over the American public and Congress and President Eisenhower."[32] His motive was not personal aggrandizement. He was seeking to balance conflicting claims in a tense and developing situation, to retain the support of public opinion, to maintain alliance solidarity, to avoid alienating the uncommitted nations, and to preserve the peace. Thanks in part to faults of method and language, he failed; and his failure will probably be enough to deny him the right to be regarded as one of the United States' greatest Secretaries of State. For it was a big failure. In his first years of office, Dulles had demonstrated his ability to appease aroused public opinion; he had brought the Korean War to an end; and his hard line had contributed to the cease-fire in Southeast Asia. But in the area that the United States Government had for twenty years regarded as of fundamental strategical importance, that is, in Europe, his style and actions had weakened the alliance that the Truman administration had forged for Europe's protection, and the violence of Eisenhower's reaction to the attack on Suez had come close to destroying NATO.

IV

And yet Dulles learned from these mistakes, and, in the wake of the crisis, he sought, with not inconsiderable success, to repair the damage done. He was doubtless aided in this by accidental factors. The implied Soviet threat to rocket-bomb London and Paris reawakened fear of the ultimate intentions of the Soviet Union, while at the same time the merciless repression of the Hungarian rising reminded people of the brutality of which the Soviet Government, despite Khrushchev's smiles, was capable. In addition, the successful launching of the *Sputniki* helped (once the initial panicky reaction was overcome) to inspire new efforts to close what now seemed to be a frightening gulf between Soviet military capabilities and those of the west.

Even so, Dulles himself deserves credit for the recovery of western

31 Murphy, *op. cit.*, pp. 392–93.
32 Finer, *op. cit.*, pp. 492–93.

unity and will. With a tact that was in sharp contrast to his behavior on previous occasions, he set about the difficult task of effecting a reconciliation with allies whom he had, not long before, arraigned before the bar of justice. By the end of 1957, he had won such a measure of success that, in a moment of anger, Khrushchev himself gave public testimony to it. The Soviet Premier called upon the United States Senate to investigate the activities and policy of the Secretary of State, an outburst that strengthened Dulles' position in his own country and simultaneously caused his stock to rise in European capitals.[33] Indeed, in 1957, when the danger of Soviet imperialism seemed greater than at any time since Stalin's death, it was reluctantly admitted that, in contrast to many wishful thinkers, Dulles had never wavered in his determined insistence that vigilance must not be relaxed, that Soviet intentions were what they had always been, and that, as he had written in 1950, there was "no greater and more dangerous illusion than that Soviet objectives can be changed by persuasion. . . . Power is the key to success in dealing with the Soviet leadership."[34]

The restoration of European confidence in the United States, badly shaken by the Suez crisis and to some extent also by the launching of the Soviet satellites, was advanced also by the sureness with which Dulles went about his work in 1958, a year that has been rightly called his greatest as Secretary of State. He found himself facing three crises in this year, and he met them all with confidence and tactical skill. In July there occurred the *coup d'état* in Iraq, and the pro-western government of Lebanon was placed in serious jeopardy. Dulles met this danger promptly and effectively, responding to President Chamoun's request for assistance by sending U.S. Marines to the imperilled country. This action dispelled the prospect of Communist domination of the Near East and made idle Khrushchev's hope that he might be able to exploit the Near Eastern troubles so as to force a summit conference on his own terms.[35]

As this situation eased, a new crisis broke out in the Far East where the Chinese Communists began their bombardment of Matsu and Quemoy in August. Despite cries of anguish raised by his liberal critics at home and in Europe, Dulles had too keen an appreciation of the potential effects of any retreat under Communist pressure to give way in this matter. Instead, he brought the U.S. Seventh Fleet into the picture in such a way as to make it clear that any Communist attempt to invade

[33] Goold-Adams, *op. cit.*, p. 255.
[34] Dulles, *War or Peace*, p. 16.
[35] Eleanor Dulles, *op. cit.*, pp. 139 ff.

the islands would lead to American intervention. After several tense days, the bombardment stopped.

Finally, in November 1958, came Khrushchev's Berlin note, with its six-month ultimatum. Dulles' first reaction to this struck many Germans as being inadequate, for it was on this occasion that he spoke to the press of the possibility of dealing with the East Germans as "agents" of the Soviet Union and said that there were possibly other routes to reunification besides free elections. These statements, which can be seen today as tactical responses to the legalism of the Soviet note, were perhaps designed to persuade critics in London and the United States that he was not wholly inflexible in his German policy and that he was capable of responding to a reasonable and positive approach from the east. But he had no intention of yielding to threats, and, essentially, his views on the possibility of reaching a viable agreement with the Soviet Union on Germany were the same as they had been when he took office. At the Berlin conference of 1954, he had asked one of his aides whether he would be satisfied if Molotov suddenly gave up all his objections and accepted free elections. "Why, yes," was the answer. "Well, that's where you and I part company," Dulles said, "because I wouldn't. There'd be a catch in it."[36] He was firmly opposed to accepting any form of agreement that did not place the essentials of the Western position under an effective guarantee, and he had no intention of giving way to military pressure before that had been realized. Despite his statements to the press, therefore, he took advantage of Anastas Mikoyan's visit to the United States in January 1959 to have a ninety-minute talk with the Soviet official, in the course of which he apparently made it clear that the United States would not yield in Berlin; and from that moment on the Soviet drive on the city began to run out of gas, although that was not immediately evident.

That was really Dulles' last significant political action. In February he made one more trip to Europe, principally to see his friend Konrad Adenauer and to explain his recent statements about Germany. At the end of the same month, he went into the hospital, and three months later he was dead.

V

What can be said, even tentatively, about his place in the history of American statecraft? Perhaps more on the negative than on the positive side. As director of the machinery of American foreign policy, he showed

[36] Goold-Adams, *op. cit.*, p. 293.

no great ability to coordinate the varied resources at his command or to use them effectively. He lived apart from the Department of State psychologically and, thanks to his penchant for travel, physically,[37] and he was never, in a real sense, its leader. Many of its officers never fully forgave him for condoning the purge effected in his first days by Scott McLeod, just as many of his ambassadors came to resent what appeared to be his willingness to disregard their reports and to supplant them in their proper functions. As the man who, with the approval of the President, was charged with the task of giving form and expression to American foreign policy, he will not be remembered for striking new conceptions, like the Marshall Plan, or for new doctrines. (It is easy to remember the Truman Doctrine, which marked a turning point in American foreign policy, but who can recall with any clarity the purpose of the Eisenhower Doctrine?) As spokesman for American goals in the world, he cannot be placed on the same level as Woodrow Wilson or Franklin Roosevelt or John Kennedy, who were able to use the wordy idealism so beloved of Americans in such a way as to mobilize energies for realistic and constructive goals. Dulles' attempts to strike the same note always sounded moralistic or boastful. Finally, as his country's chief negotiator, he was, at least until the last years, more successful in dealing with enemies than with friends, who often failed to understand his objectives and sometimes came to the point of distrusting his motives.

And yet there is a positive side which may, with the passing of time, place these negative qualities in the shadow. In a time of great danger, Dulles was a tough and determined fighter for peace and the public law, and one who recognized that these things could be maintained only by sacrifice and risk. "You have to take chances for peace, just as you must take chances in war," he was quoted as saying, in a famous *Life* magazine article in January 1956. "The ability to get to the verge without getting into war is the necessary art. If you cannot master it, you inevitably get into war. If you try to run away from it, if you are scared to go to the brink, you are lost."[38] This article brought a storm of criticism down on Dulles' head, but the London *Economist* said a little later:

> His central thought . . . is of the need for certainty. He believes that the only risk of total war is as a result of miscalculation by an aggressor,

[37] On 12 July 1956, under the heading "Stop Over in Washington Some Time, Mr. Secretary," R. H. Shackford reported in the *Washington Daily News* that Dulles had traveled a distance equal to eleven times around the earth in the last three and a half years, and he quoted Dr. Henry Wriston's opinion that less travel on the part of the Secretary of State would improve the efficiency of the Department and the morale of the chiefs of mission abroad.

[38] *Life,* 16 January 1956, p. 70.

> owing to his not knowing how far he can safely go. . . . There cannot be any certainty unless the alliance of free nations will draw the line clearly and give the aggressor no reason to doubt their determination to defend it. . . . Surely it is the lesson of the years from 1933 to 1939, which should not be forgotten so quickly that a statesman who tries to re-emphasize it, however clumsily, should be held up to obloquy.[39]

John Foster Dulles had some of the same aversion to sentimentality in politics that Bismarck possessed, and this must also be credited to the positive side of his account. He regarded with scorn those people who desired peace so avidly that they responded hungrily and uncritically to every Soviet blandishment, and he successfully resisted pressure to make concessions to the Soviet Union in the hope of getting something in return. For his steadfastness in this regard, he has been accused of pursuing a wholly negative policy,[40] a complaint that assumes greater credibility now that we have achieved something in the nature of a *détente* with the Russians than it possessed during his lifetime, when the Soviet threat was palpable and the opportunities for useful negotiation few. The historian will not be able to achieve anything like a balanced assessment of Dulles unless he can recapture the atmosphere of the 1950's and remember the sense of foreboding and even panic that sometimes affected men in responsible positions. In those circumstances, Dulles stood like a rock; and perhaps the best answer to those who now criticize him for rigidity is the evidence that the Russians had enormous respect for him,[41] doubtless because they acknowledged his sound judgment with respect to their own designs. It may even be true, although admittedly hard to prove, that his toughness and steady nerves helped to blunt the arrogant self-confidence that was so marked in their behavior in that dangerous decade and to start them on the road to what became in the 1960's a tentative accommodation with the west.

[39] *The Economist* (London), 21 January 1956, quoted in Beal, *op. cit.*, pp. 217–18.

[40] Henry A. Kissinger, *The Necessity for Choice* (New York, 1960), p. 193.

[41] So Louis Joxe, one of de Gaulle's aides, to Eleanor Dulles. *The Last Year,* p. 223.

Afterword: New Dimensions of War and Diplomacy

IN AUGUST 1965, when the Twelfth International Congress of Historical Sciences convened in Vienna, the Federal Ministry of Education provided an attractive diversion for the delegates in the form of a special exhibition on the Congress of Vienna of 1815.[1] Handsomely mounted in the imperial apartments of Emperor Francis Joseph in the Hofburg, this was a dazzling affair, showing in picture and document and artifact what Vienna and its people were like, how they lived and amused themselves in 1815, and how the statesmen who came to this greatest diplomatic gathering in history comported themselves during the deliberations that restored peace to Europe after twenty-five years of war.

One of the most popular items in the exhibition was the famous picture by the French portraitist Isabey showing the chief figures of the Congress—Metternich, Talleyrand, Castlereagh, Alexander of Russia, Humboldt, Capo d'Istria—all powdered and bedizened, in beautiful court uniforms laden down with stars and decorations, and with expressions of proud confidence on their aristocratic faces. Standing in front of this classical portrayal of the Old Diplomacy, an irreverent American was heard to say: "How those faces would have changed if they had been granted prevision and had seen Khrushchev beating his shoe on the desk in the U.N. General Assembly or Dean Rusk addressing a teach-in on Vietnam!"

There was merit in this remark. Not even by the most herculean stretching of the imagination could the men of Vienna have foreseen the coming of an age in which a significant part of a statesman's time and energy would be spent defending his foreign policy before groups of

[1] See the official program, *150 Jahre Wiener Kongress: Ausstellung veranstaltet vom Bundesministerium für Unterricht gemeinsam mit dem Verein der Museumsfreunde* (Vienna, 1965).

ordinary citizens in his own country (as American officials are constantly forced to do) or (as was true in the case of Khrushchev's egregious performance) attempting to ingratiate himself, and his country, with peoples who were entirely outside the pale of civilization in 1815.

These startling changes in diplomatic style have been the result of developments discussed earlier in this book—the spread of democracy on the one hand, and the emergence of dozens of new nations since the end of the Second World War on the other[2]—and they need no further comment here. But there have been other changes in the diplomacy of our time that are perhaps of greater significance, and these are the ones which have been caused by recent changes in the nature of war.

In the nineteenth century, war was a recognized means of advancing state interest[3] and was usually employed, except in the case of civil conflicts, in a rational manner. Despite what Clausewitz might say about its tendency to assume an absolute form, diplomacy was usually able to restrain this thrust to the utmost, and statesmen like Metternich and Bismarck—not, to be sure, without difficulty[4]—were adroit in using war as an effective instrument of policy. In the twentieth century, an age of ideology and nuclear science, there has been a dangerous tendency toward a reversal of this relationship. War, once resorted to, has become increasingly difficult to control, and the possibility of its assuming its absolute form has become at once more likely, and more frightening to contemplate, than it ever was in the age of Clausewitz.

In these circumstances, some comfort may be derived from Delbrück's demonstration that there is a reciprocal relationship between the forms assumed by war and other social institutions and that changes in one produce changes in the other.[5] This is still true today, and the increase in the destructive potential of war has had the effect of awakening a new appreciation of the essential importance of diplomacy, even in countries like our own where it has traditionally been viewed with suspicion. The growing frightfulness of war has also stimulated experimentation with new dimensions of diplomacy, in the hope that they may help avert the kind of *dénouement* to the human drama that has been portrayed in the film *Dr. Strangelove.*

In the panoply of diplomatic weapons used by the powers in today's dangerous world, bilateral diplomacy of the classical type has retained

[2] See above, Chapter 11, p. 202 f., Chapter 12, p. 208ff., and Chapter 14, p. 248 ff.

[3] See above Chapter 8, pp. 147–48.

[4] See above, Chapter 2, pp. 26, 37, Chapter 6, pp. 122–23.

[5] See above, Chapter 4, p. 72 ff.

its central importance—or, more accurately perhaps (for we must remember the attacks on the ambassadorial system after the First World War[6] and Secretary Dulles' use of the airplane to undermine it[7]), has recovered it. The ambassador resident abroad may not have the power today that Stratford Canning had in Constantinople in 1853, but he is an indispensable part of the foreign-policy machine, the principal source of information about the country to which he is accredited, and the most important channel of communication to its government. In exchanges between ambassador and foreign minister, things can be accomplished that are impossible in other diplomatic contexts. It is here that the personal element makes itself felt, as it did in the classical age.

Yet, as Quincy Wright has written, classical, bilateral diplomacy cannot in itself deal adequately "with the problems of a world with more than 110 states of diverse culture and ideology," in which "the complexity of the situation is compounded by small wars erupting sporadically in areas such as China, Vietnam, Korea, Berlin, Kashmir, Israel and the Caribbean," and where "peace is threatened by accident, miscalculation, or escalation, if not by design".[8] The dangers of the age require a wider range of diplomatic instruments and a greater number of centers of diplomatic contact and intercourse than the Old Diplomacy provided.

This has been generally recognized, and, since the end of the Second World War, it has resulted in the development of four new kinds of diplomacy which have already helped, or which promise to help, to avert the dangers of another world conflict. The first of these is regional or bloc diplomacy, the purpose of which is to form and maintain partnerships among states with common ideals or interests, to give the individual members a security they would not enjoy standing alone, and, by doing so, to avert the kind of aggression against isolated states that has in the past ballooned into major conflict. The second is the diplomacy of arms control, which is concentrated on the gravest peril of our age, the possibility that proliferation of nuclear weapons will release war from any rational restraint and make it self-generating. The third is "people to people" diplomacy in its varied forms from economic and scientific assistance programs to cultural exchange—a kind of diplomacy that is generally subverted to political purposes when practised by the great powers, but which has the potential ability, when administered

[6] See above, Chapter 12, p. 209.

[7] See above, Chapter 15, pp. 270, 272.

[8] Quincy Wright, "The Decline of Classic Diplomacy," *Journal of International Affairs* (Special Issue: "Diplomacy in Transition"), XVII (1963), 24.

through international agencies, to alleviate the conditions that are the breeding places of war and to break down the barriers of fear and distrust that exist between different races and peoples. The fourth, and most important, is United Nations diplomacy.

The special problems and techniques of the first three of these new departures are too complicated to be given summary treatment, and this listing will have to suffice. But a word must be said about U.N. diplomacy, particularly in view of all the gloomy talk of failure to live up to expectations and of imminent collapse that was heard on the occasion of the organization's twentieth anniversary in June 1965. There was doubtless some justification for these melancholy reflections. The U.N. has had its failures, and at times it has shown a tendency to take on tasks that were clearly beyond its competence. Even so, its critics tended almost wholly to overlook the splendid record of accomplishment made over the last two decades by the U.N.'s sixteen subsidiary agencies, which specialize in the kind of "people to people" diplomacy just alluded to; and they also underplayed the organization's not inconsiderable success since 1945 in de-fusing dangerous crises.

But even if the U.N.'s record had been more disappointing in this latter regard than it has been, it is hard to see where we would be without it. As Thomas Hovet has pointed out, the U.N. is the one place in the world where all blocs and ideologies are represented, the one permanent diplomatic community, and the one piece of diplomatic machinery that can be put to work at a moment's notice. It is also the one body where both traditional and democratic, bilateral and parliamentary forms of diplomacy can be brought to bear upon critical problems, so that, in moments of great danger, parliamentary diplomacy, in the General Assembly, can freeze a situation until the quieter forms of intercourse in the private offices and the corridors can find a solution for it. In a very real sense, the U.N. also supports and supplements all of the other forms of diplomacy mentioned here; and, in the case of bloc diplomacy, it alleviates its most disturbing feature, the danger that bloc-forming will lead to the clash of armed leagues, by standing ready to interpose its influence on the basis of noncommitment to any power-bloc. Finally, in Mr. Hovet's words, the very fact that "more and more foreign ministers, prime ministers and chiefs of state attend General Assembly meetings means that there is an opportunity for contact between states that is unique."[9]

The delegates to the Congress of Vienna would probably find the

[9] Thomas Hovet, Jr., "United Nations Diplomacy," *ibid.*, pp. 29 ff.

multidimensional diplomacy of our time bewildering, just as they would probably find democratic and totalitarian diplomatic styles distasteful. Yet, after reflection, they would probably see that present-day diplomacy, like their own, is struggling with the difficult problem of finding ways to adjust relations between states by rational means rather than by leaving this to the arbitrament of war; and they might even be willing to admit that their twentieth-century successors are showing considerable fertility in expedients.

Index

52922

INVENTORY '80

05